Profound Science and Elegant Literature

Profound Science and Elegant Literature

Imagining Doctors in
Nineteenth-Century America

STEPHANIE P. BROWNER

PENN

University of Pennsylvania Press

Philadelphia

10 9 8 7 6 5 4 3 2 1

Published by
University of Pennsylvania Press
Philadelphia, Pennsylvania 19104-4011

Library of Congress Cataloging-in-Publication Data

Browner, Stephanie P.
   Profound science and elegant literature : imagining doctors in nineteenth-century
America/Stepanie P. Browner.
      p.   cm.
   ISBN 0-8122-3825-7 (acid-free paper)
   Includes bibliographical references and index.
   1. American literature—19th century—History and criticism. 2. Physicians in
literature. 3. Literature and medicine—United States—History—19th century.
4. Literature and science—United States—History—19th century. 5. Medical fiction,
American—History and criticism. 6. Physicians—United States. 7. Medicine in
literature. I. Title
PS217.P48 B76   2004
813′.3093561—dc22   2004054972

To Stephen

Contents

Introduction:
What's a Doctor, After All?

What's a doctor, after all?—A legitimized voyeur, a stranger whom
we permit to poke fingers and even hands into places where we
would not permit most people to insert so much as a finger-tip,
who gazes on what we take trouble to hide; a sitter-at-bedsides,
an outsider admitted to our most intimate moments (birth, death,
etc.), anonymous, a minor character, yet also, paradoxically,
central, especially at the crisis . . . yes, yes.

—Salman Rushdie, *Shame*, 1983

The profession to which we belong, once venerated on account
of its antiquity,—its various and profound science—its elegant
literature—its polite accomplishment—its virtues,—has become
corrupt, and degenerate, to the forfeiture of its social position,
and with it the homage it formerly received spontaneously and
universally.

—Minutes of the First Annual Meeting of the American Medical
Association, 1847

The world of illness and pain is a foreign land we would rather not visit.
We distance ourselves from the sick, and those we anoint as official healers carry the burden of our most ambivalent feelings about the shame
and pleasure of living in material, mortal bodies.[1] We may wish to think
of the healer as a minor character in our lives, one who lingers in the
wings and makes only brief appearances. But we also turn to healers in
moments of great need, hoping that they, along with their expertise, wisdom, language, and therapies, will return us to the land of the healthy.
Inevitably, then, in every portrait of a doctor, nurse, shaman, or lay
healer, we hear a culture negotiating who should have the duty and privilege of entering the sick room, listening to the patient's story, attending
the ailing body, and witnessing at the deathbed.

Medical practice in the United States has two traditions—folk and
professional.[2] Throughout the eighteenth and nineteenth centuries, the
divide between the two was not rigid. A family might call in a lay healer
on one occasion and a "regular" on another, and practitioners turned

often to the pharmacopoeia and therapies of their competitors.[3] But there were important differences. Folk healers typically identified themselves with the political rhetoric of health reform, populism, egalitarianism, untutored and independent thinking, democracy, and a free market. Professional medical men, by contrast, identified themselves with advances in medical science, specialized education, and the notion of a guild. In the first decades of the nineteenth century, as a national culture began to emerge, these differences erupted into lively public battles and professional medicine lost much of its prestige. Historians agree that in 1850 professional medicine was at its nadir and "appeared to be coming apart at the seams."[4] State licensing laws were repealed in the 1830s and 1840s, competition was fierce in a crowded, deregulated market, and regulars were often branded as aristocrats bent on establishing a healthcare monopoly. One New York newspaper suggested that medicine "should be thrown open to the observation and study of all," and that "the whole machinery of mystification and concealment—wigs, gold canes, and the gibberish of prescriptions" that kept regulars in business should be destroyed.[5]

Fifty years later the battles were over, and regulars had, in large part, won the veneration they had so coveted in 1847 when they founded the American Medical Association (AMA) in an effort to recover the "homage" the profession had "formerly received spontaneously and universally." Four lavish oil paintings testify to the prestige accorded the professional doctor by the final decades of the nineteenth century: Thomas Eakins's 1875 *The Gross Clinic*, his 1889 *The Agnew Clinic*, Robert C. Hinckley's 1893 commemoration of the first surgery under ether, and John Singer Sargent's 1906 commissioned portrait of the four world-renowned doctors who were leading medical studies at Johns Hopkins Medical School.[6] Folk healers, of course, continued to practice, and as late as 1900 more dollars were spent promoting patent medicines than on advertising any other consumer product.[7] But the question of prestige had been settled, and by 1910, with support from the Carnegie Foundation, most small, proprietary medical schools, including many that trained "irregulars," had been shut down and foundation money was flowing to elite schools. In fact, by the end of the century, not only had professional medicine laid to rest the challenge from folk medicine, it had also supplanted the clergy and its cultural authority.[8] The body had replaced the soul as a person's most prized possession, and the professional doctor was, as the founders of the AMA had hoped, widely venerated as a man of profound science, elegant literature, polite accomplishments, and virtue.

Not surprisingly, given the rapidity and magnitude of the changes, historians have combed medical archives and identified scientific, economic, sociological, and ideological factors in the emergence of medicine as the most lucrative and prestigious profession in the United States. I propose to add to these efforts by looking at how fiction writers, a diverse group with its own sectarian quarrels and its own claims to knowing the body, responded. Fiction offers a rich, detailed record of anxieties raised and assuaged by regulars' efforts to professionalize and to claim exclusive somatic authority. Fiction reveals some of the terms on which medicine's professional prestige was eventually accepted and how the doctor was often envisioned as a stabilizing force in a rapidly expanding nation vulnerable to political, economic, and social troubles. It also reveals the ways in which the aesthetic imperative to make the body meaningful led fiction to resist the medicalized body, "a thing with physical, anatomical and physiological properties."[9] None of the writers I discuss denied medicine's achievements in these years. Their concern was with the political implications of medicine's ascent into elite privilege and authority and the collateral damage done by medicine as it installed its peculiar understanding of the body.

Writers were alert to medicine's class aspirations. At mid-century, when regulars were under attack from many quarters for seeking prestige and market privileges, the doctor was often represented as a stiff aristocrat. Rebecca Harding Davis, Charles Frederick Briggs, and Herman Melville, for example, suggested that elite medicine was unresponsive or even cruel to the bodies of the disenfranchised—mill laborers, minstrel performers, and common sailors. For these authors, professionalism was undemocratic. For other writers, especially later in the century, the professional doctor was just what a heterogeneous nation needed. Professional medicine promised to cure the "ills" posed by increased immigration, poverty, and urbanization, and highbrow literature often abetted the professionalization of medicine. In elite magazines of the day, for example, the fictional doctor was often a liberal gentleman who could encounter the diseased and the bizarre and remain untainted. He brought stability to worlds riven by disorder, and, like the elite fiction that represented him, he dispensed wise, temperate counsel. The doctor's scientific training was also, by the end of the century, not always evidence of elitism but of legitimate expertise, especially in fiction that negotiated gender and race issues. As an image of manly science, the fictional doctor endowed domesticity, highbrow aesthetics, and racial uplift with the prestige and seriousness of science. The image of the black physician, for example, served for some African American writers as a powerful challenge to popular images and scientific theories of innate black inferiority.

Fiction was also wary of medicine's claim to know the body. Mid-century fiction often worried that although medicine might nurture embodied democracy and corporeal equality by identifying basic somatic facts, generalizable "truths" about the body might also leave individual bodies with no history, no intimacy, no narrative particularly their own. Medicine threatened to empty the body of meaning. Nathaniel Hawthorne's tales of medical ambition, for example, warned against empiricism, suggesting that when medicine understood a birthmark as a curable lesion or the body's interior as a domain that it could colonize, it dishonored the body so profoundly that it destroyed the very thing it sought to know. Or, as Melville suggested, when medicine devoted itself to garnering prestige, making money, and rationalizing the body, it lost sight of precisely the democratic virtues it might facilitate—compassion and conversation. Later in the century, for writers such as William Dean Howells and Elizabeth Stuart Phelps, doctoring was associated with physical vigor, intuitive responses to the bodies of others, and firm grounding in empiricism. And yet, even for these writers medical epistemology was limited and incapable of responding to the diverse beauty, sexuality, history, and politics that might be written on the body. The scientific doctor (male or female) needed a mate with a fine aesthetic sensibility, and white physicians who misread black bodies needed racial education. On occasion, however, and especially for Sarah Orne Jewett and Henry James, the truly great doctor represented a sensibility that achieved both the rigor of science and the aesthetic refinement of highbrow culture, making him or her sensitive to all the complex realities and meanings of embodiment.

In short, as both medicine and literature professionalized and laid claim to widespread authority and elite privilege, their trajectories into respectability sometimes paralleled one another, sometimes reinforced each other, and sometimes were in tension. At times, fiction challenged medicine's somatic knowledge, contested doctors' ability to name and solve the body's mysteries, exposed the violence inherent in medicine's drive to epistemological mastery, and questioned science's equation of rational disinterest with white, educated masculinity. And yet fiction also found ways to use the figure of the doctor to argue for compassion as well as management, corporeal pleasure as well as normative health, sensitivity to the political history of bodies as well as somatic mastery, and appreciation of the body's mortal beauty as well as definitive diagnoses of disease.[10]

The Body in the Nineteenth Century

As scholars from a variety of disciplines have shown, sometime over the course of the eighteenth and nineteenth centuries thinking about the body changed profoundly. Francis Barker describes the change as a shift from "spectacular corporeality," in which self and body are one, to "tremulous subjectivity," in which a private, desiring self is separate from the physical body.[11] The body became something the self "loosely possessed" and something science could know.[12] With the rise of clinical studies in hospital wards and the increasing importance of dissection, the body became a material object that could be known through direct and repeated observations that yielded not just idiosyncratic interpretations of an individual patient and his or her world, but facts about all bodies.[13] The body was now a standardized, normalized, positive object that functioned according to scientific laws, and the predictability of the body, especially as known on the dissecting table, remains a defining presumption in medicine today. As one recent medical school graduate observed, it probably never "occurred to me or my fellow medical students that the human body which we dissected and examined was other than a stable experience."[14]

One result, as Catherine Gallagher notes, is that in the nineteenth century the body was considered a troubling, provocative problem and valorized as a site for definitive answers.[15] As a result, the body was measured, weighed, categorized, and dissected—work deemed serious and important. For example, in the 1840s U.S. ethnographers devoted their careers and sometimes their personal resources to collecting and measuring crania. In 1861, Abraham Lincoln allocated national resources to establishing the U.S. Sanitary Commission and also to an effort to gather information about the Union troops by measuring the "most important physical dimensions and personal characteristics" of as many soldiers as possible.[16] By the end of the century, criminologists created taxonomies of somatic features common to a "hereditary genetic criminal class" and began creating databanks of fingerprints with the hope of identifying hereditary features for various types.[17] The body became prima facie evidence, and it was hoped that by knowing the body, men and nations might build stable, healthy worlds in which disease was eradicable and social troubles manageable.[18]

In theory, the modern body is an egalitarian notion—everyone has a body that functions according to the laws of physiology.[19] But in the nineteenth century, some bodies were more visible, more measured than others. While some traits "could go unmarked, even grammatically," as Michael Warner has noted, "other features of bodies could only be acknowledged . . . as the humiliating positivity of the particular."[20] The fetishistic attention, for example, to cataloging the width of noses, the height of foreheads, the length of femurs, the color of skin, or the size of breasts made some bodies more visible than others, some features more humiliating for being a site of difference. In short, as scholars have amply documented, social categories—gender, race, ethnicity, class, and nationality—were made real, written on the body by medicine, biology, and ethnography, "naturalizing discourses of the body" that "locate difference in a pre-cultural realm where corporeal significations supposedly speak a truth which the body inherently means."[21]

The Professions in the Nineteenth Century

While those who were measured had bodies that were different and visible, those who were authorized to measure bodies seemed free of the particularizing positivity of corporeality. As Dana Nelson suggests, the "disembodied, objective, and universalized standpoint offered by Enlightenment science" became the perspective of "white manhood" in general and professional authority in particular.[22] More specifically, those who measured bodies were not part of a visible group (they were white men, for the most part), and their methods, they believed, were disinterested and rational. Of course, the U.S. doctor studying in Paris, the ethnographer cataloging skulls, the Sanitary Commission doctor measuring femurs, and the fingerprint expert collecting specimens were individuals with particular histories and perspectives. It was supposed, however, that if they were good scientists, their results would have nothing to do with them as idiosyncratic, corporeal men. By definition, in good science the measurer is immaterial and the results are reproducible. In short, bodies measured and cataloged came into view as unmediated facts, and science reproduced its authority in "captioned and ever-multiplying displays of the 'other.'"[23]

In addition to being disinterested and objective, the professional man in the nineteenth century was a liberal gentleman. He was respected as a man of learning, culture, and virtue, and in some ways he was an updated version of the eighteenth-century English gentleman. The professional was neither a capitalist nor a laborer. His prestige was not derived from wealth, and yet he was not a worker because even though he was employed by others, "he worked from a position of command . . . and was therefore never wholly at the bidding of those who employed him."[24] As a group, professionals offered an implicit contract: in return for market advantages, they would guarantee the ethical use of their special knowledge. This included establishing fair fees, adopting ethical codes, forming associations dedicated to setting standards for the profession, and providing leadership in other areas. More generally, professionals promised to be the nation's managers. As Burton Bledstein explains, the professional "excavated nature for its principles, its theoretical rules" and had "masterful command" over complex phenomena such as disease. The professional's knowledge was by definition beyond the layperson's grasp, and, as Bledstein notes, amateurs and clients alike simply had to trust the professional's mastery and his integrity.[25] As a result, the professional was often infused with what Max Weber identifies as the charismatic authority of experts, and his manners were as important as his scientific skills.[26] An 1873 *Atlantic* article, for example, suggests that the doctor cures not by "drug or knife, but by means of his counsel, and, above all, by force of his manner. . . . It is the doctor cures us, not the doctor's physic."[27]

Fiction in the Nineteenth Century

At mid-century, writing, like medicine, was open to a wide variety of practitioners. The production and availability of print materials expanded rapidly in the second half of the nineteenth century with the availability of cheap paper, less expensive presses, and better distribution of print materials. This expansion made it possible for publishers to pay authors, and authorship became an economically viable occupation open to anyone who could write. At the same time, writing became professionalized, and genres, magazines, and publishing houses became stratified according to class. Domestic fiction, for example, was women's work, sensational fiction was authored by anonymous industrial hands who were expected to produce on a schedule, and highbrow literature was the work of public figures with visible careers.[28]

Along with class and gender identities, genres were associated with particular somatic sensibilities. Sentimental and sensational fiction, for example, offered literal representations of somatic experiences—tears, crimsoned bosoms, and throbbing pulses—and readers were expected to respond similarly.[29] Maudlin death scenes were supposed to move one to tears, and seduction scenes would make a modest reader blush. Both genres, reviewers of the day warned, might agitate the body and appeal especially to female appetites for physical experiences. Dime novels aligned themselves with a masculine physicality by featuring visceral images of bodies engaged in labor and physical struggle. Realism, by contrast, shunned the body. Associated with taste, refinement, and science, realism conformed to bourgeois preferences for privatizing all things bodily. As Nancy Glazener notes, while reviewers linked sentimental and sensational fiction with alcohol, opiates, coffee, tea, and desserts, they suggested that realism was a healthy food, an effective antidote to excess and stimulation.[30]

Imagining Doctors in Nineteenth-Century America: Six Case Studies

By outlining these broad historical contexts, I do not mean to suggest that the professionalization of medicine was achieved neatly, that the limitations of scientific objectivity were never acknowledged, or that doctors never considered a patient as anything other than a material body. Nor do I mean to suggest that highbrow literature was a stable, uncontested category or that literary representations of the body always followed generic dictates. History and texts are never so simple. Indeed, the texts in this study, medical and literary texts, are useful precisely because they mediate in complex ways the rise of professional authority and the emergence of the modern body.

To gain a fuller understanding of how the tension between professionalism and the nation's democratic ideals played out in medicine, Chapter 1 focuses on a specific moment in medical history—the discovery of ether in 1846 by an enterprising dentist whose image did not conform to that of the gentleman scientist. The texts generated by the discovery of etherization and the ensuing controversies reveal the efforts of regulars to position professional medicine within and not against the egalitarian sentiments of the day. In these texts, we hear regulars presenting themselves as open to the discoveries of untutored genius, and we hear them negotiate professional medicine's relationship to a free market. We also hear, in one leading physician's enthusiasm for etherization, an argument for medical science and medicine's view of the body as fundamentally egalitarian. Pain, he suggests, is something all men suffer, and medicine's embrace of a new technology—etherization—testifies to regulars' egalitarian effort to improve the lot of all men.

Chapters 2 and 3 focus on critiques of medicine offered by Nathaniel Hawthorne and Herman Melville. In "The Birth-mark" and "Rappaccini's Daughter," Hawthorne borrows from the sensational and melodramatic tradition the trope of the mad medical experimenter who is driven by a dangerous mix of intellectual ambition, professional arrogance, and sexual energy. Essentially cautionary tales, both stories imagine a body that exceeds medicine's ambitious grasp. To Aylmer, the mark on Georgiana's cheek is a sign of pathology remediable by surgery, a diagnosis and remedy that echo contemporary thinking about lesions, perhaps the most important sign of disease in early nineteenth-century clinical medicine. But for Hawthorne, the mark is much more: indeed, it vibrates with multiple and contradictory meanings. And it cannot be erased without destroying Georgiana's body and an entire world of heightened meanings—aesthetic, erotic, psychological, dramatic, and somatic—that Hawthorne believes literature can and must honor and imagine. "Rappaccini's Daughter" is set at the moment (sixteenth-century Padua) when medicine first began to map the body's interior, and it examines the Renaissance notion of the body's interior as a continent ripe for exploration and colonization, suggesting that such colonization is akin to poisoning. As sixteenth-century anatomists put their names upon the organs they discovered, so Rappaccini marks his daughter's interior with the botanical poisons he cultivates. Significantly, Hawthorne finds medical ambition appealing as well as disturbing. Aylmer and especially Rappaccini have an intellectual interest in carnality that Hawthorne seems to have shared, and yet Hawthorne also critiques medicine's role in somaticizing a domestic middle-class subjectivity that made women and their bodies bear the burden of the unresolved psychological, sexual, and economic tensions hidden beneath a valorization of feminine purity, piousness, and self-sacrifice.

Melville's critique of medicine is based less on a sense of the body's significatory excesses and more on a love of carnality and a desire to challenge a political order in which corporeality is used to define certain classes of people as uncivilized, irrational, and deeply embodied. Melville seems to have stumbled into his interest in body politics: nakedness is a staple of exotic travel literature, and in *Typee*, Melville delights in coy descriptions of naked islanders. But in addition to celebrating the primitive's innocent carnality (and thus lamenting its destruction by Western dress, religion, and diseases), Melville also suggests that all bodies, including seemingly innocent primitive bodies, are intricately woven into a society's political and cultural life. Medicine, he suggests in later works, dishonors both the carnal and political body. In *White-Jacket*, a U.S. fleet surgeon—a figure of naval, professional, and scientific authority—is at the center of the most barbaric naval practices. He officiates at hangings and floggings, he operates a sick bay in the bowels of the frigate where there is no fresh air, while officers promenade on the deck above, and he cuts off a sailor's leg simply to flaunt his surgical skills. He presides over the destruction of bodies and the democratic fraternity that the common sailors' bodies figure for Melville. In *The Confidence-Man*, Melville considers the power of medicine to silence the body. He caricatures quacks and regulars in their efforts to persuade the public to trust them but not their competitors, suggesting that medicine's sales rhetoric colonizes the pain of others and is aimed solely at profits. But, in a rare moment of hope in a deeply cynical work, Melville also suggests that if those who claim to be healers listen to the patient and to tales of pain and injustice, the spirit of calculation that dominates human interaction may give way to generosity. Melville underscores the democratic possibilities of compassion and conversation, noting, however, that while medicine might facilitate both, sectarian battles allowed profit motives to supplant compassion and intimacy.

Chapter 4 examines the discourse of good character and cultural refinement that underpins the professional claims of both medical and literary elites at mid-century. The chapter begins by tracing the wealth, family connections, access to power, and cultural connoisseurship that helped early white male medical leaders legitimate their authority. Then the chapter turns to periodical fiction (including works by Oliver Wendell Holmes, Rebecca Harding Davis, and Henry James), tracing an alliance between regular medicine and highbrow literature in the pages of elite magazines of the day. Although regulars often came in for rough treatment in newspapers and sectarian medical journals, prestigious literary magazines rarely published articles critical of regulars, and many printed essays and fiction that defended the medical profession and celebrated the doctor's character. The *Atlantic* and similar magazines were deeply enmeshed in "the construction and justification of social hierarchy,"[31] and in these magazines the doctor is usually a white, liberal, upper-class gentleman with the virtues the AMA claimed for its members—equanimity, objectivity, disinterest, wise counsel, and ethical leadership. These virtues were also meant to characterize elite fiction itself and thus buttress highbrow literature's own cultural claims over such popular and populist genres as dime novels and sensational fiction. The good doctor, like the highbrow fiction that tells his story, manages the bodies of others, and he is a figure of stability in stories that admit and seek to contain difference, discord, disruption—forces that democracy may too readily tolerate. The chapter also notes, however, that on occasion the doctor's class affiliation comes in for close scrutiny and that the doctor is sometimes critiqued for his allegiance to an outdated class order or for his efforts to protect his class status. These stories record a resistance to the cultural claims of the AMA and an inclination to interrogate professionalism. Indeed, elite literature's willingness to envision for itself a role other than that of conservator of the status quo and handmaiden to the emergence of a class of prestigious doctors was an integral part of its image of itself as disinterested and objective.[32]

Chapter 5 focuses on the intertwined and shifting gender identities of medicine and literature in the second half of the century as women entered the medical profession, as professionalism supplanted domesticity, and as empiricism eclipsed other ways of knowing. In these years, the doctoress was featured in tracts debating what women could and could not do, in titillating images of women medical students examining or dissecting naked bodies, and in a flurry of short stories and novels by writers such as Elizabeth Stuart Phelps, William Dean Howells, Rebecca Harding Davis, Annie Nathan Meyer, Sarah Orne Jewett, S. Weir Mitchell, and Henry James. The doctoress was a topic "rich in actuality," as Howells noted, because she threatened deeply held, yet fragile presumptions about masculinity and femininity. More generally, the chapter considers how representations of medicine became a way to negotiate the taint of femininity that worried the nation and particularly threatened the arts, which were increasingly defined as a feminine complement to the manly world of science. For these writers, the good doctor is well-trained, intuitive, objective, and caring, and he or she is a professional who does important work that is both scientific and domestic, work that depends upon expertise and brings the physician into intimate settings. For some of these writers, the doctor's presence in the home makes the domestic something more than the traditional female world of home and heart. It is where the fabric of the nation is woven, and writing fiction that is good for the nation requires expertise not unlike the doctor's. But if the doctor's visits to the world of domesticity and romance endow this world with masculine virtues associated with professionalism, they also reveal medicine's limitations. Some of these authors note a possible narrowness in medicine's understanding of the body, and they suggest that health requires not only an absence of disease but also a psychological and aesthetic well-being that is literature's domain. Others offered the well-trained and well-read male doctor as a reassuring national icon of masculine vigor and cultural refinement.

Chapter 6 considers the relationship between medicine and race at the end of the century, in part by examining the political/racial work that the figure of the physician was pressed to do just when African Americans in medicine were professionalizing and challenging racist medical ideology. In 1895, at the Cotton States and International Exposition in Atlanta, black physicians founded the National Medical Association, an alternative to the AMA, and during these years they founded black-controlled hospitals that offered training for black medical professionals and health care for African Americans. Notably in these same years, between 1891 and 1901, a flurry of stories and novels took up the question of race and medicine: Francis Harper, Katherine Davis Chapman Tillman, Rebecca Harding Davis, Victoria Earle Matthews, Charles Chesnutt, and William Dean Howells all wrote fiction that made a physician living or working on the color line a central issue. Three of these—"Aunt Lindy," *The House Behind the Cedars*, and *An Imperative Duty*—place the white doctor in a racialized world, using him as a trope for medicine's racism, historical amnesia, and vulnerability to race melodrama. The others—*Iola Leroy*, *Beryl Weston*, and *The Marrow of Tradition*—imagine the black physician as a figure of hope. Not surprisingly, as black physicians gained institutional training and became venerated community leaders, the black doctor in fiction became a ready symbol of racial uplift. His success in medicine challenges racist notions of black inferiority, and he often serves as a figure of a moderate but race-proud leader. All but one of the stories consider the physician as a man as well as a professional, and in several the doctor is judged by his response to the mulatta, a figure that bears the burden of embodying and responding to the nation's gender and race psychoses. For Harper, the black doctor mediates gender stereotypes, and she makes the black male physician a figure for the promise of institutionalizing tender, maternal care of black bodies. In Harper's novel, the black doctor stands as an antidote to the caricatures of blacks as primitives that permeated U.S. culture and also as a challenge to the image of black maternal care lavished on white children and the image of black bodies bloodied and destroyed by race violence. For Harper, the black doctor cares for and loves black bodies. For Chesnutt, the black physician figures the possibility of new race relations. Always sensitive to the nation's anxiety about and fascination with the color line, Chesnutt concludes his novel about the race riots in Wilmington, North Carolina, with a black doctor heading upstairs to perform a tracheotomy on the scion of a white racist. The white body, Chesnutt suggests, needs radical surgery, and the black physician (and writer) must both cut and suture this body.

Finally, the book ends with an epilogue that looks forward into the first years of the twentieth century, when medicine moved decisively from home care into the world of regimented hospital care and from clinical medicine's emphasis on organic, narrative case histories to pathology's emphasis on somatic bits and pieces. By looking briefly at short stories by Theodore Dreiser, Jack London, and William Carlos Williams, I trace the disappearance of the beneficent master physician and the emergence of the ruthless, virtuoso surgeon and the sick doctor. As a new century dawned and a sense of a radical break with the past deepened, the coherent, unified body was no longer a reliable ground for literature or medicine. Diagnoses required examining excised tissue under microscopes, and storytelling demanded narrative fragmentation and violence.

Archives, Methodologies, Predecessors

There are two questions about texts and methodologies that should be addressed up front. Does a study that focuses only on U.S. medicine and literature endorse a notion of American exceptionalism? And is a study that focuses on "regular" medicine merely a history of the winners? Recent attention to the discourse of American exceptionalism has helped to make visible just how deeply nationalist habits are embedded in our thinking. But, as Michael Kammen points out, when evidence suggests that the United States at some moments and in some areas is distinct, then we need not run from the observation. In his study of literature and medicine in Europe, Lawrence Rothfield notes that he excludes United States literary and medical culture, despite extensive exchanges across the Atlantic, because the "history of American medicine during the nineteenth century is so different, both in professional and intellectual conditions, as to constitute an entirely separate field of inquiry."[33] Historians and sociologists of medicine agree. For example, Paul Starr notes in his introduction to *The Social Transformation of American Medicine* that "not all societies with scientifically advanced medical institutions have powerful medical professions" and that "hardly anywhere have doctors been as successful as American physicians."[34] Indeed, the distinct and remarkable success of nineteenth-century U.S. physicians both in marginalizing other medical paradigms and in becoming the most prestigious and well-paid profession in the nation has shaped U.S. healthcare ever since.

By focusing on "regulars," I do not mean to endorse the marginalization of other paradigms. The impact of "irregular" medicine (a term devised by regulars to discredit all others) on individual lives, literary discourse, and elite, popular, local, and national culture was significant and has earned astute scholarly commentary. This study seeks to provide a fresh perspective on the remarkable and rapid rise of regular medicine, even though its boundaries were not firmly in place until the first years of the twentieth century, when the Flexner report led to medical school closings and certification. And it seeks to do this by looking closely, though not exclusively, at fictional representations of doctors. Cynthia Davis, in her study of literature and medicine in these same years, examines the power of literary forms to determine the contours of bodily representations.[35] I hope to add to her fine work by examining fiction's intervention in the rise of professional medicine and the modern body.

Salman Rushdie is right: the doctor is never a minor character, not in our lives and not in nineteenth-century American fiction. Indeed, the simplest point of *Profound Science and Elegant Literature* is that representations of healers tell us much about a culture and that every portrait of a doctor, nurse, shaman, or lay healer deserves a second look. More specifically, I want to suggest that representations of doctors in the second half of the nineteenth century are particularly telling because in these years modern, scientific, professionalized medicine was established in the United States.

Historians have tended to tell two distinct though not necessarily incompatible stories of professional medicine's rise. One is an account of progress. Through access to bodies in clinics, observations at the bedside, statistical studies, the development of new tools, and conceptual innovations, there was a "gradual triumph of a critical spirit over ancient obscurantism."[36] In the second account, economically motivated regulars squeeze folk healers out of a crowded healthcare market and scientific medicine "converts the body into an object of knowledge."[37] In the first account, medical scientists discover the real body and practitioners apply this knowledge skillfully as they treat individual cases. In the second, medical scientists colonize the body and regulars seek power.

Nineteenth-century fiction considers both accounts. In some tales, the doctor is skillful, in others he is cruel; sometimes he is wise, sometimes merely ambitious; sometimes he invades the body, sometimes he is racist, and sometimes he leads a community. In short, representations of doctors interrogate the dangers posed and promises offered by the establishment of an exclusive class of esteemed, scientifically trained professional healers. The value of individual texts is that they offer local history and intervene in debates of the day. Each fictional portrait speaks to specific issues such as new ideas about interiority, the increased use of dissection, the gender identity of authorship, and the limits of empiricism. Each is also shaped by a writer's lived experience of medicine. Louisa May Alcott's uncle was active in health reform, Herman Melville watched a respected fleet surgeon authorize floggings, Henry James never forgot being dismissed with a comparative "pooh-pooh" by a Boston specialist. William Dean Howells was devastated when his daughter died despite visits to homeopaths, nerve specialists, and the renowned S. Weir Mitchell; and Charles Chesnutt considered becoming a doctor.[38] In addition to serving as individual case studies, the texts taken together testify to a broader picture, to increased acceptance of medicine's prestige and scientific authority and to continued questioning of the implications—political, physical, and psychological—of medicine's claim to exclusive and complete somatic authority.

Professional Medicine, Democracy, and the Modern Body: The Discovery of Etherization

On October 16, 1846, at Massachusetts General Hospital in Boston, a dentist anesthetized a young man while the renowned surgeon John Collins Warren excised a facial tumor. The next day the dentist anesthetized a female patient as another medical luminary, Dr. George Hayward, removed a fatty tumor from her shoulder. Alert to the possibility of fame and profit, the enterprising dentist, William T. G. Morton, immediately devoted himself to applying for a patent, to designing and manufacturing inhalers, to publishing promotional pamphlets, and to distributing a schedule of rates for the right to use his discovery. His efforts to make money offended some, his claim to being the sole discoverer was challenged by others, and the attempt to silence pain was dangerous, according to many.

The discovery of etherization and Morton's entrepreneurial schemes generated a wide variety of texts within a few years—biographies defending Morton, congressional inquiries into priority claims, articles about the role of patents in medicine, pamphlets on the nature of scientific discoveries, and medical treatises about the usefulness or danger of deadening pain. These texts are remarkably conflicted. They make logical errors, connect unrelated issues, and speak to disparate concerns at the same time. They bear witness to the uncertain status of professional medicine at mid-century, and they offer a revealing glimpse of regulars' attempts to negotiate what Paul Starr has called a "dialectic between professionalism and the nation's democratic culture."[1]

In the 1830s and 1840s, alternative healers mounted a fairly successful attack on professional medicine. They condemned regulars as elitists seeking a monopoly in the health care market, and the charges often stuck. In these years, the repeal of state licensing statutes, the popularity of Thomsonian botanics and other domestic medical practices, and a significant increase in malpractice suits were the results of a rising tide of anti-status sentiments. In part, regulars responded by consolidating their authority without the aid of legislation. State medical societies became active, doctors began to plan for a national medical convention in 1845, a year before Morton's demonstration of the anesthetic powers of ether, and in 1847 the American Medical Association was founded. These societies gave their imprimatur to particular schools, offered assistance with malpractice defense, adopted codes of ethics that often prohibited any collaboration with or referrals to nonmembers (irregulars), and debated how best to improve the reputation of orthodox physicians.[2] And yet, regulars were also sensitive to being called elitists. As loyal, prominent citizens, they had a stake in placing themselves within and not against the democratic ideals of the nation. But negotiating the dialectic between professionalism and democracy, as the ether texts suggest, was not always easy.[3]

Notably, some of the nation's most elite physicians championed Morton and proclaimed the effectiveness of ether. Henry Bigelow, a young, ambitious physician and the son of the prestigious physician Jacob Bigelow, was one of the most enthusiastic supporters of ether, and his writings reveal the degree to which some regulars engaged the egalitarian ideals of the 1840s. In telling Morton's story, Bigelow and others fashion an appealing tale of physicians working hand-in-hand with a common dentist. The tale appeals to populist sentiments in that it honors the ingenuity of the common man and yet it insists upon the importance of a professional class of wise, scientifically trained doctors who, as Bigelow suggests in a series of articles that respond to Morton's patent application, seek no special market privileges. According to Bigelow, medicine's commitment to ethics positions doctors outside and above the profit-driven world of laissez-faire capitalism. Finally, in championing ether's universal efficacy, Bigelow infuses medicine's materialist view of the body with egalitarian rhetoric. Pain, according to Bigelow, is no respecter of position; it is simply a matter of nerves fulfilling their functions. Undoubtedly, this materialist view of pain is reductionist, participating in what one scholar has called a "vast cultural shift" in which the body is almost completely lost as a site for spiritual meaning and recast as a material object of knowledge.[4] But if Bigelow's definition of pain as nothing more than nerves testifies to the power of professional medicine to install a view of the body that furthered its interests, it also testifies to Bigelow's democratic urge to understand medicine's work as essentially egalitarian. In short, Bigelow suggests that the professional physician is a democrat willing to work with those outside his profession, that professional medicine is not at odds with a free market economy, and that medicine works on behalf of all men.

Bigelow's attempts to make these arguments are variously awkward and elegant, sometimes self-serving, sometimes illogical, and sometimes passionately democratic. Indeed, I begin with the ether texts precisely because they are conflicted and because I want the study of fiction's response to medicine that I pursue in subsequent chapters to avoid the teleological habits that can bedevil efforts to read fiction in relation to history. I hope to situate fiction's meditations upon medicine and the body within a history that is attentive both to large patterns in medicine's emerging authority and to the local debates and contests the outcomes of which neither physicians nor writers could know. As June Howard reminds us, when we read literary texts within historical contexts, the goal is not to set literary texts against a "history" or "reality" whose own textuality is for that purpose repressed.[5] The ether texts are, I believe, particularly effective reminders of history's textuality. They reveal the rocky terrain of contemporary medical discussions and the efforts of regulars to position professional medicine within and not against populist and egalitarian sentiments of the day.

The details of the discovery of etherization are difficult to discern amidst the various ideological uses that have been made of the story, but most accounts agree on a basic outline.[6] Morton's educational background included a brief course of study at the Baltimore College of Dental Surgery, six months as a student and boarder with physician, chemist, and geologist Charles T. Jackson, and two lecture series at Massachusetts Medical College, where he met Dr. Warren and others on the staff at Massachusetts General Hospital. Morton first set up as a dentist in partnership with Horace Wells, but after an unsuccessful year he left Wells and worked alone. Morton was in frequent contact with Jackson, seeking advice about ingredients for a wide range of dental procedures, including deadening pain for tooth extraction, and in his partnership with Wells he probably learned about the use of nitrous oxide to reduce pain during dental surgery. According to his memoirs, Morton began experimenting with ether in the summer of 1846, and within a few months he realized that he had discovered something remarkable and applied immediately to Dr. Warren for permission to demonstrate a new compound that rendered patients insensible to pain.

Although Morton's exhibitions at Massachusetts General were probably the first successful public demonstration of the anesthetic properties of ether, his claim to being the sole discoverer of etherization was contested. Jackson insisted that he gave Morton the idea of using ether as an inhalant, and he was the most persistent disputant in what became known as the "ether controversy." Jackson wrote articles on ether and was the first to announce the discovery in Europe, where he was honored by the Academie des Sciences. He persuaded Morton to guarantee him a share in the profits from the patent; and his lawyers persuaded a Congressional subcommittee to reject Morton's request for an honorarium of one hundred thousand dollars. Horace Wells never mounted a legal challenge, but his work with nitrous oxide and his similar though less successful demonstrations in the same surgical theater two years earlier also cast a shadow on Morton's claim to be the sole discoverer of anesthesia. In 1852, with the controversy still unsettled, a third disputant, Crawford W. Long, came forward and claimed to be the discoverer of inhalant anesthesia. In 1854 the Senate passed a bill to honor and compensate Morton, but the House rejected it on the grounds that "the multiplicity of claimants" made it impossible to grant an award.[7] Morton appealed to the president, and he was promised that if he filed a suit against the government for violating his patent by using ether during the Mexican-American War without compensating him, the government would "shoulder all the responsibility" and offer Morton an appropriate reward.[8] Eight years later Morton's suit was dismissed on the grounds that the patent was not valid, and he died in 1868, poor but still defending his claims and preparing another suit against Jackson.

Most accounts of the ether controversy focus on the story just outlined. By sorting through the papers of Morton, Wells, Jackson, and Long, the evidence submitted to Congress, legal briefs, and related documents, historians have tried to name the true discoverer of anesthesia. I want to suggest, however, that the most noteworthy feature of the ether controversy was not the dispute over priority,[9] but the surprising number of physicians, including some of the most prestigious, who championed the beleaguered dentist, defended his efforts to win compensation, and enthusiastically advocated etherization before thorough testing indicated it was safe and effective. In the decade and a half following Morton's demonstrations at Massachusetts General, Henry Bigelow wrote several articles supporting Morton and etherization, and the popular magazine *Littel's Living Age* published a defense of Morton authorized by the trustees of the hospital. In addition, physicians in Boston, New York, and Philadelphia counseled Morton to appeal to the president, circulated a testimonial on his behalf, requested donations to offset his loss of income while pursuing his claim, and commissioned a biography that celebrated him as the sole discoverer of anesthesia. For some in the medical profession, telling Morton's story became a way to fashion their own story, a story of an enlightened, liberal, and ethical profession open to the discoveries of the untutored genius and yet devoted to protecting the nation from charlatans.

Defending Morton was not, however, so easy. A self-promoting opportunist eager to protect his pecuniary interests, Morton was an embarrassment to the idea of professionalism as many physicians wanted to construct it, and the history of his discovery—a story of luck and coincidence—did not conform to the conventions of more traditional histories of scientific progress. According to elite physicians, medical knowledge was gained only by the slow and painstaking accumulation of precise observations. In introductory lectures at medical schools and addresses to medical societies, the medical elite adopted a tone of impersonal reserve and constructed narratives not of individual geniuses, but of collaborative efforts that slowly and carefully added to the store of medical facts. The Paris-trained Philadelphia physician Alfred Stillé, for example, prefaced his textbook, *Elements of General Pathology* (1848), with an essay on "Medical Truth" in which he equated the "dreams of genius" with "the frauds of charlatanism."[10] Oliver Wendell Holmes, in his lectures on "Homeopathy and Its Kindred Delusions" (1842), insisted that real advances were made only after years of work by highly trained men who cared little for fame and money. For Holmes, William Harvey and Edward Jenner were examples of the selfless men whose hard work was essential to the progress of medicine. Harvey's discovery of the circulation of blood was the "legitimate result of his severe training and patient study," and Jenner's discovery of a smallpox vaccination was the culmination of "twenty-two years of experiment and researches" that he offered "unpurchased, to the public."[11] For Stillé, Holmes, and others, true scientific knowledge was untainted by the petty squabbles, self-serving secrecy, and careless errors that inevitably marred the work of ambitious men seeking glory or profit.

The emphasis on painstaking, collaborative, empirical research in such accounts of medical progress allowed regulars to distinguish themselves from irregulars who told narratives of great and original insights by untutored men. Irregulars presented themselves as men who braved ad hominem attacks from regulars in order to bring their remedies to a grateful public. Samuel Thomson, the founder of the eponymously named and widely popular botanic movement, made his story of growing up poor and learning the medicinal values of American herbs from an old Indian woman an integral part of his doctrine and appended an autobiography to his popular medical manual. Sounding the note of martyrdom, one herbalist prefaced his medical guide with an account of how he had to hold his "front bare to the bursting waves of opposition's rudest shocks, as they have poured with impetuosity from the muddy fountain of ignorance, prejudice, malice and cupidity."[12] Instead of acceptance by medical colleagues, marketplace success was the mark, in the rhetoric of irregulars, of a true remedy. Holmes and other regulars rejected popularity, however, arguing that vigorous sales were proof only of the credulity of an uneducated public bamboozled by "selfish vendors of secret remedies."[13] But Thomsonians, eclectics, patent medicine vendors, hydropaths, and homeopaths insisted that personal testimonials and estimates of the number of their followers were unassailable evidence of the truth and effectiveness of their medicines and regimens.

Morton's discovery of etherization was not a story easily assimilated into the narrative preferred by regulars. The possibility of painless surgery had not been discovered after years of empirical study, statistical analyses, and tested hypotheses by educated and reputable scientists. Rather, a poor dentist who was eager to improve his practice by advertising painless tooth extractions stumbled upon the possibility of ether-induced insensibility. Morton's investigation into the safety and universality of etherization was rudimentary, and his experiments with different inhaling apparati were cursory. More disturbingly, Morton wanted to keep his discovery a secret, and he wanted to make money. He added perfumes and burned incense during the demonstrations in order to disguise the strong and well-known smell of ether, and he called the preparation Letheon Gas, thus avoiding all mention of what he knew was the only active ingredient. Morton also refused to consider his work part of a larger scientific effort. He insisted that the discovery was his alone, and he devoted his life to disproving the claims of others to earlier, related discoveries.

Since Morton's story was more amenable to the irregulars' narratives of breakthroughs by iconoclastic and untutored geniuses than the narratives regulars told of scientific progress, we might expect the elite, professional medical men in the United States to have shunned Morton and his attempts to promote himself and his product. And, in fact, many did denounce Morton, distancing themselves from the unprofessional and unseemly affair of patent disputes and the dangerous quackery of pain-free surgery. The editor of the *Philadelphia Medical Examiner*, Robert M. Huston, wrote, "We are persuaded that the surgeons of Philadelphia will not be seduced from the high professional path of duty, into the quagmire of quackery, by this Will-o'-the-wisp." He warned that "If such things are to be sanctioned by the profession, there is little need of reform conventions, or any other efforts to elevate the professional character: physicians and quacks will soon constitute one fraternity."[14] Charles A. Lee, editor of the *New York Journal of Medicine*, suggested that Morton's supporters were "stooping from the exalted position they occupy in the profession, to hold intercourse with, and become the abettors of, quackery."[15]

But such attacks did not dissuade those among the medical elite of Boston who were determined to make Morton part of their story. Indeed, it was precisely Morton's unprofessional image and story that made him appealing to the professionals. Acceptance of Morton was evidence that could testify both to the profession's willingness to accept discoveries made by those outside the profession and, at the same time, to the profession's dedication to ethics over profits. Those who defended Morton constructed a tale of a lucky and somewhat buffoonish dentist rescued from his misguided entrepreneurial schemes by an enlightened medical community.

Henry Bigelow was one of the first and most ardent defenders of Morton, and he linked his early career and professional status to Morton's discovery. Although he had been recently appointed to the staff at Massachusetts General, Bigelow became the most public, persistent, and enthusiastic supporter of Morton and etherization. Two weeks after the first demonstration Bigelow proclaimed the advent of a new age in an address to the American Academy of Arts and Sciences on November 3, and six days later, on November 9, he read a similar paper to the Boston Society of Medical Improvement. The publication of this paper, "Insensibility During Surgical Operation Produced by Inhalation," in the *Boston Medical and Surgical Journal* (which later became the *New England Journal of Medicine*) is commonly considered the first official announcement of the discovery of anesthesia.[16] Two years later, in 1848, in the first issue of the journal of the newly formed American Medical Association, Bigelow published an account of the physiological effects of ether; and in 1848 he published *Ether and Chloroform: A Compendium of Their History, Surgical Use, Dangers, and Discovery*.[17] Notably, in all these texts Bigelow celebrates not only the discovery but also the discoverer.

In order to champion the enterprising dentist and yet follow traditional narratives, Bigelow suggests that the story of the discovery of ether began long before Morton. He implies that Morton achieved what he did because the time was ripe and that "the early narrative of the discovery" reveals "the contemporaneous and accumulating evidence of experiment" (9).[18] Bigelow writes Morton into a grand narrative that includes work done before Morton, experiments conducted after Morton's demonstration, important responses from the European community, and the numerous trials and observations recorded by reputable scientists. Bigelow clearly believes that the exchange of ideas and results among scientists throughout the world was crucial to the eventual discovery of etherization, and he even makes the bickering that followed the first demonstration part of the larger story.

In addition to writing the dentist into a longer, larger history, Bigelow uses Morton to meditate upon the role of the professional in a democratic nation. Invoking the myths of American originality, freedom from narrow training, and bold disregard for conventions, Bigelow proclaims that the United States will produce the next generation of leaders in science. The inventor, according to Bigelow, displays a willingness to reject accepted wisdom, an almost bullheaded tenacity and perseverance, and an intuitive confidence in his own ideas. Bigelow intones the names of the nation's great inventors—Franklin, Fulton, and Whitney—and adds Morton to the list. These men, he suggests, are evidence of "American ingenuity"—the nation's greatest resource (18). But having linked Morton and his medical discovery to the men who invented the bifocal, the steamboat, and the cotton gin, Bigelow suggests there are also important differences between scientific knowledge and mechanical inventions. Science requires training, and when he envisions the future contributions the United States will make to science, he warns that this will only happen if there is a greater "opportunity for education in science and unmerchantable truth." This education, Bigelow believes, will transform the "thousand nameless artisans" with a "humble genius" for invention into "true philosophers" (18). Thus Bigelow fashions a new nation out of the populist image of the United States as a land of natural inventors, suggesting that with a good education basement tinkerers will become leading scientists.

As Bigelow suggests that ingenuity and independent thinking are the nation's greatest assets, so he also suggests that U.S. leadership in science will be a natural consequence of the nation's political and economic structures. Seeking to win for U.S. scientists the same chauvinism that the U.S. political and economic systems enjoy, Bigelow notes that genius in science is often linked to genius in the political sphere. Central to Bigelow's hagiographies of Franklin, Fulton, and Whitney as scientists are their political contributions.

Franklin was a reformer; Fulton a warm advocate of the principles of free trade; while Whitney . . . anticipated the decline and overthrow of all arbitrary governments, and the substitution in their place of a purely representative system like our own. (17)

Bifocals, steamboats, and cotton gins; reform, capitalism and democracy; these are the fruits of that "uncultivated gift"—American ingenuity (18). Ether, Bigelow suggests, is another. In twenty-seven pages, he constructs a history of discoveries and inventions from Jenner to Leverrier, from Galvani to Schonbein, that ends in Boston with a common dentist. Morton's discovery, Bigelow insists, is evidence of what native ingenuity, a laissez-faire market economy, and a democratic political system can produce. In the United States, democracy and capitalism promote discovery, and medical science is both beneficiary and promoter of the nation's political and economic system. In short, Bigelow wraps modern medical science in the mantle of patriotism, and thus he refutes the charges of elitism and protectionism that were often leveled at orthodox medicine in the 1840s.

Bigelow's paean to the partnership of medical science and democracy is heartfelt, but it is not without problems. The definitions of democracy and professionalism available to Bigelow in the 1840s were in tension, and he cannot, despite his best efforts, completely reconcile his vision of professional medical science with the radical rhetoric of the Jacksonian era. Bigelow's troubles are most evident in the confusion that marks his discussion of the role of incredulity in science.

According to Bigelow, incredulity is the essential trait of all discoverers, and it is a virtue promoted by democracy and laissez-faire capitalism. Incredulity may come from "knowledge or ignorance," a crucial caveat that enables Bigelow to include Morton with those more often considered geniuses, but it always indicates a "philosophic mind [that] proposes to think for itself" (15). Such independent thought, however, was precisely what regulars would not tolerate, according to their challengers. Regulars seemed unwilling to countenance the skepticism of irregulars, and irregulars often charged the medical establishment with intolerance to new ideas and alternative therapeutics and theories. And, in fact, Bigelow balances his celebration of independent thinking with a warning about the dangers of unchecked incredulity. He cautions that "incredulity, brought to bear upon an extended system, especially the inexact sciences, is justly viewed with suspicion" and that "the world therefore justly maintains a degree of conservatism and immobility" (15). Although radical incredulity may be appropriate in the physical sciences and the mechanical arts, in medicine, Bigelow insists, we must temper such incredulity and depend upon the conservative check of a professional class of educated, experienced men. In medicine, the unsuspecting patient must be protected from the irresponsible independent thinking of practitioners who dismiss what has become accepted knowledge and practice. In other words, Bigelow reneges on his attempts to link medical science to a radical, independent democratic spirit. He claims that although medicine may advance through discoveries made by renegades and untutored minds, progress depends upon a professional class of men who can be counted on to regulate the practice of medicine and thus protect patients from practitioners who might discard the accumulated wisdom and knowledge of the profession.[19]

Bigelow's version of Morton's story—a reassuring tale in which an untutored American inventor is guided by noble, far-sighted professional men—was the tale circulated, authorized, and funded by the medical establishment. In 1848, at the request of the trustees of Massachusetts General Hospital, Richard Dana published in *Littell's Living Age* "A History of the Ether Discovery," an exhaustive account of the legal battles over priority, patents, and public recognition. Ten years later Nathan P. Rice published a hagiography of Morton, *Trials of a Public Benefactor*. Rice was hired by the "Committee to draft a Testimonial to William T. G. Morton," which met in the home of Bigelow's father,

Dr. Jacob Bigelow. Dr. James Jackson and Dr. Oliver Wendell Holmes presided and the meetings were attended by many of the leading physicians of Boston, New York, and Philadelphia, and well-known literary men such as Henry W. Longfellow, William Prescott, and James T. Fields.[20] Although both Dana's and Rice's accounts admit much of what Bigelow omits—the story of Morton's life and the unseemly details of the long, contentious legal battles over priority claims, they ultimately echo Bigelow's version. Morton represents the independent, inventive American spirit, and the physicians represent the wisdom, care, and foresight offered by educated professional men. Rice's account, for example, makes it clear that the medical profession is the hero and Morton is a madman who made a lucky discovery. He juxtaposes roll calls of the faculty at Harvard Medical School and the work of these men with Morton's work as a dentist. While the professors of medicine study and teach anatomy, physiology, chemistry, and surgery, Morton devotes his time to making false teeth, to cosmetic surgery, and—his greatest work before ether—to making a false nose attached to spectacles, with a beauty mark on the forehead to distract attention from the nose.

Within a few years, the ether histories told by Bigelow, Dana, and Rice had been widely circulated, and the discovery of ether had become institutionalized as a national tale, featuring a common, quirky dentist and wise professional men. The popular press was attentive to the story. Almost immediately after the first demonstration, the *Boston Daily Advertiser* ran Bigelow's paper in its entirety, the *New York Times* covered the congressional hearings; and in 1853 Sarah Hale published a shortened version of Dana's report in *Godey's Lady's Book*.[21] By the end of the century, the story had become a legend. In 1882 Robert Hinckley began planning an oil painting of the first surgery under ether, and he devoted eleven years to creating a suitable homage to the leading physicians of Massachusetts. Hinckley researched carefully who attended Morton's demonstration, though in the end he decided to include several luminaries who were not present, and he sought Bigelow's opinion before the painting was finished. Bigelow replied to Hinckley's request and the photograph of the painting that Hinckley included with a lengthy letter that suggests making Morton and another figure shorter and making Bigelow one-eighth of an inch taller. Bigelow also gives precise instructions about modifying his clothing, noting that "I had all my clothes from Paris, & that was then the way of making them."[22] Although the painting has not earned much acclaim and it moved about for several years, it now hangs in the Francis A. Countway Library of Harvard Medical School. A few years later, in 1891, Dr. Richard Manning Hodges published *A Narrative of Events Connected with the Introduction of Sulphuric Ether into Surgical Uses*, and on the fiftieth anniversary of Morton's first demonstration, *McClure's*

Magazine published an account by Morton's wife.[23] Hodges draws directly upon the histories by Bigelow, Dana, and Rice, and he tells essentially the same story: Morton is lucky, intuitive and entrepreneurial, and he rightly defers at the crucial moments to the superior knowledge and ethical standards of Bigelow and the medical profession. The tale begins with Morton—his "common-school education" and his work as a clerk and salesman—and it concludes with a tribute to Bigelow's "determination, his penetration into actuating motives, his executive ability,—in fact, all his sagacious and active qualities of mind and body."[24] Morton is courageous, persevering, but a man of "no extraordinary degree of scientific attainment," and the physicians and trustees of Massachusetts General are men of "discretion and moral courage."[25]

Twentieth-century versions of the ether story take the same shape.[26] As recently as 1988, in a history of famous doctors, Sherwin Nuland describes Morton and the other claimants as a "handful of alert artisans, almost all of whom were enterprising mechanics, but certainly not scientists," and he describes Warren as an "austere, highly skilled physician . . . one of the country's most revered senior physicians."[27] Nuland concludes that it was Warren's "ineluctable destiny to be the medium" through which ether was presented to the world. In short, the ether story has been told again and again in order to suggest that an established class of elite professionals is not anathema to the nation's democratic ideals. In fact, as I suggest in Chapter 4, it was not only the ether story that was pressed to do this work. Elite literary magazines in the nineteenth century offered similar portraits of the professional physician as a liberal, open-minded democrat, a man poised to dispense wise counsel to temper democracy's excesses.

Morton's story not only inspired Bigelow and others to fashion an image of professional medicine that countered charges of elitism, it also challenged regulars to articulate their relationship to the marketplace. Morton wanted to make money on his discovery, and only ten days after the first demonstration at Massachusetts General he applied for a patent. He then placed advertisements in newspapers and magazines and printed handbills in order to announce a price schedule for Letheon licenses. Four weeks later, on November 20, Morton publicly announced his patent claim, and he warned all persons "against making any infringement on the same." Two weeks later his warning was sterner:

certain unprincipled persons have, in the face of Law and Justice, without any license, instructions or authority from me whatever, used my name and attempted to Pirate said invention, endangering, from their want of skill and knowledge upon the subject, the lives of those whom they have persuaded to undergo their unwarrantable experiments.[28]

Most versions of the ether story avoid references to Morton's persistent efforts to sell licenses, and others suggest, contrary to the evidence, that when Morton revealed the ingredient in Letheon before the third demonstration, he nobly relinquished all desire for profit and thus joined the professional class of medical men who stood apart from such marketplace schemes. Bigelow, however, did not avoid the issue. But the confusion and awkwardness that marks his discussion of medical patents testify to the deep tension between laissez-faire capitalism in the professional status that regulars sought.

With the repeal of most state licensing laws, the deregulated healthcare market was crowded, and regulars competed in part by representing themselves as committed to instituting and following the highest ethical standards. One of the first tasks of the American Medical Association (AMA) when it was founded in 1847 was to adopt a code of ethics. Attracting a great deal of attention—both support and criticism—the code attempted to elevate the profession above the contentious fray of marketplace competition. The National Code of Medical Ethics, as it was sometimes called, acknowledged the almost complete withdrawal of legal regulation of medical practice but suggested that rather than lobbying for the return of state licensing, the profession was better served by regulating itself. To this end, the code called upon physicians to shun "unlicensed" or "irregular" practitioners, to refrain from quarreling with one another in public, and never to challenge the opinion of the primary attending physician of a case. Advertising was deemed "derogatory to the dignity of the profession," and all attempts to compete directly in the marketplace were deemed "the ordinary practices of empirics" and "highly reprehensible in a regular physician."[29] Thus the code suggested that the distinction between regulars and irregulars was that the former were dedicated to ethical, decorous behavior while the latter were willing to use whatever marketing schemes they could to win patients and profits.

Crucial to the profession's attempts to represent itself as ethically minded and distant from the pettiness and dishonesty of the marketplace was a condemnation of patents. The AMA code linked patents with secrecy, base profiteering, and quackery. Patents, the code suggested, fettered scientific inquiry and turned matters of truth and knowledge into business concerns.

Equally derogatory to professional character is it, for a physician to hold a patent for any surgical instrument, or medicine; or to dispense a secret nostrum, whether it be the composition or exclusive property of himself, or of others. For if such nostrums be of real efficacy, any concealment regarding it is inconsistent with beneficence and professional liberality; and if mystery alone give it value and importance, such craft implies either disgraceful ignorance, or fraudulent avarice. It is also reprehensible for physicians to give certificates attesting the efficacy of patent or secret medicine, or in any way to promote the use of them.[30]

According to the code, patents were appropriate for ideas and goods traded in the marketplace but not for the facts and truths discovered through scientific inquiry. In an 1849 report on patent medicines to the House of Representatives, one doctor warned that patents were the recourse of "the unprincipled and mercenary, [who] with fertile ingenuity, have been daily prostituting a noble science at the shrine of private interest."[31] He insisted that the medical profession opposed the "practice of granting patents for compound medicinal agents as immoral and pernicious in tendency," and he argued:

[we] oppose it not only with philanthropic views, but as exponents of an intense and universal professional sentiment, and as advocates of a large and liberal class in the body politic, whose lofty ethics repudiate exclusive rights and emoluments, forbid secrecy, and unite all its members in a common search for truth and usefulness.[32]

The argument against patents gained few adherents outside the medical profession, and the AMA's failure to persuade Congress to regulate or ban medical patents suggests the depth of sentiment against legal protection for professions. Congress was more concerned with promoting economic development than regulating medical patents, and patents were considered an effective incentive for encouraging the introduction of new inventions and ideas into the marketplace. Congress revised patent law in 1836, transforming a previously expensive and litigious application process into a relatively quick, easy, and usually successful procedure. Responding to and encouraging the emerging market culture, the new law defined ideas as private property and, more importantly, as commodities that could be developed for business and profit. Not surprisingly, then, Congress was unwilling to renege on this understanding of patents.

The belief that patents were good for the economy combined with the widespread popularity of patent medicines, made it awkward for the medical establishment to condemn Morton's patent application. Indeed, both Bigelow and Rice suggested that it was precisely the nation's free market economy that encouraged men like Morton to tinker, invent, and bring their discoveries to the marketplace and thus to the public. But their endorsement of free market principles belied the ambivalent and even antagonistic relationship between the monopoly that the medical establishment sought and laissez-faire economics.

Bigelow attempted a resolution. In his first article on etherization in the *Boston Medical and Surgical Journal*, Bigelow defends Morton's patent. He acknowledges that "patents are not usual in medical science" and that usually "fame, honor, position, and, in other countries, funds" are more acceptable.[33] But he insists that Morton's patent is necessary because it will restrict the use of ether to responsible and knowledgeable practitioners. Here Bigelow misconstrues the purpose of patents: he ignores the accepted definition of patents as economic incentives and suggests instead that patents are a form of regulation, of licensure. He seems to believe that a patent on etherization will prevent unqualified practitioners from using it. Although Bigelow seems confident in his argument, he also adds another defense, one that exposes his own ambivalence about patents. Implying that patents are part of the less prestigious and more profit-minded profession of dentistry, Bigelow suggests that Morton's patent application is excusable because patents are accepted in dentistry, the profession most likely to use ether.

Not surprisingly, it was a dentist who exposed Bigelow's misrepresentation of patents and the hypocrisy of a physician defending a medical patent. Perhaps sensitive to Bigelow's subtle insult of dentistry, Dr. Flagg, a Boston dentist, published an article two weeks later in the *Boston Medical and Surgical Journal*, suggesting that Bigelow was in defiance of the professional code of the Massachusetts Medical Society when he defended Morton's patent.[34] Flagg also points out that no one, including regulars, will ever honor Morton's patent. He notes that the physicians at Massachusetts General Hospital in particular will feel free to instruct their students in the art of etherization without compensating Morton. Most embarrassingly, Flagg exposes Bigelow's self-serving and incorrect definition of patents. Flagg points out that Morton's patent, like all patents, demands payment, not expertise, for the right to use ether as an anaesthetic.

In the next issue of the journal, Bigelow works more carefully to carve out a viable position for the medical profession on the question of patents. He argues that the medical profession is against secrecy, but not against intellectual property rights. He insists that the Massachusetts Medical Society condemns only those who seek profit by refusing to identify the contents of their drugs, not patents in and of themselves. Bigelow writes that Flagg

confounds the question of secret and that of patent, and infers that what is no longer secret is no longer patent. It is understood that the matter was secret just so long as was necessary to secure patents here and elsewhere, no longer. But the fact of its subsequent publicity does not change the question of property. The discovery and the patent rights still belong to the inventors.[35]

This time Bigelow gets it right. In the first article he invoked tenets central to professionalism—knowledge is dangerous and its use must be regulated. But confronted with the illogic of equating patents with regulation, Bigelow admits in his response to Flagg that patents protect the intellectual property rights of the patent holder, not the patient from irresponsible practitioners misusing ether. In short, Bigelow must acknowledge, as he does, that medicine would be better served by "discovery unfettered by any restrictions of law and private right." And yet, he avoids an outright condemnation of patents, insisting not quite honestly that the profession is only against secrecy and not against patents.[36]

Although Bigelow's understanding of patents was more accurate in the second article, it was a dangerous argument and one he never repeated. If, as Bigelow argued, the medical profession condemned only secrecy and not property rights, there was no basis for censuring patents at all. Patents are never secret—to apply for a patent is actually to make the new idea public in exchange for seventeen years of exclusive rights to manufacturing and marketing the idea. If Morton's patent had been accepted and honored by the medical profession, the patent would not have prohibited the use of his discovery; it simply would have required physicians and hospitals to pay Morton.[37]

Not surprisingly, in a later 1848 account of the discovery of ether, Bigelow revokes his suggestion that regulars have no objection to patents. Now, as in his first article, Bigelow suggests that Morton's patent application must be understood in light of his work in dentistry: "secrets are common . . . in the profession with which this discovery had an intimate connection in its early history."[38] Distinguishing scientists and doctors from those who work in such mechanical arts as dentistry, Bigelow insists that "in the higher atmosphere of science, which deals with abstract truth, it is not easy, nor is it usual, thus to *extort* a value for any application growing out of discovery." Determined to classify the discovery of etherization as part of science and not the mechanical arts, he now suggests that "the patent was an error of judgment as well as a violation of custom."

It is worth noting that even in this discussion, however, Bigelow cannot avoid using the language of patents.[39] Although he suggests that patents are relevant only in the world of commerce, he turns again and again to patent law for a basic definition of what constitutes a true and great scientific discovery. He begins his defense of Morton by suggesting the requirements for securing a patent are valid criteria for judging the value of an invention or discovery:

A writer upon patents has said that an invention is entitled to protection from the law, when it materially modifies the result produced, or the means by which it is produced . . . and I should in like manner, call an invention great, in proportion to the combined amount of mind invested in its production, and its intrinsic ability to minister to the supposed or real comfort and well-being of the race.[40]

Twenty pages later Bigelow concludes by citing a judicial opinion that patent rights belong to the man who "first reduces his invention to a fixed, positive and practical form."[41] Bigelow then argues that since Morton's discovery fulfills all patent requirements, his discovery must be defined as a great discovery and Morton should be acknowledged as the true discoverer. It would seem as though Bigelow can find no terms other than marketplace language and patent law by which to validate Morton's discovery. Although Bigelow insists upon the great beneficence of the discovery to all mankind, he invokes a market notion of value to identify what ether offers and what Morton deserves—"the gratitude and honor conceded by the world is a mere equivalent for *value* received" (emphasis added).

The AMA code and the medical profession's condemnation of patents were attempts to shift the terms of public debate about medical practice from questions about the freedom of the marketplace and the rights of buyers and sellers to questions about the ethical use of knowledge. But Bigelow's failure to provide a coherent argument exposes the difficulties of making such a shift. Bigelow tries to translate economic arguments into moral arguments, questions about property rights into questions about ethics, but he cannot purify medical and scientific discourse of the language and values of nineteenth-century market culture.[42]

So far I have suggested that regulars' defense of Morton testifies to their efforts to align professional medicine with democratic and free market ideals. I have also noted that their efforts are bedeviled by contradictions. Bigelow's celebration of incredulity collapses into an argument for the restraint that professional medicine can exercise upon unchecked iconoclasm, and his attempts to embrace market ideology give way to a definition of science as a discourse of truth that is removed from and above the world of commerce. The ether texts, in other words, reveal a complex portrait of orthodox medicine at midcentury in which regulars argue for their ethical and scientific superiority and yet try to remain loyal to the era's populist mood. In this section, I want to look more closely at Bigelow's discussion of the ether trials he conducted and at his career. As an ambitious young man in 1846, he was quick to adopt the most current ideas in medicine, but later in his career he resisted new trends, including developments that followed from the very ideas he had championed years earlier. In Bigelow's writings from the 1840s, we hear an early articulation of the modern notion of the body as separate from the self, but later in his career we hear him caution young doctors against this very view. In the 1840s, he understood the modern body as an egalitarian notion; toward the end of his career he worried that modern medicine was dehumanizing the patient.

According to recent histories of the body, before the nineteenth century the body was primarily perceived as an extension of the self, as an idiosyncratic, open, and fluid expression of the complex physical, spiritual, and social forces shaping an individual. As Michel Foucault and others have argued, beginning in the late eighteenth century, and as a consequence of changes in economic and social structures, the body came to be defined as a closed, well-bounded, standardized, and normalized system, a discrete object that was not an extension of the self but rather a material possession owned by the self. Knowing the body and knowing when it was healthy or ill became a matter not of listening to the patient's story but of fixing an impersonal, clinical gaze upon the body. Disease supplanted illness as the primary focus of therapeutics, and the body replaced the patient as the subject of medical knowledge. In short, the modern body is a generic body, known through statistical studies, anatomical atlases, and mathematical averages that have erased the idiosyncratic and the particular.[43]

When Morton first demonstrated ether in 1846, few U.S. physicians had adopted the new clinical definition of the body. Although many physicians studied in Paris and returned as advocates of the methods of the Paris Clinical School, many others remained committed to an understanding of illness and the patient as highly individualized. Such eminent physicians as Worthington Hooker, Paul Eve, and Josiah Goodhue argued against invariable treatments, distinguishing themselves from the earlier universalist therapeutics of heroic medicine that defined all illness as a problem of inflammation and all cures as a process of depletion, and from contemporary populist practitioners such as Samuel Thomson who claimed that most patients and most illness could be treated by one regimen or a single tonic. In 1850, for example, Eve wrote:

No two human constitutions are precisely alike. A London medical periodical has just affirmed that what cured cholera in one street, would not cure it in another. . . . We cannot, therefore, adopt any routine practice, any invariable system of treating disease; this is the blind and reckless course of empiricism; but we must, in order to apply our agents intelligently and effectually, vary them, according to the peculiar and ever changing circumstances attending each case.[44]

A belief in the individuality of each case and a rejection of therapeutic uniformity were, as Martin Pernick argues in his history of anesthesia and professionalism, central to anesthetic discourse and practice. According to Pernick, although the medical theory of individualization was, in part, an attempt to encourage "greater sensitivity toward the unique needs and individual worth of each patient," the individualist theory was also a conservative response to the republicanism implicit in Revolutionary physician Benjamin Rush's universalist theory of the body and to the Jacksonian populist ideology of cure-all therapeutics promulgated by irregulars. Pernick further suggests that when "conservative physicians" applied the theory of "individual patient differences" to the use of anesthesia, most acted on the belief that differences in pain sensitivity could be "studied, classified, and codified into detailed rules." The result, according to Pernick, was a "calculus of suffering" in which age, race, class, and gender became predictors of a patient's sensitivity to pain and need for anesthesia.[45]

Although Pernick offers a persuasive and nuanced account of how individualist theories of the human body shaped medical discourse and practice, he does not offer a history of those physicians like Bigelow who found in the discovery of ether not a justification for individualization but rather a theory of somatic egalitarianism.[46] As the son of a Paris-trained physician, Bigelow embraced the new clinical epistemology of medical science, and his study of the use and effectiveness of ether offers an early and important example in medical history of the emergence of the modern body in the United States and the influence of the ideology of Jacksonian democracy on medical discourse and representations of the body in nineteenth-century U.S. culture.

The reality of Jacksonian egalitarianism is much debated by historians. Were economic conditions relatively equal? Was it easy to move between classes? Did the common man have political power? Traditionally, historians have accepted Alexis de Tocqueville's evaluation of the United States in the 1830s and 1840s as a place of few hierarchies and widespread social, economic, and political equality. Revisionist historians have suggested that equality in the Jacksonian era was more myth than reality. All agree, however, that egalitarian ideals shaped political rhetoric and even some laws—the repeal of medical licensing requirements, for example. I would suggest that egalitarian ideals as well as Parisian clinical notions of the body shaped Bigelow's ideas about pain.

Bigelow's somatic egalitarianism and medical modernity is most immediately evident in his refusal to make distinctions between patients and their responses to pain and to ether. All men, according to Bigelow, suffer pain equally, and he writes not about patients and cases, but about *the* body, about a system that responds consistently and predictably to the anesthetic properties of such chemical compounds as ether, nitrous oxide, and chloroform. In his first report on the trials carried out by Morton, Bigelow follows convention. He introduces each case by identifying the patient's sex and age and occasionally adds a note about the patient's size. But Bigelow draws no conclusions based on these facts. He records every detail—the amount of time required for etherization, the patient's response, the degree and duration of insensibility exhibited—

and there are noteworthy differences in the data. But these differences are immaterial to Bigelow; he makes no comments and suggests no further study. Ignoring the evidence he has presented to the contrary, Bigelow eagerly claims that "Ether is capable of producing, with very rare exceptions if there be any, complete insensibility to pain."[47]

Bigelow is equally uninterested in distinguishing types, and he makes no distinction between patients based on the categories that Pernick identifies as central to many practitioners' decisions about using or forgoing anesthesia—age, sex, class, race, presenting symptoms, or surgical procedure to be performed. Indeed, Bigelow is so certain of the universal efficacy of ether that he wants to expand the uses for ether from surgical cases to such complaints as dislocations, strangulated hernia, functional pain, and muscular spasm, including cramps and colic.[48] And even when he draws upon class stereotypes to describe one case, a story about the difficulty of etherizing a big man, Bigelow is more concerned with establishing a correct method of etherization than with possible implications about types of patients and their susceptibility to etherization. He suggests that "a large and muscular man, perhaps habituated to stimulus, sometimes modifies a grimace into a demonstration of violence; objects to verbal and other interference; at last becomes violent, and if athletic, requires the united force of several assistants to confine him."[49]

But he concludes only that one should not attempt "the etherization of athletic subjects when such aid is not at hand." Bigelow draws no conclusions about the man's physiology or about variations in dose. Instead he insists that the body will succumb, as all bodies do. He instructs the surgeon to

confine the patient, and to apply the ether steadily to the mouth and nose. For some seconds, perhaps many, the patient may refuse to breathe; and bystanders unaccustomed to the phenomena, exchange significant glances. But if the pulse is good there is no real danger, and at last, exhausted nature takes a deep and full inspiration, which while it aerates the blood, is laden with the intoxicating vapour; colour returns; and the patient falls back narcotized.[50]

Thus Bigelow suggests that all bodies, even those socially marked as different, are in essence the same.

Bigelow's report on the patient's experience of the anesthetic state reveals a similar lack of interest in the individuality of each patient. Although he concludes each case study with the patient's description of the experience, he translates the patient's words into his own. Every quote is indirect, and the voice we hear is not the patient's but Bigelow's. He reports that one boy "said he had had a first rate dream," that one woman "said she had been dreaming a pleasant dream," and that another patient reported that "'it was beautiful—she dreamed of being at home—it seemed as if she had been gone a month.'" Bigelow claims to offer the patient's "own words," and yet he makes no effort to suggest his renderings of the patient's words are verbatim. Bigelow erases the marks of individuality that direct quotes seek to represent—he reproduces no syntactical oddities, no grammatical errors, no colloquialisms. For Bigelow the anesthetic state itself erases such distinctions, and he insists that under ether "the patient loses his individuality."[51]

The patient's words—the peculiarities of language, voice, and story—were irrelevant to Bigelow because the new clinical methods of scientific medicine distinguished between self and body and taught the physician that he could and must listen first and foremost to the body. Of course diagnosis and therapy continued to include close attention to the patient's report, but with the advent of the stethoscope and other techniques of physical diagnosis, medicine became increasingly confident that it could gain unmediated access to the body. The discovery of ether contributed to this confidence. Not only were doctors inventing tools for listening to and looking at the body's interior, they could now work without comments, interruptions, or resistance from the patient. Operations could be performed more slowly, more carefully, and more often. Operations also became more decorous.[52] Rather than scenes of physical struggle—strong men holding patients down, stifling screams, extending limbs taut with muscular spasms—surgery became a theater of professionals working upon a body laid out like those portrayed in anatomical atlases. Silencing the voice of the patient became, many surgeons insisted, essential to their work. And if etherization did not completely relax the body and the etherized patient moaned, resisted, or made comments on the proceedings, surgeons were to ignore such signs. In his outline of the stages of the anesthetic state, Bigelow distinguishes signs of the body from signs of the individual. Vocalizations and movements are incidental and idiosyncratic symptoms, while the primary indicators of the patient's well-being are somatic signs—pupil dilation, pulse, and breath.

Many disagreed with Bigelow. For irregulars and homeopaths, the patient's voice was not incidental. Although patent medicines were cure-alls, and thus dependent upon universalist theories of disease, advertising for patent medicine depended heavily upon personal testimonials. Filling newspaper advertising columns with detailed accounts of misery and recovery, patent medicine vendors deployed language that was rich with regionalisms and ungrammatical syntax, marking each testimonial as authentic. Similarly, in Thomsonian medicine the patient's report is primary. Thomson made personal knowledge of the body the center of his therapeutics, advising his followers—purchasers of his book—to be their own doctors, diagnosing and curing themselves in accordance with the steps outlined in his *Guide*. Homeopaths also valorized the patient's voice, suggesting that the patient's verbal response to pain was perhaps the most authentic and important sound the body ever offered. Condemning etherization, one homeopathic manual warned that "Deadening the nervous system . . . is virtually choking off Nature's voice," suggesting that the patient's words and groans were the "true physician's best guide to the seat and character of the cause of the pain."[53]

Bigelow offers a very different interpretation of pain. Refusing to sanctify pain, he insists that it is not a voice articulating any essential truths. According to Bigelow, pain is simply, and purely, a somatic experience. Bigelow rejects religious and philosophical interpretations of pain, suggesting instead that pain is a material, physical fact best understood by medical science: "Pain is the unhappy lot of animal vitality. The metaphysician finds in it the secret spring of one half of human action; the moralist proclaims it as the impending retribution of terrestrial sin . . . [but] physical suffering grows out of the imperfection of physical existence." Here Bigelow is an empiricist and a materialist, insisting that pain cannot be understood by the metaphysician and the moralist and must not be read as evidence of man's wrongs against himself or the divinity. Pain, according to Bigelow, is a mundane fact of animal life, a simple matter of "nerves fulfil[ling] their functions."[54]

In part, Bigelow's definition of pain as a mundane physiological fact is an argument against the religiosity typical of some alternative therapeutics. Many irregulars equated nature with goodness and illness with human error or depravity.[55] Thomsonians eschewed mineral cures as unnatural, botanics claimed to work with nature; hydropaths celebrated the healing powers of water, and patent medicine vendors claimed their nostrums drew upon ancient Indian knowledge of rare herbs. Irregular medicine derived its popularity in part from its successful translation of religious values into reverence for the natural. Good health was evidence of good morals, and illness was a consequence of bad living—physically, morally, and spiritually. Homeopathy, for example, suggested that pain was the "penalty we suffer for violating a physical law."[56] Bigelow's definition of pain is a radical rejection of the valorization of the natural.[57] He insists that the natural world is imperfect and that pain speaks not of our sins against nature but rather of nature's sins against man. Pain is evidence of a flawed material world.

Bigelow's definition of pain may seem to participate in what David Morris has condemned as the trivialization of pain. According to Morris, nineteenth-century scientific medicine ushered in a "vast cultural shift" that "has consistently led us to misinterpret pain as no more than a sensation, a symptom, a problem in biochemistry." Condemning the materialist interpretation of pain that Bigelow embraces, Morris laments the reduction of pain to "a mechanistic event taking place solely within the circuits of the human nervous system."[58] Morris correctly points to the nineteenth century as the moment of a crucial shift in the understanding of pain, and he is right when he notes that pain has been almost completely lost as a site for constructing spiritual meaning. But in his disenchantment with the medical profession and medical science, Morris fails to acknowledge the important cultural work done by this mid-nineteenth-century definition of pain. The success of Bigelow's definition of pain as nothing more than nerves testifies not only to the power of the medical profession to install a view of the body that furthered its interests, although it was certainly that, but also to the appeal in the nineteenth century of an egalitarian interpretation of pain. Although Bigelow's definition of pain may seem, after more than a hundred years of medical materialism, a reduction of a complex experience into a trivial malfunctioning of body parts, in 1846 it eschewed moralism and embraced an egalitarian notion of the body. All bodies suffer pain, and Bigelow believes that by using etherization, modern medicine can improve the lot of all men.

Bigelow's egalitarianism in these texts was contrary to the dominant therapeutic practice of regulars in the United States, and it was not a rhetoric he ever repeated. In the 1840s, the therapeutic practice of regulars emphasized attention to the individual: "Specificity—an individualized match between medical therapy and the specific characteristics of a particular patient and of the social and physical environments—was an essential component of proper therapeutics."[59] Although statistics on Bigelow's own use of ether are not available, he practiced at Massachusetts General Hospital, which, according to Pernick's study, was no different from other hospitals in administering anaesthesia based on the age, sex, class, and ethnicity of the patient, the patient condition, and the type of operation.[60] There is no reason to presume that Bigelow's use of ether differed significantly from the norm, and later in the century Bigelow was an ardent defender of individualist therapeutics. He was suspicious of those who promoted even more radical notions of the body as a material object, a stable fact that could be known through science and described by the laws of physiology. When some professors at Harvard wanted to increase the laboratory requirements in the medical curriculum, he argued against the reformers, warning that excessive confidence in laboratory research would train students to prescribe treatments without regard to the patient: "The student who expects to influence disease because he understands how a drug passes through the visceral cells will get into a habit of therapeutic reasoning and action very likely to damage the man or woman who owns the viscus."[61] In 1846, by contrast, Bigelow was disinclined to see differences between the effects of etherization on various patients. In truth, in 1846, he has little interest in the man or woman who owns the viscus and a great deal of interest in the universal efficacy of ether in deadening pain during surgery.

The relative merits of universalist and individualist therapeutics are difficult to distinguish. On the one hand, as Pernick notes, individualist therapies invite treatments based on race, class, and gender stereotypes. On the other, universalist therapeutics may ignore the patient and thus participate in the kind of reductionist medicalizing of the body that Morris laments and also contribute to the rise of authoritarian sciences that Foucault condemns. In practice and in most of his rhetoric, Bigelow was a supporter of individualized therapeutics. But I want to suggest that in his ether writings, and in his argument that pain is universal and ether universally effective, we hear a young physician discovering in modern medicine's approach to the body as a knowable fact an egalitarianism that excited him and that echoed popular political sentiments of the day. In his ether writings, Bigelow draws upon the language and ideology of Jacksonian Democrats, and with remarkable energy and rhetorical flourish he defines pain as the most elemental force in human life, a reminder that we all share bodies vulnerable to disease. He writes that pain "respects neither condition nor external circumstances. In the countless generations which lead us step by step into the remote ages of antiquity, each individual has bowed before this mighty inquisitor. It has borne down the strongest intellect, and sapped and withered the affections."[62]

Pain, according to Bigelow, refuses to distinguish between men, indiscriminately leveling all men to their basic animal nature. And ether also makes no distinctions, according to Bigelow's claim for its universal efficacy, and thus it can free all men: "What is pain, which the race has ceased to know in its more formidable phase, and which in another age will be remembered as a calamity of rude and early science . . . this 'dreaded misery, the worst of evils,' now lies prostrate at the feet of science."[63] Science, according to Bigelow, will liberate us from the rude leveling force of pain—science will allow "intellect" and "affections" to flourish, and science will set free talent and genius previously shackled by physical pain. In his paean to science and anesthesia, there is a democratic urge. Science, he believes, is a truly democratic force that promises to liberate every man from the limitations imposed by the physical imperfections of his animal nature and to free him to become human, to participate in the worlds he creates. Thus Bigelow attempts to reconcile egalitarianism and professionalism, defining medicine's subject—the body—as the common experience that binds together all men and knowledge of the body as the basis for medicine's authority.

Bigelow's ether writings are full of enthusiasm and youthful ambition. He eagerly imagines what medical science may achieve, he prophesies that the United States will be the next great leader in scientific inquiry, and he is convinced that professional medicine offers wise, ethical management of possibly dangerous discoveries and knowledge without trampling on market freedoms. The confusion evident in some of Bigelow's arguments suggests that the tensions between professionalism and democracy were not easily laid to rest. But his writings also bespeak a desire to understand professional, scientific medicine as an integral part of the nation's democratic ideals. For Bigelow, the professional doctor is an enthusiastic democrat. He honors the ingenuity of the common man, tempers the freedoms of the marketplace with his ethical oversight, and is devoted to freeing all men from the miseries of pain and illness. Although Bigelow was not writing fiction, he was fashioning for himself and for his readers an image of the good doctor that fiction sometimes adopted, sometimes revised, and sometimes challenged.

Chapter 2

Reading the Body: Hawthorne's Tales of Medical Ambition

> Sir William Bradshaw, a great doctor yet to her obscurely evil, without sex or lust, extremely polite to women but capable of some indescribable outrage—forcing your soul, that was it.
>
> —Virginia Woolf, *Mrs. Dalloway*

While doctors were forming medical societies in an effort to improve their public image and Henry Bigelow was envisioning how medicine might free mankind from pain, Nathaniel Hawthorne was writing cautionary tales about medicine. Hawthorne was not concerned with medicine's professional aspirations, or the class implications of professionalism. As a part of the New England elite, he had no interest in populist rhetoric and he respected professional medical men such as Oliver Wendell Holmes. But it is clear that medicine's power worried Hawthorne, and in two early tales—"The Birth-mark" (1843) and "Rappaccini's Daughter" (1844)—he considers the evil that medical scientists might do in their eagerness to master the body.

Throughout his life, Hawthorne was haunted by the power of medicine. In 1821, when he was seventeen and headed to college, he explained in a letter to his mother why he could not become a doctor: "it would weigh very heavily on my Conscience if . . . I should chance to send any unlucky Patient . . . to the realms below." Medicine, he continued, is a parasitic profession that depends upon "the Diseases and Infirmities of [one's] fellow Creatures."[1] Only a few years after "The Birth-mark" and "Rappaccini's Daughter," Hawthorne turned to the topic again, making one of the central characters in *The Scarlet Letter* a vengeful physician who pries into the heart of a man who has cuckolded him. Late in life Hawthorne returned yet again, almost compulsively it would seem, to medicine's power to do evil. One unfinished work, *Doctor Grimshawe's Secret*, is about a young American's discovery of his English past and the odd medical man who raises him. In the first draft there is no physician, but in subsequent drafts Hawthorne more fully elaborated his study of the doctor.[2] He changes from a "perfectly loveable old gentleman" whose house is filled with cobwebs to a grim alcoholic who beats the young boy and broods over his failed efforts to distill the elixir of life from spider webs.[3] In another unfinished work, "The Dolliver Romance," Hawthorne considers the fate of an apothecary who inherits the notebooks and potions of a brilliant medical scientist. The apothecary resists the temptation to experiment, but his son cannot and both the son and a townsman die as a result of ambition, vain desires, and meddling with dangerous chemicals.[4]

In all these texts, Hawthorne is both disturbed and intrigued by medicine's somatic powers. The young Hawthorne recoils from medicine when he realizes that doctors have the power to kill, and he shudders at the thought of becoming a doctor and thus profiting from the infirmities of others. As a writer, he shudders again (and would have his readers also shudder) at the thought of what ambitious medical men might do. Hawthorne's doctors are driven by a desire for knowledge. They experiment recklessly, seek mastery over the bodies of others, and believe that eventually they may be able to control life and defy death. But they always fail: their withered bodies testify to intellectual passions nurtured at the expense of their own bodies, and their desire to know and master yields only death.

Of course, the mad medical scientist was, and still is, a common trope for the arrogant desire to play God. But Hawthorne's repeated use of the trope suggests that the evil medical man was not just a stock figure for him. Indeed, Hawthorne wrote again and again about medical ambition because he was genuinely troubled by the increasingly confident claim to somatic mastery that medicine was making in those years.

Doctors had good reason to be confident in the first decades of the nineteenth century. Pathology was rapidly becoming a rigorous science that promised a radical new understanding of disease, opportunities to do autopsies were increasing, and pathologists were finding success in their efforts to correlate postmortem findings with clinical symptoms (a method still used today). With these opportunities and successes, pathologists began to "anatomize disease," to understand disease as a result of anatomical changes in internal organs (usually apparent in visible lesions) and to understand external manifestations of illness as a result of internal lesions.[5] In the new paradigm, disease was less likely to be understood as a systemic imbalance of fluids, and diagnosis was less a matter of interpreting a patient's story than seeing and reading somatic signs. The art of healing was becoming the science of medicine.

As a lover of ambiguity and "significatory excess," Hawthorne was wary of medicine's eagerness to train an empirical gaze upon the body.[6] Of course, his preference for romance, even as realism became the highbrow genre of choice, has long been understood as evidence of his resistance to empiricism in general and of a preference for shadowy worlds and symbols laden with meanings. But in "The Birth-mark" and "Rappaccini's Daughter," tales in which medical men and their experiments take center stage, Hawthorne challenges quite specifically medicine's belief that it can know the body empirically. In these tales, Hawthorne probes the manic psychology of medical ambition and thus undermines more decorous images of scientists as rational and objective. Pathologists may believe they see what is there—on the surface of the body or buried deep inside. But Hawthorne suggests that medicine's will to know is fueled and tainted by a dangerous mix of intellectual ambition, professional arrogance, and sexual desire. Hawthorne's medical men do not simply see somatic facts; rather, they reduce the body to a thing they can know and remake. But the body exceeds medicine's grasp, and medicine's desire to know the body is figured as a violation of the body, as a rape of the obdurate body.

In both tales, Hawthorne's experimenters commit acts that are akin to the "indescribable outrage" that Sir William Bradshaw commits against the shell-shocked Septimus in *Mrs. Dalloway*. According to Virginia Woolf, doctors such as Bradshaw want to force the soul, to impose order on consciousness and thus deny the fluid inner world of sensory impressions and memories. According to Hawthorne, medicine seeks to impose order on the body by reducing somatic signs to empirical data, and thus medicine is often eager to deny the many and indeterminate meanings of bodily signs. But unlike Woolf, Hawthorne is not only aghast at medicine's efforts, he returns repeatedly to writing about medical ambition because medicine's project to read and write the body was also his own.

In Hawthorne's first tale of medical ambition, a mad medical scientist kills his wife while trying to expunge a faint birthmark on her cheek. Both a tale of ambition and a coy tale about newlyweds, "The Birth-mark" was written when Hawthorne was newly married and cautiously hopeful about his own career. He began writing early in his life and worked hard, but success came slowly. For twelve years, between 1825 and 1837, Hawthorne wrote and, for the most part, failed. He wrote a historical novel that he paid to have published and then sought to suppress, a collection of tales that he tried to get published but ended up burning, and a variety of tales that appeared individually in magazines and annuals but never as a collection, despite his efforts.

At the end of this period, *Twice-Told Tales* appeared, and it was reviewed favorably. Hawthorne was both pleased and wary, noting in his journal with a touch of self-mockery: "In this dismal and sordid chamber FAME was won."[7] He was now thirty-three, and still, as Henry James noted in his biography, "poor and solitary" and still devoted to writing even though he lived "in a community in which the interest in literature was as yet of the smallest."[8] *Twice-Told Tales* would not, Hawthorne knew, bring him significant income, even if it did bring him some fame. By the end of the next year, he was engaged to be married and was perhaps even more aware that a commitment to authorship as a career was economically risky. In the next few years, he tried to make money; he worked as a salt and coal measurer in the Boston Custom House, and he joined Brook Farms and invested funds in the project. At the same time, he worried in a letter to his editors that he might never write again.

In 1842 he finally married and settled into a house in Concord, rented from Ralph Waldo Emerson's step-uncle. Now, Hawthorne must have presumed, he would write, and yet it is clear that he still worried. He noted within the year, "I could be happy as a squash, and much in the same mode. But the necessity of keeping my brains at work eats into my comfort as the squash-bugs do into the heart of vines. I keep myself uneasy, and produce little, and almost nothing that is worth producing."[9] Public success was important to Hawthorne, and throughout these years, he was attentive to the prestige and financial rewards accorded successful writers. He followed Longfellow's career, and with this former Bowdoin classmate he planned though never executed various literary projects that both imagined would be popular and aesthetic successes. Hawthorne was also sensitive to the status accorded other public officials and professionals, and shortly after they moved into the Concord house Sophia thoughtfully removed the portraits of revered clergymen in Hawthorne's study.

Not surprisingly, "The Birth-mark," written during the Hawthornes' first year in Concord, is sympathetic to ambition and to failure. By the end of the tale, Aylmer may be an egotistical, ambitious misogynist, but early on he is described as "ardent" and "imaginative." Initially Hawthorne imagined the plot would be not only about ambition and failure but also about reconciliation and acceptance.[10] In a preparatory sketch, he writes, "A person to be the death of his beloved trying to raise her to more than mortal perfection; yet this should be a comfort to him for having aimed so high and holily."[11] Although we may recoil at the suggestion that a man who has killed his wife might be comforted by the thought that her death was in the service of a high and holy aim, within the tale the narrator encourages us not to judge Aylmer too harshly. When Georgiana peeks into Aylmer's folio, we see a man both devoted to doing something extraordinary and painfully aware of his mediocrity. In what is perhaps the most disarming passage in the story, the narrator explains:

His brightest diamonds were the merest pebbles, and felt to be so by himself, in comparison with the inestimable gems which lay hidden beyond his reach. The volume, rich with achievements, that had won renown for its author, was yet as melancholy a record as ever mortal hand had penned. It was the sad confession, and continual exemplification, of the short-comings of the composite man—the spirit burthened with clay and working in matter—and of the despair that assails the higher nature, at finding itself so miserably thwarted by the earthly part. Perhaps every man of genius, in whatever sphere, might recognize the image of his own experience in Aylmer's journal. (49)

Aylmer's fear that his diamonds are mere pebbles echoes Hawthorne's anxiety that he was producing "little, and almost nothing that is worth producing." In the early 1840s Hawthorne's worries were akin to Aylmer's, and Hawthorne may even have rewritten Sophia's willingness to sacrifice her own artistic interests (she painted) to become his wife as Georgiana's willing submission to Aylmer's dangerous experiment.[12]

Ultimately, however, the tale does judge Aylmer, and although his folio may include sad confessions of thwarted dreams, he lacks a sustained awareness of his arrogant confidence in his own powers. He brags and lies without compunction, and he insists on both the difficulty of removing the birthmark and on his ability to meet the challenge. The achievement will be greater than Pygmalion's, he insists, and yet he declares: "I feel myself fully competent" (41). And he covers up his failures. In order to demonstrate his skill, he performs three tricks for his wife. The first is "almost perfect" but unimpressive—Georgiana has "some indistinct idea of the method of these optical phenomena" (45). And the second and third tricks are outright failures, with her body trumping his science. A flower he creates is blighted by her touch, and a portrait he takes is blurry except for the offensive birthmark. Ignoring these "mortifying failures" and what they suggest about somatic resistance to technological and scientific remaking, Aylmer insists he should proceed, and he brags of the "long dynasty of the alchemists" (46) and makes exaggerated claims for what science can achieve.

In other works, Hawthorne imagines that women temper male ambition. In *The Blithedale Romance* and *The House of Seven Gables*, for example, feminine purity mollifies male despotism and staves off male violence.[13] Aylmer, however, is not deterred by his wife's gentle spirit, and Hawthorne suggests that medical ambition is particularly pernicious because the physician's presumption that he knows the female body makes him immune to the tempering power of feminine purity. Aylmer's confidence of somatic mastery—he can assess the birthmark on her cheek and treat it with a special chemical brew—makes it impossible for him to see the birthmark as anything other than a problem that he can fix.[14]

Men who are not scientists find the mark on Georgiana's cheek titil-lating, a coy sign of female sexuality upon a body that is otherwise pure, and "Many a desperate swain would have risked life for the privilege of pressing his lips" to it (38). As T. Walter Herbert has noted, the erotics of imperfect purity played an important role in Hawthorne's courtship and early marriage. Hawthorne often highlighted his appreciation of Sophia's purity, insisting that he would never read the letters of his "sin-less Eve" without "first washing his hands." He called Sophia his "dove," and he imagined her as a "heavenly lily" that he might wear on his bosom.[15] At the same time, he enjoyed the teasing possibilities of a less than perfect wife, writing of his "naughty" Sophia with sly pleasure. Tropes of purity and corruption also mark Sophia's writings. In the "Family Notebook" that she and Nathaniel started keeping when they married, she purifies sexual passion, figuring it as a "wonderous instru-ment . . . for the purposes of the heart" when there is an "entire oneness of spirit" between the partners.[16] By contrast, she understood her debil-itating, chronic headaches as evidence of her impurity: "Dr. Shattuck was right when he so decidedly declared I never should be relieved 'till I hear the music of the spheres'—in other words—till I had put off corruption."[17]

Aylmer does, in fact, find the mark titillating. He cannot keep his eyes off it. But he refuses to submit, perhaps because he is "a man of science," to the erotics of imperfect purity (36). Like Hawthorne, Aylmer imag-ines the world of domesticity and marriage as a place of purity. In order to marry Georgiana, he washes "the stain of acids from his fingers" and he clears "his fine countenance from the furnace-smoke" (36). But as an ambitious experimenter, Aylmer cannot find pleasure, even naughty pleasure, in the suggestive sign on his wife's cheek. Like Dr. Shattuck and Sophia, Aylmer seems to believe that corruption must be "put off." He has spent a "toilsome youth" in the laboratory studying the "elemen-tal powers of nature," the "rich medicinal virtues" of mysterious foun-tains, the "wonders of the human frame," and the "process by which Nature assimilates all her precious influences . . . to create and foster man," and thus he believes he has the power to relieve his wife of her imperfection (42). Aylmer lays claim to domesticity's ideal—feminine purity—and believes that where nature has failed science will succeed. Moreover, as Georgiana's husband, he has the power to extract her consent to his plan. In other words, when a man is both husband and medical scientist, a blemish that might titillate a husband or earn mild therapeutic advice from a physician becomes a provocative and accessi-ble site for scientific experimentation.[18]

On one level, the tale is humorous: Aylmer is an awkward science nerd and his medical laboratory cum boudoir is more comic than gruesome. Hawthorne plays upon the tropes of sensational fiction to describe

Aylmer's laboratory as a place where scientific ambition is given free rein and male desire, unabashed and unwashed, is liberated.[19] But Aylmer is not particularly fiendish, and as he prepares to bring his wife into his laboratory he is more concerned with interior decorating than sex. Indeed, Aylmer devotes himself to transforming his laboratory, a dank room covered with "quantities of soot," filled with "gaseous odors," and inhabited by the "shaggy," "encrusted" Aminadab into an "elegant boudoir" and "secluded abode" for his "lovely woman" (50, 43, 44). Aylmer covers the walls with "gorgeous curtains" that fall from "the ceiling to the floor" in "rich and ponderous folds" that shut in "the scene from the infinite space," and he fills the rooms with "perfumed lamps" that envelop all in an "empurpled radiance" (44). The room, perhaps modeled on Hawthorne's study, which, according to Sophia, he wanted laid "with a soft, thick Turkey carpet upon the floor & hung round with full crimson curtains, so as to hide all rectangles,"[20] does not, however, produce romance or wild sex. Aylmer is often "flushed" and frequently "exhausted"; he must work to keep up his energy, and his enthusiasm is never in response to Georgiana's body. He imagines "triumph" and "ecstasy" only when he is thinking about his experiment, and it is only his assistant who sees Georgiana sexually. When Georgiana faints at the threshold of the laboratory and lies there inert and available, Aylmer is eager only to get on with the experiment. Aminadab, by contrast, sees her beauty and mutters one of the funniest lines in the story: "'If she were my wife, I'd never part with that birthmark'" (43).[21]

Georgiana, by contrast, is aroused and responsive. As the experiment progresses, she feels "a stirring up of her system—a strange, indefinite sensation creeping through her veins and tingling, half painfully, half pleasurably, at her heart" as the experiment proceeds (48). The birthmark throbs with each beat of her heart, and she feels "a sensation . . . not painful, but which induced a restlessness throughout her system" (50).[22] These coy descriptions of female orgasm, however, do not warn, as do similar descriptions in sensational fiction, that it is a woman's own physiological susceptibility to carnal desire that makes her vulnerable to seduction. Georgiana submits willingly to her husband's plan (often to the dismay of twentieth-century readers). She has read his folios, knows of his failures, retains her own independent judgment of his achievements, and yet promises him, "I shall quaff whatever draught you bring me" (51). In short, Hawthorne rewrites sensational tales of fiendish, lascivious medical scientists and easily excited women into a sometimes humorous and sometimes erotic tale of a "man of science" with a "fine countenance" and "slender figure" who directs all his sexual energy into a benighted experiment on his intelligent, willing wife.

On another level, however, Hawthorne takes seriously the possibility that sexual excitement might induce a dangerous intellectual frenzy. He read broadly in science, including occasional issues of Benjamin Silliman's *American Journal of Science and the Arts* (originally *The Medical Repository*) and a wide variety of popular science material while serving in 1836 as the editor of the *American Magazine of Useful and Entertaining Knowledge*. We also know that he read at least parts of Andrew Combe's *The Principles of Physiology of Digestion*, in which he found a case about mania that served as a source for "The Birth-mark." In a journal where he jotted down possible plots, Hawthorne notes:

The case quoted in Combe's "Physiology," from Pinel, of a young man of great talents and profound knowledge of chemistry, who had in view some new discovery of importance. In order to put his mind into the highest possible activity, he shut himself up for several successive days, and used various methods of excitement. He had a singing-girl, he drank spirits, smelled penetrating odors, sprinkled—Cologne-water round the room, &c., &c., Eight days thus passed, when he was seized with a fit of frenzy which terminated in mania.[23]

The case might have caught Hawthorne's attention because it challenged the new trend toward anatomizing disease. Philippe Pinel, the original source for the case, was a French physician who was devoted to clinical study, but who also noted that many dissections of the insane revealed no "organic lesion of the head" at all.[24] Andrew Combe was presumably interested in the case for a similar reason. Although he trained at the Royal College of Physicians of Edinburgh and in Paris with the renowned surgeon Guillaume Dupuytren, Combe, like Pinel, believed that not all illnesses were the result of lesions and that some were caused by desires too much sated or too stringently thwarted.[25]

In "The Birth-mark," as in Pinel's case, desires are thwarted, redirected, and stimulated in inappropriate ways, and the result is that a brilliant man becomes a maniac. As the narrator notes in the beginning, the tale is about the "intertwining" relationship between "love of woman" and "love of science" (36). Initially, Aylmer plans to give up his love of science for marriage. But he cannot deny his scientific desires for long, and they reappear in his obsession with the mark on his wife's cheek. Then, when he returns to his intellectual work, his sexual appetite, or "love of woman," fuels his love of science. Like the chemist in Pinel's case, Aylmer turns his laboratory into a sensual boudoir, complete with perfumes, low light, and his wife's unconscious, available body. (The case might have suggested teasingly to Hawthorne, who was himself recently married and often shut up in a room as part of his writing regimen, that male genius craves not only solitude but also sexual excitement.)

Hawthorne also takes seriously the violence that might be caused by intellectual mania fueled by repressed sexual desires, and the violence in the tale undercuts and darkens its playful sexual humor. Most obviously, Georgiana's death indicts her husband, and Aylmer is chastised by the narrator at the end of the tale for failing to understand how the "angelic spirit" is in "union with the mortal frame" (56). More disturbing are the signs indicating the violence that attends his obsession with the mark and his desire to remove it. At home, his eyes wander again and again "stealthily to her cheek," and she shudders at "his gaze" and the "peculiar expression that his face often wore" (39). Before the experiment, he dreams of "attempting an operation for the removal of the birthmark," of going deeper and deeper with a knife in an effort to "cut or wrench it away" (40). During the experiment, in response to a slight sign of independence in his wife, Aylmer grabs her arm "with a gripe that left the print of his fingers upon it" (51). His cold gaze, his dream, and the bruise make it clear that although the tale is often funny and erotic, it is also about violence.

The violence that powerful men can do to women was never far from Hawthorne's mind.[26] In "The Custom-House" he notes that his great-grandfather, Judge John Hathorne, condemned young women to the gallows during the Salem witch trials on evidence that was slight. In "Main-Street," he tells the story of a Quaker woman who was stripped to the waist and flogged as she was bound to a cart, "dragged through Main-street at the pace of a brisk walk," and given thirty lashes that drew blood after his great-great-grandfather, William Hathorne, had sentenced her.[27] In "The Birth-mark," Hawthorne focuses on the violence that an ambitious medical scientist might do.

What I have suggested so far, then, is that when Hawthorne was himself eager for success, newly married, and attuned to the language of purity and corruption, he wrote a tale about a newlywed, ambitious medical scientist determined to remove a faint birthmark from his wife's beautiful face. I have also suggested that in sexualizing medical ambition, Hawthorne was alert to the serious treatment that sexual energy was earning in scientific discourse and to images in sensational fiction of the medical laboratory as a space that licensed scientific excess and libertine expressions of male desire. By deploying the tropes of sensationalism, a language particularly adept at linking horror, humor, and sexuality, Hawthorne is able to represent Aylmer's confused mix of desire and scientific ambition as part murderous loathing, part hilarious, sleazy longing for a sexual underworld, and part medical prurience. But now I want to take the argument further and suggest that "The Birth-mark" not only draws upon popular sexualized images of the laboratory and mad medical scientists, but also posits a dark side of medicine just at the moment when medicine was seeking increased authority and increased access to the body.

In part, the tale registers a widely felt anxiety about medicine's access to the female body. The nineteenth century saw a profound shift in the physician's relationship to the patient's body. At the beginning of the century, few physicians performed extensive physical examinations, and at midcentury, physical exams, clinical study of patients in hospital wards, and the use of autopsies in medical education worried the public. But by the end of the century, physical exams were routine. The physician's access to the female body was particularly troubling. In response, doctors were eager to prove their respect for feminine purity and modesty. U.S. physicians who studied in Paris at La Pitié, a large city hospital where bodies were easily viewed, took pains to disassociate themselves from such practices. One physician acknowledged in the *New Hampshire Journal of Medicine* that while in Paris women's bodies were freely exhibited and examined, U.S. medical education would never adopt such a scandalous practice. He describes the extensive use and direct touching of women's bodies in midwifery classes and concludes by touting the modesty of American women and physicians. He writes, "How many of our American women would be thus willingly exposed? I am proud to believe not one!"[28]

In truth, female patients were used for medical education in the United States, but not without some public outcry. In 1850, for example, a University of Buffalo professor was charged with indecency after a midwifery exhibition. Those who condoned the exhibition testified that the woman was draped throughout, and students who were present reported that they saw no "front part of the woman's private parts."[29] The trial transcript suggests that at this time physicians carefully weighed the demands of medical education against female modesty. At the trial, physicians testified about the efficacy and morality of using anatomical drawings, engraved plates, life-size manikins, of "learning by touch," and of learning from "ocular demonstration."[30] Like Georgiana's inert body lying upon the threshold of Aylmer's laboratory, the female body is present but silent both in the midwifery exhibition (she is present but draped and not, it would seem, a speaking participant) and in the trial transcript (she is present but nameless and obscured by the elaborate circumlocutions devoted to avoiding explicit reference to her body).

Avoiding visual intimacy with and verbal explicitness about the female body was a concern in medical practice as well as medical education. The stethoscope was valuable, as its discoverer René Laennec noted, because it allowed him to listen to the interior of a female body without asking the patient to remove her clothes.[31] Dr. William Potts Dewees's popular midwifery manual condemned ocular pelvic exams, suggesting that "every attention should be paid to delicacy . . . the patient should not be exposed . . . even for the drawing off of the urine."[32] Parturient women were delivered while draped with sheets, and one young doctor reported that he had no idea when delivering a child if he was touching a head, hand, or foot since he steadfastly avoided looking.[33]

Such circumlocutions in language, education, and practice were not merely rhetorical strategies to appease prudish conventions. Regulars were genuinely eager to demonstrate their professional manners and their respect for feminine modesty, particularly since most of their competitors in alternative medicine did not perform physical examinations. Moreover, when studying or teaching obstetrics and gynecology, regulars at mid-century were truly embarrassed. Samuel D. Gross, the esteemed surgeon featured in Thomas Eakins's *The Gross Clinic,* described the embarrassment of his obstetrics professor: "it was seldom that he . . . looked squarely at his audience. His cheeks would be mantled with blushes while engaging in demonstrating some pelvic viscous." Dr. William Potts Dewees was less easily embarrassed. According to Gross, Dewees "did not hesitate to call things by their proper names" and never blushed in the lecture room. And yet, he insisted in his popular mid-wifery manual that students should learn from mannequins and should perform only "unsighted digital explorations of parturient women."[34]

For some, the threat that male physicians posed to women warranted an end to all-male medical care of women, and women physicians were sometimes championed as a solution to the problem of intimate care for the female body. Implicit in such debates was a concern with sexual arousal of the male physician and the vulnerability of the female patient to a lecherous physician and to her own latent desires. The reformer George Gregory, for example, published a pamphlet that concludes with a titillating warning about doctors who seduce their patients. Deploying the salacious language that was common in reform literature, the pamphlet warns of "unprincipled medical men" who have "a most familiar and confidential intercourse" with female patients.[35] The patient's "husband, being confined by business, is absent the livelong day, or for weeks and months" and the physician knows her "whims and weak points." As Aylmer uses his husbandly access and scientific authority to persuade his wife to submit to his experiment, so Gregory's imagined physician uses his husband-like medical access to a patient to visit frequently and press his suit. In language reminiscent of Hawthorne's tale, Gregory notes that the doctor fixes "his prey . . . and resist she cannot . . . she can refuse nothing—all is lost!"[36]

While Gregory's imagined scene and the trial in Buffalo may seem to us melodramatic posturing in exaggerated arguments about female delicacy, these texts suggest that anxieties about violence, eroticism, male desire, feminine purity, and medical ambition were not easily sorted out as physical examinations became more common and as medicine was increasingly devoted to knowing the body directly rather than through rationalist a priori systems or indirectly through the patient's report. Indeed, physicians' worries that physical examinations threatened domestic decorum were not unfounded. As late as 1876, Tolstoy turned in *Anna Karenina* to the specter of a full medical exam to figure women's vulnerability to the shame of physical exposure, and at mid-century, the trope of the doctor who takes advantage of his position had real currency in popular fiction. For example, Eugène Sue's best-selling novel, *The Mysteries of Paris*, published in the same year as Hawthorne's tale, draws a vivid portrait of a fiendish physician trained at La Pitié who preys upon female patients. The American edition made Dr. Griffon's abuse of women the subject of lurid illustrations, and U.S. physicians were eager to distance themselves quite explicitly from the image of Dr. Griffin.[37]

Hawthorne's tale, like Sue's novel, plays upon these concerns, and as I have suggested, Aylmer's medical ambition is in part sexual desire gone awry. In "The Birth-mark," Hawthorne seems genuinely concerned about medicine's access to the domestic world and about the sexual energy that may fuel male ambition. And his concerns were not, it would seem, unreasonable. Years later, when his oldest daughter was sick while the family was in Rome, the doctor took advantage of his access to the daughter's bedroom to press unwanted kisses upon Una's governess, Ada Shephard. In letters to her fiancé, Shephard reported that Dr. Franco was a "raging lion" who poured forth a "storm of consuming and raging passion" and "dared to force upon my cheek and lips his hateful, unholy kisses." Sophia Hawthorne also found Dr. Franco a powerful presence: she described him as "vivid, impulsive, transparent, frank" and refused to "have him blamed" for Una's continued illness.[38]

But as much as "The Birth-mark" is about scientific interests confused with and fueled by libidinal passions, it is also a significant revision of the familiar portrait of the mad doctor with access to the female body. Hawthorne invokes the specter of the sexually obsessed medical experimenter, but he warns against a danger perhaps even more worrisome than crude sexual advances. Aylmer's ambition is not about sexual access to his wife's body. The medicalized rape that the tale imagines is not, in the end, an act of carnal degradation, but rather an attempt to purify by erasure. Aylmer's ambition is not to have unrestricted access to Georgiana's body so that he might satisfy his own carnal desires (the goal Gregory and Sue suggested might motivate some physicians). Rather, his experiment seeks to purify his wife's body of its signs.

The birthmark on Georgiana's cheek heightens the visibility of her body. It draws attention to her body and to her embodiedness. Critics have variously teased out the meanings of the mark, reading it as a metonym for blood, birth, women's creativity, sexuality, imperfection, or mortality. In short, it is an overloaded sign that vibrates with multiple and contradictory meanings.[39] But it also serves most simply as a synecdoche for Georgiana's body. In fact, Hawthorne suggests that in this case not only does the part represent the whole, but that the part cannot be separated from the whole. This intimate and never-to-be-sundered relationship between the body and its signs is what medicine, according to Hawthorne, does not understand.

When Aylmer imagines that Georgiana can be separated from the mark, he presumes that the mark is alienable property. His thinking depends upon both a market notion of individualism and self ownership and the medical corollary in which the patient is presumed to own his or her body. Owning one's self was a central tenet of the rise of modern liberalism,[40] and in medicine, possessive individualism meant the body was a thing that might be studied apart from the patient. As a recent medical philosopher explains, this means that during a physical exam, "the patient responds to the request of the physician to live in his or her body . . . as a body that he or she has, not as the body that they are . . . This thing-body . . . is something merely possessed, an object, a thing with physical, anatomical and physiological property."[41] In the nineteenth century, this new model authorized the physical examinations and midwifery exhibitions that many, as I noted earlier, found troubling. According to the new model, physical examinations were not invasions of the patient's ontological being, but simply an encounter between science and its object of inquiry—the body. Splitting the body from the patient also legitimized access to the body-as-property in medical education, and medical schools promoted themselves by advertising their somatic wealth. Some proclaimed the plenitude of cadavers at their schools, Southern schools touted their easy access to the bodies of deceased slaves, and part of the appeal of studying in Paris lay in greater access to bodies—alive and dead—in clinics and in pathology laboratories.[42]

In the 1830s and 1840s, it was still possible to challenge a view that is now deeply ingrained and almost impossible to think beyond. Historians offer various accounts of the development of a Western mind/body duality. The rise of Cartesian philosophy is one major moment. The rise of modern medicine at the end of the eighteenth century is another. With this in mind, then, we should understand the popularity of the fictional evil doctor as, in part, a challenge to modern medicine's notion of the "thing body." The evil doctor's misdeed lies not only in digging up dead bodies or preying upon unsuspecting females. Rather, his greatest sin is in thinking of bodies as merely bodies.[43] Or, as Hawthorne suggests in "The Birth-mark," if bodily marks are understood as things then the body becomes vulnerable to territorial raids.[44]

Hawthorne also deploys the image of the evil doctor to make an even more pointed critique. In understanding Georgiana's birthmark as something he can remove without regard for the patient, Aylmer fails to understand that the body (and its marks) signify. In his study of the body in literature, Peter Brooks notes that although the body is a primary source for symbols, the materiality of the body seems to defy translation into language, to defy representation.[45] As a result, we try to "bring the body into language, to represent it, so it becomes part of the human semiotic and semantic project." If the body sometimes seems obdurate and unknowable, writing about the body can be a way to rediscover a "language embodied" and to create "a body endowed with meaning."[46]

In claiming to know the body directly through physical examinations, medicine believed that it might avoid the inaccuracies of linguistic translations of material facts. Early attempts to minimize the role of language in the patient-physician meeting turned to mathematical formulations. Some clinical researchers plotted the patient's narrative (the patient's description of pain, nausea, and aches) against what the doctor could know through direct examination (visible or measurable signs such as flush, temperature, pulse, breathing rate, and lesions). This "dream of an arithmetical structure of medical language" gave way, as Michel Foucault notes, to a commitment to exhaustive and exact descriptions and then to the clinical gaze, a myth in which seeing is free of language and leads directly to knowing.[47] In other words, researchers thought that ultimately the patient's words would be unnecessary. Direct examination would tell all and would never be distorted by the instability and misrepresentations of language. The discovery of lesions was central to these developments. Lesions were "prized by Paris medicine" because physicians believed they were "surer guides to pathogenesis than subjective symptoms."[48] The lesion, even more than symptomatic signs such as a rapid pulse or the "rales" of labored breathing, promised the possibility of knowing disease directly, and not through interpretation. As one historian notes, the lesion became "the most important defining characteristic of disease."[49]

Like medicine's lesion, the mark on Georgiana's cheek seems to be a somatic fact. Aylmer thinks of it as a sign of pathology, and the surgical remedy he dreams of performing would not have been out of line with medical practice since surgery was a treatment increasingly prescribed as lesions gained importance in medical thinking. But the mark on Georgiana's cheek also has affinities with the blush, a somatic sign still popular in the nineteenth century and deeply rooted in eighteenth-century novels of manners, in which it testifies to gentility as well as bodiliness.[50] Georgiana's mark suggests that she is a genteel woman and that her body discreetly betrays its desires. It bespeaks her purity and embarrassment: the red brightens when Aylmer looks at her with desire or loathing. The mark admits carnal desire: it vibrates with her pulse, is intermittent and coy, and is beyond her control. It also speaks of anger because it darkens when she reddens "with momentary anger" in response to Aylmer's involuntary recoiling from her and the mark he loathes.[51]

But whether it speaks of embarrassment, sexual desire, or anger, the mark most clearly is a symbol of the body's refusal to be known. Georgiana's birthmark is, undoubtedly, a somatic fact, something a physician might examine, and Aylmer rejects Georgiana's account of her own body and presumes he knows better. But, as Aylmer's failure makes abundantly clear, the mark cannot be known. It is too changeable—"now vaguely portrayed, now lost, now stealing forth again and glimmering to and fro" (38). It teases with the promise of meaning, but it yields nothing definitive. It is a somatic sign that cannot be plotted; it cannot be translated.[52] Medicine's approach—poke, prod, dissect—will not do. The mark reveals Hawthorne's commitment to "somatic signification" in that it dispels the fear that "the obdurate body is obstinate in its refusal to speak."[53] And yet, in its indecipherability, the birthmark also testifies to Hawthorne's commitment to significatory excess, to a view of the body not as alienable property, not as an object knowable through the "dream of an arithmetical structure of medical language."[54] Georgiana's birthmark hints at the body coming forth into an almost legible sign. And it cannot be erased without destroying the entire world of heightened meaning—aesthetic and erotic, psychological and dramatic—that Hawthorne so highly values.

Ultimately, Georgiana's mark is for Hawthorne both of the body and of language, and in the tale Hawthorne seeks both to write an embodied language and to represent a body endowed with meaning. Writing at a moment when presumably his own sexual world had been radically altered, and perhaps at a time when ownership or control of his own body had been challenged by the new carnal relations that marriage entails, Hawthorne is eager to "manage within the confines of a readable sign system . . . the challenges posed by the body" and yet to render the body as fully as perhaps his newly married state made him feel his own body.[55] Contrary to the distrust of corporeality that some critics find in Hawthorne's fiction, the pleasure of writing the body is central to the tale. When Hawthorne writes of the "triumphant rush of blood that bathed the whole cheek with its brilliant glow," he undoubtedly participates in a fantasy of the legible body. Medicine, too, participated in that fantasy. The lesion discovered in living bodies in the wards at La Pitié and in the cadavers of the pathology laboratory was for medicine the body writing itself. Expertise in this somatic language was central to medicine's claim to authority. In a challenge to that authority, Hawthorne revises medicine's stable, knowable lesion, making it a coy somatic text that yields no definitive meaning and yet is endlessly meaningful. Hawthorne's tale, like medicine, fantasizes that with its visible signs the body is asking to be read. But Hawthorne rejects medicine's fantasy of empirical somatic knowledge and offers instead romance and linguistic play as a mode of knowing the body, one less likely to do violence to the body and its meanings.

In "Rappaccini's Daughter," published twenty-one months after "The Birth-mark," Hawthorne again challenges medicine's somatic authority against a backdrop of purity, eroticism, and violence. There are, however, important differences: a birth-mark on the skin has been replaced by a poison within; a body that writes desire on its surface is now a body that kills with its breath. While "The Birth-mark" recounts a medical experiment as it is planned, the later tale begins with the experiment in medias res. In the earlier tale, the physician hopes to purify a besmirched body; in "Rappaccini's Daughter," he has bred a new body, a "commixture," an "adultery," a "mingling," a "wonder of hideous monstrosity."[56] The later tale is bleaker and more confused. It lacks the playful sexual humor of "The Birth-mark," and it considers not medicine's failed territorial raid upon female sexuality, but rather medicine's successful colonization of the body's interior, that "dim region beyond the daylight of our perfect consciousness" (114). Set at the moment when medicine first began to map the body's interior and written when pathological anatomy was assuming a central role in medicine, "Rappaccini's Daughter" figures interiority as somatic and architectural spaces—Beatrice's body and a Renaissance garden—remade and poisoned by medicine. But in poisoning his daughter and thus giving her a disturbing, diseased somatic interior, Rappaccini paradoxically also offers an honest view of the body. He destroys the idealized image of the pure, transcendent female body and understands all bodies, even female bodies, as organic matter that will ripen, putrefy, and die. All bodies harbor dark secrets.

The tension between outer and inner permeates Hawthorne's personal writings. Sometimes, Hawthorne reports, his outer self reveals nothing of his inner state. In a letter to his close friend George Hillard, Hawthorne writes of the inner agitation he feels even "when my outward man is at rest."[57] Sometimes the inner and outer are similarly disposed, but still Hawthorne reports on each. In a letter to his editor, Evert Duyckinck, Hawthorne notes that both his inner and outer selves are exhausted, explaining that his "inner man droops in sympathy" with his external self's exhaustion.[58] At times, Hawthorne coyly exposes himself and yet claims to have kept "innermost me" hidden. In "The Old Manse," for example, he insists that although some intimate details are revealed, the reader has not gone "wandering, hand and hand with me through the inner passages of my being." Hawthorne explains that he is not among those who "serve up their own hearts delicately fried, with brain-sauce, as a tidbit for their beloved public."[59]

The uneasy relationship between an outer public self and inner private self is perhaps most vivid in an undated letter written around this time. Here Hawthorne mocks himself by imagining public tours of his private chambers.

Salem.—. . . Here I am, in my old chamber, where I produced those stupendous works of fiction which have since impressed the universe with wonderment and awe! To this chamber, doubtless, in all succeeding ages, pilgrims will come to pay their tribute of reverence; they will put off their shoes at the threshold for fear of desecrating the tattered old carpets! "There," they will exclaim, "is the very bed in which he slumbered, and where he was visited by those ethereal visions which he afterwards fixed forever in glowing words! There is the wash-stand at which this exalted personage cleansed himself from the stains of earth, and rendered his outward man a fitting exponent of the pure soul within.[60]

It later turned out that the outlandish fame the passage imagines was not so far-fetched; by the early 1850s, there were print tours of Hawthorne's home for fans to purchase.[61] But before Hawthorne had to negotiate such public success, a visit to his old attic room at 12 Herbert Street prompted him to worry about his writing career and imagine a bathetic scene of public adoration that centers on a washstand. While the washstand most obviously mediates a relationship perhaps too intimate between the famous author and his adoring public, it also negotiates a relationship between the writer's outer body and the "pure soul within." The washstand make possible the cleansing transformation of the physical man necessary before embarking upon creative work, but it also gestures to everyday ablutions and uses an intimate somatic ritual to figure psychological interiority.

In part, Hawthorne's coy public staging in all these examples of an "inner man" is congruent with the fact that interiority must be publicly reproduced and yet endlessly secreted.[62] Hawthorne's need to claim and protect an "innermost me" is also a response to the public obligations of authorship. As Richard Brodhead notes, Hawthorne was among the first generation of writers who had to manage literature's emerging relations with commercial, highly public promotional efforts to sell authors, and yet produce fiction that was increasingly understood as an intimate part of the domestic sphere.[63]

What interests me here, however, is Hawthorne's inclination to represent interiority somatically and the role the physician played in his imagination and the nation's as medicine increasingly colonized the inner landscapes of the body. Anxious to protect his privacy, and yet committed to romance as a means of exploring the darkest recesses of the mind and soul, Hawthorne imagined the physician with a disturbing power to probe somatic interiority and psychic depths.[64] In *The Scarlet Letter*, for example, the narrator warns only half-humorously that "a man in possession of a secret should especially avoid the intimacy of his physician," and the image of Chillingworth digging "into the poor clergyman's heart, like a miner . . . or rather, like a sexton delving into a grave" is chilling.[65] The physician as gravedigger had widespread currency at this time, and by invoking the image, Hawthorne plays upon public anxiety about medicine's eagerness to open the body and probe its interior.[66] Chillingworth, of course, opens neither grave nor body, and yet his professional access to graves, to Dimmesdale's study and thus to the minister when he falls asleep over his books, and literally to the interior of bodies through medicinal herbs, indicates his access to Dimmesdale's heart and psyche.

In "Rappaccini's Daughter," Hawthorne takes up these issues directly, and he sets his interrogation of medicine's invasion of the interior landscape of the body at the moment and place of modern medicine's birth—the University of Padua in the sixteenth century. The center of Renaissance medicine, the University of Padua was known for anatomical studies. It was home to the major anatomists of the day—Alessandro Benedetti, Realdo Colombo, Gabriele Falloppia, Hieronymus Fabricius ab Aquapendente, and, the most famous anatomist, Andreas Vesalius, who arrived in Padua in 1537 and published the *De humani corporis fabrica* in 1543.[67] The tale is not a literal account of the Paduan medical department, but as Carol Marie Bensick has shown, Hawthorne's Italian allusions are so precise and coherent that the tale begs to be read as an historical allegory.[68]

Rappaccini is clearly one of the Paduan iconoclasts and is perhaps based on Vesalius. Like Vesalius, Rappaccini is a member of the Paduan medical faculty, and his devotion to his garden is a reminder of the link between anatomy and botany in sixteenth-century Padua (94). There were important advances in both anatomy and botany in these years, and Vesalius's *Fabrica* was published the same year Padua's first botanical garden was established.[69] Like Vesalius's anatomy theater, Rappaccini's garden features a body at the center, the medical scientist at its side, and the audience (colleagues Giovanni and Baglioni) watching from above. As Vesalius impressed everyone with his talent, and raised eyebrows with his insistence upon doing dissections himself, so Rappaccini has "as much science as any member of the faculty" and has provoked "grave objections to his professional character" with his unconventional experiments with plants and his daughter's body (99). Most importantly,

Rappaccini is, like his historical counterpart, devoted to the study of structures.

Nothing could exceed the intentness with which this scientific gardener examined every shrub which grew in his path: it seemed as if he was looking into their inmost nature, making observations in regard to their creative essence, and discovering why one leaf grew in this shape and another in that, and wherefore such and such flowers differed among themselves in hue and perfume. (95–96)

This description accurately explains a fundamental premise of Renaissance anatomy—form determines function, "shape" reveals "creative essence," and it details the role of comparative studies in botany and anatomy at this time.[70] Rappaccini also dons the garb of the anatomist and of the gardener. He defends "his hands with a pair of thick gloves" and wears "a kind of mask over his mouth and nostrils" (96). This kind of dirty, hands-on experimentation was the hallmark of the new anatomists, and in particular Vesalius, who always performed his own dissections rather than allowing a dissector to do the messy and physically demanding work of cutting up a cadaver.

Baglioni, by contrast, is a humorous portrait of a Renaissance academician, and he speaks for the traditionalists who were offended by Vesalius. He respects the old rules, and he is a man of "eminent repute" (99). He is never seen at work in a clinic or laboratory, but only amidst the trappings of unsullied academia. Unlike Rappaccini who is "sallow" and "emaciated," Baglioni is "portly" (95, 95, 106). His nature is "genial," his habits "jovial," his conversation "lively," his dinners "agreeable," and he is fond of "Tuscan wine" (99). As a dedicated Galenist, Baglioni has little tolerance for an experimenter such as Rappaccini, much as some traditionalists considered Vesalius a "mere dissector."[71] Baglioni insists that Rappaccini must not "be tolerated by those who respect the good old rules of the medical profession" (120).

In the rivalry between the two, Hawthorne captures real tensions in Renaissance medicine. Rappaccini's battle with Baglioni for Giovanni's loyalty bespeaks the power of mentors at the University of Padua, where positions were handed down from teacher to disciple and disputes were often heated and public. In 1539, for example, Vesalius published a bitter letter attacking his former teacher and other senior physicians who were unwilling to adopt new methods of venesection.[72] In another famous dispute, Gabriele Falloppia was ousted from his post in 1555 when conservatives called for a return to anatomy lessons without dissections.[73] He was reinstated only after students protested his dismissal. The "black-letter tracts" in Hawthorne's tale that record a "professional warfare of long continuance" between Rappaccini and Baglioni and are "preserved in the medical department at the University of Padua" gesture, then, to the professional bickering that marked medical science in Italy in the sixteenth century (100).

The tale is not, however, only a history of personal and methodological rivalries in Renaissance medicine. It also considers the implications of what Paduan medicine was most famous for—dissecting the human body. The success of Renaissance anatomy depended, in part, upon managing the anxiety that the opened body provokes. As Jonathan Sawday notes in his history of Renaissance anatomy, before Vesalius it was common to think of the interior of the body as the soul's domain, a habit still evident in Hawthorne's image of the washstand where the "outward man" is made "a fitting exponent of the pure soul within."[74] But, as dissection made evident, somatic interiors are not particularly clean or pure. The closed body only hints at its interior landscape, leaking phlegm, sweat, blood, and other fluids that bespeak disease and death. Dissection makes such horrors plainly visible, and looking inside the body is an uncanny experience, witnesses of postmortems report. The familiar is made strange as reassuring surface signs of individuality—wrinkles, birthmarks, and scars—disappear and the skin is peeled back to reveal some deeply shared though rarely seen human form.[75]

Vesalius's public dissections borrowed from older somatic specta-cles.[76] Medieval religious practices such as flagellation, pus drinking, and dismemberment that used the body to access the divine were not distant history in the sixteenth century, and state-sanctioned spectator-ial corporeal punishment was still practiced. Reworking these practices, the earliest anatomists claimed that the dissected body was a kind of saintly body that offered a means to higher knowledge. They also some-times acknowledged kinship with the executioner.[77] Some anatomists performed executions in order to get fresh bodies, and tickets were sold to public dissections as they were to executions. The Paduan anatomy theater was until 1594 a makeshift structure that allowed onlookers to gather much as crowds gathered at the gallows.[78] Vesalius himself did not shrink from an association with criminality; the *Fabrica*, his mag-num opus, was the result of his work on executed criminals. He publicly bragged of once lifting out a still beating heart, and wherever he lec-tured, body snatchings increased.[79] But the *Fabrica* also suggests that in the anatomy theater, body snatcher becomes revered anatomist, and the criminal body becomes a means for understanding God's greatest cre-ation—the human body.

The title page of the *Fabrica*, one of the most reproduced images from the Renaissance, makes it clear that the body, formerly hanged by the state or flayed in the name of religion, was now medicine's property.[80] A detailed and glorious rendering of an anatomy theater, the woodcut relegates animal dissection, surface anatomy, and ancient texts to the

Figure 1. Andreas Vesalius, *Fabrica de Humani Corporis*, 1543, Basel. By permission of Octavo.

margins and places Vesalius at the center beside the opened womb of a female cadaver (see Figure 1). In truth, Vesalius dissected many fewer female cadavers than male because they were harder to obtain, and his explanation of how he obtained one female body gives some sense of his audacity. She was the "handsome mistress of a certain monk," he reports, who was "snatched from her tomb by the Paduan students and carried off for public dissection." Impressed with the students' ingenuity, he continues, "By their remarkable industry they flayed the whole skin from the cadaver lest it be recognized by the monk who, with the relatives of his mistress, had complained to the municipal judge."[81] Here Vesalius thumbs his nose at religious and legal authorities and brags about medicine's power, underscoring how his students were able to erase the surface features that might reveal the biographical identity of the body without making the corpse useless for medical study. Erasure of subjectivity, as Francis Barker points out, is precisely what dissection achieves. In dissection the body becomes a "reduced and positivist body" that is "outside the pertinent domain of legitimate subjecthood."[82] The title page of the *Fabrica* admits as much. Vesalius's name is proclaimed at the top of the page, and the cadaver remains nameless; he stands ready to lecture, and she is silent; he touches her, and she feels nothing; while he creates a new science, she gives up her womb to his project. The generic, procreative female body becomes medicine's text. Medicine opens the body, probes the dark interior, and then rewrites the body as an orderly text. Unmarred by the messiness of real somatic interiors, the female body on the title page is a legible text. Indeed, on this page and throughout Vesalius's magnum opus the body is rendered orderly and beautiful both in medicine's ability to name all its parts and in images that Vesalius made sure were engraved and printed by some of the best craftsmen in Renaissance publishing.[83]

Hawthorne's tale shares much with Vesalius's text. Like the *Fabrica*, "Rappaccini's Daughter" makes the female body a text, and one whose interior invites study. As a female cadaver occupies the center of the title page and Vesalius's name is emblazoned on the ornate cartouche suspended above the scene, so Beatrice's body is at the center of the tale and her father's name is memorialized in the title. As Vesalius exposes the cadaver's womb and thus founds his own reputation and medicine's authority on scientific knowledge of female reproductive anatomy, so Rappaccini invades Beatrice's interior, claims the female power of creation by remaking her body, and expects to build a science (and his reputation) upon what he learns from her body.[84]

In writing the body as female, Hawthorne seems to follow Vesalius's lead. Like the female cadaver on the title page of the *Fabrica*, Beatrice in "Rappaccini's Garden" (and Georgiana in "The Birth-mark," for that matter) bears the burden of corporeality. Beatrice's body, much like Vesalius's cadaver, is strange, beautiful, disturbing, morbid, and yet immortal. Hawthorne also seems to have found some pleasure, like Vesalius, in flaunting protocol that sanctifies and spiritualizes the female body. In both "The Birth-mark" and "Rappaccini's Daughter," Hawthorne insists upon the materiality of the female body, and he records in detail violence against women's bodies. Moreover, the energy Hawthorne devoted in a letter (now famous among critics) to imagining a very precise and cruel punishment for women authors—they should have their faces "scarred with an oyster shell"—may seem akin to the delight Vesalius takes in the flaying of the monk's mistress.

But "Rappaccini's Daughter" and "The Birth-mark" critique those, including perhaps Hawthorne himself, who would deface the female body. Aylmer and Rappaccini are judged precisely on the grounds that instead of worshipping the female body they presume to have power over it. And it is in his rendering of the female body that I want to suggest that Hawthorne parts company with Vesalius. Both Hawthorne's tales imagine female resistance to male power and to men's efforts to rewrite and disfigure their bodies. In "The Birth-mark," as noted earlier, Georgiana reads her husband's journals and honestly appraises his skill. In "Rappaccini's Daughter," the female body can bruise and poison. In fact, the later tale revises Hawthorne's earlier account of female docility by more fully acknowledging female anger. Although Beatrice seems like a dutiful daughter, at the end of the tale she challenges her father, asking, "wherefore didst thou inflict this miserable doom upon thy child?" She also boldly challenges Giovanni as he waxes hot and cold. She responds to his "gaze of uneasy suspicion" with a "queenlike haughtiness" (112). When he reaches to pluck the strange sister flower in the garden, she grabs his arm and leaves a "purple print like that of four small fingers, and the likeness of a slender thumb upon his wrist" (115), a mark much like the one Aylmer leaves on Georgiana. Beatrice's embarrassment and anger is also registered in the "tinge of passion" that colors her cheek. In short, she talks back, and both the blush on her face and the bruise she inflicts give somatic testimony that the body on the title page of the *Fabrica* cannot. Although created by medicine, Beatrice's body cannot be reduced by it to a tame, positivist fact.

In its retelling of sixteenth-century Paduan science, the tale also suggests that medicine's violation of the body is not redeemed by the knowledge it constructs. By setting the tale in the first half of the sixteenth century, Hawthorne invokes Renaissance notions of the body's interior as a continent ripe for exploration and colonization.[85] As Renaissance anatomists such as Falloppia put their names upon body parts, so Rappaccini colonizes his daughter's body. In part, Rappaccini is a generic caricature of the mad scientist. He lacks "warmth of heart" and "cares infinitely more for science than for mankind" (95, 99). His "patients are interesting to him only as subjects for some new experiment," and he would "sacrifice human life . . . for the sake of adding so much as a mustard seed to the great heap of his accumulated knowledge" (99). But Hawthorne's critique is also more pointed. Rappaccini's masterpiece—a "monstrous offspring of man's depraved fancy"—is sister to Vesalius's female cadaver, and Beatrice's body underscores not the glories of medical mastery over the somatic, but rather the "estranged" body created by medical knowledge. Although "more beautiful than the richest" flowers in the garden, this uncanny, perilous body can be "touched only with a glove" (97). She is naturally beautiful, yet artificially brilliant, and her breath, no longer a sign of a "pure soul within," bespeaks a somatic interior that Rappaccini's science has made a place of poison and death.

But if Beatrice's body seems artificial, it seems equally clear that in making it poisonous, Rappaccini has created a more realistic somatic text than Vesalius. Vesalius may have wielded the scalpel himself when he taught anatomy and eagerly plunged his hands into messy, dead bodies, but his anatomy atlas ordered and beautified somatic materiality. In doing so the atlas offered a sanitized body, a body neatly mapped. The anatomy atlas avoids the disturbing, uncanny horror and fascination that real encounters with the material body (especially when it is opened up) produce. Rappaccini's creation, unlike the body in Vesalius's atlas, is monstrous as well as beautiful.

As Rappaccini is based in part upon a sixteenth-century anatomist, so he is also derived in part from nineteenth-century pathologists. Originally called morbid anatomy, modern pathology began with a 1761 treatise, *On the Seats and Causes of Disease*, by Giambattista Morgagni, a Paduan.[86] The first English study was Matthew Baillie's 1793 *Morbid Anatomy of Some of the Most Important Parts of the Human Body*, and a few years later, the specialty was fully launched with Marie-François-Xavier Bichat's *Treatise on Membranes* (1800). This was quickly followed by important works by René-Théophile-Hyacinthe Laennec in 1819 and Pierre-Charles-Alexandre Louis in 1829. Although led by the French, morbid anatomy was not limited to Europe. Many U.S. physicians encountered the new pathology when they studied in Paris. Those who stayed home had access to Baillie's book, which went through three U.S. editions, to Bichat's, which was translated and published in Boston in 1822, to Laennec's, which was widely distributed upon its publication in 1823 in the United States, and to Louis's, which was translated by the respected Boston physician Henry I. Bowditch in 1836.

The tale's response to the new pathology is complex. On one level, it rejects pathology's commitment to empiricism and to anatomizing disease, to "literally putting one's finger on that abstraction 'disease.'"[87] When Baglioni condemns his adversary as an "empiric," he makes a charge that would have had pointed meaning for nineteenth-century readers. Although the term had a long tradition of being applied to folk healers, by the 1830s elite physicians had adopted the term, despite its common association with quackery, to indicate their rejection of rationalist theories and their commitment to clinical studies and postmortem dissection. Hawthorne has little sympathy for such epistemologies. In "The Birth-mark," he suggests that the body and its signs cannot be known through empirical, positivist science, and "Rappaccini's Daughter" ends with the narrator's sharp critique of the inadequacies of empiricism: "There is something truer and more real than what we can see with the eyes and touch with the finger" (120).

But this caution, while heartfelt, is not where the energy of the tale lies, and the tale finds in the new pathology a sensual model of somatic interiors and an image of the pathologist as an artist willing to plunge into the dangerous, erotic, morbid depths of the human body. This was an image that nineteenth-century pathologists sometimes cultivated, and the darkness of the body's interior was a popular trope among pathologists. Bichat's famous dictum—"Open up a few corpses: you will dissipate at once the darkness that observation alone could not dissipate"— champions the courage of the dissector who voyages into the strange world of somatic interiors.[88] Although Bichat presumes that pathologists will bring light into this new world, for him and others somatic interiors are dark, deep, mysterious. As Foucalt explains, pathologists believed that medicine was now beginning to travel "along a path that had not so far been opened to it; vertically from the symptomatic surface to the tissual . . . plunging from the manifest to the hidden."[89] He adds that medicine saw "a new space opening up before it; the tangible spaces of the body, which at the same time is that opaque mass in which secrets, invisible lesions, and the very mystery of origins lie hidden."[90] Inevitably, even living patients, at least those in hospitals, were recast by the new medicine. They were now defined as strange and fascinating case studies, and the "museological display of patients as pathological specimens in Parisian clinical teaching" became common practice.[91]

Rappaccini's passion for direct, sensory knowledge of the "hue and perfume" of "malignant influences" would have marked him for nineteenth-century readers as a model of this new breed of doctors (96). He shares with his real world counterparts a fascination with the sights and smells of disease, and his intimacy with the dangerous plants of his garden parallels the "morbid education of the senses" that was essential to clinical medicine. Similarly, Giovanni's training in the sensory world of Rappaccini's garden laboratory is akin to nineteenth-century medical education at the Hotel-Dieu, La Pitié, and other Parisian hospitals where instruction included "drilling students to interpret the sights, sounds, and smells of disease."[92] For Hawthorne this work is creative as well as awful. Thus, although Rappaccini's fanatical devotion to discovering the secrets of poisons surely played upon popular fears of a medical profession now consumed with disease and death and Hawthorne would have us recoil from Rappaccini's work, he also seems to delight in the "pale man of science" who devotes, "as might an artist," an entire life to "achieving a picture" of the mortal human body (126). The pathologist's portrait of the diseased body is for Hawthorne both "terrible" and "beautiful" (127), and in the discourse of disease, Hawthorne finds a "symbolic language" that richly renders the "thrill of undefineable horror" that attends intimate somatic knowledge (98, 121). Rappaccini's interest in poisons is in the end more interesting than Aylmer's desire for purity and erasure and preferable to it.

The "thrill of undefineable horror" that a pathologist such as Rappaccini knows gestures to an erotics of disease that the tale explores most fully in the character of Giovanni. While Rappaccini brings a father's seasoned patience and an experienced physician's equanimity to the horror and beauty of the mortal body, Giovanni, a young medical student full of professional ambition and naive sexual desire, is both more excited and more troubled by a body that is beautiful and poisonous. His encounters with Beatrice are alternately hot and cold, erotic and medical. Initially, he spies on Beatrice, believing that he is sneaking a look, when in fact this is a privacy staged for him by Beatrice's father. Like a student in an anatomy theater, Giovanni looks down upon a tableau created by his would-be mentor that is meant to draw him into intimacy with the subject—Beatrice's body. Falling for the ploy, Giovanni gains direct access to this strange body in the most sexually suggestive scene in the tale. To meet the strange beauty, the young man pays his landlady to guide him through "several obscure passages" to the garden, which he enters by "forcing himself through the entanglement of a shrub that wreathed its tendrils over the hidden entrance" (109). The overripe garden, however, is too much for a young man who fancies purity more than carnality, and Giovanni's desire cools. His entrance into the secluded garden is not the climax it should be, and the narrator muses upon the medical student's "untimely" loss of desire in a passage we might also read as a comment from Hawthorne, who was now in his second year of marriage and perhaps no longer intoxicated by conjugal pleasures.[93]

How often is it the case that, when impossibilities have come to pass and dreams have condensed their misty substance into tangible realities, we find ourselves calm, and even coldly self-possessed, amid circumstances which it would have been a delirium of joy or agony to anticipate! Fate delights to thwart us thus. Passion will choose his own time to rush upon the scene, and linger sluggishly behind when an appropriate adjustment of events would seem to summon his appearance. (109)

Suddenly, with Beatrice's disturbing body near at hand, Giovanni is no longer an eager lover but a cold medical scientist: "now there was singular and untimely equanimity within his breast" and he begins "a critical observation of the plants" (110). Although Giovanni is at times seduced by Beatrice's odoriferous carnality, at other times he finds her body and its smells "ugly" and "loathsome" (124).

Giovanni is much like Aylmer in his failure to love that which is imperfect. When Giovanni is repulsed by Beatrice's body, we may decide he is a callow young man who fails to love that which is mortal. But do we really believe he should ignore the strange smells that suggest hers is a dangerous body? Poison is a more disturbing trope for the mortal body than a faint birthmark, and Hawthorne never minimizes the threat posed by Beatrice's body. Georgiana's birthmark is titillating, but it threatens no one. Beatrice's strange condition, by contrast, is threatening; she seems to be contagious as well as erotic.

Poison was a common term in popular and medical discourse for all disease-causing agents, and in sexualizing Beatrice's contagious condition, Hawthorne provocatively explores the psychosexual anxieties that attend disease. Disease transmission theories of the day identified direct contact, proximity, and smell as modes by which disease might be passed from the infected to the healthy. Direct contact, proximity, and smells are also, as Hawthorne notes, the ways in which lovers know each other and share their passions. Thus Giovanni is deeply and perhaps legitimately ambivalent about intimacy with Beatrice. The signs he has to interpret are truly worrisome. Rappaccini is cautious when he works in the garden. He makes sure that there is "no approach to intimacy" between himself and the poisonous flowers in his garden. He avoids "their actual touch or the direct inhaling of their odors" (96), and still he has an "air of insecurity" in the garden as if "one moment of license, would wreak upon him some terrible fatality" (96). Beatrice and her sister plants are so contagious that her father has quarantined her, a common practice during cholera epidemics, and he keeps the garden locked.[94] The strange sweet smells associated with Beatrice are also worrisome. Foul-smelling miasmas were widely understood as a cause of disease, and bad odors in and of themselves often seemed dangerous. In his 1842 report on London sanitary conditions, for example, Edwin Chadwick insisted that "All smell is, if it be intense, immediate, acute disease," and public health measures in the United States were often aimed at cleaning up noxious smells.[95] Putrefying organic matter was presumed to be a major source of contagious miasmas, and in Rappaccini's garden, the "oppressive exhalations" from the "luxuriant vegetation" betray the beginning of putrefaction under the opulence of growth. Beatrice's breath has a richness that bespeaks a ripeness moving towards decay. Her touch is also unsettling. When she grabs Giovanni's arm, he feels an electric shock that may be erotic, but the mark she leaves behind indicates that he is now infected. In short, Beatrice's body is beautiful and malignant. Less than two years after representing the female body as sweetly marked by a faint, titillating birthmark, Hawthorne represents it (as known and remade by pathology) as darkly alluring and poisonous.[96]

Significantly, what intrigues Hawthorne about the mix of thrill and horror that might attend the work of pathology is the psychological depth that such conflicted feelings create. To confront the dark truths hidden within the body, to discover that the smells of the female body are not fragrant perfumes but organic exhalations that testify to the morbidity of human matter, is to discover that inner and outer are not always one. With Georgiana, the surface was besmirched but there was little doubt of a pure, inner spirit; Aylmer's failure lies in his desire to make the outside as pure as Georgiana's inner soul. But with Beatrice, Hawthorne mounts a more disturbing challenge to fantasies about female purity. To be near Beatrice, to see, smell, and touch her is to encounter the organic, carnal body. For Giovanni, to enter the garden is to fall from a young man's Eden in which desire is pure and uncontaminated by carnality. As it turns out, Rappaccini's garden is not an Eden, and to discover that all bodies, even the idealized body of a beautiful woman, carry the signs and smells of disease, putrefaction, and death is, according to the tale, a kind of poisoning. Giovanni is in the end poisoned not only because Beatrice touches him and he inhales the smells of her body and Rappaccini's garden, but because he has encountered a female body that he cannot idealize. Now, as the narrator explains, a "lurid mixture of the two"—desire and loathing—becomes a "fierce and subtle poison" that "produces the illuminating blaze of the infernal regions" (105). Or, put another way, an encounter with Beatrice's uncanny body produces a dark interiority in the superficial young man. Medicine, and in particular pathology, the tale suggests, is the snake in the garden, bringing knowledge of the mortal body and thus psychological interiority. Medical knowledge of disease and somatic interiors infects naive fantasies of somatic purity with reminders of the body's morbidity. In focusing much of the tale on Giovanni's reactions to Beatrice as he tries to make sense of her body, Hawthorne charts a young man's discovery of female carnality and the psychological interiority—conflicted and diseased—that develops as a consequence.

Hawthorne's inclination to use the tropes of pathology to figure complex psychological interiority was widely noted. Shortly after his death, critics summed up Hawthorne as a writer with a "morbid sensibility" who dwelled on "morbid psychology."[97] Earlier, Edwin Percy Whipple's review of *The Scarlet Letter* faulted the book for its "almost morbid intensity," lamenting its "painfully anatomical" exhibition of "psychological details," and Duyckinck began his review of the romance by celebrating it as a "study of character in which the human heart is anatomized, carefully."[98] More intimately, in an 1850 letter George Hillard asked Hawthorne, "How comes it that with so thoroughly healthy an organization as you have, you have such a taste for the morbid anatomy of the human heart, and such knowledge of it too?"[99]

The use of "morbid" in commentary on Hawthorne is not surprising for two reasons. First, the increasing importance of morbid anatomy in medical science was widely noted, and medicine's need for dead bodies worried many. In 1824 and 1830, there were riots at medical schools to protest body snatching and dissections, and between 1830 and 1850 five states passed but then repealed anatomy laws that sought to respond to medicine's increased need for cadavers. Not surprisingly, during these years figurative uses of the term morbid became common. Although 1777 is the first the *Oxford English Dictionary* gives for morbid used figuratively, the dictionary notes a flurry of new uses in the early nineteenth century. Citations include an 1834 reference to "morbid vision," an 1842 comment on "morbid melancholy," and an 1853 reference to "morbid enthusiasm." The first citation the *OED* offers for "morbid anatomy" used figuratively is 1851, the same year Hillard asked Hawthorne about his taste for the subject. Significantly, the *OED* citation is also literary: in "Pleasures, Objects, and Advantages of Literature," Robert Aris Willmott asserts, "Books . . . belong to the study of the mind's morbid anatomy."[100] Literature, much like pathology it would seem, seeks to know dark, diseased interiors.

Second, Hillard and others turned to the language of pathology to describe Hawthorne's work because his somatic obsessions were noteworthy. Unlike realists who ceded the body to sensationalist, gothic, and sentimental fiction, Hawthorne held tenaciously to his somatic interests. In the 1840s, the divide between lowbrow and highbrow genres was deepening, and the body was increasingly taboo for writers with lofty aspirations. As Nancy Glazener points out, lowbrow fiction was demonized as addictive and dangerous because of its interest in and appeal to somatic desires. In 1860, for example, E. P. Whipple warned that sensational fiction is "whiskey for the mind," and in 1855 a *Putnam's* reviewer worried that sentimental fiction stimulated physical experiences in the reader and thus by working "upon the sensibilities" such fiction stimulated an appetite for more sensation.[101]

Hawthorne's interest in writing the body shares much with sensational fiction. In both "The Birth-mark" and "Rappaccini's Daughter," Hawthorne imagines, as do many penny press tales, the mad experimenter's laboratory as a place far from bourgeois decorum. In the penny press, the laboratory was the place where medicine seized upon its object of inquiry—the material body—free from bourgeois expectations that all bodies should be treated with respect, even dead bodies. At mid-century, as one historian notes, there was a "fascination with dissection rooms" and an eagerness "for shocking representations of opening, destroying, and peering inside a corpse."[102] Hawthorne shares this fascination with medical work, and, in "Rappaccini's Daughter," he borrows the tropes of sensational fiction.[103]

But the tale also challenges the tendency in both popular fiction and highbrow literature that would have character writ clearly upon the body.[104] In sensational fiction, intemperance is visible in a ruddy face, greed in an ugly leer, promiscuity in oily skin, purity in a snow-white bosom. Beatrice's body is not so legible. What does Beatrice's body reveal about her character? If she is truly pure, is her body lying? Or does the perilous malignancy within tell us something about her character? Giovanni cannot escape the belief that her body must say something about her character. When he spies on her, he is struck by the "simplicity and sweetness" of her face, and yet he finds her repulsive (102). The contradiction between body and character "made him ask anew what manner of mortal she might be," and he asks, "beautiful, shall I call her?— or inexpressibly terrible?" (102, 103).

The reader, of course, is allowed to feel superior to the shallow Giovanni and his "uneasy suspicion" (112), and we might conclude, as Bensick suggests, that Giovanni fails because he insists that bodies signify something beyond the material. According to Bensick, Giovanni's final betrayal of Beatrice comes from his inability to accept the idea that a pure spirit might inhabit a sick body.[105] Bensick's point is the same as Susan Sontag's in her important work on illness and metaphors. For Sontag, illness is not a metaphor. Literary habits notwithstanding, illness tells us nothing about the ill; disease reveals nothing about the patient. According to Bensick, Giovanni's failure lies in his inability to realize that Beatrice's body tells him nothing about her character.

But I want to suggest that although Giovanni might be a kinder young man if he were not so quick to turn Beatrice's body into a metaphor with secret signification about her character, Hawthorne is not recommending that we understand the body as mere matter. Baglioni's antidote kills rather than cures Beatrice precisely because Baglioni has reduced her condition to a physical problem, like Georgiana's birthmark, that can be cured with the right chemical brew. Giovanni should know better, but in

an act of desperation, he accepts Baglioni's diagnosis and takes the antidote to Beatrice because he wants to deny what he has learned. He wants
to believe that what he smells in the garden and on Beatrice's breath is
a material problem that can be solved. But this is vain grasping after the
fantasy of empirical solutions. Rappaccini, by contrast, knows better. His
"inward disease" marks him as a man who has the complex interiority
that comes with a real awareness of the deep tension between our desires for purity and immortality and the reality that we inhabit mortal,
diseased bodies, between a fantasy of spiritual love and the realities of
carnal desire.[106]

By imagining a body that is a strange mix of purity and carnality, the
virginal and the violated, Hawthorne deploys both medical and gothic
tropes to imagine an interiority—psychological and somatic—that is not
idealized, but diseased, morbid, dark, smelly, thrilling, and horrible.
Thus, although Renaissance anatomy and nineteenth-century pathology
might be charged with stealing the body's interior from religion and
with colonizing and poisoning the body's interior landscape, Hawthorne
also found in the new pathology a deep, alluring, and profoundly
untranscendent body that was a suitable house for an interiority more
complicated than suggested by clichéd notions of a "pure soul within."

Written after Sophia's first pregnancy ended in miscarriage and after
the birth of a daughter, "Rappaccini's Daughter" envisions bodily realities that may owe something to Hawthorne's deepening sense of bodies,
his own and others, as he encountered in the daily intimacies of domestic life the mysteries and truths—beautiful and terrible—of living bodies. Medicine's eagerness to open the body and claim expertise about
the body's inner landscapes troubled Hawthorne, and he was inclined to
resist its authority, but in the pathologized body he found a compelling
image of a luxuriant and putrefying body that may well have spoken to
a man who was now a father and a husband. In short, Hawthorne both
shared medicine's desire to know and write the body and was deeply
troubled by the loss of somatic meaning with the rise of modern medicine.

Chapter 3

Carnival Bodies and Medical Professionalism in Melville's Fiction

> One of the effects of civilization (not to say one of the ingredients in it), is, that the spectacle, and even the very idea of pain, is kept more and more out of the sight of those classes who enjoy in their fullness the benefits of civilization. . . . All those necessary portions of the business of society that oblige any person to be the immediate agent or ocular witness of the infliction of pain, are delegated by common consent to peculiar and narrow classes: to the judge, the soldier, the surgeon, the butcher, and the executioner.
>
> —John Stuart Mill, "Civilization," 1836

Although Herman Melville did not write about medical men as often as Hawthorne, the fictional doctors that do appear in his works suggest a similar attentiveness to medicine's ambitions, and resistance to professional discourses of somatic mastery. Melville was friends with some of the most eminent physicians of the day, including Oliver Wendell Holmes, John Wakefield Francis, and Augustus K. Gardner, and yet his representations of medical men are sharply satirical. In *White-Jacket*, a U.S. navy surgeon is a vicious butcher. In *The Confidence-Man*, the marketplace machinations of an herb-doctor reveal the profit motives behind medical sectarian squabbling. And in *Billy Budd, Sailor*, Melville ascribes narrow mechanistic thinking to another ship surgeon. In all three portraits, the medical man is oblivious to pain. The fleet surgeon in *White-Jacket* barely notices the death of a common sailor whose leg he has needlessly amputated, the herb-doctor's sales pitch is a barrage of words that silences his customers, and the ship surgeon on the *Bellipotent* takes pride in a "scientifically conducted" hanging he directs.[1] In other words, while witnessing or inflicting pain was, as John Stuart Mill noted in 1836, increasingly "delegated by common consent to peculiar and narrow classes," Melville was committed to writing about pain and somatic spectacles, spectacles that Mill suggested were "kept more and more out of the sight of those classes who enjoy in their fullness the benefits of civilization."

Critics have commented on Melville's interest in the body. Sharon Cameron notes a brutal literalness about bodies in *Moby-Dick*, Robert K. Martin discovers homosocial desire in Melville's passion for writing about male bodies, and Peter Bellis suggests that "bodily-identity" is central to Melville's fiction. To these incisive readings, I hope to add an awareness of Melville's interest in the body as a resistance to the management at the center of nineteenth-century professionalism. By writing about the body—its pleasures and its pains—Melville distances himself from and critiques an emerging professional class that, as Dana Nelson suggests, depended heavily upon Enlightenment notions of disembodied reason and physical self-management. Although by birth Melville had entrée into the ruling elite of the nation, he preferred in his writing to sojourn in carnival worlds—Marquesan island, U.S. man-of-war, Mississippi steamboat—and to develop a politics responsive to the unmanaged body. To put this another way, although in the nineteenth century both physicians and authors increasingly claimed authority by standing "apart from and above the carnivalesque scene as a transcendent, single, unified subject," Melville preferred to write about the body from the ground level and to immerse his readers in spectacular somatic worlds.[2] To develop these suggestions more fully, I begin with a discussion of Melville's first novel because in this early work he fashions a politics of embodiment central to his critique of medical professionalism.[3]

Melville's interest in somatic spectacles is evident in the first pages of *Typee: A Peep at Polynesian Life*. The opening chapter features two tales of public nakedness. The first tells of natives stripping a missionary woman. Initially, the natives are beguiled by her calico dress, and they believe she is "some new divinity."[4] As she becomes familiar to them, however, they seek "to pierce the sacred veil of calico" in which she is "enshrined." Before long, their "idolatry was changed into contempt: and there was no end to the contumely showered upon her by the savages." Finally, "to the horror of her affectionate spouse, she was stripped of her garments, and given to understand that she could no longer carry on her deceits with impunity." The "gentle dame" is not "sufficiently evangelized" to endure the exposure. She demands that her husband "relinquish his undertaking" of "reclaiming these islands from heathenism," and they flee (6–7).

In the second tale, exposure is voluntary: an Indian Queen admires the elaborate tattoos on a U.S. sailor's chest and lifts her skirts in order to show her own decorated body. As the narrator explains, because the French colonial leaders pride "themselves upon the beneficial effects of their jurisdiction, as discernible in the deportment of the natives," they are eager, when a U.S. man-of-war comes into port, to arrange for the King and Queen of Nukuheva to make a formal visit to the U.S.

Commodore. Melville describes in detail the festive formalities: "a gig, gaily bedizened with streamers" carries the royal pair to the U.S. frigate, and in return, "we paid them all the honors due to royalty;—manning our yards, firing a salute, and making a prodigious hubbub." As "their majesties" stroll the deck, the French officers are "wonderfully pleased with the discreet manner in which these distinguished personages behaved themselves." The King sports a "magnificent military uniform" and a "huge chapeau" with "waving ostrich plumes." Devoted to expressing the "gaiety of their national taste," the "tailors of the fleet" have given particular attention to the Queen's "adornment." She wears a "gaudy tissue of scarlet cloth, trimmed with yellow silk" and a "fanciful turban of purple velvet, figured with silver sprigs, and surmounted by a tuft of variegated feathers" (7–8).

As it turns out, the French effort is for naught. Haute couture cannot conceal the primitive body. The King's chapeau does not hide the "broad patch of tattooing stretched completely across his face," and fine silk cannot conceal the "spiral tattooing" on the Queen's legs. Haute couture also cannot curb the primitive's love of flesh. When the Queen spies "an old *salt*, whose bare arms and feet, and exposed breast were covered with as many inscriptions in India ink as the lid of an Egyptian sarcophagus" she pulls open his shirt, rolls up his trousers, and hangs "over the fellow, caressing him, and expressing her delight in a variety of wild exclamations and gestures." To demonstrate further her appreciation, she "bent forward for a moment, and turning sharply round, threw up the skirts of her mantle, and revealed a sight from which the aghast Frenchmen retreated precipitately" (8).

As a narrative device, the occasional glimpse of skin makes Melville's *Peep at Polynesian Life* a titillating striptease. In these opening accounts of nakedness, we know from the beginning that there will be a climactic disrobing, and the teasing delay of gratification serves as verbal foreplay. This is particularly true in the second account. We know the Queen is not shy of "exhibiting her charms," and so the reader may savor Melville's elaborate descriptions of French costume even while awaiting the Queen's nakedness. There is, in fact, throughout the book a coy delight in describing risqué or disturbing somatic spectacles (even the remains of a cannibal feast) in formal, modest, and circuitous language. Thus the humor in the second account of disrobing depends not only upon the contrast between a French love of fabric and a native preference for tattoos, but also upon a playful disconnect when refined language is used to describe a primitive, childlike scene in which "I'll show you mine since I've seen yours" is the operative principle. In short, Melville begins his account of life on a Pacific Island by plunging his readers into a carnivalesque world in which high and low mix irreverently.

French finery is flung off so that a Queen can show her tattooed backside, a gentle missionary woman is stripped naked, and highbrow, literary language is used to recount "low" events.

Attentive to Melville's high style and his somatic interests, Richard Brodhead rightly notes that for Melville "the literary" was not necessarily "in opposition to unrepressed bodily life."[5] But Melville's interest in the tensions between the high culture of literary language and the low world of naked bodies is not only about expanding highbrow aesthetics to include representations of bodily life. It is about challenging a political order in which corporeality serves as a marker of people and cultures deemed uncivilized, unrefined, less rational and more physical. Melville's carnivalesque challenges middle-class decorum and the implicit class hierarchy that accompanies it. As Peter Stallybrass and Allon White explain, "bourgeois democracy emerged with a class which, whilst indeed progressive in its best political aspirations, had encoded in its manners, morals and imaginative writings, in its body, bearing and taste, a subliminal elitism."[6] The two scenes of nakedness that open *Typee* reject refinement and bourgeois embarrassment and disgust with things somatic.

The politics of nakedness were not lost on Melville's U.S. publisher. *Typee* appeared in England in February 1842 and in the United States in March. A second U.S. edition, entitled the "Revised Edition," appeared four months later. Both U.S. editions, supervised by John Wiley of Wiley and Putnam, were bowdlerized.[7] In the first U.S. edition, probably a rush-job, deletions and changes are few but pointed, with four of the five coming in the first seventeen pages. Two of these are aimed at the accounts of disrobing in Chapter 1. Melville's jab at religion in his editorializing on the missionary dame's response to being stripped must have worried Wiley. He deleted the ironic suggestion that more religion would have made her more tolerant of being exposed, changing "not sufficiently evangelized to endure this" to "could not endure this." In the account of the Queen of Nukuheva's display of her tattooed backside, the first American version deletes "threw up the skirts of her mantle." Wiley also excised a reference to the "unholy passions of the crew and their unlimited gratification," a change that required resetting ten lines.

The extensive changes made with the "Revised" edition (the only version readily available until the Melville revival of the 1920s) have the same intent as the changes made in the first U.S. edition; they delete or minimize Melville's references to somatic pleasures. In the Revised Edition, the "naked houris" become the "lovely houris," and Typee damsels "anoint my body with a fragrant oil" instead of "my whole body with a fragrant oil." Wiley also deleted references to Tommo's burning cheeks and his "bashful timidity" when he takes his first river bath, and he deleted Melville's ironic observation that it was "foreign benefactors"

who introduced venereal disease to the islands. A chapter explaining
the open, casual sexual relations among the Typees was also heavily
edited. Perhaps most dramatic, though, was Wiley's editing of accounts
of nakedness. He deleted in their entirety both accounts of nakedness in
Chapter 1, and he also excised an account in Chapter 4 of a French
admiral wearing a richly decorated frock coat and laced chapeau-bras
while he attempts to persuade a naked Tior King to give away his people's independence. In all three instances, expurgation of references to
naked bodies serves a more basic goal—minimizing Melville's critiques
of missions and imperialism.

On one level, the transgression in both tales of nakedness is fairly
direct. To be stripped is to be violated, and most readers, even liberal
readers inclined to question the value of evangelism, surely wince at the
image of a gentle Christian dame being stripped by suspicious natives.
The Queen's bare skin is less obviously transgressive. She is not Western,
she disrobes herself, and she is not embarrassed by nakedness. And if her
nakedness insults those around her, we might easily forgive her act as
naive rather than aggressive. But the tale emphasizes the transgressive
nature of her act. If Melville had reported on the Queen's nakedness as
part of a larger ethnographic account of naked islanders, then the scene
might be read as respectable, scientific reporting. But the account is not
offered as a contribution to scientific understanding of native customs.
Flipping up one's skirt during a formal affair with Western men is a gesture that is sexually bold and even pornographic, at least to Westerners.
When the Frenchmen flee, we understand that the "sight"—her backside—has violated their deep sense of the privacy and shame of the
naked body. According to Western etiquette, gentle dames should not be
stripped and queens should not display their rumps.

On another level, the tales chronicle a more disturbing transgression
than the violation of middle-class decorum. The natives' indecorous mis-
deeds—their violations of Western sartorial customs—are retaliation
(conscious or unconscious) for what has been done to them. In *Typee*,
Melville records the brutal consequences of Western attempts to civilize
the natives, and in the opening tales of nakedness, he suggests that they
fight back by stripping off the deceit of clothing. The tale of the Queen
offers this lesson humorously. When dressed in French finery, the King
and Queen look ridiculous. A chapeau with ostrich feathers atop a tattooed face makes him look like "royalty in goggles," and she, with silver
sprigs and a tuft of variegated feathers on her head, looks "ludicrous."
The scene is explicitly attentive to the importance of cultural performances—including clothing—to the French, and thus we should
understand that the Queen's customs must be important to her. The tale
of the dame's stripping is a reminder of the shame of being dressed (or

undressed) in the fashion of another culture. Thus, although the Queen's retaliation (lifting her skirt) is unconscious and funny, her bare backside challenges French imperialism (at least their attempts at sartorial uplift), and the pleasure she takes in an old salt's body aligns her regal innocence not with middle-class manners but with the somatic customs of America's working class. The scene suggests that the delight in tattoos a U.S. sailor and a native Queen share bespeaks a common political plight—both suffer tyrannies in which their bodies are deemed inferior and dispensable.

The tale of the missionary dame's disrobing makes a similar though more barbed case against somatic hierarchies and the violence of imperialism. Melville's readers might have understood the natives' initial belief that the dame is "some new divinity" as evidence of the heathens' unconscious understanding of the superiority of Christianity, Christians, and Western ways. But the tale is sympathetic to the natives' anger when they discover she is not a god. The tale suggests that her calico is, in fact, a kind of deception, and that the natives' anger may be a legitimate response to the missionaries' confidence in the superiority of their religion and civilization. Melville's source for this incident is a self-congratulatory account of missions by William Ellis, and he clearly mocks the condescending beneficence and piety of his source when he suggests that a woman who was "sufficiently evangelized" would not mind being stripped, that a truly religious woman would not mind the exposure that she is, like the heathens she seeks to uplift, merely a body.

Several chapters later Melville makes an explicit connection between Western bourgeois culture and the destruction and enslavement of native people. He notes that back home money is collected for missionary projects: "benevolent-looking gentlemen in white cravats solicit alms" and "old ladies in sober russet low gowns, contribute sixpences," all to help uplift heathens. And the result in the colonies is that "Neat villas, trim gardens, shaven lawns, spires, and cupolas arise" for European missionaries and colonialists, while "the poor savage soon finds himself an interloper in the country of his fathers" (195). The fruit of the land is "devoured before the eyes of the starving inhabitants, or sent on board the numerous vessels which now touch at their shores," and the natives are "civilized into draught horses, and evangelized into beasts of burden" (196). Given the mantle of respectability, piety, and polite manners that cloaks the violence of imperialism, stripping off a missionary's calico dress is not an insignificant response.

In their study of the politics and poetics of transgression, Stallybrass and White warn that the "exhilarating sense of freedom which transgression affords" is not always a sign of "political progressiveness."[8] But I want to suggest that the transgression enacted by Melville's carnivalesque is radical. The exhilarating freedom that Melville imagines the natives feel when they expose the dame for what she is—a human body—is a sign of the freedom they might gain by undoing a hierarchy of bodies and cultures in which they are deemed inferior. And the act does free them, if only briefly, from yet another Western attempt at evangelism. The dame and her husband leave. The exhilarating freedom figured in the Queen flipping up the skirts of her mantle is similarly radical. The French have not only dressed her in their clothing, they have also, as Melville notes in the middle of this account, "slaughtered about a hundred and fifty" natives. Thus when her naked body and the pleasure she takes in showing her body and in looking at the sailor's body make the French retreat, it is a brief moment of success in a political battle for control of the islands and the life of the island people.

In these tales, Melville's tone as well as his topic is subversive. By posing as a naive reporter Melville challenges emerging discourses of professional science that gave the imprimatur of empiricism to the stratification of bodies and cultures that authorized Western imperialism. Most simply, Melville's pose of innocence contrasts with the mastery associated with professionals. In the preface, he presents his account of island life as nothing more than a sailor's account of a "curious adventure." Writing of himself in the third person, Melville coyly notes the author's "deficiencies" as an expert: the author has spent most of his time "tossing about on the wide ocean," and as a mere sailor he can only describe and not explain the "singular and interesting people among whom he was thrown" (xiii). In fact, Melville drew heavily upon sea tales and accounts of Pacific Island natives by missionaries, captains, and explorers, but he dispenses with the authoritative tone typical of his sources. Tommo (Melville's alter ego) is neither a captain nor an explorer, only a common sailor, an everyman who unwittingly stumbles into an adventure and a political lesson simply because he is weary of life on a whaler and jumps ship in the Marquesas.

The sly, impish, childlike delight that Melville's narrator takes in low, somatic pleasures also challenges the equanimity, refinement, and empiricism adopted by professionals when dealing with fleshy materials. In general, the naked body in the nineteenth century was a private matter. As an artist notes in Nathaniel Hawthorne's *The Marble Faun*, "'Now-a-days, people are as good as born in their clothes, and there is practically not a nude human being in existence.'"[9] Legitimate nakedness was, more or less, limited to two venues—museums and scientific treatises. In the museum, the nakedness of classical statuary (but not of contemporary bodies) was acceptable because these bodies were understood as symbols of spiritual purity, beauty, and intelligence. As Hawthorne's artist explains, the Greek sculptor "found his models in the open sunshine, and among pure and princely maidens." Contemporary artists, she notes, can only "steal guilty glances at hired models."[10] And, in fact, nudes by contemporary American artists were not widely accepted until the second half of the century.[11]

In science, naked bodies were data (and thus not troubling), and naked native bodies were useful in ethnographic studies that measured and cataloged the human form in order to establish graduated hierarchies of bodies more or less classically beautiful, and thus more or less civilized. In one source that Melville used to write *Typee*, a Marquesan man is measured in order that he might be compared with the *Apollo Belvedere*—a Roman statue (copied from a Greek statue) that was widely admired as a paragon of classical beauty.[12] In such studies, the classical body serves as a somatic symbol for the virtues of high culture. Monumental, elevated, closed, homogenous, well proportioned, the classical body figures transcendent individualism and is associated with rationality, "economy of utterance," "parsimony of explanation," spirit, and thought over corporeality.[13] These were the virtues professional scientists claimed for themselves and their discipline, and they were also the virtues the West believed it brought to the islands.

These are not, however, the virtues Melville celebrates in *Typee*. The naked bodies in Melville's opening scenes are not classical bodies; in the somatic hierarchy of the day, they are grotesque bodies of carnival. Both scenes feature undressing, and the emphasis is on the exposed body and thus on the most private parts of the body. And although both scenes foreground bodies that might be deemed beautiful, the emphasis on female clothing—a calico dress stripped off and skirts lifted—teasingly brings to mind the exposure of what skirts hide, that is the lower parts of the body.[14] What Melville offers, then, in *Typee* is not an ethnographic study in which nakedness serves science and bodies are data. Rather, he offers a glimpse of the somatic theater and politics of islanders.

In noting the natives' political use of the body, Melville deconstructs the myth of the primitive's natural body. Tattooing and cannibalism—somatic practices that make Tommo very anxious—suggest that the primitive body is not natural or innocent. Unlike the gentle missionary dame, the tattooed Typees can never be stripped of their social dress. They may seem to live in unmediated bodies, but in fact they make such intimate use of the body that there can be no distinguishing a natural body from its theatrical forms. Tommo's companion, Fayaway, is "very little embellished," and her nearly unmarked body allows Tommo to indulge Western fantasies of natural natives. He explains that by going naked she "clung to the primitive and summer garb of Eden" (86–87). But the "hideous old wretches" in the Houlah Houlah grounds who are green from their tattoos challenge Tommo's primitivist romance because their bodies figure not naturalness but a theater of the body that Westerners cannot understand.[15]

The green men, and the somatic practices of the Taipi more generally, also undermine the ethnographer's fantasy of the body as a knowable, measurable material fact. As Judith Butler explains, "insofar as power operates successfully by constituting an object domain, a field of intelligibility, as a taken-for-granted ontology, its material effects are taken as material data or primary givens."[16] This is the move of "empiricist foundationalism," and a move nineteenth-century race studies made by positing the existence of a visible, racialized body. Once posited, the racialized body, including the Marquesan native, becomes material data that science may study objectively. Melville's account unsettles the empiricist foundation that is at the heart of nineteenth-century scientific authority. According to Melville, the native body is not measurable; it is not a stable fact because native somatic practices, especially tattooing and cannibalism but also nakedness, make the body a spectacle, a sign that is used, manipulated, tattooed, displayed, and sometimes even ingested.[17]

The body as spectacle rather than fact initially delights Tommo, and then it terrifies him. Melville, however, was not as unnerved by somatic stagecraft as his alter ego.[18] Contemporary readers commented on Melville's stagecraft, insisting that the whole book was more dedicated to theatrical thrills than to accurate reporting. The *London Spectator* noted Melville's "tendency to make too much of things," and Evert Duyckinck suggested that Melville's savages were like "performers in a rich ballet."[19] Notably, although more recent critics have focused on tattooing and cannibalism, of all the somatic spectacles in Melville's savage ballet, Wiley was more concerned with nakedness. He removed neither the descriptions of Karky entreating Tommo to be tattooed nor the scene in which Tommo discovers "the disordered members of a human skeleton, the bones still fresh with moisture, and with particles of flesh clinging to them here and there" (238). These scenes endorse the civilized man's horror at the savage's supposed intense somatic life and thus endorse ethnography's myth of the bodiliness of natives. By contrast, the scenes of nakedness that Wiley excised render somatic delights rather than horrors, and they remind us that the body, even the native's body, is always "materialized" under particular conditions. Melville loves the radical materiality of the body, and thus he delights in the Queen's bare backside (which is, of course, a sign of the material body only because bourgeois codes so define it). But he also knows that the body can never be known apart from the political and linguistic world in which it comes into visibility. The Queen's rump is never simply flesh. In fact, it is tattooed with the signs of her culture, and it is made visible in an act of cross-cultural solidarity with a U.S. sailor and in an act of defiance of French customs.

It is worth noting that in writing *Typee*, his first book, Melville seems to have discovered that writing about the body was something he was good at.[20] Although reviewers warned of the novel's licentiousness, they admitted that they were seduced by Melville's language. Most reviewers responded to Melville's wit, applauded his style, even if they condemned the subject, and described *Typee* as fresh, entertaining, and eminently readable.[21] Indeed, Melville's language is coy, seductive, ornate, excessive, sometimes ironically "arch" (as Margaret Fuller noted in her review), and often humorous.[22] Melville takes pleasure in the teasing possibilities of innuendo, in the disparity between Tommo's linguistic circumlocutions and his fascination with savage bodies, in the play between fiction and fact, and in his power to speak boldly of politics and bodies. Unlike his later focus in *The Confidence-Man* on the politics of pain and his dismay at the powerlessness of language when confronted with the pervasive influence of the marketplace, in his first novel Melville is drunk with the discovery of a language that can speak of bodily pleasures and politics.[23]

Although *White-Jacket*, like *Typee*, celebrates bodily life and satirizes those who claim authority over the bodies of others, there is a bitterness in Melville's fifth novel not present in the first. *White-Jacket* focuses on pain rather than pleasure, and as a result Melville's stylized language is more disturbing. In *Typee* there is comedy as well as politics in the discrepancies between a self-consciously literary language and the physical pleasures of native life this language describes. In *White-Jacket*, the indirection of literary language used to render the relentless misery of mistreated sailors produces irony more biting. In fact, the discrepancy between refined language and physical cruelty serves as a constant reminder of the book's main concern—the discrepancy between civilization's pretenses and its barbarity. Based on Melville's fourteen months service on the U.S. Navy frigate *United States* as he headed home at the end of three years in the Pacific and written eight years after the experience, *White-Jacket* makes flogging the central symbol of civilization's brutality. Flogging, as one biographer notes, is deeply offensive to Melville not only because it may be ordered for venial transgressions but also because it is "conducted with all the formality of institutionalized civilization."[24] As the professional who presides at every flogging and as a man eager to operate just to keep his surgical skills polished, Cadwallader Cuticle, M.D., the surgeon of the fleet, is a particularly powerful symbol of civilization's brutal treatment of bodies deemed dispensable.

In many ways, Cadwallader Cuticle, M.D., is a stock character. Like Hawthorne's medical men, for example, Cadwallader Cuticle is educated and accomplished. He is "a gentleman of remarkable science," an "Honorary Member of the most distinguished Colleges of Surgeons both in Europe and America" and the "foremost Surgeon in the Navy."[25] Also like Hawthorne's doctors, he has bizarre, grotesque interests (he is devoted to "Morbid Anatomy"), he is so unflappable as to be "untouched by the keenest misery coming under a fleet-surgeon's eye," and his withered body testifies to intellectual fervor nurtured at the expense of physical health (248–49).

It is also clear, however, that Cuticle is more than a stock character. Melville devotes four chapters exclusively to the fleet surgeon (more than to any other character), and one of these chapters, "The Operation," is the longest chapter in the book. We also know that Melville worked to make the information in these chapters accurate. He makes reference to the best contemporary treatise on gunshot wounds and several other medical texts. He read and borrowed from at least six articles in *The Penny Cyclopedia of the Society for the Diffusion of Useful Knowledge*, including entries on amputation, anatomy, gunshot wounds, William Hunter, the human skeleton, and tourniquets. We also know that when he traveled after completing *White-Jacket*, Melville made a point of continuing his somatic studies. He picked up a copy of Johann Caspar Lavater's *Essays on Physiognomy*, he visited the Paris morgue, and he probably visited an anatomical museum in London.[26] The morgue was popular with tourists who had a taste for the grotesque, and Melville may have known about it through his friend Dr. Augustus K. Gardner who had studied in Paris and written a guidebook to the city. We know that Gardner gave a copy of *Old Wine in New Bottles; or, Spare Hours of a Student in Paris* to Melville and that he gave Melville housing recommendations.[27] He may also have recommended the morgue, or perhaps Gardner's guidebook description piqued Melville's interest:

Iron frames supporting inclined boards to the number of eight or ten were arranged around the room. . . . On these, directly underneath the collection of clothes, were outstretched the bodies of their wearers, stripped naked, with the exception of a slight covering of small size about the loins. . . . [On each] a constant shower of water was projected . . . from a cock, which was fixed above.[28]

Two days after visiting the morgue, a sight Melville seems to have gone out of his way to see, he made a trip to view specimens at a pathology museum. The Musée Dupuytren was probably recommended to Melville by his New York friend Dr. John Wakefield Francis. Francis was a fan of medical museums, and he had known Guillaume Dupuytren. In fact, Francis may have regaled Melville with stories about medical luminaries while Melville was writing *White-Jacket* and attending regularly Francis's lively soirees.[29]

In addition to being well researched and indicative of Melville's abiding interest in the body and the grotesque, the chapters devoted to Cuticle are noteworthy because this portrait is the only one in *White-Jacket* that departs radically from its historical counterpart. Unlike the imaginary Cuticle on the *Neversink*, the real surgeon on the *United States* in 1843 was widely admired as a skillful physician and a good administrator. But instead of honoring the surgeon, Melville develops at length a satirical portrait of a cruel man, and Melville's writing in these chapters is the most energetic in the book. The amputation chapter, as Wai Chee Dimock notes, is full of "expository violence," "verbal torrents," a "maniacal exactitude of language," and a kind of linguistic mania that Dimock reads as evidence of Melville's vexed relationship with his readers.[30] Dimock's argument is persuasive, but I want to suggest that the rhetorical excess in these chapters is also evidence of Melville's disgust with professional authority and with professionals who use their authority to legitimize brutality.

As noted in Chapter 1, regulars were under attack in these years, and many retreated from earlier efforts to tighten licensing regulations, seeking instead to represent themselves as ethical men and to adopting ethical codes, including the 1848 National Medical Ethics Code. The result was that regulars were somewhat successful in shifting the focus of the debate about professionalism from economics to ethics. In his 1847 paper on etherization, for example, Henry Bigelow suggested that major advances in medical science made it increasingly important to protect the public from profiteering quacks and that such protection was precisely what an ethically minded, self-regulating profession could offer. With Cadwallader Cuticle, Melville challenges the image of the ethically minded professional. Since populists and irregulars were eager to accuse regulars of vanity and ambition, when Melville makes an elite surgeon on a flagship of the U.S. Navy a self-serving, career-minded butcher, the satire cuts to the core of a sensitive issue for the medical profession.

Cuticle's vanity is most evident in his need for an audience, and Melville devotes some of his most elaborate prose to Cuticle's interaction with his colleagues. When a difficult case presents itself, Cuticle calls the surgeons from the other ships to watch him amputate. It was common for other ship surgeons to gather for consultations and to watch and assist at a dangerous operation, but Cuticle wants an audience not because he needs help or because he wants to teach but solely to parade his power. He mocks and belittles the other surgeons who are fawning accomplices to his butchery, and he misrepresents the facts of the case in order to justify amputation. He flaunts his knowledge of major medical texts, and the topic of his long lecture before the amputation is career building.

Young gentlemen . . . seeing you here reminds me of the classes of students once under my instruction at the Philadelphia College of Physicians and Surgeons. Ah, those were happy days! . . . The town, the city, the metropolis, young gentlemen, is the place for you students; at least in these dull times of peace, when the army and navy furnish no inducements for a youth ambitious of rising in our honorable profession. Take an old man's advice, and if the war now threatening between the States and Mexico should break out, exchange your Navy commissions for commissions in the army. From having no military marine herself, Mexico has always been backward in furnishing subjects for the amputation-tables of foreign navies. The cause of science has languished in her hands. (257)

In part, Melville follows tradition here since an eagerness for victims is a staple of the mad doctor stereotype. But it is particularly horrifying to suggest in 1850, only two years after the end of the bloody U.S.-Mexican War, that a military surgeon (and Melville underscores Cuticle's pedigree by making him a former professor at the prestigious Philadelphia College) might view the carnage of war as a career opportunity.

Interestingly, Melville omits the sexual undertones that often play in mad doctor tales. Typically the mad doctor's patient is female, and, as I noted in Chapter 2, the heightened sense of corporeality associated with the female body is often figured as an incitement to the fiendish physician's sexual desires that he then sublimates into scientific ambition. Cuticle has no such thwarted desires. Melville's surgeon is devoid of psychological interiority and sexual desires. Cuticle is concerned only with his performance before his colleagues, and in Melville's cautionary tale of the mad doctor, the danger lies not in the physician's lewd desires but solely in the ambitious doctor's eagerness for advancement.

In addition to tapping mid-century anxieties about careerism among professionals, Melville's satire of the fleet surgeon challenges presumptions about the relationship between mind and body, intellect and brawn, rationality and physicality. As scholars have shown, throughout much of the nineteenth century these polarized notions were used in both crude and subtle ways to map distinctions between male and female, white and nonwhite, upper and lower classes. As Robyn Wiegman and others have noted, the category of citizen was essentially bodiless, while other categories—women, nonwhites, and workers—bore a burden of a heightened corporeality, and an "asymmetry of corporeality" permeated nineteenth-century representations.[31]

On the surface, Melville seems to indulge this kind of thinking in his tendency to romanticize the body. In *Typee* the natives seem to be more physical than Westerners, and in *White-Jacket* the common sailor is "of the body" in a way officers are not. But just as Melville both uses and complicates the myth of the natural savage in *Typee*, suggesting that although the natives may have an enviable physicality their bodies are not as innocent of cultural inscriptions as we might think, so in *White-Jacket* he probes our presumptions about the disembodied rationality of science and the physicality of the working man.

According to Melville, the sailor is intensely physical in part because his body is always taxed and in danger. Physical discomforts, labor that does not renew and is not adequately compensated, frequent floggings, and the looming threat of the death penalty make the sailor's body the primary site of his oppression. Indeed, physical vulnerability so shames one common seaman that he fears meeting his brother, a midshipman on another ship, because "he [is] an officer and I a miserable sailor who at any moment may be flogged at the gangway, before his very eyes" (244). And yet, Melville also understands the sailor's body as a site of fraternity, rebellion, and nobility. Friendships on the *Neversink* are fueled by physical empathy, and rebellion against tyranny is based on the sailors' love of their own bodies.[32] In a deeply moving account of what he calls the "Rebellion of the Beards," Melville rewrites the 1842 Somers mutiny, a complex affair that ended with three sailors being hanged, as a tale of the common seaman's physical nobility. Melville refers to the "old tars" who lead the revolt against an order to shave as "sculptured Assyrian kings" and Roman senators, and Melville's paean to facial hair bestows honor and nobility upon bodies (and men) more often deemed dirty and dispensable (362–63). In the preceding chapter, White-Jacket sits beside a dying fellow sailor in an unventilated sickbay while officers stroll the promenade above. The moral is clear: class oppression consigns sailors to steamy sickbays, the ship surgeon does nothing to intervene, and sailors build a brotherhood of the oppressed by caring for each other's bodies.

In the context, then, of oppressed but noble sailor bodies, the fleet surgeon's pathetic body takes on particular significance. On one level, Melville seems to accept the popular notion that mind and body are in opposition. Sailors are lusty and Cuticle has a decrepit body, we are given to understand, because his intellectual pursuits have taken a toll on his body.

He was a small, withered man. . . . His chest was shallow, his shoulders bent, his pantaloons hung round his skeleton legs, and his face was singularly attenuated. In truth, the corporeal vitality of this man seemed, in a good degree, to have died out of him. He walked abroad, a curious patch-work of life and death, with a wig, one glass eye, and a set of false teeth, while his voice was husky and thick; but his mind seemed undebilitated as in youth; it shone out of his remaining eye with basilisk brilliancy. (248)

This image of the physically withered but mentally brilliant medical man echoes many others of the era. But Cuticle's body is not simply a body worn away and thus less present, visible, or significant. Indeed, Melville's attention to Cuticle's attenuated body only makes it more visible and revealing. For both Hawthorne and Melville, the intellectual interests of a medical man would seem not only to vitiate his body but also to leave telltale signs of the dark side of medicine's somatic obsessions. Aylmer's trembling body, for example, bespeaks medicine's prurient fascination with female sexuality, and Rappaccini's sickly, odoriferous body is both a direct result of his botanical experiments and a powerful symbol of the dark interiority that pathology presupposes. Like Rappaccini's body, then, Cuticle's body testifies to medicine's morbid interest. His missing body parts gesture humorously to the role of dissection in nineteenth-century medicine, to medicine's interest in disease and decay as well as health, and to Cuticle's own eagerness to collect parts and to amputate. Cuticle's nearly dead body reminds us that it is "largely through interrogation of the dead that doctors aspire to know the diseases of the living."[33]

In addition, Cuticle's attenuated body gestures to medicine's habit of locating itself in what Denise Albanese has called "an artificial space of evacuated materiality."[34] As Dana Nelson notes, nineteenth-century, professional scientific authority was essentially occluded. In medicine, as I noted in Chapter 2, the new emphasis on clinical studies entailed a belief in the primacy of observation and in the possibility that observation leads directly to knowing. In what Foucault has called the myth of the clinical gaze, clinicians believed that seeing might be free of language. To put this another way, the professional—his expertise, his body, his part in constructing knowledge—is occluded because knowledge springs unmediated from the positive bodies of the patients in the wards. The observer (typically a white, upper-class professional medical man) stands outside the frame of reference.[35] The confidence in the possibility of an epistemology of pure knowing is evident in Oliver Wendell Holmes's suggestion that science is free from "servile adherence to territorial limits." Science is not limited by terrestrial perspectives: it is, he believed, "like the atmosphere."[36]

Cuticle's body suggests a very different image of science. His body is, like those he works on, profoundly material. In fact, Melville is so taken with the humor of Cuticle's patch-work body as a mirror image of the bodies that medical discourse creates (the body understood as parts and not as a whole) that he has the surgeon remove his jacket, his kerchief, his false eye, his false teeth, and his wig before the amputation begins. With this darkly humorous dismantling, the professional becomes literally and ironically "disembodied" and thus becomes a grotesque, carnivalesque body—a parodic image of the idealized classical body. At the moment of surgery, Cuticle is not an emblem of disembodied rationality, but a brutal, fragmentary, corporeal man, and Melville devotes some of his most maniacal "exactitude of language" to rendering this irony:

Now the Surgeon of the Fleet and the top-man [the patient] presented a spectacle which, to a reflecting mind, was better than a church-yard sermon on the
mortality of man. Here was a sailor, who, four days previous had stood erect—a
pillar of life—with an arm like a royal mast and a thigh like a windlass. . . And
who was it that now stood over him like a superior being, and, as if clothed himself with the attributes of immortality, indifferently discoursed of carving up his
broken flesh, and thus piecing out his abbreviated days? Who was it, that in
capacity of Surgeon seemed enacting the part of Regenerator of life? The withered, shrunken, one-eyed, toothless, hairless Cuticle; with a trunk half dead—a
memento mori to behold! (259)

The ironies are multiple, and Melville's anger and vitriol are palpable.
The surgeon is not a rational man; he is as much "of the body" as his
patient although at the same time he is much less of a man. Or, perhaps,
it would be more accurate to say that he is much less of a body than his
patient and yet has the power to take his life.

In keeping with his decrepit body and his avidity for amputations,
Cuticle has a passion for brutality and brutal language. He has little tolerance for the Latinate scientific language of his colleagues, mocking
such language as nothing more than a feeble attempt to sanitize medicine's work and to distance the physician from the fleshy material that
is his work. Surgeons Bandage, Patella, Wedge, and Sawyer give advice
to Cuticle in elaborate circumlocutions. While rising up on tiptoe,
Surgeon Wedge explains that if the bullet has shattered and divided "the
whole *femur*, including the *Greater* and *Lesser Trochanter*, the *Linear aspera*,
the *Digitial fossa*, and the *Intertrochanteric*," he recommends amputation
(253). But Cuticle has no patience with such language. He fashions
himself an iconoclast, perhaps akin to a man like Vesalius who, as I
noted in the previous chapter, eschewed professional decorum and
boldly plunged his hands literally and publicly into the bloody work of
medicine. But Cuticle's honesty about bodies, unlike Vesalius's, does not
make him revere the body. Medicine is power for Cuticle. And, even
though his own body bears humiliating evidence of mortality, Cuticle
understands the bodies of others not as an opportunity for empathy or
fraternity, but as an opportunity to exercise his power.

As with other fictional portraits of mad surgeons, Cuticle's nearly insa-
tiable desire for surgery is complemented by a cold-hearted equanimity. The American Medical Association urged self-control. The minutes
from the first meeting note that "professional duty requires of a physician, that he should have such a control over himself as not to betray
strong emotion," and they caution that although "many medical men"
may be "possessed of abundant attainments and resources," many are
also "so constitutionally timid and readily abashed as to lose much of
their self-possession and usefulness at the critical moment."[37] Melville's

physician never loses his self-posession, but the satire of medical equanimity is not only familiar, it is also dark and disturbing.

Surrounded by moans and shrieks, by features distorted with anguish inflicted by himself, he maintained a countenance almost supernaturally calm; and unless the intense interest of the operation flushed his wan face with a momentary tinge of professional enthusiasm, he toiled away, untouched by the keenest misery coming under a fleet-surgeon's eye. Indeed, the long habitutation to the dissecting-room and the amputation-table had made him seemingly impervious to the ordinary emotions of humanity. Yet you could not say that Cuticle was essentially a cruel-hearted man. His apparent heartlessness must have been of a purely scientific origin. It is not to be imagined even that Cuticle would have harmed a fly, unless he could procure a microscope powerful enough to assist him in experimenting on the minute vitals of the creature. (251)

The passage ends with a retreat into absurdity—a surgeon operating on a fly, but it begins with moans and shrieks that are all too real in a novel dedicated to representing the misery and physical degradation of sailors.

Melville also satirizes with edgy humor medicine's intimacy with the grotesque. This is particularly clear in his description of Cuticle's "unsightly collection of Parisian casts" (249). Cuticle's stateroom is crowded with "all imaginable malformations of the human members, both organic and induced by disease," and Melville devotes a long paragraph to a loving description of one specimen—the head of an elderly woman. He begins by noting her "singularly gentle and meek" aspect and then the details of her "hideous, crumpled horn, like that of a ram, downward growing out from the forehead, and partly shadowing the face" (249). Only half jokingly, Melville notes that "as you gazed, the freezing fascination of its horribleness gradually waned" and "your whole heart burst with sorrow, as you contemplated those aged features, ashy pale and wan" (249). Cuticle, of course, responds neither with horror, as does his cot boy, nor with sorrow, as does the narrator. The surgeon simply uses the horn as a hat stand.

In part Melville delights in body humor, but his tone shifts from dark humor to sober realism when the amputation begins. The cut is made "near the trunk and the vitals," while large tubs catch the blood and an attendant sits in "readiness to grasp the limb, as when a plank is being severed by a carpenter and his apprentice" (261). The sailor's body is like a fly's readied for experimentation, and when Cuticle barely reacts to the sailor's death after the amputation, the humor of the preceding pages evaporates and there is a real and disturbing sense of the power of professionals over the lives of others. The top-man does not have to die; Cuticle kills him out of professional zeal to practice his surgical skills and show off before his colleagues.

Of course, it is not realism to suggest that fleet surgeons are so eager to amputate that they will risk killing a patient, that doctors are unmoved by death, that the bodies of medical men bear witness to their brutality, or that careerism makes them hope for war casualties. But at the end of the four chapters devoted to Cadwallader Cuticle, M.D., it is clear that Melville is not only playing with a form—the stereotypic evil doctor—but satirizing with intense rhetorical energy a profession he had no obvious reason to hate. In fact, Melville's distaste for ship surgeons was so strong that it resurfaced years later in "Billy Budd." In this unfinished, late story, Melville concludes the climatic scene of Budd's hanging with a conversation between the purser and the surgeon about the lack of motion (erection and ejaculation) at the moment of hanging. Since Melville had witnessed a hanging in London during his 1848 trip and had read many accounts of hangings, he probably knew that, as the purser says, "this muscular spasm" is "in a degree more or less invariable in these cases." The purser believes it must mean something that there is no spasm when Budd is hanged. Throughout the story, Budd's body—its beauty, innocence, and stutter—shimmers with possible meanings for readers and the purser. But the surgeon, in a mean-spirited antireaderly moment, scoffs at the purser's efforts to interpret Budd's body. The purser wonders if the absence of any spasm might be a sign of Budd's willpower or evidence of euthanasia. But the surgeon brusquely dismisses both terms; they are not "included in the lexicon of science." The surgeon is a "saturnine, spare, and tall" man in whom "discreet causticity went along with a manner less genial than polite."[38] He is proud of the hanging he directed, and he is annoyed by the purser finding oddities and seeking meaning. Notably, in earlier drafts the exchange between the purser and the surgeon was brief and attached to the end of the chapter about Budd's hanging. But late in the composition process, Melville revisited the exchange between the purser and the surgeon, revising it heavily and expanding it into a separate chapter that develops more fully the surgeon's narrow thinking and cruel rejection of meaning.[39]

So why did Melville hold ship surgeons in such low regard? As he points out in *White-Jacket,* the ship surgeon officiates at every hanging and at every flogging, and yet he rarely interferes. Melville saw 163 floggings in his fourteen months on the *United States.* Presumably the much admired fleet surgeon officiated at every one. In a particularly disturbing chapter on "Flogging Through the Fleet," a punishment in which the sailor is whipped on every ship, Melville explains: "In some cases the attending surgeon has professionally interfered before the last lash has been given, alleging that immediate death must ensue if the remainder should be administered without respite" (371). But whenever possible the punishment does continue. When "the surgeon officially reports [the sailor] capable of undergoing the rest of the sentence, it is forthwith inflicted" (371). The description of flogging through the fleet is horrific—blood on every ship and shreds of flesh left behind—and the fact that a surgeon, a man trained to care for bodies, would authorize such violence seems to have deeply troubled Melville.

Seven years after imagining a U.S. Navy fleet surgeon as an opportunistic butcher keen for war casualties, Melville turned from studying medicine's bloody ambitions to depicting medical salesmanship. On a man-of-war, a surgeon has absolute power, and he does not have to market himself. On a Mississippi steamboat, by contrast, a medical man must woo a skeptical public, using his linguistic talents to earn the confidence and dollars of potential customers.

Much changed for Melville between 1850, the year *White-Jacket* was published, and 1856, when he began writing *The Confidence-Man*. In the first few years following *Typee*'s success, Melville devoted himself to making a living as a writer, and even though none of the four subsequent sea novels (*Omoo, Mardi, Redburn,* and *White-Jacket*) sold well, he remained hopeful. Shortly after he had completed *White-Jacket* and had just started *Moby-Dick*, he imagined even loftier goals than commercial success, wondering if he might be one of those "masters of the great Art of Telling the Truth."[40] But low sales and some sharp reviews made Melville increasingly aware of the difficulty of authorship as a career. Failure to finish *Moby-Dick* on time led him to borrow money, the dismal sales of *Pierre* left him unable to pay back the advances *Harper's* granted him, and *Israel Potter* and the magazine stories did not bring in enough money to release Melville from the hard work of full-time farming. The extent of Melville's depression elicits various appraisals, but most agree that his despair was probably deepest as he began *The Confidence-Man*.

During these years, Melville also struggled with health problems. In 1853, he began to suffer back pain, probably rheumatism, and throughout the summer of 1855 he was in pain from a debilitating bout of sciatica. With these problems, he began to worry that he would no longer be able to farm, and yet he and his family knew that long writing sessions also aggravated his back troubles. In a letter to President Franklin Pierce requesting a consulship for Melville, a friend reported that although Melville had "contributed to our Literature much that is instructive and delightful," he was working too hard and needed a government position: "he is toiling early & late at his literary labors, & hazarding his health to an extent greatly to be regretted."[41] The pace had indeed been frantic: in the six years from 1846 to 1852, Melville had published seven novels, and between 1853 and 1856, he published fourteen short pieces and one more novel. Given these worries—physical and financial—it is not surprising that in *The Confidence-Man* Melville devotes six chapters to one who traffics in pain, profits, and words.

For most critics and readers, *The Confidence-Man* is a dark, difficult book. The central character, a con-man, takes on an impossible array of identities, and there is no plot, simply a series of philosophical dialogues in which the knave tries to fleece the fool. Set on the *Fidèle*, a southward-bound Mississippi steamer, the book imagines the radical instability of a carnivalesque world in which almost every human interaction is (or might be) a confidence game. The result is a book in which, as Cecilia Tichi notes, Melville seems to have given up on his earlier passion for sorting out political and ethical questions. Focusing on the book's linguistic density, Michael Gilmore notes that "Syntax goes awry, double negatives accumulate, and clauses spin out of control until sense becomes elusive if not impenetrable."[42] And for both Wai Chee Dimock and Elizabeth Renker, *The Confidence-Man* lacks human warmth. Words "eclipse their human speakers," and the novel's "dizzying masquerade of faces" reduces human characters to mere letters on the page.[43]

Even bodies on the *Fidèle* are not what they seem since throughout the novel the con-man changes not only his clothing, his business, and his personality, but also his voice, his hair color, his stature, and his skin color.[44] As the cosmopolitan, another avatar of the con-man, sums up near the end of the book: "You can conclude nothing absolute from the human form."[45] Or, as Michael Rogin notes, on the *Fidèle* "there are only the costumes with no one inside . . . the body is no more real than its veils."[46]

This view of the body is a significant departure from the politics of corporeality that mark the earlier works. In *Typee* and *White-Jacket*, Melville is both sensitive to ideologies that reduce natives or sailors to nothing more than bodies, and devoted to representing and celebrating the body. In both works, finding language that adequately represents somatic pleasures and pain is important to Melville and to his politics. And the violence done to the bodies of natives and sailors serves in each work as powerful evidence of the evils of Western civilization. In *The Confidence-Man*, by contrast, Melville no longer seems to trust that the body might serve as a ground for political or ethical judgments. The body, it seems, is as untrustworthy as language, as likely to be manipulated as words.

This unnerving sense of the body's plasticity is established in an early scene that is useful since it raises some of the same issues (the commodification of the body and of pain) that Melville interrogates more fully in the herb-doctor chapters. In the first chapters, the con-man appears as a "grotesque negro cripple" who dances for the passengers on the *Fidèle*, using a coal sifter for a tambourine. Black Guinea has something "wrong about his legs" that leaves him "cut down to the stature of a Newfoundland dog," and he has a "good-natured, honest black face" that he rubs "against the upper part of people's thighs" to ingratiate himself with his audience (10). The scene raises unsettling questions about authenticity, charity, and race. As Eric Lott notes in his history of minstrelsy, performances such as Black Guinea's were popular precisely because blackness had become by mid-century "a marketable object of white interest."[47] Destitution was also marketable, and advice to philanthropists often encouraged them to scrutinize closely all appeals for alms.[48] Should Black Guinea's audience believe him or not? Should the reader feel pity? Melville's answer is yes, but not because he meets authenticity criteria. Whether he is black or not, crippled or able-bodied, Black Guinea is a corporeal man, and his performance takes a toll on both his spirit and his body.[49] This is particularly clear when, in an effort to keep his audience interested, he adopts an even more ingenious and degrading form of supplication.

as in appearance he seemed a dog, so now, in a merry way, like a dog he began to be treated. Still shuffling among the crowd, now and then he would pause, throwing back his head and opening his mouth like an elephant for tossed apples at a menagerie; when, making a space before him, people would have a bout at a strange sort of pitch-penny game, the cripple's mouth being at once target and purse, and he hailing each expertly caught copper with a cracked bravura from his tambourine. (11)

Catching pennies in this fashion was a common trick. According to an *Atlantic Monthly* article on the origins of minstrelsy, T. D. Rice borrowed the costume for his first blackface act from a black man who "won a precarious subsistence by letting his open mouth as a mark for boys to pitch pennies into at three paces, and by carrying the trunks of passengers from the steamboats to the hotels" in Pittsburgh.[50] In the *Atlantic*, the black man's penny-catching trick is comic, though also persuasive evidence of his financial desperation. In Melville's account of penny catching, there is more bite since his version attends not only to the beggar's talent for making a spectacle of his body and thus for making money, but also, briefly, to the real, physical pain of trading on one's body.

To be the subject of alms-giving is trying, and to feel in duty bound to appear cheerfully grateful under the trial, must be still more so; but whatever his secret emotions, he swallowed them, while still retaining each copper this side the oesophagus. And nearly always he grinned, and only once or twice did he wince, which was when certain coins, tossed by more playful almoners, came inconveniently nigh to his teeth, an accident whose unwelcomeness was not unedged by the circumstance that the pennies thus thrown proved buttons. (11–12)

Although the passage begins by noting Black Guinea's skill at hiding the humiliation of accepting alms tossed at his mouth, it ends by admitting that he cannot conceal humiliation or physical pain. The passage insists upon the emotional and physical costs of turning the body into a commodity, and Black Guinea's wince suggests that this carnival scene is not only about the marketability of blackness or disability, but also about the reality of pain even when turned into a spectacle.

Melville takes up both the marketability and reality of pain more fully in the herb-doctor chapters, in which he chronicles how medicine seeks to profit from pain and thus often drowns out the authentic sounds of pain. Medicine, according to Melville, appropriates the patient's experience in much the way South Seas missionaries colonize the bodies of islanders and the U.S. Navy appropriates the bodies of sailors. In focusing on an herb-doctor, Melville does not seem to target regulars, but in the deregulated healthcare market of mid-nineteenth-century America, regulars and irregulars alike had to sell themselves and Melville's herb-doctor employs language used by all practitioners in their efforts to win the public's confidence.

Most specifically, Melville's doctor is a parody of Thomsonian herbalists, and, more broadly, of patent medicines. Launched by Samuel Thomson in 1822 with the publication of *New Guide to Health; Or Botanic Family Physician, Containing a Complete System of Practice*, Thomsonianism condemned mineral and chemical remedies and the heroic therapeutics of regulars, recommending instead natural medicines made of herbs and roots. Thomson eschewed professional schools and societies, and he censured the high fees of regular physicians. He insisted that laymen could treat themselves, and his promotion of a democratic medicine based on self-healing made his method widely popular, particularly in rural areas and along the frontier. Thomson claimed to have sold more than one hundred thousand copies of the *Guide* within a decade and a half of its first publication, and he battled criticism, suits, and legislation aimed at limiting or ending his practice.[51] Although the Thomsonian movement lost coherence when its leader died in 1843, a more broadly defined botanical movement had developed by then, and in many states Thomsonianism and its derivatives rivaled regular medicine.

Melville's herb-doctor, a frontiersman traveling down the Mississippi, makes a Thomsonian-style populist appeal. Insisting that "a plain man . . . might rightly question an eminent physiologist" (78), he condemns "chemical practitioners" for their elaborate "tinctures, and fumes, and braziers, and occult incantations." He labels a popular German water cure a "fatal delusion" and scoffs at respirators for tuberculosis (79). As an alternative, he recommends his Omni-Balsamic Reinvigorator that, like Thomson's much-touted remedy, lobelia, is a cure for every illness and for all patients. It is cheap, widely available, and, of course, made only of natural ingredients. And, just as Thomson claimed to have learned herbs as a child in rural New Hampshire under the tutelage of an old woman, so the herb-doctor describes himself "staff in hand, in glades, and upon hillsides, go[ing] about nature, humbly seeking her cures" (79).[52]

Not surprisingly, given the novel's sharp examination of Christian ethics, Melville is particularly attentive to the religiosity of alternative medicine. In response to the scientific claims of orthodox medicine, some alternative practitioners charged regulars with a sacrilegious pride in human understanding, suggesting that atheistic theories were typical of the European scientific tradition. Botanical medicines, they claimed, were based upon a simple science that never presumed to explain the inscrutable ways of God and nature.[53] As one Thomsonian explains in *The Botanico Medical Reference Book,* the principle of life is "in many respects undefined and perhaps forever undefinable," and he warns against "philosophy and physiology which teach that life is the effect of some particular association of matter."[54] Melville's herb-doctor sounds the same note. He calls chemical practitioners "Pharaoh's vain sorcerers, trying to beat down the will of heaven" (78); he warns that belief in human invention implies a "kind and degree of pride in human skill, which seems scarce compatible with reverential dependence upon the power above" (79); he calls his medicine the Samaritan Pain Dissuader; and he suggests that the theories of other healers have "the appearance of a kind of implied irreligion" (79).

In addition to targeting herbalists and patent medicine, Melville spoofs the well-known squabbling among regulars and irregulars that typically included fairly obvious efforts to discredit others and champion one's own sect. Among irregulars this often meant proclaiming the democratic nature of one's medicines while also providing a guarantee of exclusivity. Melville's herb-doctor, for example, claims that his cure is natural and available to everyone, while he marks his vials with a secret trademark and thus assures his patients that his medicine is special—an authentic, limited-edition remedy that cannot be reproduced at home or purchased in a generic form at a cheaper price. "Take the wrapper from any of my vials and hold it to the light, you will see water-marked in capitals the word '*confidence*,' which is the countersign of the medicine, as I wish it was of the world. The wrapper bears that mark or else the medicine is counterfeit" (83).

The herb-doctor asks for confidence and yet encourages wariness, an awkward position all salesmen must negotiate, and Melville lampoons trademarks, testimonials, patents, and attacks on others that were widely used in these years as marketing strategies. In the *Mobile Advertiser* of July

6, 1849, for example, an advertisement for Dr. Townsend's Sarsaparilla cautions that at least one imitation, made by a Dr. Townsend who "is no doctor and never was," may confuse those who want the original. The column-long ad explains that although "any person can boil or stew the root till they get a dark-colored liquid," it is only in "Genuine Old Dr. Jacob Townsend's Sarsaparilla" that "every particle of medical virtue is secured in a pure and concentrated form."[55] Thomson similarly protected his economic interests. He obtained a comprehensive patent for his medicinal compounds, patented the treatment regimen he recommended, charged twenty dollars for a license to use his system and demanded a vow of secrecy from all licensees.[56]

Melville's satire of the language of confidence and distrust, counterfeit and genuine, also targets regular medicine. The National Ethical Code of the American Medical Association, for example, encouraged physicians to trust only regulars and to have nothing to do with other healers. Medical schools often administered oaths of allegiance, and physicians were encouraged to be wary of consultations with other practitioners and to manage carefully a patient's request for a second opinion. It was recommended that the principal physician should always enter the sick room first and leave last, thus denying a second practitioner any opportunity to undermine the primary physician's authority. One medical journal editor even admitted in print that the profession was full of "jealous, quarrelsome men, whose chief delight is in the annoyance and ridicule of each other."[57]

Melville's satire of medicine's language in these battles is precise and pointed. The herb-doctor counsels a sick man to trust his remedy, but not anyone else's:

Nay, think not I seek to cry up my treatment by crying down that of others. And yet, when one is confident he has truth on his side, and that it is not on the other, it is no very easy thing to be charitable; not that temper is the bar, but conscience; for charity would beget toleration, you know, which is a kind of implied permitting, and in effect a kind of countenancing; and that which is countenanced is so far furthered. (77)

Regulars similarly counseled suspicion of others while urging confidence in themselves. One medical college, for example, required its graduates to swear that they would "neither countenance nor affiliate with any system of irregular practice, nor engage either in the manufacture, sale, or recommendation of 'quack' nostrums or patent medicines, nor countenance the practice of senseless dogma of hydropathy, homeopathy, or Thomsonianism."[58] Although reluctant to call for a return to licensing in an era enamored of market freedoms, regulars worried, like the herb-doctor, about the consequences of tolerating, permitting, countenancing, and thus furthering the theories and therapeutics of others. Regulars and irregulars, like Melville's herb-doctor, found it "no very easy thing to be charitable" toward their competitors.

Tolerance comes in for particularly sharp words in Oliver Wendell Holmes's famous 1842 diatribe against irregulars, a speech first delivered to the Boston Society for the Diffusion of Useful Knowledge and later published as "Homeopathy and Its Kindred Delusions." Holmes raises two issues. One, he admits that on occasion alternative medicines may work: "So long as the body is affected through the mind, no audacious device, even of the most manifestly dishonest character, can fail of producing occasional good to those who yield it an implicit or even a partial faith."[59] This seems reasonable, but in admitting that faith might play a role in healing, Holmes wanders into dangerous waters. Appeals to faith were typically represented by regulars as a mark of fraudulent medicine. Only quacks require patients to have faith in the remedy. Scientific medicine works regardless of what the patient thinks. Not surprisingly, Holmes immediately qualifies his first statement, insisting that any broader claim that quacks make for their remedies based on the occasional good gained by the patient's trust is a crime akin to counterfeiting U.S. coins: "The argument founded on this occasional good would be as applicable in justifying the counterfeiter and giving circulation to his base coin, on the ground that a spurious dollar had often relieved a poor man's necessities." According to Holmes, if the quack's occasional success leads to a general countenancing of his practice, the result will be as disastrous as allowing a base coin wide circulation.

Holmes's analogy is telling: a sick man is a poor man, a homeopath is a counterfeiter, and nostrums are base coins that must be kept out of circulation. Money was a delicate issue for regulars. As I discuss in the next chapter, regulars avoided public discussion of their fees, claiming ethical service rather than profit was their motive. Discussions of their role in a market economy, as noted in Chapter 1, often led to conclusions they did not want to endorse. In this case, Holmes's analogy suggests a corollary that he would probably never have asserted publicly, but might well have accepted privately. That is, if nostrums are base coins, then the medicine of regulars must be akin to genuine money. Holmes may well have wanted to assert that scientific medicine should be the legal tender of the health care economy, but he probably would not have wanted to make an explicit analogy between medicine and money. This might suggest too explicitly that every pill swallowed is another coin in the doctor's pocket, precisely what regulars often said about quacks. Thus, when Melville's herb-doctor, sounding remarkably like Holmes, claims that his own medicines are legal tender and his competitors' are base coins, he makes an argument made by regulars and irregulars alike. According to

Melville, sectarian quarrels are not about what is best for the patient but fierce, bitter battles about who will earn the confidence of the public and who will profit.[60]

In suggesting that Melville's satire extends to regulars, I do not mean to suggest that he made no distinctions between regulars and irregulars, between quackery and science, or between the upper-class educated physician and the patent-medicine salesman. In addition to maintaining a friendship with Dr. Francis in New York City while writing *White-Jacket*, Melville socialized with other regulars, including Holmes, who was a longtime family friend. In fact, Holmes's early poem "Last Leaf" immortalized Melville's paternal grandfather as a Revolutionary War hero.[61] When Melville lived in Pittsfield, Holmes's country home was nearby, and Holmes was among those who climbed Monument Mountain in an 1850 outing now famous for the literati gathered there and for the beginning of the short but intense friendship between Melville and Hawthorne.[62] Melville also turned to Holmes for medical help. Elizabeth Melville called in Holmes when her husband was disabled by sciatica, and some have read "I and My Chimney" as, relating in part to Holmes, Melville's Pittsfield home, and his physical troubles.[63] Melville's amicable relations with doctors also included a brief friendship with a Dr. Taylor whom he met in 1849 en route to England. Melville was impressed with Dr. Taylor's learning and wit, and he detailed in his journal their lively conversations and their plans to tour Europe and the Middle East together (which they never did). Melville also stayed in touch with his uncle, Dr. Amos Nourse.

Given these friendships and class affiliations, it is likely that Melville valued the educated sensibilities of well-to-do regulars and shared Holmes's contempt for quackery. Undoubtedly, then, his satire is aimed first and foremost at patent medicine and herbalism. But the similarities between the herb-doctor's arguments and the rhetoric of regulars suggest that Melville was also ready to poke fun at regulars by noting just how much they shared with their less decorous brethren. Indeed, the divide between regulars and irregulars was not as deep as Holmes wanted to claim. Regulars borrowed from the armamentarium of irregulars, and some offered their testimonials for use in patent medicine advertising. In an 1850 prize-winning essay, "Lessons from the History of Medical Delusions," the esteemed Yale medical professor Dr. Worthington Hooker admitted that regulars shared more with quackery than they wanted to admit.[64] And as historian Thomas Richards notes, regulars and patent medicine vendors shared basic presumptions, including "that all diseases can be cured; that cures will be technical in nature; that disease is not to be blamed on circumstance, or more precisely, the capitalist system; that symptoms of disease are generally manifestations of individuality; that experts know best; and that the body's needs can best be met by consuming various kinds of therapeutic commodities."[65] Regulars and irregulars, Richards suggests, were "two corporations competing for the same market," offering distinct versions of essentially the same message, and the ubiquity of patent medicine contributed to a "medicalization of life" that served the interests of regulars and irregulars alike.

Stylistic differences, of course, were real. Patent medicine, in many ways, was a sanctioned inversion of regular medicine, and its carnivalesque advertising and bold claims served as counterexamples to the decorum that regulars cultivated. Broad, body humor was often a part of medicine shows where patent medicines were sold, and print advertisements for nostrums featured images of the troubled body that were not unlike the bodies presented in freak shows and the extravaganzas of P. T. Barnum and other impresarios.[66] Oliver Wendell Holmes and others held themselves aloof from the carnival world of such advertising, and they often positioned themselves firmly among the nation's elite, as I discuss in the next chapter. They represented themselves as men of learning and culture, and they took up leading positions in civic institutions. But Melville was an iconoclast, and by 1856 any allegiance he might have had to the ruling class of professionals had largely disappeared.

In addition to spoofing medical squabbles, the herb-doctor chapters interrogate the implications of speaking for those in pain. Black Guinea's wince early in the novel suggests that pain cannot be disguised, even by the most talented con-man, and the six chapters devoted to the herb-doctor focus on the reality of pain, thus achieving a gritty realism absent in the rest of the novel. Although the novel is always intellectually challenging, it is rarely emotionally engaging. It is often difficult to distinguish knaves from fools, and there is little incentive to care for any particular character. In the herb-doctor chapters, however, the fool and the knave are easily identified; one man is in pain, the other is not. In other chapters, the con-man dupes such unappealing fools as a sly student, a suspicious barber, a misanthropic philosopher, and a fellow knave. These scams raise abstract ethical questions, but they do not touch us emotionally. By contrast, when a doctor convinces a tubercular who has tried every remedy to buy with renewed hopes a nostrum and when a doctor charges a dying, miserly old man for a useless vial of Omni-Balsamic Reinvigorator, the con-game is particularly cruel. Moreover, the herb-doctor chapters are punctuated by quiet but pointed descriptions of pain. In these chapters, compelling descriptions of coughs, twisted bodies, missing limbs, and hopelessness make it clear that Melville understands medicine as a con-game that fleeces those who cannot speak their own pain.

The herb-doctor's first patient, a consumptive, can barely speak. Initially, he offers only a "feeble dumb-show" (78). Having given up on doctors and their babble, the tubercular shoos the doctor away with gestures that mean, according to the narrator, "Pray leave me; who was ever cured by talk?" and "Pray leave me. Why, with painful words, hint the vanity of that which the pains of this body have too painfully proved?" (78). Words are useless, and when the consumptive finally speaks, it is the sound of his voice—and not his words—that testify most powerfully to his misery. His voice is like "the sound of obstructed air gurgling through a maze of broken honey-combs" (79).

In the next scene, the herb-doctor solicits another man who finds language inadequate. The Titan limps onto the *Fidèle* as if he were a wounded god or oversized ancient hero who has battled valiantly against the gods. His body bespeaks the hardships of the natural world and the human world. His beard is "blackly pendant, like the Carolina moss, and dank with cypress dew," and his countenance is "tawny and shadowy as an iron-ore country on a clouded day" (85). Unlike the restorative natural world celebrated by Transcendentalism or health reformers, nature weighs heavily upon the Titan's body. His "tall stature [is] like a main-mast yielding to the gale, or Adam to the thunder" (86). His body also bears evidence of man-made troubles—war, industrialism, and racism. His labored walk, we are told, may be the result of service in the Mexican war. His voice is "deep and lonesome enough to have come from the bottom of an abandoned coalshaft," and his daughter is a frail half-breed (86). The metaphors inscribe his body with images of a scarred national landscape, and as a symbol of the nation's ills, his stooped body challenges the herb-doctor's relentless alliegiance to a doctrine of facile optimism.

Eventually, the Titan rebuffs the herb-doctor directly. Finding that averting his face or offering only short answers does not dissuade the herb-doctor from chattering, the Titan finally explains to the optimist that there are some ills that cannot be righted. He insists that "some pains cannot be eased but by producing insensibility, and cannot be cured but by producing death" (87). Unwilling to accept this, the herb-doctor answers with more optimistic pronouncements, and neither the Titan's silence, nor his bowed "shaggy form" propped up with a "heavy walking-stick of swamp-oak," nor the stunning bell-like voice he uses to proclaim the profundity of his suffering, can break the verbal barrage of the herb-doctor. Finally, in one of the most powerful moments in the novel, the Titan strikes the doctor. But the blow, and thus this climactic moment, comes to nothing. The herb-doctor never falters; he chatters on, using the bruise inflicted by the Titan as another opportunity to demonstrate the effectiveness of his Samaritan Pain Dissuader.

Frustrated by the endless words of the herb-doctor and by his slippery, pollyannaish philosophy, we, too, want the doctor to shut up so that the somatic evidence of pain—the Titan's labored walk or the consumptive's husky voice—might register. The Titan's desperate blow makes the cruelty of the herb-doctor's obliviousness evident. But it also suggests the consequences of rejecting language, and the scene is more ambiguous than simply the enactment of the retribution the doctor deserves. The Titan is likable enough in his grandeur as a large, silent man with a small girl-woman in his care. And he may speak a grim truth. But he is also an angry misanthrope. His smile is "hypochondriacally scornful," and when he hits the doctor his countenance is "lividly epileptic with hypochondriac mania" (86, 88). He is, Melville suggests, one who finds a philosophy and an identity in pain.[67] And, while the Titan's suffering deserves our sympathy and the herb-doctor's facile chatter is offensive, the Titan's hypochondriacal malaise rejects what the confidence-man does offer—conversation.[68]

As Elaine Scarry notes, pain "does not simply resist language but actively destroys it, bringing about an immediate reversion to a state anterior to language, to the sounds and cries a human being makes before language is learned."[69] Thus when we are in pain, we often turn to others to translate our cries and groans into words, or to ask us about the pain and thus help return us to the world of language.

For the Titan and the tubercular, the herb-doctor's language is particularly offensive because it trivializes their misery, offers false hope, and seeks profits. When the herb-doctor claims to understand the suffering of others and when he offers remedies to soothe their pain, their bodies become props—commodity spectacles—in his marketplace performance. The Titan and the tubercular suspect this, and they are right. The herb-doctor manages, like a master of ceremonies, the words of his patients. To bring the fool into the scam, he invites him into conversation. Then once the scam is completed, the doctor silences his patient. He tells the miser, "But your voice is husky; I have let you talk too much" (83). He promises the tubercular that his "rough voice" will be soothed and quieted by a bottle of Omni-Invigorator. In managing these conversations, the herb-doctor privileges his own words and voice. In contrast to the husky voices and taciturn silence of those in pain, the herb-doctor's voice is smooth, his words glib. Compared to the rapid Mississippi that "runs sparkling and gurgling, all over in eddies" (77), his voice bubbles with facile promises and drowns out the quieter sounds of pain and suffering. This is particularly clear when he stands before a group, proclaiming his eagerness to give half of his proceeds to some "benevolent purpose" (90). When no one steps forward as an agent of a charitable organization, he asks any needy passenger to come forward. Deafened by his own, self-promotional chatter, he fails to hear the quiet crying of "an unhappy-looking woman, in a sort of mourning, neat, but sadly worn" (91). Her sobs attract the attention of the other passengers, and she earns the reader's sympathy as one truly in distress, but the doctor is deaf to her cries. Although much in *The Confidence-Man* is masquerade and performance, the widow's sobs, like Black Guinea's wince, are genuine.

For the most part, Melville suggests that the private, quiet, hidden pain is more likely to be authentic than public displays of suffering. The Titan, the sobbing widow, the tubercular, and even Black Guinea are quiet about their pain.[70] But in a chapter devoted to "the soldier of fortune," Melville considers the power of language, offering the soldier, Tom, as an instructive contrast to the Titan.

Tom's troubles began when he saw a gentleman kill a working man. As a valuable witness for the prosecution, Tom was detained in a damp jail cell until the trial, while the other witnesses and the accused gentleman got out on bail. At the trial, Tom testified that he saw "the steel go in, and saw it sticking in," but the murderer was acquitted because he was a gentleman and had wealthy friends (95). From prison, Tom was transferred to the Corporation Hospital, where he spent three years receiving the inadequate care that was common in public hospitals. He worsened, grew tired "of lying in a grated iron bed alongside groaning thieves and mouldering burglars," and left the hospital a cripple and a beggar (95).[71] Tom, formerly a cooper, is now homeless, penniless, and ill.

The herb-doctor responds with his usual optimism.[72] He suggests that while the acquittal may "speak prosaically for justice, it speaks romantically for friendship," since it is through the efforts of friends that the gentleman evades conviction. The herb-doctor's optimism, overbearing in every case, is particularly hollow this time. And he admits as much when he acknowledges that "the government might be thought to have more or less to do with what seems undesirable" (98). Most significantly, Tom's story leaves the herb-doctor "silent for a time, buried in thought" (97). The herb-doctor, indeed the confidence-man in any guise, is almost never at a loss for words. But this time he is, and Tom achieves by telling his story what the Titan could not with his blow—he makes the herb-doctor pause and acknowledge a very grim reality.

Tom's bitterness is profound. Much like the herb-doctor's other patients, he initially responds with nothing but "morose ogreness" to the herb-doctor's chatter, and he tells his tale of woe only because he hopes to disillusion the optimistic doctor. Likened to a hyena, Tom cackles that this is his chance to "get hold of the Happy Man, drill him, drop the powder, and leave him to explode at his leisure" (94). But, in telling his tale, Tom makes further conversation possible, and the scene is dramatically changed when the doctor offers Tom a free bottle of tonic. For

Tom, the offer casts the herb-doctor's willingness to talk and listen in a new light. He tells the doctor, "You have borne with me like a good Christian, and talked to me like one" (100). The offer of a gift—unsolicited and despite Tom's incivility—seems to make real a generosity that had, up to that point, been merely verbal. As a result, a man previously "toughened and defiant in misery" is now at peace. Unlike the Titan, Tom has found comfort, and as the herb-doctor exits, "the cripple gradually subsided from his hard rocking into a gentle oscillation. It expressed, perhaps, the soothed mood of his reverie" (100).

Tom's repose might be, in some ways, a sad image. He is at peace, we might argue, only because he has been duped. He may think that the herb-doctor cares, but presumably the herb-doctor only seeks to improve his reputation, and giving a cripple a box of useless liniment is a cruel way to do this. But the final image of Tom rocking gently on his crutches is powerful, and I want to suggest that Tom's reverie is an important moment. In a work dedicated to exposing the corrosive effects of the calculating spirit, the herb-doctor's gift giving stands as an important alternative to the brutal dynamics of the marketplace, if only momentarily.

It is easy to be skeptical of the authenticity of gift giving. The power that comes to those who give and the burden that falls upon those who receive has been much noted. In 1651, Thomas Hobbes commented that "no man giveth, but with intention of good to himself." In 1844, Ralph Waldo Emerson mulled over the trials of giving and receiving—the "law of benefits is a difficult channel, which requires careful sailing, or rude boats"—and he suggests that "We do not quite forgive a giver." Likening gifts to chains, Friedrich Nietzsche cautioned that gifts make recipients feel inferior and vengeful; and in his 1925 study on gifts, Marcel Mauss noted that in some traditional societies gift giving could be an aggressive and competitive practice.[73] More recently, Daniel Hack has studied how nineteenth-century British writers cultivated a professional identity in part to avoid becoming charity cases for those eager to buy the title of benefactor of the arts.[74] Personally, Melville probably knew all too well the burden of receiving gifts. When he struggled financially because writing would not pay, he accepted help from his family, as had his father before him. As a struggling but optimistic dry-goods merchant, Thomas Melvill turned repeatedly to his own father for funds. Similarly, Melville accepted assistance from his father-in-law, thoughtfully defined as loans against Elizabeth's inheritance. Presumably, Melville was sensitive to his position, and perhaps he winced, much like Black Guinea, when he found himself compelled to accept such gifts.

With Tom, however, Melville considers the possibility that a gift might produce not awkward emotions and a sense of debt that cannot be repaid, but rather a moment of peace. According to Jacques Derrida, the gift exists "beyond calculation."[75] And Melville also intuits that something other than calculation may be possible. For Derrida, the gift creates an *aporia*, an impasse, because a pure act of generosity is essentially impossible since in giving we cannot but anticipate the pleasure of the credit that will redound to us. We are always calculating, it would seem. But Derrida suggests we should push against this impasse. The gift is "an expenditure without reserve." "In a moment of madness," we do "something for once without or beyond reason."[76] In 1843, Carlyle, a man Melville greatly admired, made a similar plea: "Cash Payment is not the sole relation of human beings" (*Past and Present*), and in *The Confidence-Man*, Melville imagines a mad, carnivalesque world that might allow a gift to be given and received without calculation. Given the impasse that attends gift giving, Derrida admits that "one is never sure that there is a gift, that the gift is given."[77] And Melville seems to agree. As the herb-doctor leaves, Tom thanks him, and offers to pay: "Here is the money. I won't take nay. There, there; and may Almighty goodness go with you" (100). Perhaps the words "There, there," indicate a transaction. It seems likely that Tom has made the herb-doctor accept payment. Thus we might conclude that the herb-doctor's scam is successful; Tom has paid for useless medicine. Perhaps by paying, Tom relieves himself of the burden of receiving a gift and thus annuls the gift. But the herb-doctor's gesture, even if it disappears almost immediately, has consoled Tom. In this chapter, the herb-doctor's silence is an authentic, uncalculating response to Tom's tale of injustice, pain, and misery, and possibly his gift is an act "without or beyond reason."

Throughout his life, Melville was suspicious of easy truths. The era's facile optimism easily seduced men into arrogant self-satisfaction, he believed, and led them to have little interest in unpleasant, hard truths. The slaughter of Pacific Island people, the miseries of the common sailor under constant threat of flogging and hanging, and the anger of a man crippled by a careless justice system are truths no one wants to hear. Echoing the Titan, a merchant on the *Fidèle* insists, "Truth will not be comforted." But as Elizabeth Foster notes in her astute and generous reading, for all his "unremitting truth-seeking" and commitment to skepticism as a necessary response to "cheating optimisms," Melville was deeply worried by "the prospect of a world without charity."[78] Charity, for Melville, was most likely when bodies—their pleasures and their pains—were fully and compassionately acknowledged. In *Typee*, Melville challenges a political and representational order in which the burden of corporeality is carried by some and not by others and the pain of some is deemed insignificant. In *White-Jacket*, he celebrates the possibility of embodied democracy but underscores the managerial violence that threatens at all times. In *The Confidence-Man*, the herb-doctor is first and foremost a satire of the smooth-talking quack who preys upon the physical miseries of men and women, turning their bodies into spectacles for his profit and then dismissing his patients with confident predictions for rapid improvement. But he is not only villainous, he listens and he gives away real silver coins. In compassion, conversation, and charity, Melville finds a glimmer of hope for a democracy that delights in the body.

Henry Bigelow believed etherization was a promising sign of what medicine might achieve and he understood medicine as dedicated to freeing all men from pain, but Melville was less optimistic. Ship surgeons were all too willing to lend their authority and expertise to cruelty, and irregulars as well as regulars were out to win the public's confidence. Melville had little confidence in professional medicine or folk therapeutics. Indeed, by 1857 he was a disillusioned man. But in the chatter of an herb-doctor, Melville also finds a spirit of excess that may, if the healer pauses to listen to the patient, inspire a generosity that might revive democratic fraternity.

Chapter 4

Class and Character: Doctors in Nineteenth-Century Periodicals

> It is the doctor cures us, not the doctor's physic.
> —*Atlantic Monthly* (1873)

Historians agree on the basic outlines of the rise of professionalism in America. Between 1750 and 1830 the traditional, "liberal" professions (medicine, law, ministry) were successfully established through the founding of self-regulating institutions. Between 1830 and 1870, with the rise of anti-elitist sentiments, they lost prestige and power, though all three professions continued to garner some respect and to build institutional power. After 1870, Americans increasingly accepted professionals as experts worthy of trust, autonomy, and status.[1] Indeed, the culture of professionalism that has prevailed now for more than a hundred years is so deep that it is easy to take the prestige and power of professionals as natural and inevitable. Experts, we believe, deserve our respect and special compensation for their work—not just a paycheck but the power to govern themselves (who else could provide oversight of such complex fields). We presume that professionals prize mastery of esoteric knowledge over riches and that they put their knowledge to work for the public good. In return, society grants the professions prestige, market privileges, and exemption from outside regulation.

But, as many historians also note, professions have not always made good on their part of the bargain. For example, in the nineteenth century, regular physicians did not necessarily provide better care than their competitors. A commitment among regulars to active treatments (bleeding, purging, and blistering) meant that alternative remedies (typically less aggressive) were sometimes more effective, and usually less damaging, than the heroic therapies that regulars prescribed.[2] Nor were regulars immune to economic self-interest. Although many believed that more demanding training was desirable, in a deregulated market and with the proliferation of medical schools, few institutions, even elite ones, were willing to raise standards and thus risk lower enrollment and income.[3]

What, then, can explain medicine's success in establishing itself by the end of the century as the most prestigious profession in the nation? On what grounds did regulars eventually gain the veneration so desired by the first president of the AMA and his brethren?

As sociologists remind us, ultimately the privileges accorded professionals must come from the state, either explicitly in the form of licensing laws or implicitly through gate-keeping institutions such as exclusive societies, professional associations, prestigious universities, and accredited hospitals. To establish such institutions or to gain licensing regulations, professionals must persuade those in power, and society as a whole, that their knowledge is not accessible to laymen and that they are an ethically minded, coherent group deserving and capable of self-regulation. As one historian of the medical profession puts it, the privileged position of any profession is "secured by the political and economic influence of the elite which sponsors it."[4] This is not to suggest a conspiracy between professionals and the ruling class to seize power or even endless, bald-faced efforts to rally support from legislators (though doctors have testified before Congress on matters regarding professional autonomy). Rather, prestige and power is secured as professions, and distinct groups within each profession, form alliances, or in Gramsci's words "organic" ties, with significant factions of the ruling class, which, of course, itself consists of changing coalitions.[5] In other words, the history of the medical profession in the United States is in part the history of medicine's affiliations with particular factions and coalitions of the nation's elite.[6]

In this chapter, I tell a part of this history by examining ties between regulars and highbrow literature as recorded in elite magazines—those magazines that were able to achieve a national readership and to identify themselves with an emerging and professionalizing literary culture. As I noted in the Introduction, although regulars often came in for rough treatment in newspapers and sectarian medical journals at mid-century, in the pages of the nation's elite magazines they were usually honored. In the *Southern Literary Messenger*, for example, an 1843 editorial insists that, contrary to popular opinion, doctors are religious men and are never hard-hearted.[7] A few years later the *New Englander* published an address by Yale medical professor Worthington Hooker. Speaking to entering students, Hooker explains that the professional doctor is distinguished not so much by successful treatment (perhaps an attempt to respond to the fact that regulars did not have a higher rate of cures than irregulars) as by his character.[8] And the next year, *Putnam's* ran two articles championing doctors for their kindness, common sense, and steadiness.[9] Support for regulars in the pages of elite magazines is not particularly surprising. These magazines, as Nancy Glazener notes, were

deeply enmeshed in the "construction and justification of social hierarchy," and in the celebration of the doctor's good character we can see
the forging of an alliance that served the interests of both medicine and
literature.[10]

Significantly, the fiction published in the nation's elite magazines
offers a more complicated record than did the non-fiction essays of the
alliance between profound science and elegant literature, presenting on
occasion a less appealing portrait of the doctor's character than Hooker
sketched. While the fictional physician in mid-century periodical literature is often a liberal, upper-class gentleman who brings stability to the
world he inhabits, in other stories the doctor may be critiqued for his
unbending allegiance to an outdated class order, exposed as one who is
eager to marry into the upper-class, or satirized as in mad-doctor tales.

The range of roles imagined for the physician testifies to a complex
relationship between literature and medicine at mid-century. In the
uncritical stories, the virtues of the professional doctor echo those the
AMA sought for its members. These are also the virtues that elite fiction
claimed for itself as it established an authority premised upon its distinction and distance from the "low" character and illegitimacy of popular and populist genres such as dime novels and sensational fiction.
The "good" doctors, like the highbrow fiction that tells their story, are
figures of stability that might well have appealed to an audience worried
about democracy's tolerance for discord, disruption, and change. Critical stories, by contrast, show a resistance to the cultural claims of the
AMA, a willingness to interrogate professionalism and literature's sense
of itself as objective and disinterested (virtues that then validated literature as a critical, independent discourse free of suspect class allegiances).

Although the stories examined here vary in their judgment of the
physician, all are marked by anxieties about social instability. These worries were prompted by a wide range of political, economic, and cultural
factors—the depression of the late 1830s and early 1840s, the European
revolutions of the 1840s, the panic of 1857, immigration, divisive debates about defining new territories as slave holding or free soil, the rise
of a commodity culture in which copies and originals seemed indis-
tinguishable, and fears of miscegenation that led, according to Shirley
Samuels, to a "fatal desire to pull apart one body from another."[11] Mid-
nineteenth-century anxieties about the nation's stability were registered
at the very deepest somatic levels, and the figure of the doctor negotiates
these anxieties. As images of confidence men and painted ladies reflected the nation's fascination with and fear of the fluid social order and
hybrid identities that seemed to make and threatened to unmake America
before the war, so the image of the doctor—noble or mad, steady or in-
flexible—registers a deep though conflicted desire for national stability.

The image of the doctor as a wise, temperate, liberal, well-to-do gentleman has deep roots, and to understand how mid-nineteenth-century
periodical fiction invokes and resists this image, I turn first to real doctors. Early professionalizing efforts were successful in part because
the country's medical leaders were sons of elite families and thus had
ready access to social, political, and economic structures.[12] Most of the
renowned physicians of the colonial northeast, for example, were born
into wealthy families, benefited from education at select academies, and
tended to be politically conservative and wary of democracy.

John Morgan, often called the father of American medicine, came
from a successful mercantile Philadelphia family, and he studied at the
elite West Nottingham Academy in rural Maryland, which was directed
by the Reverend Dr. Samuel Finley (the future first president of Princeton College and Benjamin Rush's uncle). Morgan earned an M.D. at Edinburgh, toured the Continent after his studies, and returned to found
the first medical school in the country. During the Revolutionary War,
Morgan was appointed by Congress to serve as director-general for the
army hospital, and during his tenure, he persuaded Congress to make
army medicine more exclusive by requiring examinations of all regi-
mental surgeon candidates.[13]

Benjamin Rush, another Philadelphia physician and patriot, was born
on a large farm outside the city; his father and mother came from established families, and he, too, attended Nottingham Academy. Although
still a young doctor in 1774, Rush had good connections and socialized
with delegates visiting Philadelphia for the First Continental Congress,
including John and Samuel Adams and George Washington. In 1776 he
married Julia Stockton (daughter of a New Jersey Supreme Court justice) and attended, along with his father-in-law, the Second Continental Congress. Rush supported rebellion (he signed the Declaration of
Independence), but like many Federalists he worried about the tyranny
of "ignorance and licentiousness."[14] In the *American Museum*, for example, he warned of the dangers of a single legislature and called for two
legislative bodies (that is, an aristocratic Senate as well as a populist
House). Believing in the importance of professional expertise, he wrote,
"Government is a science . . . and can never be perfect in America, until
we encourage men to devote not only three years, but their whole lives
to it. I believe the principal reason why so many men of abilities object
to serving in Congress, is owing to their not thinking it worth while to
spend three years acquiring a profession which their country immediately forbids them to follow."[15]

Like their Philadelphia brethren, the leading medical men of Boston
were also from patrician families and active in public affairs. John
Warren and his brother Joseph Warren were from a landed family that

owned more than ninety acres by 1755; their father was a selectman of Roxbury, Massachusetts, and their mother was the daughter of a doctor and granddaughter of a clergyman. Joseph Warren apprenticed with a wealthy, esteemed Boston physician, whose patients included many colonial aristocrats, though he sided with the Whigs and befriended and treated many leading Whigs of the day. He played a major role in colonial Boston politics, had a hand in what one biographer calls the "largest patronage system" outside the official government of the state, and did much to shape colonial policy and opinion before and during the struggle for independence.[16] Along with Samuel Adams he was a leader of the Liberty Party, he spoke in favor of dumping tea in Boston Harbor, he may have boarded the *Dartmouth* and even acted as a leader of the treasonable act, and he died at Bunker Hill.[17]

John Warren, one of the most influential physicians in Boston at the turn of the century, studied under his older brother, married the daughter of Rhode Island's governor, and was a founding member of the Massachusetts Medical Society and the medical department at Harvard. A Federalist who like Rush was wary of too much power in the hands of the untrained, Warren joined other urban, Federalist-identified physicians to rebuff the attempts of rural, Jeffersonian physicians to seize control of Boston's medical establishments and open the profession to physicians with less formal education. Warren's son, John Collins Warren, was equally eminent, active, and influential. He studied at Harvard, succeeded his father as the Hersey Professor of Anatomy and Surgery at Harvard, and helped to found Massachusetts General Hospital and the *Boston Medical and Surgical Journal*, premiere institutions in U.S. medicine, and performed, as noted in Chapter 1, the first operation under ether.[18]

In short, family connections, access to power, and wealth allowed early medical leaders to create policies and institutions (especially schools, societies, and hospitals) that made professional medicine's authority and prestige legitimate, visible, and exclusive. When founding the first medical school in the country, Morgan aimed quite consciously to establish an institution that would produce, and authorize in the eyes of the public, a venerated elite medical profession. In his celebrated *Discourse Upon the Institution of Medical Schools in America* (1765), he provided explicit guidelines for his brethren based on what he had seen abroad. He encouraged physicians to eschew the work of apothecaries and surgeons (tradesmen in Britain), he called for a colonial Royal College of Physicians to guide all other societies, and he insisted that honorariums were preferable to fee schedules.[19] Some of these imported notions never caught on among colonial physicians—shunning surgery and having no set fees, for example. But they testify to the gentlemanly status that Morgan sought for American physicians. According to Morgan, whereas surgeons and apothecaries needed only practical skills, physicians needed a classical education (including Greek and Latin), formal instruction in medical theory, and a "genius for deliberation, reasoning, judgment, and experience."[20] Although Morgan believed that theoretical knowledge and familiarity with classical languages made a physician a better healer, he probably also understood these accomplishments as indications that a formally educated physician was a gentleman with an aptitude for analytic thought, an interest in the ancients, and time for esoteric studies.[21]

Morgan's curriculum was realized with the opening of the Medical College of Philadelphia. The school trained more physicians than any other in its day, and it began to distance American medicine (elite medicine, at least) from practical arts and local trades, occupations traditionally learned through apprenticeship. Morgan's own training in America had been as an apprentice, and apprenticeship continued to be used for medical training into the nineteenth century.[22] But a formal medical education, he believed, would help establish in young physicians a sense of camaraderie, an esprit de corps. As Gramsci notes, camaraderie, pride, and a sense of natural group coherence are based, in part, upon a sense among professionals of the "uninterrupted historical continuity" of their discipline, and this allows professionals to "put themselves forward as autonomous and independent."[23] The professional's independence was something U.S. physicians were particularly keen to foreground. The doctor was in no one's pocket, regulars insisted. Or, as explained by James Jackson, Sr., one of the most eminent physicians in the nation, the professional medical man was a freeman and a slave to no one and no single theory. In his *Letters to a Young Physician*, Jackson argues that education in a "liberal profession" must not be through apprenticeship—"an apprentice is a servant. . . . He works for his master's benefit, and at his master's bidding." Jackson acknowledges that in the past in Europe apothecaries and surgeons "learned their arts" in this way. "But," he continues, "it was never so as to physicians. They did not pursue their studies under bonds, but like clergymen and lawyers, as freemen."[24]

Jackson's representation of the physician as a man who serves no master was not universally accepted. While some believed that the professional's training might lift him above the fray and teach him, in Morgan's words, "deliberation, reason, and judgment," others noted the alliance between professionals and those in power and were suspicious of it. Indeed, the professional man's economic interests, class allegiances, and political debts were thorny issues debated and finessed by medical leaders and scrutinized, as I discuss later in this chapter, by periodical fiction.

Federalists, both in medicine and politics, championed the professional as a source of wise counsel on difficult subjects. Alexander Hamilton, for example, suggests in one of the *Federalist Papers* that the professional is, unlike the average man, attentive to "the general interests of society." The professional is an "impartial arbiter," according to Hamilton, and as a group the professions form "no distinct interest in society." Professional men, he insists, are the "objects of confidence and choice of each other and other parts of the community.[25] James Madison makes a similar argument for a strong federal government when he suggests that the nation should put its trust in experts much the way a patient trusts his doctor. Madison likens America to a patient with a "disorder daily growing worse" and in need of a physician. As he explains, the patient, "after coolly revolving his situation, and the characters of different physicians, selects and calls in such of them as he judges most capable of administering relief, and best entitled to his confidence."[26] The analogy is telling. For Madison, national instability (a possible consequence of unrestrained popular rule) is akin to disease, and as the ill man calls in a medical expert, so the country must call in political experts. Citizens have the right to choose their government, and patients have the right to choose their doctors. But once a choice is made, citizens and patients should, unless there is good reason to the contrary, follow the experts' advice—the laws and the therapeutics of the professionals in whom they have put their trust. Smart patients and smart citizens, Madison suggests, allow professional experts to manage their bodies and their country.

Physicians eager to elevate the profession made similar arguments for their expertise. Morgan insisted that medicine is a "difficult" science, and he contrasted college-trained physicians and military generals—the elite corps who see the big picture—with apothecaries, surgeons, and soldiers who dig in the trenches.[27] Rush, probably the single most influential physician in the nation at the turn of the century, similarly valued school accreditation. He taught for years at the medical school in Philadelphia, founded a liberal arts college, and valued medical theory as the foundation of medical practice (a notion that, like a formal curriculum, sought to define medicine as a science rather than an art or craft). Other physicians challenged these views as elitist. In Connecticut and Massachusetts, for example, rural physicians called for a more open profession. Stiff qualifications, they argued, served wealthy urban physicians with access to universities and hospitals and discriminated against those trained through apprenticeships. Federalist physicians answered that high standards were simply in society's best interest. Thus, when Jeffersonian physicians sought to establish a second medical society in Massachusetts with licensing powers, a society that would have challenged the increasing power of Harvard's medical professorate, Jackson, John Warren, and others from Harvard and the Massachusetts Medical Society insisted that *they* acted merely as the "guardians of science" and "patrons of the healing arts."[28] The challengers retorted with a sharp satire, in a Boston newspaper, mocking the Warren family as a dynasty bent on controlling medical practice in Boston. The town needed a new fire company, the satire began, but "Captain Squirt" (Warren) and his son "young Squirt" (John C. Warren) stood in the way. In the end the Warrens prevailed, and as one historian of these battles concludes, elite physicians continued to control medical societies that regulated the profession and they continued to direct "powerful and heavily endowed incorporated medical institutions" because they had affiliations with "the institutions and social groups in which political, financial, and cultural power resided."[29]

Of course, elite physicians were willing to acknowledge that they had selfish interests. In his *Letters to a Young Physician*, Jackson admits that physicians may be motivated in part by a "desire for profit and reputation." But the physician's "true" interests—"love of science and humanity" in Jackson's words—intersect with what is best for society.[30] Thus in arguing against a second medical society, John Warren insisted that two societies would fracture professional cohesion and that what was bad for the profession was bad for healthcare in Massachusetts. Similarly, his son and Jackson solicited funds for what would become Massachusetts General Hospital by suggesting that a hospital would be good for the city and good for professional medicine. In a remarkably adroit open letter to Boston's upper crust, Jackson and Warren suggest that the poor and the rich, the city and the medical profession, humanity and science, will all be served by the founding of a hospital. They note the increasing number of "faceless people," predicting that as men and women move into a city and have little or no extended family, they will not be able to take care of themselves when they are sick.[31] The almshouse, they point out, is more a "house of correction" than a hospital and the worthy poor want nothing to do with such a place. A "well-regulated" hospital, by contrast, will appeal to the worthy poor, and it will make them healthy and capable of returning to work. In short, by contributing to a hospital, Boston's wealthy will be ensuring civic order, quelling the dissent that ill health might breed among the city's lower classes, and, as Warren and Jackson point out, helping medical science. The hospital will be a facility "for acquiring knowledge" that will be useful to "students in the medical school established in this town." Noting that the only school of eminence is in Philadelphia (the one Morgan founded), they also play to civic pride, promising to build a medical community to rival Philadelphia's, and in one neat sentence they link what is good for the medical profession with what is good for Boston: "A hospital is an institution absolutely essential to a medical school, and one which would afford relief and comfort to the thousands of the sick and miserable."[32] They conclude by saying that a hospital will honor the city's leading citizens, those who serve as "treasurers of God's bounty." The edifice will be "a most honorable monument of the munificence of the present times, which will ensure its founders the blessings of thousands in ages to come."[33] In short, a hospital would help the deserving poor, reduce social and political instability caused by untreated disease, demonstrate the philanthropy of Boston's rich, nurture medical science, and increase the professional opportunities and power of Boston's medical leaders.

As it turned out, Warren and Jackson were right. All were served, and probably served well, as Massachusetts General quickly became a large, well-run, prestigious institution. It served the sick; more than a thousand were treated each year.[34] It also served the medical elite. It was a premier site for gaining experience and professional prestige and was renowned for such achievements as the first operation under anesthesia (John C. Warren was the surgeon). The hospital also served Boston's elite. Designed by Charles Bullfinch and built by convict labor, the building became a city landmark and a sign of the munificence of Boston's rich. The hospital was also a way for Boston's elite to protect and increase its wealth.[35] Although major contributors to the Hospital did not want their names emblazoned on plaques in the wards or even in an entrance foyer, they were clear about keeping control of the hospital.[36] The hospital remained free from governmental and public control, and it became part of a consortium of private, not-for-profit corporations that served, though "discreet elite management," the financial interests of the city's wealthy.[37] The hospital was financially tied to an insurance company devoted to providing trust management and loans for Boston's elite.[38]

Not surprisingly, the hospital had some critics. As one historian notes, "the private control of the institution" and "the great wealth, status, and ambition of the doctors" might explain why some lower on the economic ladder worried that Massachusetts General was not first and foremost dedicated to the welfare of the poor.[39] In fact, control of the hospital— on the wards and on the board—was in the hands of Boston's elite. Nineteen of the twenty-four trustee officers between 1820 and 1850 were among Boston's wealthiest, sixteen of twenty-one attending physicians and surgeons between 1817 and 1851 were officers or sons of officers of the Massachusetts Medical Society, and eight physicians came from the same families as the trustees. Populists might also have wondered about the hospital's association with prestigious Boston cultural institutions. Many of the names that appear on the hospital's rosters of trustees and attending physicians also appear on lists of trustees and donors for the cultural institutions of the city. For example, 46 percent of the trustees for the Boston Athenaeum (a private, gentleman's library that some republicans found offensive) also served on the board of the hospital.[40]

Massachusetts General was not the only medical target of populist ire. Anti-elitist rhetoric detected power plays in scientific language, in the display of diplomas and certificates of society membership, and in the familial status of elite doctors. The most popular domestic medicine manual of the day, for example, announced on the title page that it was written "In Plain Language, Free from Doctor's Terms."[41] Similarly, a regular, full-page advertisement in *Harper's Weekly* for Graefenberg tonics derided elite physicians of Boston and New York for their dependence upon the trappings of professionalism. The druggists and physicians at Graefenberg, the ad explained, "make no professions of position. They merely claim to cure disease, and are willing to rest their case upon the testimony of those they have cured, and not upon any position or honors awarded by a self-constituted medical board."[42] Political radicals, alert to the fact that elite physicians were often from patrician families, included professionals in their attacks on class oppression. As one union organizer declared, "the capitalists, monopolists, judges, lawyers, doctors, and priests . . . know that the secret of their own power and wealth consists in the strictest concert of action. . . . Unions among themselves have always enabled the few to rule and ride the people."[43]

These were not, we should remember, merely rhetorical attacks. Although a small coterie of physicians, including those practicing at Massachusetts General, were able to maintain their status, wealth, and power, the profession in general experienced a real decline in public confidence. Licensing patterns make this clear. In 1830 all but three states had medical licensing regulations; in 1860 almost none had such laws.[44] Although these laws never fully regulated medical practice, they had distinguished one class of practitioners as legitimate, but with the repeal of licensing laws, regulars could no longer claim a distinction sanctioned by law.[45]

In response to the populism of the day, regulars scaled back some of their professionalizing efforts. Many retreated from their commitment to licensing regulation, and many schools lowered entrance and graduation standards. The result was that medical training became more accessible, practices formerly defined as trades (dentistry, for example) became professionalized, and distinctions between medical sects diminished. And yet, many regulars, including the founders of the AMA, continued to believe that they had a peculiar claim to veneration and confidence based on the fact that they were, as a group, men of good character.[46]

Attempts to claim authority, as Max Weber notes, typically draw upon three justifications: tradition, rational argument, and character.[47] There was a tradition for physicians to point to, and so they did. Medical schools, societies, and journals regularly paid homage to medicine's grand past, and in his president's address at the first meeting of the AMA, Nathaniel Chapman reminded his brethren that their profession was "once venerated on account of its antiquity," earning homage "spontaneously and universally."[48] Rational arguments were also made: regulars suggested that their authority derived from the fact that they had rigorous training in medical science. And yet, appeals to tradition and expertise were risky given the political climate, and such arguments were largely unpersuasive among those who believed and sometimes saw that a folk remedy might do as much good as a visit from a regular. Thus, in an effort to regain the nation's confidence, regulars also trumpeted their good character.

A claim to authority based on regulars' good character avoided the charge of elitism because it was widely understood that character was not a matter of family status. The potential for good character might be found in all men, including those born in the meanest corners of society. As Francis Lieber (a friend of John C. Warren) suggested in his popular 1846 *The Character of the Gentleman*, any man might become a gentleman by cultivating particular virtues. Of course, character traits varied, and some men might be more capable of developing the virtues of a gentleman, but it was precisely this diversity of talents and temperaments that allowed character to legitimize class hierarchies. Distinctions between men based on character rather than family ancestry, Lieber suggested, resulted in a natural hierarchy, a meritocracy. Thus, when regulars claimed they were men of good character, they sought both to claim distinction and, at the same time, to avoid elitism.[49] They avoided elitism because, according to the ideology of character, every man is self-made, and history, politics, economics, and class play no role. They claimed distinction by suggesting that if the regular doctor is a good man, it is because he has made himself so through rigorous self-discipline.[50] Of course, self-making was not an option for everyone: Jews, the Irish, slaves, and many other marked groups were presumed to have predictable, inherited character traits, and for them the potential for self-making was profoundly circumscribed. But for most middle-class white men, self-making was a duty, and when done well self-mastery was precisely what fitted one for shouldering the responsibility of leadership and management.[51] Power and authority were the rewards for mastering one's passions and making oneself reliable, ethical, and honorable.

The claim to good character also served regulars in their efforts to gain public confidence because, in theory at least, good character could not be faked. Although there was a national fascination with and fear of confidence men and painted ladies, as Karen Haltunnen has shown, there was, in the discourse of character, the presumption that the con-man could never quite completely pass as a man of good character.[52] And, conversely, a man with a well-developed, strong, good character would never, in the end, be taken in by a con-man. Con games depended upon something a little slippery on both sides. Of course, in the rhetorical battle between regulars and other sects (a war in which character defamation was a common stratagem), regulars allowed that good men might be duped by quacks. While maligning the character of alternative healers and boasting of their own trustworthiness, regulars were careful never to suggest that patients were to blame for quackery's success. The sick man is particularly vulnerable, more vulnerable than he might be in any other situation because he is sick and because as a layman he cannot evaluate medical expertise (an assertion alternative healers dismissed). A man may assess the value of a consumer commodity, and a bad purchase is not disastrous, but a sick man is desperate to make a good decision, and yet cannot assess the value of a doctor's prescription. Thus the patient must consider the doctor's character, as James Madison noted. Character, unlike expertise, can be discerned and evaluated. Indeed, the mid-century popularity of phrenology, a science of discerning character through visible cranial signs, testifies to the eagerness to believe that character is legible.

Of course, regulars did not call in phrenologists to prove their trustworthiness. But they did understand the importance of making their good character visible. When the founders of the AMA drafted a code of ethics (an attempt to shift debates about professional authority away from a populist emphasis on market freedoms and toward a concern with professional ethics), they were particularly keen to delineate the character qualifications they valued and that they expected of their membership. To do this, they borrowed, as did many local medical societies before them, from Thomas Percival's eighteenth-century tract on medical ethics, quoting directly his suggestion that doctors inspire "gratitude, respect, and confidence" because they unite "*tenderness* with *firmness*, and *condescension* with *authority*" (original emphasis).[53] In this passage, the good doctor balances emotional responsiveness with firmness because he is a caring man with a doctor's expert understanding of disease and death. He balances condescension—in the eighteenth-century this meant the superior man's ability to put himself on the same level as those beneath him—with a clear sense of the authority and responsibility that comes with a command of medical knowledge.[54] In short, according to the AMA, the good doctor wins his patients' trust because he is both a democrat sympathetic to their human condition and a reliable, disinterested expert who through his will and understanding (the faculties most highly valued in eighteenth- and nineteenth-century faculty psychology) provides trustworthy advice.[55]

In addition to adopting the right bedside manner, regulars demonstrated their good character through public displays of cultural refinement. As

Pierre Bourdieu has suggested, an "aristocracy of culture" permeates society's class distinctions. Despite constant challenges to elite culture and a full awareness that taste is culturally produced, there lingers in every epoch since the seventeenth century a sense that the aesthetic is rooted in an "ethos of elective distance from the necessities of the natural and social world." The "taste of necessity" seeks physical satisfaction, while the "taste of liberty" seeks beauty and style. The former is base, ordinary, "lower, coarse, vulgar," while the latter constitutes the "sacred sphere of culture." The aristocracy of culture, in other words, affirms the "superiority of those who can be satisfied with the sublimated, refined, disinterested, gratuitous, distinguished pleasures," and it makes visible the "moral excellence" of those with a "capacity for sublimation."[56]

In the nineteenth-century United States, cultural refinement was particularly associated with Europe, and study abroad was highly valued among ambitious physicians. In the seventeenth century, well-to-do physicians went to Leyden; between 1769 and 1819 more than three hundred studied in Edinburgh, and between 1815 and the 1850s more than a thousand studied in Paris.[57] The cachet of such trips was significant. Doctors often returned enthusiastic about having studied with some of the most famous European medical men and with a sense that they had imbibed European culture because, although these trips were largely devoted to medical studies, they bore some resemblance to the gentleman's grand tour.[58] Morgan, for example, returned from his European travels with the beginnings of an art collection (paintings, engravings, and original manuscripts) that eventually became a much admired mature collection.[59] He could also boast of having met, as an 1828 biographer noted, "the first medical and literary characters" of Europe, including Voltaire in Geneva and the renowned pathologist Morgagni in Padua.[60] Rush also met Europe's cultural luminaries during his trip, including Sir Joshua Reynolds, Samuel Johnson, Oliver Goldsmith, and Diderot.[61]

The next generation also returned from their travels with a sense of cultural superiority. Some physicians flaunted what one doctor called "Parisian polish," using French phrases and resisting a reacculturation to what some saw as the provincial manners of the United States and to the anti-intellectual mood within the U.S. medical community.[62] Of course, European polish was offensive to some homebred physicians and to those wary of elitism, and yet, medical leaders from Morgan to the founders of the AMA to Abraham Flexner in the early twentieth century sought to position medicine alongside highbrow culture. Having gained support from European luminaries for his medical school in Philadelphia, Morgan appended to their letters of recommendations the observation that these were men "distinguished for their superior knowledge in literature" as well as men "eminent in everything which relates to medical science."[63] Eighty years later, in his first address to the AMA, Nathaniel Chapman noted that the medical profession had formerly earned respect not only because of its antiquity but also because of "its various and profound science—its elegant literature—its polite accomplishment—its virtues."[64] And another eighty years after Smith's address, Abraham Flexner, the man who almost single-handedly reformed medical education at the beginning of the twentieth century with the help of Carnegie Foundation money, similarly linked medicine with literature. In an introduction to a reprinting of Morgan's *Discourses*, Flexner championed the entry requirements and curriculum of Johns Hopkins as a continuation of Morgan's early understanding of the importance of a "sound education in literature and science."[65]

To those who believed that truths were self-evident, that the vox populi needed no managing by experts, and that regulars had nothing more to offer than their polished images, the argument that cultural refinement bespoke good character was not persuasive. But it was an argument that drew upon widespread notions of highbrow culture—art, literature, ancient languages, erudition, etc.—as pursuits far removed from the crass world of commerce. The politics of cultural refinement are relatively simple in that regardless of whether good taste is learned or innate, it signals a sensitivity to beauty and truth that marks the man of good taste as superior. If good taste is innate, then those who have it are naturally responsive to the aesthetic, naturally appreciative of the sublime. If good taste is learned, then it is a virtue earned through self-discipline, through a dedication to a pursuit that brings no monetary rewards, only aesthetic and perhaps spiritual refinement. Taste, according to this way of thinking, is an index of character: men with good taste are men with good character. Neither taste nor character can be faked. Both require discipline, both testify to an appreciation of the importance of balance and proportion in all things, and both gesture to innate talents.

The power of taste to certify those fluent in highbrow culture as worthy stewards of the nation is significant. As Glazener notes, in the nineteenth century competency in highbrow culture became an important indicator of a deserving and natural aristocracy in the United States. With no sumptuary laws or titles to fix prestige upon a select group, and because of popular resistance to entrenched patrician power, the nation's elite distinguished itself by claiming that education, expertise, good character, and good taste made them legitimate and trustworthy managers and leaders in a democratic nation. In other words, regulars found in the discourse of character and taste the possibility of distinguishing themselves as men of culture as well as men of science. Indeed, the alliance between regulars and highbrow culture, and specifically be-tween "profound science" and "elegant literature" has a long, appealing history from John Morgan collecting European paintings to Oliver Wen-dell Holmes writing for the *Atlantic* to Oliver Sacks penning literary accounts of neurological cases for the *New York Review of Books*. The doc-tor as a man of cultured sensibilities is, for many, a reassuring image of science and culture, knowledge and compassion, tenderness and firm-ness, condescension and authority united in one man. Significantly, one historian's survey of early-twentieth-century medical journals suggests that doctors understand the value of cultural capital. Again and again journal articles insist that cultured doctors attract educated, middle-class patients who pay their bills and further add to a doctor's social status.[66]

The ideology of character was not, however, simply a tool to be used at will by regulars. The study of character was precisely what the bur-geoning world of fiction claimed as its specialty, and in periodical fiction we see literature interrogating the doctor's character.

Caught in class politics of its own, nineteenth-century writing was, like medicine, open to a wide variety of practitioners and was often stratified along class lines. As Richard Brodhead notes, writers and readers under-stood the cultural distance that separated the *Atlantic* from *Frank Leslie's Illustrated Newspaper* but often traveled quite casually between the two worlds. Louisa May Alcott, for example, contributed to both, while also understanding that the one conferred cultural status and the other did not.[67] Medicine, as I have just suggested, was similarly both open and stratified. It was relatively easy to get a diploma at midcentury (from an "orthodox" or alternative school), and many doctors drew upon a variety of theories and therapeutics without regard for the prestige associated with any particular sect. And yet, there was little doubt about a hierar-chy within medicine, a hierarchy visible in institutional and society affil-iation as well as in family name. Both doctors and patients knew full well that John C. Warren was eminent and powerful and that the local herb-doctor was a common man. The periodicals I consider here were, for the most part, like Massachusetts General Hospital, in that they were run by and affiliated with the elite. Thus these magazines often celebrated reg-ulars as men of good character. But as Glazener reminds us, *Harper's*, *Putnam's*, the *Atlantic*, and other magazines with highbrow pretensions record both assertions and violations of elite literary sensibilities, and thus they both endorsed and challenged the class ideology implicit in the refinement and authority that regulars claimed.

The intersection of elite medicine and literature is perhaps most clearly visible in the career of Oliver Wendell Holmes. Doctor, writer, and regular contributor to the *Atlantic*, Holmes embodied the virtues that elite professionals in both literature and medicine wanted to claim—education, taste, expertise, compassion, understanding, and will. Holmes was born into a religiously orthodox family with a fine New England pedigree. His father, a minister at the First Church of Cambridge, sent him to Phillips Academy and then to Harvard College, where Holmes made friends with others who would become part of the next generation of a powerful, liberal New England aristocracy. After college, he studied law for one year and then turned to medicine. In 1839, Holmes was briefly a professor of anatomy and physiology at Dartmouth, and, in 1843, he delivered a paper on "The Contagiousness of Puerperal Fever" to the Boston Society for Medical Improvement. The suggestion (thirty years before Pasteur introduced the germ theory) that childbed fever was carried by doctors and nurses as they examined one woman after another without attention to antisepsis was Holmes's greatest contribution to medicine. This discovery, along with three Boylston prizes for medical essays and an impressive record of lectures, made Holmes one of the preeminent physicians in New England, and in 1847 he was named the Parkman Professorship of Anatomy and Physiology at Harvard.

Not surprisingly, given his background and achievements, Holmes defined himself as a gentleman and a scientist. He adopted the latter label in Paris, where he learned the "numerical method" of Pierre Louis in the wards at La Pitié. Louis's theories probably had little impact on daily practice across the United States, but study in Paris offered both cultural capital and scientific legitimacy. In a letter home to his parents, Holmes claimed that he was gaining modern training and knowledge that could never be matched by the usual rounds of house calls and bedside treatments in the United States.

Our physicians of the old school have not the slightest idea of the confidence and certainty with which such a man as Louis speaks of his patients. If I was asked: Why do you prefer that intelligent young man, who has been studying faithfully in Paris, to this venerable practitioner who has lived more than twice as long? I should say: Because the young man has experience. He has seen more cases, perhaps, of any given disease; he has seen them grouped so as to throw more light upon each other; he has been taught to bestow upon them far more painful investigation . . . merely to have breathed a concentrated scientific atmosphere like that of Paris must have an effect on anyone who has lived where stupidity is tolerated, where mediocrity is applauded, and where excellence is defied.[68]

In this passage, Holmes moves from championing the empirical method of Louis to snobbish disdain for American mediocrity. In fact, for Holmes and others, Paris represented an elite scientific training unavailable in the United States that promised to distinguish regulars from other healers and to vanquish, in Holmes's words, stupidity and mediocrity.

Although Holmes and others were enthusiastic about science, they also insisted that they were gentlemen.[69] They warned of the excesses of science: too much science might brutalize a doctor, ruin his character and make him ruthless and fanatical. It became a commonplace among U.S. physicians that the French were good scientists but not good doctors, and at mid-century the image of the sinister clinician became an important trope against which regulars defined themselves. The evil Dr. Griffon in Eugene Sue's *Les mystères de Paris* (1843) came to stand for what U.S. physicians wanted to reject, and Holmes condemned the heartless experiments depicted in the novel.[70] In fact, few U.S. physicians devoted themselves to clinical studies upon their return to the United States. Holmes, for example, never really distinguished himself as a medical researcher. His work, including that on puerperal fever, was based not on experimental science or clinical studies, but on a gentleman's pursuit of knowledge—reading in ancient and modern medical texts and conversation with practicing physicians.[71]

In literature as in medicine, Holmes was a modern, democratic, scientific, and cultured gentleman, negotiating with finesse the distinct ideologies implicit in this hybrid identity. His literary style was a mix of modern iconoclasm and traditional, upper-class Yankee humanism. Holmes moved in New England literary circles that included Lowell, Emerson, and Longfellow, and he was the epitome of all that the *Atlantic* represented. He not only named the magazine, he was also its most consistent contributor for years, and he was a regular member of the exclusive Saturday Club—an informal group of liberal, learned gentlemen of Boston. To this world of "elegant literature," Holmes brought the empirical methods he had learned in Paris. Throughout his literary works, Holmes attacks the traditional doctrines of his father and of New England Calvinism, and critics have rightly traced his ideas on limited free will and biological determinism to his scientific training.[72]

And yet, Holmes's literary works now strike us as wooden because of an elitism that was inseparable from the way he constructed authorship. In the poems, the essays, and the novels, the narrator is always a gentleman who holds himself apart from the contentious fray on which he comments.[73] In the series of Breakfast Table essays that Holmes wrote for the *Atlantic*, he offers the "talk" of an educated gentleman addressing others at an imaginary breakfast table in a New England boardinghouse. The scene has populist possibilities: the leveling moment of early morning breakfast among boarders who are known not by family, social standing, or previous history, but simply by their words. But Holmes's breakfast table is not democratic. At the center of each series is one figure—an autocrat, poet, or professor—whose words and ideas dominate. At times he draws out others or is the object of a clever observation that momentarily one-ups him at his own game of wit and insight. The heart of the series, however, lies in the "talk" of the autocrat and his ability to encapsulate familiar truths or brief flashes of insight in witty analogies that include both a little homespun wisdom and a large dose of paternal condescension. The autocrat, the professor, or the poet is a liberal, modern gentleman who by virtue of his superior education and class is a man of equanimity, knowledge, and social grace.

Holmes's vision of a cultural elite—in literature and medicine—was shared by many of the Yankee humanists who wrote for the *Atlantic*. As Ellery Sedgwick notes in his history of the *Atlantic*, the founders, editors, and early contributors were politically progressive, and most believed in the extension of individual rights to all, regardless of class, race, or gender. Holmes, for example, fought for women's right to attend Harvard Medical School, he supported the admission of three African Americans in 1850, and he was a fierce advocate of free speech.[74] But about majority rule, the magazine was "deeply ambivalent, particularly in matters of intellect, aesthetics, and morality," and many contributors "had strong convictions advocating the social responsibility of the educated individual."[75] Cultural stewardship, as Glazener notes, was a privilege and a duty the Brahmins embraced. In founding service institutions such as the Massachusetts General Hospital, the Boston Dispensary, and the Lowell Institute, as well as cultural institutions such as the Boston Athenaeum and the *Atlantic*, the Boston Brahmins made visible to themselves and others the legitimacy and "desirability of their social and cultural leadership."[76] The modern physician—a man of science and culture—was, for Holmes and others, an attractive embodiment of such leadership.

The claims that Holmes, the AMA, and other regulars made for the character of the professional physician were often echoed in the fiction published in the *Atlantic, Harper's*, and *Putnam's* in which doctors mediate the exotic, offer narrative control, and resolve plot entanglements. Like Holmes's autocrat at the breakfast table, the professional doctor mitigates the dangers of democracy. He has an egalitarian commitment to the health of the nation, he recuperates the ill body to the standards of a somatic norm, and he has a professional's immunity to the dangerous contagion of the wild ideas and behavior of the populace. This professional disinterest is akin to the narrative distance of highbrow literature. It is a stance that both acknowledges the unruly and yet contains the dangerous liberties that democracy permits.[77]

During the first two years of the *Atlantic*, a doctor appears in three stories. In the inaugural issue, a short story by Calvin Wheeler Phillio deploys stereotypes often used at mid-century to mock the professions.[78] In "Akin by Marriage," makes a parson buffoonish and out of touch with the modern world and a young lawyer slick and ambitious. The doctor is treated more gently. He is no genius, but he is more respected than the others, and the respect depends not upon his display of knowledge or skill but rather upon his common sense and steady habits, the same credentials that Hooker and others insisted should be the basis for widespread acceptance of medicine's authority. The next year L. P. Hale's story "The Queen of the Red Chessmen" features a doctor who is both practical and imaginative.[79] The story dabbles in the supernatural and offers the doctor as a symbol of moderation, a man who understands the claims of opposing worlds—the practical and the romantic, the real and the supernatural.

In the next issue of the *Atlantic*, Rose Terry's tale "Eben Jackson" features a doctor in a Louisiana hospital as he listens on a hot evening to a sailor's tale, a Melvillean sea adventure replete with marriage to a native island woman.[80] The sailor speaks in a rough dialect, and his tale is the romantic heart of the story. But the frame and the control in the story lie with the doctor. He carries the tale back to the gentler clime of New England, and he tells it in gentler words to the sailor's betrothed. Reassuring her that the sailor died thinking of her, the doctor turns an exotic tale into a conventional tale of faithful love for the New England girl back home. The distance and equanimity the doctors maintain in both Hale's and Terry's stories is akin to the distance and narrative control that marks "literary" fiction in which detached, ironic treatment of characters is common. Transcendence marks both elite medicine and highbrow fiction: Holmes studied in dirty Parisian wards to learn the truths of medical science, and *Atlantic* contributors Hale and Terry place fictional doctors in less than genteel adventures only to have them emerge clean and wise.

Two stories in *Harper's* similarly turn to doctors as managers, but to resolve economic rather than romance troubles. "The Infant Heir" features a doctor who determines who is the appropriate heir to a great fortune, and in "Mary Rankin" the doctor presides over the return of property to a disinherited daughter.[81] In both stories, wealth originates with an aristocratic patriarch and is passed, ultimately, to a deserving daughter or granddaughter, but not without some handwringing. The female heirs have married out of their class, in each case to a poor artist, and thus have incurred the wrath of their fathers. The stories speak to anxiety about aristocratic privilege and resolve this anxiety by transferring wealth to a couple that unite the feminine virtues of the aristocracy—breeding and beauty—with the democratic virtues of a self-made artist who struggles to make a living. These marriages, like those in Cooper's *The Pioneers* and Hawthorne's *The House of the Seven Gables*, are mixed marriages that seek to resolve competing claims to American property. The stories also legitimize the doctor's authority as he presides over the dissolution of the aristocracy and the establishment of a new social order that is both democratic and stable.

In both stories the doctor validates the new inheritance laws of antebellum America. By 1850 many states had liberalized women's control of inherited property, not out of a new sense of women's political rights but with an eye to protecting husbands from being devastated by creditors in the aftermath of the Panic of 1837. Women seemed a good place to secure, or hide, wealth against future national economic crises. The revised marital laws were also an attempt to codify law, that is, to make it more fully articulated in statutes and less dependent upon common law.[82] This would offer, many believed, a stronger and more visible legal order.

Both "The Infant Heir" and "Mary Rankin" are stories of anxiety that find resolution in the doctor's endorsement of the new and essentially conservative inheritance laws. They are not only comedies in which the world is turned upside down for pleasure. Rather, they are stories that seek to rectify mistakes that seem all too possible, and they depend upon the doctor to turn the world right side up again. In both, inherited wealth is problematic and cannot simply be handed to the next generation. Deserving descendants ultimately get the money, but inheritance is tainted money, and in each case the money must be cleansed before it is passed on. This is the role the doctor plays. He disinfects the money and authorizes the transference of wealth. He does this in part by testifying to the moral worthiness of the recipient. His friendship speaks to the character of the heiress. But he also authorizes the transference because he is disinterested in wealth. His interest is health and the body. Unlike lawyers who traffic in such matters, the doctor is removed from the juridical and thus can testify and enter into such matters as one who is committed only to somatic truths and scientific facts.

These issues are articulated elegantly in the account of the death of John Randolph in the December 1850 issue of *Harper's*.[83] Excerpted from a biography by Hugh A. Garland that was published by Harper and Brothers, the account describes the final days in 1833 of the infamous Virginian politician whose barbs, witticisms, and unrelenting conservatism made for a tumultuous political career that included a duel with Henry Clay in 1826. Randolph's biographers, from Garland in 1850 to Henry Adams in 1882 to Russell Kirk in 1951, struggle to make sense of the man and his politics.[84] Garland's solution depends upon the trope of the trustworthy character of the good doctor. According to Garland, Randolph induced a doctor to travel with him as he headed north to make amends to his Northern opponent Henry Clay, and he demanded the presence of several doctors when he was on his deathbed and wanted to free his slaves. The accuracy of Garland's account is not supported by other evidence, and its primary purpose is political. Writing seventeen years after Randolph's death, Garland uses the Virginian to promote a national unity that Randolph in fact rejected. The story imagines, just when the nation is moving toward division, a conservative Southern politician who recants his divisive politics under the wise gaze of a bevy of doctors. Notably, in Garland's account Randolph has no use for clergymen, even though he is on his deathbed. By 1850 the clergy were profoundly disestablished, and Garland's account testifies to the waning authority of the clergy and the rising status of physicians. In Garland's account, the doctor, with his strong, steady, and quiet charismatic presence, is a man who can attend the nation in troubled times. Like the patriarchs in "The Infant Heir" and "Mary Rankin," Randolph is cantankerous and demanding, and in all three texts, the order of the fathers is passing and a new order is emerging. The doctor is the figure who can both appease the dying fathers and authorize a new order.

Although "The Infant Heir," "Mary Rankin," and Garland's account of Randolph's last days imagine the doctor as an economically disinterested man well suited to handling wills and the establishment of a new social order, other stories suggest that the professional man has his own class aspirations. These stories interrogate the doctor's attempt to remain aloof from the marketplace, suggesting that his relationship to money and class is more vexed than professional societies such as the AMA were inclined to admit. As noted earlier, professionalism was defended in the mid-nineteenth century, in part, as an implicit contract in which society grants self-governance, social status, exemption from free market competition, and significant financial rewards in return for commitments to high ethical standards, knowledge, and expertise.[85] In this model, high fees are legitimate because the physician must be free from financial worries lest such concerns influence a medical decision or corrupt his character. Although the rhetoric of professionalism at mid-century rarely speaks directly of this implicit contract, many physicians privately acknowledged the importance of economic security. Early in his career, Elisha Bartlett wrote to his father that "a few years will place me above the fear of want.—I believe I can rely with confidence on the character I have gained and am gaining—and so long as *that* remains unimpaired I have little to fear."[86] Adept at understanding the physician's interest as coincident with society's, Jackson made essentially the same point when he suggested that physicians should be paid well: "Our profession has attached to it great labors and great responsibility. It is for the public good that it should hold out due reward, so as to attract to it young men of talents and sound learning."[87] The professional's eagerness to get his "due reward," or, more modestly, to be "above the fear of want," is the subject of tales by Holmes and Henry James, two writers whose own class inheritance and professional aspirations give them vested interests in the subtle negotiations of a class identity for professionals in a democratic society.

Holmes's first novel, *Elsie Venner*, which was serialized in the *Atlantic* from January 1860 to April 1861, speaks directly to the professional's need for economic security.[88] The novel makes familiar use of the doctor to frame a sensational story. There are three doctors in the novel. The first is a professor of medicine who narrates the strange tale of Elsie Venner, who has inherited the demonic wildness of snakes because her mother was bitten while pregnant with her. The second physician is an old country doctor who knows the secrets of the Venner family and figures as the stereotypical calm, composed doctor who chuckles at ridiculous deacons who debate outdated theological issues at boring parties. The third doctor is a young Brahmin who has not yet finished his training and who, because of his youth, is enthralled by the girl's strange beauty. Unlike his elders, the young doctor lacks equanimity and money. The two, Holmes admits, are connected. Financial need puts the professional man in an awkward relationship with his clients. Echoing Jackson, the narrator notes: "The clergyman, the physician, the teacher, must be paid; but each of them, if his duty be performed in the true spirit, can hardly help a shiver of disgust when money is counted out to him" (171).

The Brahmin, the professional par excellence for Holmes, is a scholar by nature who does not always fare well in the commercial world of capitalism, and his financial failures testify to his love of ideas and disinterest in money.[89] Thus ideally the professional has an income more secure than the fees he collects. In this romantic comedy, the solution is marriage; the young doctor marries the "daughter of—of—why, the great banking-firm, you know, Bilyuns Brothers & Forrester" (356). The stuttering acknowledges the embarrassment of marrying money, of the professional man needing money. The young physician might have married a penniless young lady of good breeding who, like him, loves ideas. But by marrying money, he need not spend his time "squeezing out" money from his patients (354). Thus Holmes gives his effete Brahmin professional the robust inheritance of a banker's daughter.

In *The Autocrat of the Breakfast Table*, Holmes worries quite openly about class. On the one hand, he sees the need for a cohesive class of well-educated men who can lead and manage the nation. On the other, he is scornful of the nation's wealthiest, both the new merchant class and conservative patrician families. Holmes himself was from a mixed family. His father was learned but from rural Connecticut, while his mother was from a very distinguished Boston family. As a result, perhaps, he was torn between celebrating the self-made man and believing in the superior talents of men from elite families. Early in his essays for the *Atlantic*, he favors men born of good family, while in later essays he suggests that the nation is best served by tapping the talent of ambitious young men no matter what their family background. But the rawness of these men worried Holmes. They needed refining. Thus in *Elsie Venner* he imagines a union between money and intellectual ambition as a solution that offers not only money in support of good intellect, but also money in support of building the physical and cultural well-being of the nation's leaders. In his next-to-last essay in the *Autocrat*, he wrote,

We are forming an aristocracy, as you may observe, in this country,—not a *gratia-Dei*, nor a *jure-divino* one,—but a *de-facto* upper stratum of being, which floats over the turbid waves of common life like the iridescent film you may have seen spreading over the water about our wharves,—very splendid, though its origin may have been tar, tallow, train-oil, or other such unctuous commodities. . . . Of course, money is the cornerstone. Money kept for two or three generations transforms a race, —I don't mean merely in manners and hereditary culture, but in blood and bone. Money buys air and sunshine . . . good nursing, good doctoring, and the best cuts of beef and mutton . . . The physical character of the next generation rises in consequence.[90]

For Holmes, men with intellectual talent (and these men might well come from undistinguished families) must have enough money, not only to guarantee that they will be free of want but also so that their progeny will benefit and found a physically robust, national aristocracy of talent.[91]

As Holmes has a culturally elite Brahmin professional marry into the commercial aristocracy, so in "A Most Extraordinary Case" (April 1868), Henry James marries a modern doctor into old money.[92] Here the doctor is a well-trained scientific man who has been called in to care for an upper-class Civil War veteran who has had a nervous breakdown. For Holmes, the professional doctor comes out of the scholarly traditions of the Brahmin class, but for James, the doctor is primarily a scientist. James's doctor has a strength of character that goes beyond gentlemanly equanimity; he has a hardness that derives from his scientific training. The soldier's nervous weakness, by contrast, calls up familiar stereotypes about aristocratic debility. Perhaps a bit viciously, the story ends when the doctor marries the rich girl the soldier had presumed would be his. In James's story, the traditional order is replaced with a new order that marries the professional to the aristocrat, masculine science to feminine culture. The marriage achieves what the AMA sought for its members—"profound science" and "polite accomplishments"—and the story both endorses this resolution and distances itself from the self-serving maneuvers of the professional doctor in the world of emotional relationships. In these stories, Holmes and James establish a new class for the physician—a hybrid class that brings together the wealth of commercial entrepreneurs, or the old aristocracy, and the learning of the professional man. And although each story unabashedly limns the professional's crass desire to join the upper class, they both justify this desire as essential to the progress promised by a professional class that is, in Bartlett's words, "above the fear of want."

Two other stories, one published in the *Atlantic* the same year Holmes's novel was serialized and the other a few years earlier in *Putnam's*, also focus on the doctor's class. But whereas Holmes and James imagine the doctor who needs money (and thus give him democratic appeal), these stories indict doctors for elitism. Although the AMA understood condescension as both a democratic and gentlemanly ability to understand those one advises and manages, in these stories the doctor cannot sympathize across class boundaries. His class allegiance and anxieties make him incapable of responding to new ideas or defiant identities. In Rebecca Harding Davis's 1861 *Atlantic* story, "Life in the Iron Mills," the doctor cannot imagine any response to a destitute ironworker beyond a condescending philanthropic notion that someone should give the poor man some money.[93] Hugh Wolfe, an untutored sculptor, an immigrant, a worker with the "taint of schooling on him," and a man with some stirrings of class consciousness, defies easy categories (48). He is a character rarely seen in periodical fiction of this period because no one, including Davis, quite knows who he is and what he wants. The doctor tries to understand Hugh, but in the end he retreats from economic truths that might demand something of him. In this instance, the doctor is not so much steady, composed, and reliable, as stiff, imperceptive, and unimaginative, and his failure is deeply disturbing.

Dr. May's part in Davis's story is small but telling. He responds to the nude, muscular female statute that Hugh has made from iron refuse (korl), but he fails to understand the body as a primary site for establishing class distinctions, a central theme in Davis's story. Bodies shaped by class are everywhere in this story. The mill workers are "brawny" and half-naked or hunchbacked, colorless, and ravaged. The mill owner's son refers casually to the workers as "his hands," which they are since it is their labor that creates his wealth. And Mitchell, a visitor to the mill and well-to-do cynical philosopher who coolly notes the cruelty of class oppression, has the body and the bodily aesthetics of his class: the well-built body of an "amateur gymnast," an "anatomical eye," and a refined "white hand" adorned with "the bloody-glow of a red ring" (51). Hugh, perhaps because he is a sculptor, is painfully aware of the class politics of somatic aesthetics, of the contrast between his own flesh "muddy with grease and ashes" and "the pure face, the delicate, sinewy limbs" of Mitchell (58). He feels a "quick pleasure" when Mitchell's graceful hand adorned with the ring catches his eye, and afterward Hugh looks at himself with "loathing." But, Hugh's korl woman challenges the aesthetic that engenders self-loathing. There is "not one line of beauty or grace in it," and yet the korl statue is compelling and Dr. May finds the figure unsettling (53).

Initially, Dr. May understands the power of the statue to lie in Hugh's mastery: "'Look,' continued the Doctor, 'at this bony wrist and the strained sinews of the instep!'" Then, when Hugh explains that the woman "be hungry," Dr. May is eager to point out anatomical inaccuracies. "Oh-h! But what a mistake you have made, my fine fellow! You have given no sign of starvation to the body. It is strong,—terribly strong" (53). Ultimately, the doctor cannot reconcile transgressive class politics in an aesthetic work. Even when Hugh makes a more explicit explanation—the woman is hungry for what will "make her live, I think,—like you," and Mitchell and the mill owner's son have a discussion about equality and class oppression, Dr. May remains "vexed, puzzled" (54). He feels something, and, after listening to a dead-end discussion of class inequality, he sighs, "a good honest sigh, from the depths of his stomach" (55). He has a good heart, as a good doctor should; he goes to Hugh and puts "his hand kindly on his arm," intending to do good. "Something of a vague idea possessed the Doctor's brain that much good was to be done here by a friendly word or two," and so, the doctor gives Hugh a brief lecture in self-making. He explains that a "man may make himself anything he chooses," and so the doctor puts himself at ease with a "glowing" sense of "his own magnanimity" (56).

Although Davis is clearly suggesting that most philanthropy is empty talk, she allows that the doctor is, in fact, magnanimous, and that the possibility of self-making is exactly what Hugh hungers for: "The puddler had drunk in every word, looking through the Doctor's flurry, and generous heat, and self-approval, into his will." But will is precisely what the doctor lacks, and this intimate moment between grimy worker and kind-hearted town physician crumbles. When the doctor tells Hugh, "Make yourself what you will," Hugh responds, "Will you help me?" Davis's repetition of and play upon the word "will" underscores the tension between the doctor's professional commitment to autonomy and the puddler's deep awareness of the necessity of fraternity. Ultimately, the doctor cannot rise to the puddler's request, and he turns to his companions and laments, "I have not the means" (56). The doctor cannot think or feel his way out of his class privilege. He translates a request for help into a request for money (which it may well have been, though Hugh might have accepted help in a variety of guises), and the doctor concludes that raising up one man would be pointless. So each night he imagines his duty is done when he prays "that power might be given these degraded souls to rise" (58). Davis underscores the thinness of his kindhearted gestures and words later in the story when we get a brief description of the doctor's response to a newspaper report on Hugh. Sitting at the breakfast table, the doctor reads aloud to his wife that Hugh has been sentenced to nineteen years for robbing Mitchell. He exclaims indignantly, "Scoundrel! Serves him right! After all our kindness that night! Picking Mitchell's pocket at the very time!" His wife concurs, and they go on "to talk of something else" (65). Davis's point is clear: the professional doctor's failure to see his own class privilege makes him obtuse and culpable.

C. F. Briggs's *Putnam's* short story "Elegant Tom Dillar" offers a similar and equally powerful example of a doctor's failure to understand somatic politics and to respond to bodies that challenge traditional categories.[94] Like Dr. May, Dr. Laurens so values the comforts of his privilege that he will do nothing to endanger his status. Like much of Briggs's fiction, the story is critical of precisely what Holmes wanted, "an established elite," and exposes the instability of class identities built on economic speculation and confidence games.[95] It also considers how minstrelsy might destroy a rich doctor's fantasy that he can both indulge the pleasures of working-class art and maintain his public reputation. Brigg's plot is clever. The protagonist, Elegant Tom Dillar, is a rich, elegant man of European ancestry who is tricked into making a bad investment. He loses all his money and disappears from high society, only to return a few months later rich and elegant once again. No one, however, knows how he makes his living until one night a doctor, the father of his fiancée, is called from the audience to attend a renowned Ethiopian minstrel who has fallen on stage. Although the doctor promises not to reveal Tom's new identity as Higgins the great minstrel artist, within hours everyone knows and shuns Tom, who then retreats to Europe.

Elegant Tom's identity is a conundrum. On the one hand, he is the archetypal good fellow who is wronged by all—stock adviser, high society, fair-weather friends, and even the doctor. And yet, he is not a conventional emblem of honesty; he is a slippery character who remakes himself three or four times. He is a natural aristocrat, then a financially ruined, unshaven, homeless man wandering the streets, then he is wealthy again and even more elegant but deeply mysterious, then an Ethiopian minstrel or "sham darkey" as the story labels him, and finally a Parisian aristocrat who has no use for his American countrymen. He is, it might seem, a trickster figure, but he practices no tricks. He proposes to make his living as a professional artist, a song and dance man in a minstrel show, although this "profession" is available to him precisely because he can adopt the face, manners, accent, gestures, and dance of another, of *the* Other in nineteenth-century America. Tom's body is malleable and performs well any role he chooses, and the story celebrates his talents by elevating minstrelsy to a reputable profession. As an aristocrat, Tom has only accomplishments and no education in a profession. He has a fine voice, a sense of rhythm, a handsome face, good manners, and, it would seem, a talent for adopting the identities of others, a bold suggestion that aristocracy is primarily a matter of manners and gestures. That Tom sees how to use these accomplishments to make money testifies to his resourcefulness and suggests that he is as American as the dollar that his last name invokes. Inverting the literary habit of reducing the poor to metonymic body parts, Briggs makes Tom an impressive somatic genius who finds personal and professional fulfillment on the minstrel stage.

The doctor, by contrast, gains his authority not through somatic talents but through his claim to somatic expertise and through his professional identity as a man of good character and of cultural refinement, and it is fitting that the doctor, a man who is authorized to work with bodies, has the power to expose Tom. But the doctor's deed is not as simple as it seems. When Dr. Laurens tells his cronies at the Manhattan Club that Tom makes his living as a minstrel dancer, he is not exposing the "real" race identity of either Tom or the character he plays on stage. The revelation is not that a white man plays the part of Dandy Jim. Minstrel shows were premised on such passing; and in the story, public billboards identify the artist behind the darkey Dandy Jim as the renowned Higgins. Tom's crime is not to pass for black, but to pass for working class. The minstrel show was working-class entertainment, produced by and for the working class. Indeed, the doctor should not be in the audience, but he, protected by his professional identity, can slum when the opera is not on and indulge in this quintessential American art form. Tom, however, cannot be associated with minstrelsy; his social status is more vulnerable. Thus, when the doctor tells Tom's secret at the Manhattan Club, he knows that this will result in Tom's expulsion from the ranks of the city's socialites.

Dr. Laurens was probably read by contemporaries as a spoof on the wealthy, prestigious New York doctor John Wakefield Francis. As I noted in the previous chapter, Francis was a patron of the arts and renowned in New York medicine. He was a founder and president of the New York Academy of Medicine, brought the first Italian opera to the United States, and had an infamously bawdy sense of humor.[96] He held nightly soirees for New York artists and writers, gave Melville medical information for *Redburn* and *White-Jacket*, and charged actors and musicians reduced rates for his services.[97] In fact, as Francis's home was the "center of the intellectual galaxy of this metropolis" and his imprimatur could bolster a reputation, so Dr. Laurens's love of minstrelsy lends legitimacy to this working-class art form.[98] Briggs delights in playing with the class affiliations of distinct art genres. Dr. Laurens goes to both the opera and minstrel shows, but there is no doubt which he prefers and which is more democratic. At the opera, Dr. Laurens maintains professional composure; he listens to the "prima donna as though she were a patient." But minstrelsy, and in particular the "incomparable Higgins," makes him lose his self-possession.[99] He "never fail[s] to drop in" when Higgins performs, which was "nearly every night," and he carelessly trades on his class privilege to gain admittance to a sold-out hall. In short, minstrelsy makes the elite physician responsive to the art and body of the Other.[100]

Briggs, not surprisingly, is a bit wary of the seductive, somatic pleasures of minstrelsy, and he imagines the minstrel theater as a raucous scene. Tom's performance ends when "the frenzy of the spectators" is at its peak and a boy throws an orange peel onto the stage that makes Tom slip and thus brings Dr. Laurens to his side. But Briggs's tale is less concerned with misbehavior at the theater than with the doctor's cruel exposure of Tom. Although entertained by the talent on the minstrel stage (and perhaps titillated by minstrelsy's crimes against established social codes), Dr. Laurens fails to act on the democratic potential of fascination with the Other. In the slippery world of class hierarchies where market fluctuations can remake the social order, a man performs his class identity, as Briggs notes, through his aesthetic choices. In other words, while Dr. Laurens may enjoy the libidinal pleasures of the show, he dare not let minstrelsy's vulgarity contaminate his family's reputation.[101] Tom may ravish him, but not his daughter. Thus, when called in his professional capacity to attend the body of the fallen minstrel, the doctor does not give Tom the same kind of attention he gives the opera diva. Rather, he asserts his authority, rejects Tom's talents for play, deception, and fluidity, and casts him out to become a foreign body. The moral energy of the tale climaxes in a condemnation of the doctor's betrayal of a body he so admires. The doctor banishes the Continental, aristocratic Tom, the Irish immigrant Higgins, and the negro Dandy Jim with one act of ripping off the mask, and thus the tale condemns the doctor for capitulating to antidemocratic ideologies that would fix race, class, and national identities upon the body. In short, the tale condemns the doctor for a cruel act, a betrayal of a body that he admires because he is eager to protect the whiteness and class status of his family from the taint of burnt cork and poverty.

It is important to note that both Briggs's and Davis's stories have vexed relationships with the elite literary world. Critics have noted that Davis's story defies the conventions typically associated with the *Atlantic*, and Briggs's story challenges bourgeois cultural politics. Hugh's unfocused yearnings and resentment threaten the social order that the *Atlantic* implicitly endorsed, and "Elegant Tom Dillar" celebrates the democratic potential and rowdy freedom of lowbrow minstrel shows. Both stories also explicitly condemn the professional as a man unwilling to do anything for his social inferiors. Both satirize doctors as concerned only with their own wealth and status, and in both tales doctors, presumably dedicated to somatic welfare, betray men with aesthetic talents and financial need. Of course, critiques of class politics in elite magazines were, and still are, an integral part of elite literary culture. As Glazener notes, nineteenth-century, highbrow literary culture both "sought to secure some of the status privileges created by capital" and understood its "public mission in the more or less loyal critique of capitalism's excesses."[102] In other words, authors such as Davis and Briggs might hope to build successful careers while using their pens to expose class inequities. Both were often critical of the nation's elite, and yet both wanted to be a part of that world. Davis believed that although the Boston literati "thought they were guiding the real world," in fact they "stood quite outside of it, and never would see it as it was," and yet she valued having her work appear in the *Atlantic*.[103] Similarly, Briggs was wary of the elite literary world of New England transcendentalists, and yet as a founder and editor of *Putnam's*, he was eager to publish the best American writers (and he did). Not surprisingly, both Davis and Briggs found that their politics did not always agree with those of their publishers and reviewers. Although Davis's story appeared in the *Atlantic* to much acclaim, her second manuscript made James T. Fields nervous, and he required extensive revisions.[104] Davis also came in for sharp words from Henry James, who insisted that even though she had "made herself the poet of poor people—laborers, farmers, mechanics, and factory hands," she had failed to describe these oppressed folks in the "rational English which we exact from writers on other subjects."[105] Briggs also encountered resistance to his social commentary: his serialized tale for the *Knickerbocker* about an orphan victimized by the corruption of the rich was cut short after only two installments.

While Holmes and James gently probed the professional physician's need for economic security and Davis and Briggs critiqued the class allegiance of well-to-do doctors, other periodical fiction took up medical technology. Two light, comic mad-scientist tales appeared in the *Atlantic* at mid-century—F. J. O'Brien's "The Diamond Lens" and Moncure Daniel Conway's "My Lost Art".[106] Both tales are about medical ambition, and both follow the conventions of sensational fiction. And yet there is no concern with the mad doctor's access to bodies, a theme in penny-press tales of fiendish doctors eager to seduce women and to dissect still warm bodies. Neither tale experiments with the macabre, and neither risks the political critique that is sometimes a feature of more radical sensational fiction. Both humorously suggest that medical ambition may be dangerous, but the threat is only to the mad doctor, and the descent of the mad doctor into monomania is described with such florid, luscious, and energetic prose that the literary performance eclipses whatever vague warning the tales offer. In these stories, highbrow literature goes slumming in genteel ways.

Most explicitly, both tales challenge medicine's enchantment with new visual technologies. As Foucault has suggested, with the development of the microscope and the stethoscope medicine began to lay claim to the interior of the body, and Holmes and other physicians believed that the new instruments provided accurate, unmediated access to truth. In an 1859 *Atlantic* article, for example, Holmes claimed that with the stereoscope "nature scales off its surface for us" and in that surface—in the form, light, and color—"we have the essence of the thing."[107] Holmes celebrated the power of photography in another *Atlantic* essay two years later and again in 1863.[108] In each article, Holmes marveled at the new technology and gracefully called these God's gifts, but he suggested that such technological advances were really the fruits of modern science.

Literary representations of the new visual technologies offered a very different understanding. While medicine championed the accuracy of a scientific gaze, mad doctor stories noted the unreliability of the gaze and the new visual technologies. As Jonathan Crary notes, the clinical gaze and the myth of unmediated seeing did not go unchallenged by theorists of perception who insisted that the visible is "lodged in the unstable physiology and temporality of the human body."[109] This is the suggestion made by the *Atlantic* stories. Each is a playful tale about a scientist who believes he sees objectively but who, in fact, sees only what his deranged mind creates. These mad doctors mistakenly believe that their machines will extend the power of human vision and allow them to see more than others but instead they fall into strange, fantasy worlds. In short, in contrast to the objectivity many scientists and doctors claimed for the new visual and diagnostic technologies, both stories insist that vision is subjective. The stories do not, however, end with that assertion. They do not moralize about the dangers of such subjectivity or even about the dangers of a deranged vision. Rather, both stories use the madman's vision as an excuse to indulge a linguistic virtuosity that is impressive and luscious. The doctors, who are fanatic scientists and thus emblems of the seductive powers of science that worried many Paris-trained physicians, move beyond science and become visionaries and poets. They see beautiful things and report with florid eloquence what they see. Both stories use first-person narration, which licenses flights of linguistic excess, and in both stories, technology becomes a means for the protagonist, and the author, to escape the mundane and to legitimate in highbrow fiction extravagant displays of sensational language.

In "The Diamond Lens," a scientist discovers a beautiful woman in a drop of water. In an effort to escape from his mad love for her, he goes to the theater to see a "celebrated danseur." The cure does not work because she is thick-limbed and earthbound compared to the female form on the "stage of his microscope." Mid-century regulars might have objected to O'Brien linking the worlds of medicine and theater, but such a comparison was not far-fetched. Shows featuring the latest medical discovery—nitrous oxide, ether, stethoscopes, microscopes—were popular entertainment in nineteenth-century America. Indeed, O'Brien's story and such popular shows remind us that ideas, machines, and discoveries exist not only within the discipline and discourse of their origination. In Moncure Daniel Conway's "My Lost Art", a mad doctor who devotes himself to making daguerreotypes of the highest resolution of Jupiter discovers on the surface of the planet "Art" — and not nature. In both tales, science pushed to its limits yields art, and madness liberates a flight of raucous linguistic play that is not typical in the *Atlantic*. In these tales the doctors are sensual and energetic, and the language is romantic and exalted. The doctors are distinctly unprofessional, and the stories themselves lack restraint, composure, equanimity, and sobriety.

As David Reynolds notes, "sensational literature, the erotic and the pseudoscientific were often linked in the antebellum imagination," and subversive literature, widely disseminated in "yellow-covered novels" and penny-press newspapers, appealed to a national anxiety about and fascination with violence, revolution, anti-elitism, and eroticism.[110] And yet, when translated into the highbrow literature of magazines such as the *Atlantic*, the democratic excesses of this tradition are lost. The sensational elements become more a matter of aesthetic delight than radical political imagining. Thus O'Brien and Conway play with the subversive possibilities of sensation fiction, but in the end they only play. The stories do not mock the staid worlds of elite fiction and professional medicine, and they do not challenge the power of the nation's cultural leaders and its professional men. Rather, they link a medical underworld of techno-enthusiasts with the literary underworld of sensationalism, and in these stories, carnival worlds invite play but pose no real challenge to the status quo.

By the end of the nineteenth century, medicine was well on its way to becoming the most lucrative and esteemed profession in the United States, and highbrow literary fiction had become a well-defined genre and cultural establishment. To explain how medicine achieved its privileged status, historians note various factors, including the founding of medical societies, urbanization, changes in medical education, and the rise of hospitals. To explain the rise of a self-consciously artistic and professional literary practice, scholars often note the role of prestigious national magazines in "establishing American literary culture as an author-sustaining formation" and in shaping the reading practices that produced and sustained a cultural elite.[111] I would suggest that the partnership between literature and medicine also played a role in the rise of both professions. The project of mutual cultural authorization depended heavily upon the figure of the doctor. The image of the steady, gentleman doctor served the interests of regulars and the interests of highbrow literature, and it also addressed widespread national anxieties about fluid identities, blurred class boundaries, confidence games, and economic instability. This image was also challenged by writers such as Davis and Briggs, who found in the doctor a symbol of elitism and class division.

The partnership of "profound science" and "elegant literature" is a deep cultural habit in the United States—both in real lives and in fiction. In the second half of the nineteenth century, the James family produced a writer and a professor of medicine, the literary Putnam family produced a daughter who became a prestigious physician, and Sarah Orne Jewett, daughter of a physician, turned to medicine for a model of professional authorship. From Holmes to Sir Luke Strett in *The Wings of the Dove* to Oliver Sacks, the cultured physician is both an appealing and troubling image in a nation that has never quite resolved the tensions between democracy and the elitism inherent in professionalism.

Chapter 5

Gender, Medicine, and Literature in Postbellum Fiction

In the second half of the nineteenth century, women began to enter the medical profession, and the popular press took note. In 1847, Elizabeth Blackwell entered the Geneva Medical College in New York; in 1849, Lydia Folger Fowler, wife of the phrenology publisher Lorenzo Fowler, entered Central Medical College in Syracuse, where she also briefly served on the faculty before the college closed in 1852. By 1868 more than 300 women had earned medical degrees, and the topic of women doctors was newsworthy enough for *The Galaxy* to run a long article reassuring the nation that most doctoresses were "gentle, modest, and womanly."[1] Two years later *Frank Leslie's Illustrated Newspaper* jumped into the debate with an article on women doctors that included sensational images of women engaged in the brutal, gory, and intimate work of anatomical studies.[2] One illustration features a modest female medical student bent daintily over a cadaver as she probes the muscles of a flayed lower leg (see Figure 2). Another depicts an anatomy lecture at the New York Medical College for Women, showing the female lecturer standing next to a partially dissected cadaver and a room full of women students watching. A third illustration is a cartoon of women medical students gathered around the open chest of a male cadaver with the hope, as the caption explains, of "finding out with the aid of a lancet the peculiarities of the masculine heart." By the 1880s, novelists were also weighing in on the topic. Rebecca Harding Davis published a short story about a doctoress in 1878 in *Harper's New Monthly Magazine*, Elizabeth Stuart Phelps took up the subject in 1880 and 1882, and before the century came to a close, William Dean Howells, Sarah Orne Jewett, Henry James, and S. Weir Mitchell had all offered their version of the woman doctor.

But this chapter is not only about the doctoress; rather, it is about the intertwined and shifting gender identities of medicine and literature in the second half of the century as healthcare moved out of the home, professionalism supplanted domesticity, and empiricism eclipsed other ways of knowing. Thus I frame my discussion of the doctoress in fiction by

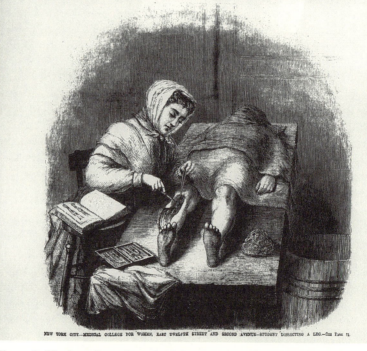

Figure 2. "Student dissecting a leg." *Frank Leslie's Illustrated Newspaper*, 16 April, 1870.

beginning with a discussion of two Louisa May Alcott novels that yoke medicine's masculine authority to a feminist, domestic agenda and by ending with a consideration of the refined male doctor in James's fiction as a figure that bridges the gender and epistemological gap between science and culture. This framing suggests that representations of the doctoress were not only about women entering medicine but also about how representations of medicine became a way to negotiate a taint of femininity, or in Martha Banta's phrase the "scandal of failed masculinity," that worried the nation and particularly threatened the arts, which were increasingly defined as a feminine complement to the manly world of science.[3]

Before turning to Alcott's novels, however, I want to outline in broad terms the relevant context. Thus in the next section I take up briefly four trends in the second half of the century: one, women's entrance into the medical profession and the role of domesticity in this development; two, the masculinization of empiricism; three, the emergence of the doctor as a national icon of refined masculinity; and four, the rise of a new culture of letters in which literature is valued not for the moral purposes it might serve but for its aesthetic achievement and the true artist is imagined as "an (almost) ungendered figure of self-disciplined professional devotion."[4]

Before the 1860s, women were largely excluded from professional medicine. This is not to say that women were not healers. In the seventeenth and eighteenth centuries, folk medicine was practiced by women as well as men; female nurses offered primary and extended care in cases where money, access, or severity of the illness made it difficult or unnecessary to call in a physician; teenage girls often served sick relatives; well-to-do mothers sometimes hired female infant-care specialists; and midwifery was almost exclusively practiced by women. And yet, women had no major role in professional medicine, and colonial laws neither admitted nor barred women because, as Regina Morantz-Sanchez notes, "woman *physician* was still a contradiction in terms."[5] In the nineteenth century, women's lay opportunities in healthcare diminished as professionalized gynecology and obstetrics almost completely eliminated the role of midwives, new medical theories of sexual dimorphism mirrored and legitimized the ideology of separate spheres, and women's bodies and female reproductive physiology were increasingly defined as complex systems best managed by expert, professional doctors. This history of the marginalization of women in healthcare with the rise of professional medicine has, however, been augmented recently with attention to the role of domestic ideology in expanding opportunities for women outside the home. Separate spheres rhetoric undoubtedly widened the gap between public and private and in many ways narrowed women's work, but the valorization of the home and of women's role as mothers politicized the domestic and allowed reformers and feminists to argue that what made women naturally good in the home would also make them good outside the home.

This corollary to domestic ideology seemed particularly applicable to medicine. The health reform movement often touted women's unique talents as healers—"In sickness there is no hand like a woman's hand," insisted one water-cure journal—and middle-class white women were active in the movement.[6] One third of the members of the American Physiological Society were female, Ladies Physiological Societies sprung up across the nation, and women gave lectures and wrote for health reform journals.[7] In fact, women's significant and visible contributions to the movement offered a "powerful stimulus," as one historian notes, to women's entrance into the medical profession.[8] It was relatively easy to reshape arguments for women's role in securing a healthy citizenry into arguments for women's role in professional medicine. If women's maternal inclinations, talent for domestic science and economy, and high moral sense made them the best stewards of home and children, and even made them excellent nurses, then these same virtues might also make them capable doctors. And the arguments were persuasive. Women earned degrees from sectarian and "regular" institutions, founded their own schools, built dispensaries and hospitals to provide clinical training, and entered the medical profession at a higher rate than any other profession except teaching.[9] By the end of the century, about five percent of the profession nationwide was female (a number that did not rise again until the 1960s), and in the Northeast the percentage was higher. In Boston, women made up 14.9 percent of the profession in 1880 and 18 percent in 1890.[10]

The rapid rise of the "doctoress" in fact and in popular awareness did not, however, undo the gender-essentializing tendencies of the century; nor did women's entrance into the medical profession undermine the habitual somaticization of women or the masculine identity of empirical science. In large part, women chose medicine and were able to gain a foothold in the profession because the suggestion that they were naturally good at taking care of infirm bodies did not overturn the status quo. Elizabeth Blackwell, for example, was convinced that women, because of their very nature, would make valuable contributions to medicine, and she made arguments to this effect throughout her life. In 1889, for example, Blackwell celebrated women's talent for the "subordination of the self to the welfare of others."[11] In many ways, Blackwell's arguments for what women might offer harked back to what was becoming by 1889 an old-fashioned notion of the gentlemanly physician who, as

Percival argued in the eighteenth century and the AMA seconded in the 1848 Code of Ethics, unites "tenderness with firmness, and condescension with authority." Although for Percival and the founders of the AMA, these manly virtues defined the good doctor, in the second half of the century the doctor was increasingly valued for his scientific knowledge and objectivity and not his character. Thus, as I noted in Chapter 4, the good doctor in fiction at mid-century was valued for his equanimity, compassion, cultural refinement, and discerning moral sense, while later in the century and as women entered the profession, the good doctor was increasingly imagined as a scientist with an unyielding commitment to empiricism. It is, of course, impossible to determine if the shift toward manly empiricism in representations of medicine was a response to the fear that women physicians would feminize the profession, but it is clear that this shift included a renewed assertion of medicine's masculinity.

For Blackwell and many other women who entered the profession in the second half of the nineteenth century, defining medicine as compassionate as well as scientific, moral as well as intellectual, was in many ways a countermove to the emphasis on masculinity and empiricism, and her definition of medicine sought to align good medicine with feminine talents. Of course, nineteenth-century women physicians understood their relationship to medicine variously, and yet, according to Morantz-Sanchez, most would have agreed with one doctoress's suggestion that "every woman is born a doctor. Men have to study to become one."[12] Given these habits of thought, it is not surprising that women gravitated towards medical specialties and paradigms identified with service, uplift, and compassionate patient care. Although hospital records suggest that women did not differ significantly in therapeutic styles from their male colleagues, the records do indicate that women devoted more time to interacting with their patients, that female-run institutions were slower to adopt new technologies than male-led institutions, and that women physicians were more likely to develop social programs and to found patient-focused institutions than to pursue research.[13] In short, even as women entered the medical profession in significant numbers, a gender gap remained. Women might be good at the art of healing, but empirical science required skills defined as masculine.

Science and femininity were not always at odds, as Londa Schiebinger has shown. In classical iconography, the sciences were typically represented as women. Mathematics, chemistry, botany, astronomy, physics, medicine, and other branches of science, just like poetry, reason, and justice, were all personified as women. A voluptuous Scientia dominated the frontispieces of scientific texts up through the eighteenth century, and her image lingers today on the back of the Nobel medals for chemistry and physics, which feature a toga-clad Scientia unveiling the face of a bare-breasted Natura. The feminine icon did not mean that the pursuit of knowledge was a feminine activity or that women scientists were common, although the image may have endorsed elite women's intellectual activity in salons and at court. Rather, science was personified as a woman because she figured the promise of a "creative union" for the male scientist with the "secrets of nature or the rational soul."[14] But as empiricism replaced rationalist paradigms and as science was increasingly understood as the pursuit of knowledge through direct observation, a female guide became superfluous, and by the mid-nineteenth century science no longer had a feminine face. Indeed, femininity and science became, by definition, incompatible: Kant banished metaphysics from philosophy, calling her a "matron outcast and forsaken"; Rousseau called for military vigor in science; and scientific language eschewed poetry and rhetorical ornament, styles increasingly defined as feminine. As Schiebinger concludes, "feminine" became a term applied to "a style of scholarship, a set of values, and a way of knowing to be excluded from the new scientific order."[15]

Concurrent with the increasing emphasis on the masculinity of science was the somaticizing of women. Or, as Londa Schiebinger notes, as the idealized Scientia disappeared from frontispieces, the anatomized female body began to appear within medical texts. When the eighteenth century began, only one anatomical atlas included an illustration of a female skeleton; by the end of the century, drawings of female skeletons abounded. There was in these years, as Thomas Laqueur has documented, a revolution in medical thinking on sex and gender. Previous presumptions about the female body as a lesser but essentially similar version of the male (thus it did not need to be included in anatomy atlases) gave way to an understanding of the two sexes as incommensurate, biological opposites.[16] Formerly, anatomists understood the uterus as a modified penis, and they made models explicitly female only in illustrations of reproductive organs. By the end of the century, the uterus had no relationship to male organs, and illustrations of female skeletons often enshrined sexual difference by broadening the pelvis and shrinking the head.[17]

As medicine embraced empirical methods and deepened its masculine identity and as anatomy sought biological evidence of gender difference, visual representations shifted from an emphasis on the doctor's gentlemanly and scholarly pursuits to clinical scenes. In her seminal study of gender in images of medical science, Ludmilla Jordanova reminds us that the schism between magic and empirical science that we take for granted was the result of a self-conscious effort that "really only gathered momentum in the eighteenth century" and depended upon redefining knowledge from that which is arcane, hidden, and mysterious to that which can be seen. Science was, unlike magic, committed to an empirical method, to the "open study of what could be viewed," and thus valid knowledge came to lie "exclusively in the public domain," while secret knowledge and secret remedies became evidence of unprofessionalism and quackery.[18] The clinic became the paradigmatic scene for representing medical empiricism: the space was public and the object of study, often the female body, was laid out for all to view.

In Chapter 2, I discussed the distinctive title page of *De Humani Corporis Fabrica*, which features Andreas Vesalius at work on a female body, even though the majority of the cadavers he worked on were male. Vesalius's work and this image were groundbreaking at the time. By the nineteenth century, however, the image of the male doctor at work on the female body was a common and powerful representation of the masculinity of medicine. Reworking a host of meanings associated with veiled and unveiled women (sexuality, femininity, truth, nature, beauty, decency, and shame), this trope makes the doctor a man who can manage the knowledge and dangerous forces unleashed by the naked female body. In fact, the images in the 1870 *Frank Leslie's Illustrated Newspaper* article that show women doctors dissecting male cadavers are comic or sensational precisely because to make the observing scientist female and the unveiled body male is to go against a deep gender-encoding of who looks at whom.

Thomas Eakins's 1889 oil painting *The Agnew Clinic* updates Vesalius's title page and offers a dramatic example of how this trope served to masculinize and refine the intimate somatic work of medicine. As Anthony Rotundo has noted, the masculinity of medicine in the nineteenth century was not always secure.[19] Women were gaining a foothold in the profession, and medicine's intimate relationship with bodies and homes and its lack of involvement with the world of business and commerce made medicine, like religion and the arts, in danger of seeming less manly. Similarly, medicine's association with refinement was not always obvious. Surgery, for example, had a history that set it apart from the tradition of the gentlemanly physician, and the efforts of dentists, apothecaries, and others to be included under the mantle of medicine's professional status often undermined the cultural refinement and class affiliation that elite physicians wanted to claim for themselves. And yet, by the end of the century, the doctor/surgeon was readily imagined, as in Eakins's painting, as a refined gentleman comfortable in a public, professional, institutional world in which his masculine vigor triumphantly manages disease and the female body.

The Agnew Clinic was the largest canvas Eakins ever painted, and it was his second portrait of a doctor in a surgical theater. The earlier painting, *The Gross Clinic*, offers a dark, almost melodramatic image of a

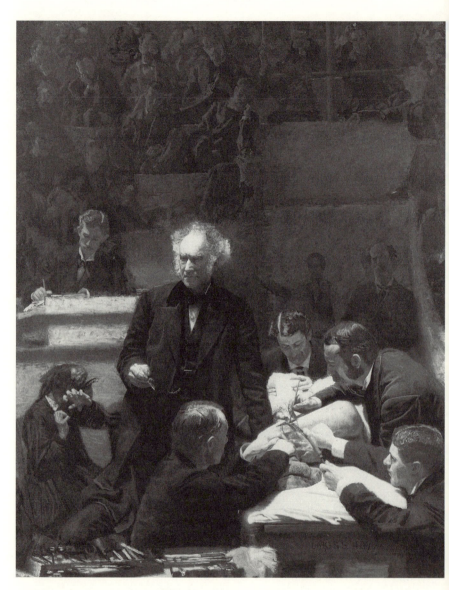

Figure 3. Thomas Eakins, *The Gross Clinic*, 1875. Courtesy of Jefferson Medical College of Thomas Jefferson University.

scientist/surgeon (see Figure 3). In a dark suit, against a dark back-ground, the white-haired and mutton-chopped Dr. Gross holds a scalpel in his bloody hand. Below him lies the patient on the surgery table with the body distorted through extreme foreshortening. Sitting to the doc-tor's right is a woman who covers her eyes with hands stretched taut with fear, a sign of feminine delicacy reacting to surgical gore. In dark shadows behind the doctor are a handful of viewers seated in the steeply tiered seats of the surgery theater. The painting teasingly echoes the images of dark, dank, basement medical theaters featured in sensational tales of fiendish anatomists cutting bodies into parts. But the painting also revises this stereotype. Dr. Gross is not a fiend: the velvet lapel on his suit, the gold watch chain, and the thin-lipped, steely eyed stare directed away from the wound held open by three assistants indicate his social class, his rank in the medical hierarchy, his refinement, and his commit-ment both to direct knowing and to the abstract ideas that empirical science yields. He has worked directly with the materiality of this body; his blood-stained hand makes this evident and the patient himself is more material than human since we see only body parts that do not cohere readily into a recognizable and complete human form. The doc-tor has looked, touched, and bloodied his hands, but at the moment we see him, he is looking away. He is neither enthralled nor repelled by the body; he seeks knowledge not somatic thrills. Standing tall, with a white light reflecting off his brow, he dominates the painting, figuring the senior doctor's physical vigor, absolute emotional control, and intel-lectual mastery.

In the later painting, the potentially titillating allure of the unveiled female body rather than the gory realities of surgery takes center stage (see Figure 4). The surgeon works not on an unidentifiable bony body part but on a woman whose human form is legible. The ether cone has been pulled to one side, and her cheek, nose, closed eyelids, eyebrows, and hairline are all visible. Her clavicle is delicately shadowed, a brightly lit right breast with a dark aureole and nipple carefully rendered falls not too heavily to the side, and her shoulder and arm are white and pleasingly rounded. The assistants seem to work on the patient with respect and care. The one who holds the ether cone is touching her tem-ple and looking intently into her face, presumably to check her level of unconsciousness, another leans over her legs with a sponge in one hand as he peers up the length of her body with concern, and the senior assis-tant works with both hands, holding a scalpel in one, to do what seems to be delicate work on her left breast. In this painting, the students in the theater are visible, and although the painting was commissioned by the students and unveiled at the commencement ceremonies on May 1, 1889, they are rendered with the broad strokes of a gentle satire upon youthfulness. Several seem to be asleep, some are languidly draped over fellow students, a few lean forward, some are curious, and some almost leer. By contrast, a stern-faced nurse with a starched white cap figures the propriety they cannot muster. But neither the students nor the nurse, nor even the surgeon's assistants who touch the patient with kindness, achieve the self-possessed, master-of-all gaze that Dr. Agnew directs upon the entire scene.

Like Dr. Gross, Dr. Agnew has a scalpel in hand and seems to have paused in order to explain something to the auditors. But while Dr. Gross stands next to the table, Dr. Agnew has stepped away, and his gaze has less intensity and more equanimity than Dr. Gross's. If the first painting is about the doctor as master of the somatic world and the brutal work of surgery, the second is an allegory of refined masculinity and professionalism. The first foregrounds the doctor's interiority, not his refinement, and the shadows bespeak the doctor's solitary, brooding intensity at the surgery table as his somatic expertise is put to the test. In the later painting, the doctor surveys the entire scene, and his gaze bears witness not to intensity or interiority but to accomplishment and composure. Eakins's interest in masculinity fully and gracefully achieved

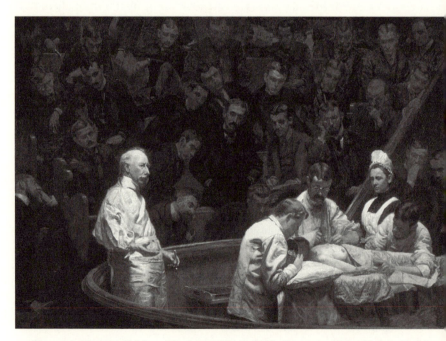

Figure 4. Thomas Eakins, *The Agnew Clinic*, 1889. Courtesy of the University of Pennsylvania.

becomes apparent when we compare the painting with the photograph from which he worked (see Figure 5). The photograph represents medicine as an all male world with little hierarchy. In revising the photograph, Eakins constructs a fairly precise professional hierarchy. The students watch, the nurse stands ready to assist, one assistant monitors vital signs, a specialist administers ether, a surgeon (or assistant) closes the wound, and Dr. Agnew, the paragon of medicine, stands apart, lecturing to the students. Eakins's decision to change the leg operation in the photograph to a mastectomy further dramatizes medicine's professionalism—the bare breast that catches the viewer's attention is of no interest to doctors—and raises gender issues only to dismiss them.

By 1889, women had entered the profession at the highest levels, but they had also met resistance, as I noted earlier. One of the most public battles happened at the Pennsylvania Hospital in 1869, when thirty-five students from the Women's Medical College entered the surgery amphitheater to attend a lecture. Women students had been attending clinics at another hospital in the city for a year, and Dean Ann Preston

Figure 5. Photograph by George Chambers, 30 March, 1886, used by Thomas Eakins for *The Agnew Clinic*. From the Collections of the University of Pennsylvania Archives.

had secured permission in advance from the managers of the Pennsylvania Hospital for this visit. But, the male students jeered, threw things at the women, spat on them, and followed them out of the theater in order to continue to harass them. The incident was reported in newspapers throughout the region, and the hospital managers decided that women could attend only one clinic a week and that lecturers had the right to dismiss students if a case was indelicate. Dr. Agnew was not among women's supporters. He, along with other esteemed colleagues, signed a petition against admitting women to the theater; He even resigned for a short period from the Pennsylvania Hospital in order to avoid lecturing to women, and he argued passionately against women becoming doctors, claiming that when women learn to "amputate limbs, make perineal section, or cut for stone," they and society will forfeit "all those qualities now the glory of the sex."[20]

Whether Eakins paid attention to the gender battles in medicine, we do not know. But it is significant that between the two paintings Eakins's reputation soared, then collapsed over the issue of nudity, and then was restored as he turned to explicitly national themes. In the years after *The Gross Clinic*, Eakins was appointed to a professorship of drawing and painting at the Pennsylvania Academy of the Fine Arts, and he became celebrated as "the first of Philadelphia artists." He also increasingly devoted his time to photographic studies of the nude, and with his students he photographed nude models in a series of standardized poses. He worked at the University of Pennsylvania with Eadweard Muybridge, the pioneer of motion photography, and he put anatomy studies at the center of his studio classes.[21] This emphasis on the body unsettled many, and Eakins was asked to resign from the Academy in 1886 because of rumors about his use of nudity in the studio and his sexual relations. Eakins spent the next two years writing letters to supporters and critics alike, although he also undertook a series of portraits of Philadelphia's prominent scientists, spent ten weeks at a ranch in the Dakota Territory in order to improve his health, perhaps at the suggestion of his friend Dr. S. Weir Mitchell, and befriended and painted Walt Whitman. In these years, Eakins also experimented with what one scholar calls "the portrait of a woman as a vision of elegance."[22] In short, between *The Gross Clinic* of 1875 and *The Agnew Clinic* of 1889, Eakins's interests shifted from the body to the nation, from anatomy and photography to Western landscapes, cowboys, prominent men of science and poetry, and beautiful society women. This shift had a profound impact on the painter's understanding of his own craft, and also, significantly, on his representation of the clinic.

As Michael Fried has shown in his magisterial study of *The Gross Clinic*, the operation represented in the painting essentially ratifies "the violence that the body has already been subjected to by its placement and treatment in the composition."[23] A viewer must work hard to make sense of the patient's body, and there is a "quasi-sexual note of violence in the climatic recognition" that what we see are "stockinged feet, a length of naked thigh seen mostly from below, and a bony posterior, the last of which raises but conspicuously fails to answer the question of the body's gender." As Fried concludes, what confronts us is "an image at once painful to look at (so piercingly does it threaten our visual defenses) and all but impossible, hence painful, *to look away* from (so keen is our craving for precisely that confirmation of our own bodily reality)" (original emphasis). Amid this representational and medical violence, stands the "master healer," a paternal yet almost menacing figure. In a persuasive Freudian reading of the violence in the painting, Fried concludes that while the terrified seated woman figures a feminine reaction to castration ("chaotic, hysterical, and unassuageable") that the painting almost mocks, the doctor figures a "regulated, masterly, and in the end healing" response.[24]

In *The Agnew Clinic*, there is no Oedipal complex, no castration thematics, and no violence, at least no male-against-male violence. Female viewers may wince at the thought of the not-quite-visible mastectomy being performed, but no one in the painting finds the scene disturbing, and there is no representational violence—everything is legible. A mastectomy is not a horrific occasion, at least according to the painting, but rather a procedure that young male students casually watch and the master surgeon performs with ease. In fact, by the end of the century, extensive experimentation with mastectomies, ovariotomies, and hysterectomies had enabled the invention of new techniques and had been central to surgery's rising legitimacy and professional status. Dr. Gross's face testifies to the violence of surgery in an earlier era when bone-setting and amputations dominated surgical practice. By contrast, Dr. Agnew's calm countenance suggests the extent to which the surgeon had become an icon of masculine self-management. The taxing, strenuous, unsettling work of surgery takes no toll on the doctor, and the painting enshrines the doctor not as one who has just this moment achieved the self-management that surgery requires, but rather as a man at home in his profession. In fact, the painting makes institutional authority an explicit theme: the name of the institution (the University of Pennsylvania) that commissioned Eakins and employed the famous Dr. Agnew is emblazoned on the sheet under the patient.

In her study of the career of the nineteenth-century gynecologist J. Marion Sims, Dana Nelson suggests that gynecological practice and especially the development of new, aggressive surgeries, "provided a symbolically satisfying avenue for establishing white male professional expertise" and for extending "the purview of professional male authority over culture."[25] Making a broader but similar point, Robyn Wiegman explains, "the reduction of woman to her anatomy provides the difference against which masculine *disembodiment* can be achieved: the rationality of the mind surpasses, even as it appropriates, the physical limitations of the body" (original emphasis).[26] Although Dr. Agnew wears a white gown that hints at surgery's old affiliation with the knife trades, his authority, unlike Dr. Gross's, is a disembodied authority. Dr. Gross's authority is wrested through a physical, even violent mastery of the body, while Dr. Agnew's authority is a tidier, easier mastery over a decorous albeit exposed female body. The only violence in the scene is in a dramatic support beam that plunges diagonally towards the patient's body. But the doctor's gaze cuts across this diagonal and reclaims the scene, making her body the site for a reassuring representation of institutional medical professionalism and disembodied masculine rationality.

In Chapters 2 and 3, I noted that both Hawthorne and Melville explore the humor, irony, and pathos of medicine's efforts to claim somatic authority while also holding itself aloof from the messy realities and unsettling carnality of the body. The wan, emaciated bodies of Aylmer, Rappaccini, and Dr. Cuticle Cadwallader suggest that they have pursued somatic interests at the expense of their own physical vitality. Indeed, the enervated scientist was a popular caricature in the nineteenth century because he is both a figure of masculine intellect and, and a comic figure of failed masculine vigor. But the effete scientist was replaced in the second half of the century by the image of the vigorous doctor. As medicine's prestige and status skyrocketed, and as health and vitality were valorized, the doctor was increasingly represented as a man of vitality and strength. This strength also suggested that the excessive corporeality of women, nonwhites, and laborers, which needed to be managed for the sake of national stability, would be well managed by men like Dr. Gross and Dr. Agnew who can master themselves, including their own bodies and the unbounded, diseased, and excessively corporeal bodies of others. Dr. Gross, however, achieves his mastery through violence, Dr. Agnew through refinement. Fried likens *The Gross Clinic* to Stephen Crane's *The Red Badge of Courage*, suggesting that Eakins honors in the painting a kind of brutal truthtelling that realists/naturalists valued. *The Agnew Clinic* also honors a literary style, though fourteen years later it is not the brutality of naturalism that interests Eakins. Rather, Dr. Agnew embodies a Jamesian cultural refinement, intellectual mastery, and sophisticated indirection. From a decorous distance, Dr. Agnew casts his knowing gaze over the action, much as Sir Luke Strett casts his knowing gaze over the action in *The Wings of the Dove*. For Eakins and James late in their careers, masculinity is not a matter of physical prowess but the composure and equanimity that comes with refinement.

As scholars have noted, anxieties about literature's gender affiliation permeate nineteenth-century print culture, and these anxieties particularly plagued writers who wanted to be taken seriously. On several occasions Hawthorne noted the popularity of women writers, and Howells conceded that the "man of letters must make up his mind that in the United States the fate of a book is in the hands of the women."[27] And Hawthorne and Howells were right.

A rapid rise in the number of published women writers, an expanding literary market, and a reorganization of work, family life, and gender roles meant that reading and writing were often understood as feminine activities.[28] And yet, at the same time, realism and literary professionalism were both aggressively encoded as masculine. As Nancy Glazener notes, although we cannot know if the gendering of realism and authorial professionalism was a response to "the emergence of unprecedented numbers of women readers and writers" or simply the mobilization of a gender-identity already in place, "serious" literature sought to identify itself with such masculine virtues as distance, self-discipline, restraint, and an inclination to transcend the quotidian and engage important issues.[29] An 1876 essay in *Scribner's* entitled "Literary Virility," for example, offers a robust assertion that virile literature is concerned not with small matters but with "the great affairs, the great questions, the great pursuits of life."[30] Manly realism, as Glazener summarizes, "required mobilizing a feminine-coded felicity with details but subordinating it to a masculine-coded process of judgment and generalization, and it also required possessing a feminine-coded susceptibility to emotion but subordinating it to a masculine-coded power of restraint."[31] Thomas Eakins's *Dr. Agnew* embodies this version of masculinity, and Eakins's paintings came to be celebrated at the end of the century for their Americanness, objectivity, and masculinity, or in the words of one critic for their vision of "dignity and unbridled masculine power."[32]

But gender codes are always unstable, and while Hawthorne, Howells, Eakins, and the anonymous author of the *Scribner's* essay might proclaim the vigor of the arts, elite culture, especially when understood in opposition to the world of science, remained vulnerable to charges of dandyism. Literature also remained vulnerable to charges of effeminacy as health and physical vigor were enshrined as virtues that distinguished America from older, declining civilizations. In 1894, for example, Theodore Roosevelt, the self-proclaimed embodiment of American manliness, mocked the "undersized man of letters" for his "effeminate sensitiveness." The effete artist cannot, according to Roosevelt, "play a man's part among men."[33] These charges were not easily dismissed, and in the pages that follow I consider the gender-encoding of medicine and literature as writers engaged contemporary presumptions and anxieties about the gender of science and culture, empiricism and aesthetics. I begin with Louisa May Alcott and her efforts to position the medical expert within the domestic world and thus to give domesticity's moral agenda scientific and masculine legitimacy while also challenging the discourse of masculinity. Then I turn to fictional accounts of the "lady doctor" written by some of the nation's most ambitious and productive writers, accounts that engage and sometimes seek to revise the gender codes that make medicine masculine and literature feminine. I conclude by looking at Sarah Orne Jewett's and Henry James's efforts to rewrite conventional gender codes as they imagine the doctor, male or female, as one who brings together scientific and aesthetic ways of knowing.

Significantly, all the writers I discuss in this chapter accept medical authority. In striking contrast to Hawthorne's coldhearted medical experimenters and Melville's cruel ship surgeon and garrulous quack, the doctors in these post-Civil War works are good healers. They are well-trained experts and naturally intuitive, they care about the well being of their patients, and they never send a bill for their services. They are not the kind of heroes we might expect, however, given medicine's deepening connection in the second half of the century with universities, laboratories, and hospitals; we do not follow them into the halls of academia or the crowded wards of urban hospitals. Some of these works are nostalgic for a passing world of domestic medicine, and they sometimes imagine the good doctor at the bedside and not in the laboratory, but these works accept the doctor as a well-compensated, professional expert. There is little or no critique of the doctor's class ambitions, as sometimes appeared in periodical fiction in the 1860s; rather, the issue is the shifting gender identity of the professions—literary and medical—and of distinct ways of knowing.

In two popular juvenile novels, *Eight Cousins* (1874) and *Rose in Bloom* (1876), Louisa May Alcott advances feminist arguments of the day. She condemns the medicalization of the female body and medicine's tendency to define the female body in terms of its reproductive capabilities. She rejects the theory of sexual dimorphism that physicians used to argue for separate educational programs for boys and girls, and she refuses to consider female puberty a medical crisis. But she does not completely reject medical authority. In fact, while critiquing certain conservative medical theories on gender, Alcott also uses medicine's prestige to validate her own work—the moral instruction of young girls—and she makes the doctor an appealing spokesman for domestic virtues by suggesting that his advice on physiology and fashion is for the good of young girls and the nation. Ultimately, however, fashion politics and nationalism bedevil Alcott's progressive agenda. Like other reformers of the day, she naturalizes and nationalizes her critique of modern fashion, invoking scientific authority in her battle against what she believed were corrosive consumer desires spawned by capitalism and nurtured by European culture. Thus Alcott's domestic agenda becomes a nationalist project that participates in what David Noble has called "the metaphor of two worlds" that posits an innocent, natural world against a fallen world of culture.[34]

In the years when Alcott was writing, gynecologists offered advice on women's education, exercise, and clothing. In 1868, for example, T. Gaillard Thomas published *A Practical Treatise on the Diseases of Women* and listed the most common causes of uterine disease as lack of exercise, too much education, and improper dress. A teacher and practitioner at several New York hospitals, Thomas was one of the most respected gynecologists in the profession, and his *Treatise* was typical of gynecological handbooks of the day and was well-accepted—a second edition appeared in 1869 and a third in 1871. At the center of Thomas's work are the presumptions that nature and culture are in opposition and that the former is good and the latter fraught with perils. Drawing heavily upon this two-world metaphor, Thomas cautions that women, like the nation, must be true to the dictates of nature and must resist the seductive appeal of modern culture. According to Thomas, American women had fallen into a weakened state because of "the customs of civilized life" and the habits of "luxurious and indolent lives."[35] Thomas explains that girls who dance at parties every night risk displaced uteri, inflammation of the glands of Naboth, and other uterine disorders. For Thomas and others, the menstrual cycle loomed as a momentous event in the physiological, emotional, and social lives of women and maintaining the perfect "form and vigor" of the reproductive system, the sanguineous system, and the nervous system required knowing when and when not to exercise, what clothes to wear, and the best educational plan to follow.[36]

As the work of Carroll Smith-Rosenberg and other historians suggests, female education was a topic many gynecologists felt compelled to address, and frequently they warned that the education and care of pubescent girls required particular awareness of the physiology of the maturing ovaries and uterus. The most famous treatise on the subject, Dr. Edward Clarke's *Sex in Education* (1872), appeared two years before Alcott's *Eight Cousins*. Invoking the increasingly popular Darwinian notion of sexual dimorphism, the Harvard professor insisted that although "in childhood boys and girls are very nearly alike . . . as maturity approaches, the sexes diverge."[37] For Clarke, the changes in the male body were relatively uninteresting. But the changes in the female body were, for the scientist, awe-inspiring and for the nation a moment of supreme importance:

The growth of this peculiar and marvelous apparatus [the uterus] in the perfect development of which humanity has so large an interest, occurs during the few years of a girl's educational life. No such extraordinary task, calling for such rapid expenditure of force, building up such a delicate and extensive mechanism within the organism,—a house within a house, an engine within an engine,—is imposed upon the male physique.[38]

Like Thomas, Clarke also posited the dangers of culture for women's health, warning that "the milliner's stuffing, the colorist's pencil, the druggist's compounds" were ruining "the race of strong, hardy, cheerful girls, that used to grow up in country places."[39] Health, by this time, had become a moral imperative; political choices were defined as healthy or unhealthy, and even political questions might be answered by reference to the laws of physiology:

The problem of woman's sphere . . . is not to be solved by applying to it abstract principles of right and wrong. Its solution must be obtained from physiology, not from ethics or metaphysics. The question must be submitted to Agassiz and Huxley, not to Kant or Calvin, to Church or Pope.[40]

Not everyone accepted Clarke's assertion that science would do away with political debates by providing definitive answers based on natural laws. But he was right about the authority that medicine wielded when it spoke and the degree to which the body rather than the soul had become the primary arbiter of social questions.

Alcott, like Clarke, Thomas, and others, was also concerned with the physical health of teenage girls. In her earlier novel *Little Women*, illness was a sign of heightened spirituality. Drawing heavily upon what Susan Sontag has identified as a romantic and moralized view of illness as an etherealizing force that enables a character to move away from the gross desires of the physical body and toward virtuous, self-sacrificing behavior, Alcott makes the sickly Beth March an emblem of the spiritual world. By the 1870s, however, health had become a virtue, and the sentimental, pious, and aesthetic valorization of illness had lost currency. Thus, in *Eight Cousins* and *Rose in Bloom*, Rose Campbell's sick and weak body reveals not a highly developed spiritual nature, but rather the effects of too much culture, that is, sentimental novels and modern habits (tonics, pills, frequent naps, limited activity, and corsets).

Alcott frequently delights in physically lively female bodies. In *Little Women*, Beth's weak body is upstaged by Jo's wild body. Jo cannot contain herself—her intellectual energy spills over into her body—and Alcott marks Jo as the most interesting character in the novel by celebrating her undisciplined physicality. Physical energy is also a sign of health and happiness in *Eight Cousins* and *Rose in Bloom*, but the problem has shifted from too much physical vitality to too little. In *Little Women*, Jo's somatic expressiveness must be harnessed, and Alcott suggests that excessive physical energy is a sign, after a certain age, of a failure to attain a fully feminine subjectivity. By contrast, Rose Campbell is too feminine and too enthralled with modern culture, and instead of learning feminine restraint, she must cultivate an energy that Alcott acknowledges many consider masculine. Under the tutelage of her bachelor uncle, Dr. Alec, an energetic man who announces his arrival by climbing up a trellis at dawn to prod the groggy Rose into action, Rose learns to swim, row, ride horses, run, and play with her seven male cousins. Not surprisingly, the boys also benefit from Rose's company, learning to eschew the vices of modern urban society—alcohol, cigarettes, gambling, flirtation, and way-wardness. Alcott's point is clear: contrary to what Clarke would have predicted, because coeducation serves as an antidote to the false and exaggerated femininity and masculinity that tempt teenage girls and boys, Rose prospers under coeducation.

Notably, although Alcott, like Clarke and Thomas, suggests that modern culture is unhealthy, unlike the medical experts she has little interest in the future reproductive duties of American women. Both *Eight Cousins* and *Rose in Bloom* offer a program for guiding a young girl into healthy womanhood and into a good marriage, but they remain persistently silent on the subject of motherhood. Health is a moral imperative in the novels, but illness and health are not gender specific. Rose must learn to care for her body, but so must her cousins and her uncle. When she stays out in the cold too long, she catches pneumonia, but men also get sick: Uncle Alec is stricken by a life-threatening flu, and her cousin and future husband Mac strains his eyes and is confined like a female neurasthenic to rest in a dark room for several months. Illness is gender blind, and when the children learn anatomy there is no need for gender segregation—to the dismay of the aunts—because the fundamental structures and functions of the body, Alcott insists, are not marked by gender. In their anatomy class, the children study a skinless, fleshless, genderless body—a skeleton.

Alcott's resistance to the somaticization of gender is noteworthy. As I mentioned earlier, skeletons were no longer by this time typically genderless. Indeed, as the deepest, hardest structure of the body, the skeleton had become in the nineteenth century an important site for making gender difference visible. Thus, in having the children study a skeleton with no sex markers, Alcott suggests that gender differences may not be as deep as some believe. Alcott's silence on Rose's reproductive future is also remarkable. Even one of the leading women medical scientists of the day, Mary Putnam Jacobi, often fell into using gender stereotypes. For example, in her 1886 rebuttal to conservative medical opinion that deemed women unfit for higher education, Jacobi sums up the distinct contributions of men and women to reproduction by noting that "the superior contribution of the nutritive element of reproduction made by the female is balanced by an inferior dependence upon the animal or sexual element: in other words, she is sexually inferior."[41] Thus Jacobi leaps from minimizing the physiological demands of menstruation to defining women as less sexual than men. Alcott, by contrast, assiduously avoids making women's biology a direct explanation for anything.

Gender difference is central to Alcott's novels, but for her the difference is social rather than biological. In those instances when Rose needs a different education than her cousins, it is not because her body is different, not because she has ovaries or because she menstruates, but because she will work at home and not in the public sphere. The difference between men and women, according to Alcott, lies not in anatomical or physiological differences but in the distinct work assigned to each sex. Alcott does not propose a radical restructuring of male and female labor—Rose learns domestic economy and her cousins learn business—but she refuses to somaticize gender differences. In fact, both Rose and other Alcott heroines consider and sometimes pursue work outside the home.[42]

As part of her efforts to deessentialize gender codes, Alcott also makes the domestic sphere an important site for the formation of male identity and the exercise of male authority. In *Little Women*, Alcott banishes men to the periphery of the domestic sphere. Mr. March is an absent patriarch who rules through language. His letters home intrude only slightly into the private domestic world of his daughters; his words "my little women" are merely a genial reminder of the final goal of their education, and he has little to do with the daily work of guiding his daughters into womanhood. In *Eight Cousins* and *Rose in Bloom*, by contrast, Alcott situates her heroine in the middle of a family of men, and she replaces Marmee with an avuncular medical man.[43] Unlike Mr. March, Dr. Alec is not a distant patriarch dispatching letters that encourage Rose to become a good woman, and contrary to the notion that virile professional men attend to important issues and not petty details, Dr. Alec is concerned with the smallest and most domestic details of raising children. He has an appropriately masculine history—he has sailed around the world, traded on the international market, and studied medicine—but his authority depends upon his identification with the domestic. He is skilled at sewing on buttons, choosing dresses for Rose, planning outings for boys and girls, and most importantly giving Rose the education and guidance her aunts cannot. He is not only a substitute father but an excellent mother.

Perhaps most importantly, Alcott links Dr. Alec's medical authority to the domestic. Dr. Alec, not surprisingly, educates Rose according to the

ideals of the health reform movement: plenty of exercise, fresh air, natural foods; lessons in physiology and hygiene; and self-control and moderation in all things. Alcott mocks Latinate language and the increasing
dependence upon German laboratory science when she makes Mac look
foolish for holding forth at a party about "the globular forms of silicate
of bismuth at Schneeburt and Johanngeorgenstadt," and she makes Dr.
Alec's science reassuringly comprehensible and his therapeutics homespun.[44] As Lora Romero notes, Alcott and other champions of domesticity not only valorized the home but also the quotidian, suggesting that
domesticity, like empiricism, values what is visible, ordinary, and obvious over what is theoretical, obscure, and cloaked in obtuse language.
Thus Dr. Alec proves the success of his educational program with two
before-and-after photographs that mix the domestic, populist delights of
portraiture (the aunts are enchanted by the likenesses) with the incon-
trovertible evidence of photographic technology. Photography is both
an appeal to emotions and empirical evidence. And so Dr. Alec is both a
family member and a man who knows facts. He offers none of the detachment considered essential to modern medicine. He is not disinterested—he was once in love with Rose's mother. And he woos Rose to his
simple therapy of fresh milk and brown bread by plying her with trinkets
and promises of fun outings. Alcott eschews the language, diagnoses,
and authority of physicians such as Clarke who boldly pronounced on
the health of the nation's women. And yet Dr. Alec speaks with the
authority of empirical science. Perhaps, Alcott coyly suggests, leading
physicians should spend more time raising girls before pronouncing on
the nature of all women.

As Alcott domesticates medicine, so she also draws upon medicine's
authority and prestige to legitimize her literary project—the moral
instruction of young girls—and she ultimately accepts medicine's premise that the body is the final arbiter of social and moral issues. In *Little
Women,* children are socialized through what Richard Brodhead has
called the "disciplinary intimacy" of the mother's presence.[45] In *Eight
Cousins* and *Rose in Bloom,* a doctor replaces the maternal figures of
Alcott's earlier fiction. And with a doctor as the disciplinary presence
rather than a maternal figure, the somatic becomes Alcott's primary
concern even as moral choices remain central.

Alcott's attempts to formulate a morality linked to the body are clear-
est in her condemnation of fashion. In *Little Women,* fashion threatens
a woman's character and not her body. When Meg wears a borrowed,
fashionable gown to a ball, she feels "queer, and stiff and half-dressed."[46]
She no longer looks like herself, her closest friend fails to recognize her,
and she misbehaves by drinking champagne and flirting. Again, years
later when Meg is married, she loses a sense of who she is when she

indulges her fashion fancies. Swayed by the presence of a rich friend and seduced by violet silk at bargain prices, Meg "can't resist" and she buys yards of the luxurious fabric in order to make a new dress, wasting fifty dollars that was intended for a new coat for her husband.[47]

In *Eight Cousins*, Alcott suggests that fashion is dangerous not only because it ruins a woman's good character but also because it threatens the health and freedom of her body. In a chapter entitled "Fashion and Physiology," Rose fancies a dress that is "loaded with plaited frills" and "heavy fringes, bows, puffs, ruffles, and revers." Ostentatious in its "profusion of ornaments," the dress, the narrator tells us, "made one's head ache to think of the amount of work wasted" on it.[48] In *Little Women*, Alcott suggests that the excessive frills of party dresses must be rejected in favor of old, familiar dresses. The important features of Meg's old dresses are that they come from home and are her own. In *Eight Cousins* it is not enough to wear the familiar and thus be true to one's self and one's family. Good dresses must also be true to the body, and so the best suit for Rose is not, in fact, an old dress, but a new one chosen by a medical expert—Dr. Alec. Good dresses, the doctor teaches, promote an energetic and healthy body as well as the development of a strong and moral character. At the doctor's suggestion, Rose puts on a blue flannel dress that will keep her warm and allow her to run and jump with her cousins. In the "freedom suit," Rose can swing herself over the back of a sofa and run down the hallway; she can "sit without rumpling any trimming" and need not be "thinking of my clothes all the time."[49] The suit liberates Rose from tight corsets, animates her body, and rescues her from a vapid and morally bankrupt fashion ideology that, according to Alcott, threatens women's bodies as well as their character. By making Dr. Alec a fashion consultant, Alcott suggests that medical knowledge about the body is essential for distinguishing between good and bad dresses and that moral instruction is concerned not only with behavior but with the body itself.

According to Karen Haltunnen, morally good fashion is true to the self in antebellum sentimental culture. But by the 1870s, with an increasing sense that the nation's stability and strength depended upon the physical health of its citizens, good fashion had to be good for the body as well as good for the wearer's character. In Chapter 4, for example, I noted Oliver Wendell Holmes's sense of the physical improvement possible in a few generations for those who could afford country estates, choice cuts of meat, the best nursing for their children, and other amenities. The results, he imagined, would be fitter and better men.

Not surprisingly, with this valorization of the body, sartorial morality came to be concerned not only with what effect a dress might have on the wearer's character but also the effect it might have on her body. As

Casey Finch explains in a history of Victorian underwear, a new sartorial iconography emerged in the second half of the nineteenth century that collapsed the distinction between the naked condition and a clothed condition, between the body and its clothing.[50] Thus when Alcott has Rose choose a practical, modest dress, the dress makes Rose's body practical and modest. The "freedom suit" may allow a young girl to act as a boy, and in this way it is liberating (and feminist, perhaps), but it also redirects desires that the novel identifies as unlicensed feminine appetite—the carnal taste for sumptuous excess, sensuality, and pleasure. In fact, one of Rose's aunts is alert to just what effect the blue flannel dress will have—it will not encourage admiring second glances—and Dr. Alec's presence, his medical authority and knowledge, serve to validate the domestic lesson in modesty and moderation Rose must learn. Choosing the right dress, it turns out, is both a moral and a physiological issue. In short, although Alcott rejects Clarke's presumptions about the special needs of female physiology and resists a shift in health care discourse away from the domestic to the scientific, like Clarke she makes the body the final arbiter of complex social questions and she makes the doctor the best judge of what constitutes freedom.

Alcott's domestic agenda is a good example of the contradictory gender politics of nineteenth-century domesticity. As Lora Romero notes, domesticity is not inherently radical or conservative. Domestic ideology helped to produce images of selfless women, but it also condemned patriarchal culture for "violence against the integrity of female selfhood."[51] Domesticity leant its support to the health reform movement and the dress reform movement, identifying the physiological dangers of heroic medical therapies and, as the Beecher sisters noted, the "monstrous fashions" that impeded natural development and brought "distortion and disease" to the female body.[52] But the feminist critique of fashion offered by Alcott and the Beechers also valorizes the natural. And in making physical health and a doctor, albeit a domesticated one, the arbiters of her political agenda, Alcott depends upon and deepens medicine's somatic authority to define what is natural and healthy. In calling upon physiology to decide questions about fashion, Alcott and other feminists ceded cultural authority to science and endorsed the reification of scientific knowledge. Fashion, unlike science, understands the body as something that can be made, while critiques of fashion often deploy a language of authenticity, suggesting that fashion degrades the "natural" body and nurtures false desires spawned by capitalism and patriarchy.[53] Thus in fashion critique, and more generally, in critiques of consumption, culture is opposed to nature, artificial desires to natural, organic, healthy needs. In short, for Alcott and others, fashion is a fall into representation, or misrepresentation, of the body.

Alcott did not always understand fashion as a fall. In her thrillers, she has a fine sense of just what costume and lighting might achieve, suggesting in *Behind a Mask: or, A Woman's Power* that women might well manipulate appearances to get power. But when writing for girls, Alcott embraces the language of authenticity and cautions her readers against desires she deems unnatural and unhealthy. Thus, in *Eight Cousins* and *Rose in Bloom,* the body is the final arbiter of what is good for girls, and medicine, albeit a domestic medicine, is the best judge not only of food, but also of clothing, books, and educational curricula for teenage girls. Notably, at the end of *Rose in Bloom* Alcott tries to find a place for culture, and she has Rose marry the only man who might be better than Dr. Alec, her cousin Mac. No longer infatuated with scientific jargon, he is now a poet/doctor and thus worthy of replacing Dr. Alec in Rose's life because he is devoted to knowing both the body and the soul.[54] The ending, however, is unconvincing, and although Alcott may want to make room for a poet in a world best known by science, Mac is a weak attempt to limit scientific authority.

As Alcott leans upon medicine's scientific and masculine authority to legitimize her domestic agenda, so Rebecca Harding Davis, William Dean Howells, Elizabeth Stuart Phelps, Annie Nathan Meyers, Sarah Orne Jewett, and Henry James use medicine to legitimize and masculinize literature. But even as they reify the doctor and endorse the masculinity of medicine, so they also seek to articulate medicine's epistemological limits. In fact, by having her heroine marry a poet/doctor, Alcott anticipates the efforts of other writers to define an aesthetic sensibility that is beyond medicine's grasp and to suggest, as Alcott does with the figure of the poet/doctor, that medical knowledge is incomplete unless coupled with aesthetic ways of knowing. Not surprisingly, efforts to infuse medicine with an aesthetic sensibility were often bedeviled by gender troubles. By the last decades of the century it was almost impossible to imagine what science knew and what it did not know without encoding the former as masculine and the latter as feminine. In fact, it was precisely these deep gender codes that made the topic of the "lady-doctor" particularly interesting, or, as James told Howells, "rich in actuality."[55] The rising number of female practitioners had prompted some concern about what this might do to gender proprieties. Some worried that exposure to the gory realities of medicine would damage women's delicacy, while others suggested that women physicians could not be mothers (or good mothers) and that the nation needed mothers more than it needed women doctors.

In response, as I noted earlier, some leading female physicians suggested that feminine talents made them particularly adept at healing, while others rejected gender arguments and sought coeducation and access to the most elite training in order to battle the ghettoizing of women into the world of alternative medicine, a world increasingly deemed domestic and unscientific. And, in fact, regular medical schools were reluctant to admit women. By 1893 only 37 out of 105 orthodox institutions accepted women, and the prestigious *Boston Medical and Surgical Journal* opposed coeducation in medicine, suggesting (disingenuously) that women could get an equally good education at all-female schools.[56] And yet the rise in the number of women physicians was a fact, and the doctoress was "rich in actuality" because her success was a gage of feminism's success and because she threatened deeply held and yet fragile presumptions about masculinity and femininity.

One of the earliest representations in fiction of the lady doctor, "A Day with Doctor Sarah" by Rebecca Harding Davis, appeared in *Harper's New Monthly Magazine* in September 1878. Endorsing the popular assumption that women who become doctors are politically rather than romantically inclined, Davis makes her lady doctor a passionate feminist and a strong woman who is not eager to marry. She is, however, susceptible to the needs and appeal of children. When we meet Doctor Sarah, she has given up her profession for political activism. With "thin lips and broad forehead," Doctor Sarah has "very few of the qualities which go to make a happy marriage." She is, however, a "born mother."[57] Thus, although she can resist her former lover when he returns, she cannot resist the call to care for his children when he is killed in a train accident. She, too, is on the train, headed to Washington, D.C., in order to speak to a congressional committee about women's rights, but rather than catching another train, she stays behind, forever. As an indignant friend laments, "There is always an obstacle in the way with women. . . . But why must it always be a man or a baby."[58] What has been derailed by the train wreck is not, however, a woman's professional career but "only" her political activism. Presumably, Dr. Sarah will return to her medical career: one of the children needs extended medical care, and with no husband to disapprove Sarah might well be able to raise children and practice medicine, but she will have no time for trips to Washington, D.C.

While Davis does not suggest that medicine and motherhood are mutually exclusive, she does suggest that medicine and politics are at odds. Dr. Sarah is an appealing alternative to the politically obtuse mill doctor in Davis's earlier novella *Life in the Iron Mills* (see Chapter 4). Unlike Dr. May, she is sensitive to the needy, ready to act, and eager to devote herself to political efforts, but her real and most admirable talents lie in helping individuals. Throughout her career, Davis took on tough political issues, and consistently her work, both in style and content, foregrounds and values the unruly complexities of local, participatory democracy. As one critic notes, for Davis "the most productive form of relation comes not through representivity but in contiguity, through the day-to-day forming of inter/subjectivity."[59] Thus, although Davis values the expertise of professionals, feminists, and activists eager to speak as representatives to Congress, she gives Dr. Sarah a different role in changing the nation, a role of helping individuals day-to-day. Because of the valorization of the local and quotidian, it is tempting to read Dr. Sarah as evidence of a feminist politics still linked to domesticity, but this would be to define Davis's politics too narrowly and to perpetuate the habit of defining a commitment to the local as a strictly feminine value. Dr. Sarah's decision to care for the children thrust upon her by a train accident is not one she makes because this is a woman's duty or what women are best at. Rather, it is how she or any professional can make a difference. Medicine and feminism, according to Davis, work best when they engage the local. Thus, for Davis, the doctoress raises questions not about what women can and cannot do, but about what is the most productive form of political action. Medicine, she suggests, like feminism, must not succumb to the allure of grandiosity.

William Dean Howells and Elizabeth Stuart Phelps also limit medicine's power, not by suggesting it is most effective in the local context, however, but by delimiting its expertise. Many scholars have paired Howells's *Dr. Breen's Practice* and Phelps's *Dr. Zay* for a number of obvious reasons: both novels are about women doctors, they were published almost simultaneously, Howells and Phelps knew each other, and the novels offer very different answers to the question of women's fitness for medical practice. *Dr. Breen's Practice* is a comic novel about the unfocused philanthropy of a woman who has decided to help the world by becoming a doctor, even though she finds the study of medicine repulsive. Grace Breen's motivation is disappointment in love, and she devotes her life to medicine "in the spirit in which other women enter convents, or go out to the heathen lands."[60] She has a womanly knack for "distinction in dress and manner" and no talent for medicine. She is, Howells makes clear by depending upon conventional gender codes, a lovely woman better suited to the world of romance and marriage than the rigors of medicine. By the end, Grace has renounced most of her medical ambitions, married, and, not unlike Davis's Dr. Sarah, turned her philanthropic inclinations and medical training to "treating the sick children among her husband's operatives" (15–16, 269).[61]

Howells's ending, while disappointing then and now to feminists, was not without a basis in reality. As Howells suggests, some women doctors did quit medical practice when they married, limiting their post-marriage medical efforts to occasional charitable work. These women were, however, a minority. Other life choices that lady physicians made, and that

Howells does not consider, included lifelong relationships with other women physicians, adopting children as single women (as Doctor Sarah does), and marrying other professionals (including physicians). The problem of whether and how a woman physician might combine marriage, motherhood, and a medical career was a real one, and women physicians wrote about their decisions in diaries and spoke openly to their female students about these issues.[62] The antifeminism in Howell's treatment of the lady physician, then, lies not only in his suggestion that women are better suited to marriage than to medical careers, but in the light treatment he gives to what was for many a serious issue.

Howells was not usually careless in thinking about gender issues, and he was sensitive to the importance and difficulty of writing about women's lives: "novelists are great in proportion to the accuracy and fullness with which they portray women," he insisted.[63] But his portraits of independent women are rarely optimistic. After *Dr. Breen's Practice*, he wrote three more novels in which women abandon careers for marriage.[64] And yet, Howells encouraged many women writers, including Charlotte Perkins Gilman, though he could also fall into competitiveness and patronizing superiority when dealing with women. When Phelps came to him with her plans for *Dr. Zay*, he "listened with a mixture of amusement and anxiety," and he added, against Phelps's wishes, a preface to her novel when it ran in the *Atlantic*, proclaiming her innocent of borrowing from him. When he later learned that two others were also considering the topic, Howells bragged in a letter to Samuel Clemens: "You know I had two rivals in the celebration of a doctoress; now comes a pretty young doctoress who had written out her own adventures."[65] Apparently, when Howells took up the question of the lady physician, he did not want to share the field with women writers. In fact, the same condescending tone he adopts toward the "pretty young doctoress" in his letter (and toward Phelps in his preface to her work) marks his treatment of Grace Breen. As one critic notes, Howells's novel ends not only with the lady doctor giving up her career but with a scene in which she is childlike and vulnerable. As she awkwardly proclaims her love for her suitor, she covers her eyes "with the beautiful, artless action of a shame-smitten child" (258). The scene underscores the hopelessness of her earlier attempts to cultivate the self-control and independence of a professional doctor.[66]

In taking up the lady physician, Phelps seems to rebut Howell's conservative tale of the doctoress, and her agenda is explicitly feminist. Phelps had been a contributor to *Sex in Education*, an answer to Clarke's *No Sex in Education*. She challenged Clarke's authority directly, claiming that he wrote as if he were "a theorist who does not desire to be answered." She also insisted that neither "the proportions of the gray and white matter in the brain" nor the "exquisite machinery of the viscera" can tell us much about the "exact position of women in the economy of a cursed world."[67] For Phelps, fiction was more likely than medicine to say something useful about women in society, and charting the actual and potential opportunities for women in the economic world was what Phelps aimed to do in her novels. In *Hedged In* (1870), she wrote about single mothers, in *Silent Partner* (1871) she exposed the harsh consequences of marital laws that deprived married women of private property, and in *The Woman's Journal* and the *Independent* she published articles about women's health and education. And in *Doctor Zay*, Phelps charts one doctoress's successful career in rural Maine where she drives about on her own, earns $5000 a year, and can marry without abandoning her career.[68]

Most critics have taken Howells and Phelps at their word, evaluating both novels as responses to women's efforts to gain entrance into higher education and the professions. In this light, Howells emerges as an unenlightened patriarch and Phelps as a staunch feminist.[69] But I would like to suggest that the novels actually share a great deal in their representations of medicine, if not in their treatment of women doctors. Both authors reify medicine, suggesting that physicians are born, not made, both understand professional authority as essentially masculine, and both suggest that literature is medicine's equal and complement. As Alcott makes the ideal husband a poet/doctor, so Howells and Phelps imagine the ideal marriage as a union of medicine and literature.

Howells's novel features not only a woman doctor who gives up her career, but also a male doctor who, unlike Grace Breen, is a "true" doctor. In general, Howells treats his characters with a gentle irony that makes them pathetic, laughable, and occasionally endearing. The minor characters are all cartoonish exaggerations of narrow types, and even the heroine is a caricature of the self-deluded New England girl who takes herself too seriously. Howells's touch is light and his tone encourages detached amusement. But in the depiction of Dr. Mulbridge, Howells sounds an uncharacteristic note of sincerity. Dr. Mulbridge has a politically unsavory history: he is the grandson of a former slave ship captain who cast his "dying vote for General Jackson" and the son of a "tolerated Copperhead." The doctor is an insensitive, unmannered man with Southern sympathies and contempt for women, a boorish bully who wears a rough coat and still lives with his mother. A few decades earlier, such characteristics might have made Dr. Mulbridge a figure of the crude physician insensitive to the delicacies of the sickroom. But Dr. Mulbridge is a fine physician, not despite his rough manners but precisely because he cares not a wit for the world of manners and the extraneous, insignificant details that consume the attention of more nervous, sensitive humans. When Dr. Mulbridge enters the sick room, he is the epitome of the "natural" physician. In a tone distinctive for its lack of irony, Howells writes:

The large, somewhat uncouth man gave evidence . . . that he was all physician, and that he had not chosen his profession from any theory or motive, however good, but had been as much chosen by it as if he had been born a physician. He was incredibly gentle and soft in all his movements, and perfectly kind, without being at any moment unprofitably sympathetic. He knew when to listen and when not to listen,—to learn everything from the quivering bundle of nerves before him without seeming to have learnt anything alarming; he smiled when it would do her good to be laughed at, and treated her with such grave respect that she could not feel herself trifled with, nor remember afterwards any point of neglect. (107)

In most of his fiction, Howells is attentive to how we misperceive others and ourselves. We all lack full self-awareness and cannot help but read the world with reference to our own hopes and fears. The good doctor, at least at the moment of a medical crisis, is different. At the bedside he is "all physician": he has no self that obscures his perception, he has no interests of his own to distract him, and he can see past the manners, affectations, and poses of the patient. He is, in short, the consummate detached, disinterested professional clinician, though he is also kind and gentle. He knows the patient's body directly (much as doctors who studied in the Paris hospitals believed was possible through the new clinical methods), and yet he is still an American doctor—attentive to the patient and not just eager for medical knowledge. At Mrs. Maynard's bedside, Dr. Mulbridge watches "beside his patient, noting every change with a wary intelligence which no fact escaped and no anxiety clouded; alert, gentle, prompt; suffering no questions, and absolutely silent as to all impressions" (179).

Phelps's doctor is also born to the profession. Dr. Zay's father was a physician, and she discovered her passion for science as a girl. Her hands show "unusual signs of strength" and she has a "firm and fearless touch" and a natural enthusiasm for dislocations, fractures, medical treatises, and long nights.[70] Most importantly, she transcends her female nature: she is a doctor even more than she is a woman. As her patient and suitor Waldo Yorke notes, she is blind to romance and she is oblivious to the conventions of male/female relationships. She never indulges him, she refuses his attempts at repartee, she answers his declaration of love with a diagnosis that he is nervous, and even her abrupt departures are evidence that her professional bedside manner trumps any feminine inclination to linger in conversation with a possible suitor. In short, Phelps depicts Doctor Zay as a true professional, which, in the gender codes of the day, means she is unwomanly. When she is in a hurry, the doctor drums her fingers on the table "with that nervous protest . . . which is a more natural expression of irritation among men than women," she has a cool scientific eye rather than any sensitivity to beauty, she lacks the spirituality and religious faith that women traditionally offer the world, and in even the most demanding situations she can keep "her dangerous and sacred feminine nerve under magnificent training" (110).

It is not surprising that Phelps's representation of a fine female physician is ensnared by gender. Howells can make Dr. Mulbridge a good doctor without reference to his gender. Professional virtues—detachment, self-control, expertise, and stamina—are masculine virtues. In representing a female physician with such talents, Phelps cannot but wrestle with the fact that what counts as womanly is the opposite of what counts as professional. Dr. Zay can be a good professional only if she is less than womanly. And yet, to underscore her masculine habits reminds us that she is female and thus she achieves self-control not by nature but by effort.[71]

In part, Phelps suggests that Dr. Zay is a good doctor precisely because she is female, an argument many women physicians used to campaign for women's admission to medical schools. As a girl, Dr. Zay nursed her mother and admired the women doctors who attended her mother. Now, as an adult, she devotes her life to helping women and children. Phelps also takes care to make Dr. Zay feminine. She has "the curves of femininity," and as one observer notes, "There's woman clear through that girl's brains" (97, 101). Phelps also makes Dr. Zay a homeopathic practitioner, perhaps because women entered homeopathy in larger numbers than regular medicine, and perhaps because homeopathy was seen as a gentler therapeutic since it did not call for bleeding or purging.[72] Thus Phelps insists upon Dr. Zay's innate womanliness, while at the same time coding her professionalism as masculine.

Central to the masculinity that both Phelps and Howells associate with professional medicine is a physical vitality that is set in opposition to manners, language, and culture. Both Dr. Mulbridge and Dr. Zay eschew chatter and figurative language, cut through polite conversation, set aside social conventions, ignore the opinions of others, and wrestle with the facts of life and death. Dr. Zay can ligate arteries, revive a drowned mill worker, and nurse the town through an epidemic of scarlet fever and diphtheria because of her physical and mental strength:

She had bread to eat that he knew not of. . . . Her splendid health was like a god to her. She leaned against her own physical strength, as another woman might lean upon a man's. She had the repose of her full mental activity. . . . She moved on her straight and narrow way between life and death, where one hysteric moment would be fatal, with a glorious poise. (110–11)

Dr. Mulbridge has a similar physical strength, though Howells feels no compunction to explain this strength, as Phelps does in noting Doctor Zay's ability to hold hysteria at bay. Dr. Mulbridge stays up all night, eats with an appetite that offends proper ladies, and refuses polite conversation. Neither he nor Dr. Zay, however, understand love, desire, or aesthetics. When Dr. Mulbridge proposes to Grace, he leans over her, explaining the "reasons" that oblige her to marry him (226). Unlike the suave Mr. Libby, who anticipates her desires, Dr. Mulbridge bears down on Grace, telling her that, although he is not very good looking and although "such things weigh with women," she should accept his proposal since style really is a trivial matter (227). In the presence of a sick body, Dr. Mulbridge is an intuitive man understanding every need, but in the presence of a healthy woman he fails to read her body and to tune his energy to hers. Phelps also makes her doctor deaf to the language of love. Although Waldo pursues Dr. Zay with the finesse of a finely bred Bostonian, the doctor barely notices. Her suitor has a literary sensibility that attends to details. In the Maine forest he becomes a "worshipper in Nature's cathedrals," in his sick room he notes the wall hangings, the carpet, and the vase of apple-blossoms, and after each visit from Dr. Zay he mulls over the implications of her words and gestures. But Dr. Zay is oblivious to such matters, and she accuses Yorke of "strangling in allegory" and tells him that he "speak[s] in figures" while she is "a person of facts" (132, 131). When she looks at him, she does not see the beauty of his pale skin and dark eyes, but only the signs of a medical condition. Medicine can understand illness but not desire. Or, as Phelps reminds us, "the doctor was not an artist" (161).

On this Phelps and Howells agree, and also on the appeal and power of masculine refinement. Both Howells and Phelps make the man of fine sensibilities an effeminate wanderer who has little sense of purpose or vocation, and thus they explicitly consider the feminization of literature and high culture and the attendant concern that art has lost its social purpose and cultural authority. Mr. Libby and Waldo York lack energy and purpose. Libby has "done nothing but enjoy [him]self since [he] left college" (147), and Waldo has an eye for beauty, an ear for language, a profession he has never practiced, and an injury that lands him in bed for most of the novel. But for all their dandyish lounging, both men are thoroughly heterosexual and adequately masculine. Libby is honest, courageous, and strong, as we learn when he risks his life to save a man. And Yorke, perhaps because he is a feminist's hero, proves his masculinity by being man enough to love a woman as independent at Dr. Zay.[73] For Howells and Phelps, literature offers an important antidote to the narrow thinking of modern science. Both writers depict the humorous and embarrassing missteps of physicians in love, and both use the wit of romantic comedy to underscore the unimaginative language of medicine.

Thus, although the two novels differ in their conclusions on women's role in professional medicine, they both use medicine as a foil to define a literary sensibility that is sensitive to style, wit, beauty, art, and love and is embodied in a debonair aesthete who gets the girl.

In many ways, the heterosexual marriage that ends both Phelps's and Howells's novels essentializes gender complementarity, even as both novels challenge the feminization of culture and aesthetics. Henry James and Annie Nathan Meyer, by contrast, offer portraits of medicine in skirts without using a heterosexual ending to assuage the gender anxiety that the doctoress provokes.

The Bostonians appeared in 1885 (serially in *The Century*), three years after *The Portrait of a Lady* and Howell's *Dr. Breen's Practice* had been reviewed together in the *Atlantic*. The reviewer, Horace Scudder, preferred Howells's novel because it "introduces us to people whom we know" and it has a "naturalness" that James's does not.[74] Most critics today would disagree with Scudder. Howells's *Dr. Breen's Practice* is usually considered a slight achievement, but Scudder's review may have stung James and shaped his treatment of the doctoress.[75] There is neither feminine sweetness nor feminist ardor in Dr. Prance. She is "[s]pare, dry, hard"; she has cropped hair, no aptitude for social niceties, and no interest in the feminist reform efforts of the women around her who presume that because she is a woman doctor she will be sympathetic to their cause.[76] James refuses to assuage fears that medicine will masculinize women, and he makes it clear that the lady physician needs neither feminism nor a family. Dr. Prance plays only a minor role in the plot, but as the only stern realist in the novel she is a substantial presence, and James valorizes her judgments as the no-nonsense opinions of a practical-minded medical scientist. Like Howells and Phelps, James admires medicine's rigor: "Doctor Prance dealt in facts," and she is "addicted neither to empty phrases nor to unconsidered assertions" (307, 302).

In several earlier works, James indulges the stereotype of the doctor as a narrow scientist. In *Daisy Miller*, he notes that while doctors offer indisputable truths about the "villainous miasma" of the night air at the Coliseum, poets are sensitive to the "historic atmosphere."[77] In *The Portrait of a Lady*, a London specialist is cold and imperious, and in "Lady Barbarina," James mocks a medical man who is a renowned researcher but ignorant about human behavior. Notably, in one of his earliest works, *Washington Square*, James offers a more complex portrait of the doctor, but the result is only a more damning critique of medical arrogance. Dr. Sloper is culturally refined, and he has a novelist's interest in plot, irony, and character, but he ruins his daughter's life because he fails to understand her "in anything but material terms."[78]

Like Dr. Sloper, Dr. Prance also prefers material, empirical explanations to sentiment, and both novels suggest that the scientific view lacks sensitivity to the human element. But Dr. Prance is probably less guilty of this limitation than Dr. Sloper. Although she is "tough and technical," she is also keenly aware of the battle between Basil Ransom and Olive Chancellor for the heart of Verena Tarrant, and she is responsive to Basil's aesthetic and psychological intelligence. She finds Basil more interesting than the feminists who champion her, and in the only tender chapter in the novel she walks with Basil on the beach, teaches him to cast, and indulges the dying Miss Birdseye's sentimentality. Everyone in the novel except Prance and Basil is shrill, obtuse, or greedy. Olive is prone to melodrama, the Tarrants are hungry for publicity, and the rich women who dominate Boston are trivial. By contrast, Dr. Prance deals in facts, and when Basil sees the social world for what it is she concurs, giving his observations the added authority of her science. They are kindred souls, eschewing reform, sentimentality, and crass commercialism for brutal honesty about human relations as well as material facts.

Several critics have taken offense at James's lady physician, reading her as a masculinized woman. And, in fact, to Basil she seems like a boy, a naughty boy who would cut school to do experiments. And yet, although Dr. Prance's curveless body may be a jab at the femininity of lady physicians, only in a world where women must perform their femininity is Dr. Prance "unwomaned" by her profession. In fact, what is most distinctive about Dr. Prance is James's refusal to suggest that she needs the enlightening influence of culture. While Phelps and Howells (and a host of popular twentieth-century films about doctors) tell tales of brilliant doctors who become kinder after being exposed to the humanizing influence of culture, James rejects this claim.[79] Neither a Southern aristocrat nor New England feminists have anything to teach her. And yet, Dr. Prance and Basil are a couple. James does not close the gender and epistemological gap between science and culture with a heterosexual marriage, but Basil's aristocratic, refined aesthetic sensibilities and writerly interests in words are neatly matched by her hard-edged commitment to empirical facts.

A few years after *The Bostonians* was published, Annie Nathan Meyer offered an equally unsentimental portrait of the tough lady physician. In *Helen Brent, M.D.* (1892), Meyer positions a female physician neither in relation to men or children nor as a complement to refinement, but as a leader in the field. Meyer's doctoress founds a medical school devoted to laboratory training and prides herself on her own scientific sophistication. She is the new breed of doctor; she studies in Germany and is bold enough to direct a campaign against venereal disease. Both esteemed and popular, she establishes a national reputation by performing "difficult gynecological operations, the success of which had interested the entire medical profession—operations that required nerve, coolness, daring, skill, a steady hand, and a delicate one."[80]

Gynecological surgery came of age in the 1880s, and gynecologists, as I noted earlier, established the field's legitimacy and elevated their own professional status by making aggressive use of surgery for a wide variety of ailments. This "orgy of gynecological surgery," in the words of one historian, and the emphasis on radical surgeries (the complete removal of ovaries and uterus or the entire breast and underlying muscles, for example) has rightly earned sharp criticism.[81] But the development of surgical solutions was not solely motivated by professional ambition. Gynecologists believed they were responding effectively to real and often intractable gynecological problems. In making Dr. Brent a leading gynecological surgeon, Meyers suggests that women in medicine will offer not just feminine compassion but also new insights into disease because they may not make the same presumptions that male physicians make.

Meyer was active in promoting women's professional opportunities, devoting several years, for example, to raising money to found Barnard College. Meyer knew many leading women professionals of her day, and it is possible that Brent is modeled on Mary Dixon Jones, a gynecological surgeon who became well known in 1888 for performing the first complete hysterectomy. Jones was unusual in her day for pursuing professional advancement in male-dominated arenas and through male-dominated networks. Jones presented specimens at meetings of the New York Pathological Society, she published in specialty journals and served as editor of several, she was the chief medical officer of the Women's Dispensary Hospital in Brooklyn, and she was an ardent advocate of surgical remedies for female troubles. She also gained public notoriety in 1892 when the Brooklyn *Daily Eagle* ran a series of articles portraying her as a knife-happy surgeon. As a result, Jones was indicted on manslaughter charges and was the subject of eight malpractice suits, although she was eventually cleared of all charges.[82]

Brent, like Jones, is aggressive in pursuing her career. She is not just eager to help the sick; she is dedicated to the self-promotion that was part of any doctor's rise to professional eminence. Unlike Dr. Prance and Dr. Zay, she is not a homeopath, and while there are only hints that Dr. Prance dissects, Dr. Brent is an aggressive surgeon. Meyer gives a nod to the gender anxieties raised by the successful doctoress, and she makes Brent feminine as well as competent. Thus, although she wears practical clothes, she is beautiful, and, when, on one occasion, she dons a lavish gown with soft lace she shows that she can be a "queenly lady" as well as a doctor (176). Meyer also suggests that Brent is marriageable. She is betrothed to a lawyer, but he treats her poorly and breaks off the engagement when she gets her degree and insists upon going to Germany to continue her studies. She is, we suspect, better off without him, and yet at the end of the novel, after his wife has died, he writes to Brent to tell her that some-day he will come to her "broken" and "suppliant" (196). Notably, a re-viewer for the *Atlantic Monthly* found the return to the marriage question at the end of the story an insult to women doctors everywhere: "How the genuine woman-doctors must loathe these travesties on their real life!"[83]

Although this comment suggests the extent to which the woman doc-tor was no longer a radical idea by 1892, the review remains silent on what is radical in the novel—the suggestion that women doctors might take an active role, surgically and politically, in women's healthcare. Fem-inists have often lambasted surgical solutions to gynecological problems as evidence of medicine's aggressive and arrogant use and abuse of women's bodies. But, as Regina Morantz-Sanchez suggests, surgical solu-tions for gynecological problems might have been prompted not only by an eagerness for professional advancement, but also by what we might read as a feminist understanding of disease. Dixon Jones's interest, for example, in outside (microbial) causes of disease rather than internal, systemic causes was not only a logical pathology theory for a surgeon, but also an etiology that might have been appealing to a woman. An emphasis on outside causes (poor hygiene, husbands passing venereal disease to wives, poor care of parturient women) for pelvic disease "freed the female body from its association with inherent pathology."[84] By mak-ing Dr. Brent both a surgeon and an advocate for public awareness about venereal disease transmission, Meyer joins Dixon Jones in suggesting that medical thinking on gynecological disease must be freed from presump-tions about the female body's susceptibility to disease. According to Meyer, this is a contribution women physicians and surgeons might be able to make.

Both James and Meyer have little patience with conventional gender codes. Superficially, Dr. Prance may be pigeonholed as a masculinized woman, but James suggests that she is right when she tells Basil that "Men and women are all the same to me. . . . I don't see any difference. There is room for improvement in both sexes. Neither of them is up to the standard" (37). Gender is a fetishized category that James has no interest in turning into a biological fact. Meyer also refuses to ascribe innate, biological feminine or masculine traits to her characters, but unlike James, she has little faith in science as a gender-free world. In making Dr. Prance uninterested in feminine styles and feminist politics, James suggests that science's commitment to knowing the material world means that it stands apart from contemporary debates about gender. Dr. Brent, by contrast, is a scientist who by virtue of her commitment to women's political concerns can see how gender ensnares even science.

In the last two sections of this chapter, I look at fictional physicians, one female and one male, who represent a synthesis of aesthetic and scientific ways of knowing, and I consider the appeal of the doctor as one who might be able to transcend the gender battles of the nineteenth century. This may be a transcendence we want to challenge as a false leap out of gender politics, but both Sarah Orne Jewett's *A Country Doctor* and James's *The Wings of the Dove* suggest that the true professional, writer or doctor, is defined not by gender but by an all-consuming "self-disciplined professional devotion."[85]

For Jewett, medicine offers a model for healing not just the sick body, but a deeper malaise that threatens society. In *A Country Doctor*, medicine bridges the opposites that mark Jewett's fictional world—new and old, city and country, the natural and the social, the individual and the community, and, like Howells, Phelps, James, and Meyer, Jewett celebrates the sense of vocation that medicine demands. Indeed, like all the authors I consider in this chapter, Jewett endows her own literary project with a seriousness that borrows from medicine, though it is not medicine's masculinity that she admires.

Like Alcott, Jewett is wary of urban modernity, and the novel opens with several vignettes of rural folk sharing stories, taking care of each other, and burying their dead. This is the old world passing. In the city, lonely women and men who lack "high aims or any especial and fruitful single-heartedness" lead "unimportant and commonplace" lives.[86] In "self-centered Dunport," Miss Prince, a woman of "rare capacity," wastes her talents on managing a fine house, Miss Fraley feels as if she "were not accomplishing anything," and George Gerry lacks "stern determination which wins its way at all hazards" (193, 177, 152, 215). According to Jewett, while the city might offer financial opportunity and social amenities, it provides no sense of purpose or duty. And although the country offers the spiritual inspiration of the natural landscape and a long tradition of hard work, rural culture is disappearing and what is left cannot address the distinctive problems of the modern world.

According to Jewett, the modern malaise is a kind of physical disease. Embracing the somaticization of American culture I noted in Alcott's later novels, Jewett understands poor health and enfeebled bodies as signs of the degeneration of American society. She warns that "few people know even what true and complete physical life is" (139). She insists that the body is "the soul's instrument of action and service in the world," and she laments the "inferior bodies which come to us through either our ancestors' foolishness or our own" (139). In part, Jewett's diagnosis echoes the warnings that were at the center of health reform. Modernity is marked by intellectual mediocrity, spiritual emptiness, and moral vacuity, and she finds at the root of these failings a lack of physical vitality.

But Jewett refuses to literalize the links between moral, spiritual, and physical decline, and she shuns programmatic reforms such as exercise regimens, self-help lessons in physiology, and homemade bread. In fact, the body is largely absent in Jewett's novel. She never invokes mere physical energy as an ideal in the way that Alcott, Howells, and Phelps make the sheer physical vitality of their doctors crucial evidence of their moral integrity and professional dedication. Instead, Jewett transforms physical health into spiritual grace, intimating that the latter cannot be achieved merely by adopting a good diet or putting on the right dress. Jewett suggests that the somatic malaise that she diagnoses is in the end an aesthetic illness, a disease of wrecked sensibilities. Furthermore, she reworks the warnings that Alcott and other domestic novelists issued about the corruption of domestic and religious morality by the intrusion of unchecked consumerism into the private, familial sphere into a warning about the loss of aesthetic sensibilities, of disciplinary rigor, and of high-mindedness with the advent of modern banality. Jewett abhors the "half-alive people who think it no wrong to bring into the world human beings with even less vitality than themselves," and she bemoans the "thousands of shipwrecked, and failing, and inadequate, and useless lives" (139).

Medicine, according to Jewett, offers a cure, and doctors can teach us how to live useful lives. But rather than an avuncular doctor who knows how to bake bread, we need expert, well-trained doctors, and she offers the medical profession as an exemplary discipline that demands all that the modern world lacks—purpose, energy, and intelligence. Superficially, Dr. Leslie has much in common with Dr. Mulbridge and Dr. Zay. Like them, he has curative powers that depend less upon medical therapies than upon his presence. He is "singularly self-reliant and composed," his eyes show a "rare thoughtfulness and foresight," and he "instinctively" takes command (26–27). Nan, the girl Dr. Leslie raises and introduces to medicine, has a similar intuitive ability to respond to the complexities of pain and illness and an authoritative presence that allows her to take charge without presenting credentials or answering questions. Like Phelps and Howells, Jewett also suggests that doctors have little interest in or talent for courtship. Dr. Leslie has no love interest (his wife and child died years ago), and Nan is only briefly tempted by a suitor. But Jewett never implies that Dr. Leslie or Nan, or their way of knowing, is inadequate, solely masculine or feminine, or in need of a complement. For Jewett, the doctor is the modern sage, and while a rural male doctor serves the old world, he can also mentor a young female doctor (notably Nan studies in Germany) who will serve the urban modern world.

Although in some ways Jewett's understanding of the malaise of modernity as a loss of physical vitality participates in the somaticization of social questions, she does not make the body the final arbiter; rather, she suggests that medicine is concerned with more than bodies. Thus, while Howells and Phelps define medicine narrowly, Jewett suggests that good doctors must attend to the patient's body and spirit and to the physical and spiritual health of the entire community. Dr. Leslie rarely practices medicine in Jewett's novel. Unlike Dr. Zay and Dr. Mulbridge, he does not sit beside patients, and his own body is never threatened or worn down by the effort of his work. In fact, Dr. Leslie is not identified with the somatic at all. Rather, he talks, muses, and visits. He talks as easily with his old friend Dr. Ferris about bodies, souls, faith, and disease as he does with Mrs. Graham about the "old place" and the loss of traditional values. He is known, respected, and loved by all, and he knows the details of life in Oldfields—the histories and dark secrets of all the families. But he also maintains a distance that allows him insight into greater issues than the personal and the mundane. He watches the opening burial procession from afar, and he offers insights into the connection between "spiritual laziness and physical laziness" (84).

In many ways, Dr. Leslie figures both a passing medical world—home visits and an intimate relationship with the entire community—and a willingness to modernize. He raises Nan, bringing scientific knowledge as well as domestic wisdom to the job in order to teach her how to "work with nature and not against it" (80, 78). Nan learns to direct her love of nature and her abundant energy into mastering the details of *materia medica*, and so Dr. Leslie guides her into an adult life that makes the most of her talents and strengths. Alcott's Dr. Alec also raises a little girl. But unlike Dr. Alec's program, which values commonsense truths, Dr. Leslie's program preaches distinction and excellence. Furthermore, Dr. Leslie's success is not that he charts the troubled waters of gender identity for his young charge as does Dr. Alec, but rather that he guides his charge into a profession and gives her a vocational passion that defines her role in the world. Thus Jewett jettisons Alcott's domestic agenda and valorization of the quotidian for an emphasis on professionalism, dedication, and distinction.

Many critics have read Jewett's works in the context of a female, domestic tradition. Ann Romines writes that Jewett's work "teaches, validates, and preserves the language of domestic culture."[87] Margaret Roman argues that Jewett "creates a woman's imaginative universe" and "subverts the male-dominated form."[88] But as Richard Brodhead claims, Jewett differs in important ways from her female predecessors. The domestic tradition presumes that "literary discourse is continuous with, not differentiated from, the discourses of piety and domestic instruction." Jewett, by contrast, is part of a late nineteenth-century "high-cultural presentation of literature as a sphere of its own value in itself."[89] As

Brodhead notes, in high culture "the good in a work of art is put there *through its art*, through the disciplined application of a craft specific to that mode of creation" (emphasis original).[90] In this paradigm, art is good—morally and aesthetically good—not because of any explicit agenda it might present, but because it embodies distinction, excellence, and a disciplined commitment to craft.

For Jewett, medicine offers a cure for the malaise of modernity not because it addresses the physical degeneration that attends the loss of spiritual and intellectual energy, but because it offers a model for the kind of commitment required to heal the aimlessness and lack of purpose that mark modern society.[91] Medical work itself does not capture Jewett's imagination, but the image of the doctor devoted to transforming, like an artist, every experience into greater knowledge and understanding is at the center of the novel. Jewett makes the comparison between art and medicine explicit in a gloss on what makes Nan a good student of medicine:

There must be an instinct that recognizes a disease and suggests its remedy, as much as an instinct that finds the right notes and harmonies for a composer of music, or the colors for a true artist's picture, or the results of figures for a mathematician. . . . there is something needed beside even drill and experience; every student of medicine should be fitted by nature with a power of insight, a gift for his business . . . and as the great poet tells the truths of God, and makes other souls wiser and stronger and fitter for action, so the great doctor works for the body's health, and tries to keep human beings free from the failures that come from neglect and ignorance. (138–39)

It is tempting to read this passage as an elevation of medicine to the status of art, but perhaps it is more accurate to read it as an attempt to endow literature with the prestige and authority of medicine. No doubt in finding parallels between medicine and the arts, the latter gains the masculine seriousness accorded medicine, and yet in the above passage Jewett assiduously avoids all gender-specific language. She uses no pronouns and thus never makes the doctor, the visual artist, or the great poet male or female.

Like Jewett, James also sometimes imagined the doctor as endowed with a unique "power of insight." In *The Bostonians*, for example, Dr. Prance gives an impressively astute answer to Basil Ransom's inquiry about how Olive and Verena are doing after the death of Miss Birdseye—"you can hear the silence vibrate." Similarly, in *The Wings of the Dove*, Sir Luke Strett understands what others do not. Unlike Dr. Prance, however, Strett is also a man of taste and style. There is no roughness about this doctor; he is, like Eakins's Dr. Agnew, the consummate physician and master of all—life and death, the body and the psyche—and a man of refinement.

Before turning to *The Wings of the Dove*, I want to briefly consider a story James wrote seven years earlier that also features a culturally refined doctor. In "The Middle Years," James pairs a young, "ardent physiologist" with an ailing writer who is wrestling with the realization that he may die before producing his best work.[92] The writer finds consolation in the company of the literate doctor, and the doctor is thrilled to know a writer he deeply admires. The two meet as Dr. Hugh is "lingering" over a novel, "credulous" and "absorbed" (261). Initially, Dr. Hugh does not realize that Dencombe is the author of the book he is reading—*The Middle Years*. But when the writer puts down the book he is carrying, and Dr. Hugh picks it up and sees that it is a copy of the very novel he is reading and that it is marked with possible revisions, he suddenly understands that chance has brought him face-to-face with the idolized writer. The realization makes the doctor blush, and the sudden exposure makes the novelist faint. Dr. Hugh helps Dencombe back to his hotel and takes over the case. Conveniently, in addition to being Dencombe's ideal reader, he is also his ideal doctor: Dr. Hugh's medical expertise is just what Dencombe needs, and Dencombe's attending physician relenquishes the case because he recognizes that as a lover of Dencombe's work, Dr. Hugh has a "peculiar right" (269). Moreover, Dr. Hugh is eager to repay Dencombe for the literary pleasures he has bestowed upon the world. Thus when Dencombe admits his desire for "an extension" on life in order to write more, Dr. Hugh declares exuberantly, and in language that anticipates Sir Luke Strett's injunction to Milly Theale, "You *shall* live" (270). Indeed, Dr. Hugh is so enchanted by Dencombe's description of what he might write next (should he live) that he promises his profession will "hold itself responsible for such a life" (272).

As it turns out, however, Dr. Hugh takes on the new case at a significant cost to himself.[93] The doctor is already employed to care for a countess, and when he shortchanges her in order to spend more time with Dencombe, the countess leaves the resort, writes Dr. Hugh out of her will, and dies. As Dr. Hugh explains to Dencombe, "I chose to accept, whatever they might be, the consequences of my infatuation" (275). In short, the doctor chooses to serve art rather than money. Unlike the early James story I discussed in Chapter 4, in which the doctor wins an inheritance when he marries his patient's rich girlfriend, in this story the doctor forsakes money and is true to his patient and to his love of literature. By 1893, it would seem, James is less interested in the doctor's class ambitions than in his good taste. He is also, we should note, less interested in the economics of marriage and more interested in rendering passions between men. In some ways, "The Middle Years" is a familiar story of medicine's limitations and literature's sophistication. The doctor is young, eager, and optimistic, while Dencombe is a mature man facing mortality and the loss of possibility. The doctor reads fine literature, Dencombe writes it. It is also a tale of love—of admiration and intimacy. But by figuring an intimate relationship between a doctor and a writer as a relationship between two men, James breaks with the tradition that would have the professions joined through heterosexuality and eliminates the question of gender identity of either profession. In short, by writing about a young male doctor ardently serving an older male writer, James neither joins the hand-wringing about the feminization of literature or medicine nor joins in the assertion of the strenuous masculinity of either.

In *The Wings of the Dove*, James again joins empirical and aesthetic epistemologies, ways of knowing usually presumed to be incommensurate, but this time by embodying both in one figure. Sir Luke Strett, the great London doctor who treats Milly Theale, knows and understands the ineffable with the assurance and positivity of a man with the best training in medicine and science and also with the refined sensibility and fine intelligence of the artist who registers fully, in James's phrase, "a direct impression of life." Sir Luke Strett epitomizes the Jamesian "disposition of withheld involvement," a disposition that James's contemporary critics often found insufficiently patriotic and insufficiently masculine.[94] In 1883, for example, James was castigated for his "pseduo-Americanism," his "polished prose," and his failure to engage the "daily struggles" and "urgent life of America." In 1904 a reviewer complained that James and other dilettantish writers were "untouched by the forces . . . seething around them."[95] Twenty years earlier, in *The Bostonians*, James did address urgent topics by taking up gender anxieties and the cultural wars between North and South and science and culture.[96] But in *The Wings of the Dove*, James addresses what he believed was one of the most urgent struggles, the tension between the desire to live and an intense consciousness of mortality.

In his preface to the New York edition of *The Wings of the Dove*, James notes that although he had long thought of writing about a character "stricken and doomed, condemned to die under short respite," he had also worried that such a topic was a "formidable" theme. But he had finally changed his mind, coming to see, perhaps after taking up the subject in "The Middle Years," that representing "a person infirm and ill" might be, if not treated as a " 'frank' subject," a topic with "secrets and compartments."[97] James's personal knowledge of the world of illness and medicine was extensive.[98] Beside his own "obscure hurt," his father had lost a leg, suffered bouts of depression, and was close friends with a physician; his brother William suffered from neurasthenia, earned a medical degree at Harvard, and taught anatomy and physiology; and his sister Alice was an invalid throughout her life. James also wrote often about illness. In *The Portrait of a Lady*, Ralph Touchett's slow wasting away from tuberculosis structures the end of the novel and hangs over Isabel as a reminder of the limitations of her freedom. Rose Muniment, the invalid sister of the anarchist leader in *The Princess Casamassima*, is a stoic whose transcendence over her bodily privations serves as an alternative to the sensual, aesthetic, and political pleasures her brother indulges. In "The Beast in the Jungle," May Bartram retreats into a "chamber of pain, rigidly guarded," that is forbidden to John Marcher, and in *Daisy Miller*, James does not disallow the harsh judgment that the "little American flirt" contracts malaria as punishment for "going round at night." It is in *The Wings of the Dove*, however, that James makes illness and medicine's response not a "frank" matter but an opportunity to probe what interested him most in his late work—the heavy weight of knowing. Illness, he finally decided as he reports in the preface, is deeply "interesting" since this condition intensifies "consciousness of all relations."[99]

By the end of the nineteenth century, the transformation of American medicine from speculative rationalism to empirical materialism was essentially complete. Medical practice was still eclectic—newspapers advertised doctors who were expert in bloodletting, Mesmerism, and constitutional pathology, and members of the James family sought relief in hydropathy, hypnosis, and galvanic electrical currents as well as morphine and surgery. But well-publicized advances in bacteriology and discovery of X-rays made it clear that medicine would never again be the art of interpreting illness as a dialectical interaction between body, mind, and environment.[100] The definition of disease as a specific "lesion-based entity that reenacted itself in every individual sufferer," first articulated by such Paris-trained physicians as Elisha Bartlett, had become widely accepted by the end of the century.[101] In short, the new and now dominant paradigm privileged body over mind, matter over spirit, and observable, measurable facts over less tangible realities.

Given the emphasis on naming disease, identifying afflicted body parts, and discovering the somatic etiology of disease, James's refusal in *The Wings of the Dove* to diagnose Milly's illness is noteworthy. The refusal is not the coy move that James makes in *The Ambassadors* when he avoids naming the presumably crass consumer item manufactured by the Newsomes in Woolett, Massachusetts. Rather, James's refusal to name Milly's illness is an explicit rejection of the empirical materialism of scientific medicine and a refusal to participate in the somaticization of illness. James rejects the legitimacy offered by medical diagnosis. He makes it clear that Milly does not have tuberculosis, the cause of which was discovered in 1882; Mrs. Stringhman announces that it is not a case of American nerves, another name for neurasthenia; and Milly suffers none of the ignominies of illness—the smells of medicine and the scheduling of treatments. And yet, James insists that it is a "real" disease. In the preface, James writes of the difficulties of "making one's protagonist 'sick.'"[102] Sir Luke Strett discovers "something" when he examines Milly, her physical decline is evident throughout the novel; and in the final scenes there is little doubt that she suffers. The critical attention lavished on diagnosing Milly's illness—tuberculosis, chlorosis, neurasthenia have all been suggested—also testifies to its reality for readers.

James's refusal to diagnose Milly is particularly striking given his sister's longing "for some palpable disease" throughout her life as an invalid and how she felt "driven back to stagger alone under the monstrous mass of subjective sensations."[103] Presumably James knew this and knew that she felt an "enormous relief" when the doctor diagnosed breast cancer, finally giving her an "uncompromising verdict" that lifted her out of the "formless vague" and set her "within the very heart of the sustaining concrete."[104] James himself sought medical and social legitimacy for what he later called his "obscure hurt" when he went to visit a Boston surgeon in 1862. Like Alice, he also knew the humiliation of being denied such legitimacy when the surgeon failed to "warn, to comfort, or to command—to do anything but make quite unassistingly light of the bewilderment exposed to him."[105]

James's refusal to offer a medical term for Milly's illness, then, is not a denial of its reality or legitimacy, but a refusal to limit its meaning, which James suggests is best comprehended not empirically but through impressions. Thus we learn that Milly attracts attention not only because she is an American in England, a rich girl of marrying age, and an orphan, but because she also bears some other distinguishing characteristic that no one can quite identify. We are told that she works upon "the sympathy, the curiosity, and the fancy of her associates," that she is considered strange, bewildering, and confusing, that she is "so queer to behold."[106] But no one can be more specific, no one can name what makes Milly strange. In fact, Milly's "strangeness" is best represented by a painting. The viewing of a painting by Bronzino, a portrait that has, as both Milly and others immediately understand, an uncanny likeness to her is a crucial scene in James's development of the legitimacy of Milly's illness. The Bronzino scene makes it clear that although no one can name Milly's illness—no character can quite articulate what Milly and the woman in the portrait share—a great painting can capture the immanent reality of illness that medical terms would only trivialize.

The Bronzino scene is also a reminder that everyone wants to interpret Milly, but James makes it clear that each character's response reveals more about the observer than about Milly or her illness. Kate, Densher, Mrs. Lowder, Susie Stringham, and even Milly fail to understand illness fully because each has too much invested. Sir Luke Strett, however, has no investment. He is interested but uninvolved, and if the "unspotted princess" can be known only through the "windows of other people's interest in her," then it is Strett who offers the best view.[107] Like Jewett's Dr. Leslie, Strett knows much more than is revealed by the positivist empirical methods of medicine, and both characters are examples of the acceptance in America's elite intellectual circles that the physician, and not the judge or priest, had become the wisest, most discerning counselor and thus "the most appropriate guardian of the rights of society and the individual."[108]

In the New York preface, James admits, though not without a good bit of ironic self-consciousness, that indirection is, in part, a deferential response to the patient's delicate sensibilities and her need for privacy. As Alice rejected William's appropriating sympathy, so Milly resists the prying, pitying, and morbid curiosity of the healthy who want to look into her world of illness. She avoids "all inquiry into her own case"; she recoils from the "lingering eyes" of the guests at Matcham; she allows Kate to summarize inaccurately—"you are well"; and she warns Densher "off the question of how she was" by telling him "to ignore my interesting side" (185, 142, 242). With Strett, however, Milly feels that she is known. As she tells Kate in a rare moment of confidence, "he knows all about me, and I like it. I don't hate it a bit" (151). With Strett she feels "completely free" and "disposed to undue volubility" (153). Unlike the prying, scheming, and pitying interest of all around her, Strett's interest is the disinterested attention of the scientist. She is certain that he knows her "scientifically, ponderably, proveably—not just loosely and sociably" (150). Most importantly, she feels that he sets before her a "crystal clean . . . great empty cup of attention" (150). The metaphor makes it clear that what he offers is disinterested interest—an empty cup of attention. Perhaps an early exploration of the role of the psychiatrist and the dynamics of transference, James's representation of Strett suggests that it is precisely disinterested interest that leads the patient inexorably into the difficulties of self-knowledge.

We know very little about the doctor. We see glimpses of an individual—the man who is particular about his "numerous effects" when preparing to board a train and has a small interest in art and antiques—but he is always the doctor. Others reveal themselves, others confront truths, but not the doctor. He is, we might surmise, enchanted by his young American patient. He is willing to "discreetly indulge" Milly, but he is always her doctor (158). He visits her in Venice, but he makes the trip because he already had it planned. He comes to the party she gives in his honor, but his "strong face and type" remain "less assimilated by the scene perhaps than any others" (335). In short, Strett is the consummate professional—detached, proficient, unflappable, wise, inscrutable.

He is "half like a general and half like a bishop" (151). He has the "highest type of scientific mind" and a penetrating look. We might assume that Strett's detachment is the consequence of medical training and that his thoughts, opinions, and conclusions are legitimate because they are scientific. But James offers no such explanation. Nor does he define Strett by reference to medical science. He never studies medical texts, he has no association with a hospital or laboratory, he uses no scientific language. In fact, the only reference to the details of medicine comes in a brief reference to "interrogation, auscultation, exploration" (159). Unlike the 1999 film version of the novel in which Strett is identified as a blood specialist and radiologist, in the novel the great doctor proffers no certifying evidence of his medical authority. What makes him a professional, an authority, is not training in a specialty or science at all, but his detachment, his reserve, his disinterested interest. As art, according to the new high-culture aesthetic, is removed from social concerns, so the doctor's office is a place removed from the vested interests and calculations of the public world; it offers silence and space for reflection. Strett is, as Milly notes, priest as well as doctor; he serves as a modern confessor and as a mirror.

In "The Art of Fiction," James defines the novel as "a direct impression of life" and suggests that its value "is greater or less according to the intensity of the impression." Strett, we gather from the responses of those who meet him, offers such impressions. He returns to those who come to him impressions of themselves, of their lives, of their choices. James acknowledges that every impression is "personal," but he also argues that "the deepest quality of a work of art will always be the quality of the mind of the producer" and that "as that intelligence is fine" so "the novel, the picture, the statue partake of the substance of truth and beauty."[109] Clearly, Strett's intelligence is fine, and James suggests that as the Bronzino painting prompts every viewer to sense that some truth and beauty about Milly is captured in the portrait, so Strett's presence similarly makes others feel that they have encountered an important truth about the meaning of illness. The Boston surgeon who dismissed the young James with a "comparative pooh-pooh" failed, as Strett does not, to understand the richly complex relationship between somatic facts and life.

During his last encounter with Strett, Densher realizes that everyone has hovered "outside an impenetrable ring fence," ignoring "the fact of her condition," and he comes to understand that there has "reigned a kind of expensive vagueness, made up of smiles and silences and beautiful fictions and priceless arrangements, all strained to breaking." Everyone, he now admits, "fostered suppressions which were in the direct interest of everyone's good manner, everyone's pity, everyone's quite generous ideal." He concludes, "It was a conspiracy of silence, as the cliché went, to which no one had made an exception." Echoing Alice James's condemnations of William's sympathy, Densher's realization of his part in the cruel tiptoeing and dishonest smiles that have denied the "pain and horror" of Milly's illness is given a surprising amount of authorial privilege. Densher's epiphany is not just his—it is a warning for all. And he comes to this understanding in the presence of Strett. The great doctor strips away the deceit and vagueness that has surrounded Milly and protected everyone else from the truth of the body, from "the great smudge of mortality across the picture." In Strett's presence, "The facts of physical suffering, of incurable pain, of the chance grimly narrowed, had been made, at a stroke, intense" (388–89).

In *The Agnew Clinic*, Eakins offers the senior surgeon much as James offers Sir Luke Strett as a man of power and equanimity, a detached yet involved witness and participant in the "facts of physical suffering." And both Dr. Agnew and Sir Luke Strett preside over women's suffering. But James revises the gender politics of Eakins's painting. Milly Theale may be sick, but she is no more defined by her body than any other character, and she suffers not a female disorder that the male doctor masters but rather an intensifying of consciousness that the doctor nurtures. James is not oblivious to gender. In the preface, he notes that in an earlier treatment of illness he violated gender stereotypes, noting that the "happy effect" Ralph Touchett produces "could never in the world" have been the "fact of sex; since men, among the mortally afflicted, suffer on the whole more overtly and more grossly than women, and resist with a ruder, an inferior strategy." In *The Wings of the Dove*, Milly's graceful decline may, in James's mind, be more typical of women than men, but gender is not foregrounded. Strett is not a master of bodies—male or female—but a fine witness to the "process of life" as it "gives way fighting," to "the whole course of . . . disintegration" and "the whole ordeal of . . . consciousness."[110] In this, James suggests, femininity and masculinity play no significant role.

The emergence in the second half of the nineteenth century of what Burton Bledstein has called a "culture of professionalism" reconfigured authority in the United States. In medicine, technological and scientific knowledge of the body as "a mechanism opaque to all but those with medical training" replaced an emphasis on the "patient as a social being and family member," and, as a result, medicine's authority shifted from domestic to institutional.[111] Lay practitioners lost power because they did not have access to institutions, and Americans, it is generally agreed, depended increasingly upon the specialized knowledge of trained doctors and less upon the lore, traditions, and family medical guides that had formed the basis of much medical care in the first half of the century. In these same years, literature also distanced itself from the domestic and embraced professional values. In the shift from Alcott's avuncular Dr. Alec to Jewett's cultured Dr. Leslie and James's brilliant Sir Luke Strett, for example, we can see an increasing acceptance of medicine's status and an increasing emphasis on the aesthetic (rather than the domestic) as literature's primary concern.

As scholars have noted, medicine's rise to professional eminence entailed a loss of democratic possibility as alternative practitioners were shouldered out of the healthcare market and as somatic management and mastery rather than somatic freedoms came to the fore of the national agenda. Similarly, the rise of an elite, highbrow aesthetic entailed a loss of democratic formlessness and a denial of refinement's politics. The marriage of empirical science and refined sensibility as figured in Jewett's Dr. Nan, James's Sir Luke Strett, and Eakins's Dr. Agnew might be seen, then, as a worrisome entrenchment of authority through mutual cultural authorization. This book began in part out of my desire to unpack the politics of what I saw as a mutual back-slapping, self-congratulatory tone when "profound science" and "elegant literature" join forces. For example, when Oliver Sacks weaves into a medical case study the refined pleasures of high culture, both discourses profit. A high culture affiliation endows medicine with a refined and humane public image, while the detached rationalism of science gives highbrow aesthetics a feel of universal value. The refined doctor, in other words, is an image that reassuringly masks the antidemocratic politics of elite literature and professional medicine. And yet, I also want to suggest that although Dr. Nan, Sir Luke Strett, and Dr. Agnew all offer a false escape from class and gender politics, these three doctors are also an attempt to value a way of knowing beyond empiricism, an imaginative way of knowing that just might, if embodiment is not something only some classes of people suffer, enable an expansion of democratic compassion for both the "whole course of disintegration" that is an inevitable part of living in material bodies and "the whole ordeal of consciousness" that attends embodiment.

Chapter 6

Social Surgery: Physicians on the Color Line

In *The Souls of Black Folk* (1903), W. E. B. Du Bois imagined a future beyond racism if the nation was willing to undergo radical surgery:

> If, while the healing of this vast sore is progressing, the races are to live for many years side by side, united in economic effect, obeying a common government, sensitive to mutual thought and feeling, yet subtly and silently separate in many matters of deeper human intimacy,—if this unusual and dangerous development is to progress amid peace and order, mutual respect and growing intelligence, it will call for social surgery at once the delicatest and nicest in modern history.[1]

That Du Bois turned to surgical metaphors when writing about racism and race violence is not surprising. On one level, the passage testifies to the confidence increasingly placed in surgery at the end of the nineteenth century. On another level, Du Bois's call for social surgery underscores the urgency of the race problem. Surgery is always a radical therapeutic even when it is the best choice. Significantly, Du Bois does not call for surgery as a remedy for the cancer of racism. Healing this sore will take time: racism, he seems to suggest, is a systemic problem. Surgery, ironically, is the therapeutic he recommends for maintaining peace, "surgery at once the delicatest and nicest in modern history" is what is required for the races to live "side by side" and yet "subtly and silently separate." Surgery—precision cutting, careful splicing, and delicate suturing—is what it will take for a black man to live next to a white man peacefully.

Although the chapter "Of the Training of Black Men" is famous for its description of a "talented tenth" who must lead the race, it also includes a vivid description of black anger. How to keep "these millions from brooding over the wrongs of the past" is Du Bois's question. "The dangerously clear logic of the Negro's position will more and more loudly assert itself," and a "gospel of revolt and revenge" may gain ground.[2] Managing this kind of anger, according to Du Bois, requires surgery. And college-educated leaders. In calling for a talented tenth to lead the race, Du Bois was fully aware that African Americans were suffering not only political racism but also medical racism. In his 1899 study of Philadelphia, he devotes a full chapter to the high mortality rate among African Americans in the city, and he notes with some optimism a rise in the number of "young doctors, who have spared no pains to equip themselves at the best schools of the country."[3] In fact, as Du Bois surely knew, in 1903 black physicians were uniquely situated to perform a "social surgery at once the delicatest and nicest in modern history."

Between 1868 and 1904, eleven medical schools were founded to train African American physicians, with eight opening between 1882 and 1904, and the number of black physicians grew from 909 in 1890 to 3,885 in 1920.[4] The first black medical journal, *The Medical and Surgical Observer*, began publishing in 1892, and in 1895, at the Cotton States and International Exposition in Atlanta, black physicians founded the National Medical Association.[5] During these years, the health crisis among African Americans was severe, and death rates were so high in the 1870, 1880, and 1890 census reports that some analysts predicted black extinction by the year 2000.[6] Responding to this crisis was one goal of the NMA; another was the creation of institutions that would make medical training, professional careers, and community leadership real possibilities for black physicians. The NMA was explicit in its political work—it called upon physicians to serve their own and it founded the *Journal of the NMA* (now the longest continuously publishing African American journal) to air medical, professional, and political matters.[7]

Du Bois's use of surgical metaphors also points indirectly to the role of medicine in the discourse of race. Medicine played a major role in the somaticization of race in the nineteenth century, with some of the nation's leading medical scientists insisting that human races were distinct species.[8] Dr. Charles Caldwell, one of the first and most passionate proponents of polygenesis, was an esteemed physician and professor. He studied medicine under Dr. Benjamin Rush, received his degree from the University of Pennsylvania, practiced in Philadelphia, and later moved west where he founded two medical departments in Kentucky, one at Transylvania University in Lexington and one at the University of Louisville. Unlike his mentor, Rush, who believed that "the Black Color" is "derived from leprosy," Caldwell argued in *Thoughts on the Original Unity of the Human Race* (1830) that although the sun might "efface, in time, the fair tints of the European skin," it could not turn a European into an African.[9]

A few years later another esteemed medical scientist took up the question of race difference and distinct origins for each race. Dr. Samuel George Morton published two comparative anatomy treatises: *Crania Americana* in 1839 and *Crania Aegyptiaca* in 1844. In these works, replete with careful documentation of his quantitative work, Morton set out to document racial differences not on the surface of the body (skin, hair, and facial features), nor in more subjective characteristics (intelligence, temperament, character), but inside the body. In studying crania, Morton focused on a body part that seemed measurable (he calculated the volume of crania by filling them with pellets) and deeply meaningful. The size of a skull surely meant something about the capacity of the brain it contained. Morton's studies identified a norm and range of cranial capacity for each race, and he found, not surprisingly given the beliefs of the day, a hierarchy of size that put Caucasians at the top and Negroes at the bottom. Morton's credentials were impeccable, and he believed his scientific method was unbeholden to politics.[10] He received his medical degree from the University of Pennsylvania, practiced in Philadelphia, and taught anatomy at Pennsylvania Medical College. He published regularly, held weekly soirees, and was elected secretary of the Academy of Natural Sciences in 1831, a position that led him to correspond with experts across the world. Morton was a part of the medical elite; he studied at Edinburgh, and he was willing to reverse himself in public if empirical studies and clinical experiences proved him wrong. In an 1834 article on tuberculosis, he advocated bleeding, blistering, and lead. Then in 1837 he published a second article on tuberculosis, dismissing heroic methods as "utterly inadmissible."[11] Morton began collecting crania in 1820 to prepare anatomy lectures. By the 1830s, with the help of physicians, scientists, naval officers, and explorers, he had the largest collection in the world. Morton also traded crania with other physicians, including Dr. John Collins Warren, the eminent Boston surgeon who helped to found Massachusetts General Hospital (see Chapter 4) and performed the first operation under ether (see Chapter 1).

Polygenesis was not a theory that spread far or lasted long. It was not widely accepted in Europe, and after 1859 few polygenesists remained. But even as a common origin for all men became the dominant theory, medical scientists did not stop documenting anatomical and physiological differences. Although Morton's polygenesis theory was discredited, his numbers and method seemed like good science, and a good bit of medical science in the second half of the nineteenth century was dedicated to measuring bodies in an effort to document race differences. While biologists, natural historians, anthropologists, and sociologists all made contributions to anatomizing race, physicians probably played the most important role in racialized anthropometrical studies.

Government and institutional funds were often devoted to race studies. In 1861, for example, Lincoln called for the establishment of a U.S. Sanitary Commission. Among its tasks was an understanding of the physical and moral condition of troops (a concern after the Union's defeat at Bull Run). The commission went about this task by setting out to measure "the most important physical dimensions" of as many soldiers as possible.[12] Not surprisingly, the survey attended to race, and medical physicians received a questionnaire about the physical build and intelligence of Negro soldiers in particular.[13] Armed with an impressive array of tools—andrometer, spirometer, dynometer, facial angle, platform balance, and calipers—army doctors measured among other parts, the distance between nipples and between eyes; the distance from the finger tip to patella; the ratio of arm length to leg length; the circumference of the pelvis and chest. They also measured feet, necks, heels, and heads. Results, commentary, and updates appeared in *Popular Science Monthly* and *Science*, among other journals, and measurements tabulated according to race (white, full black, mixed race, and Indian) were published in 1869.

Having accumulated statistics on 15,900 soldiers, the Sanitary Commission sought to continue reliable measurements after the war by distributing its tools to colleges and research institutions. There was also a new effort to discover race differences inside the body. A surgeon in the U.S. Volunteers made a study of brain weight based on autopsies of 24 white and 381 black soldiers, all performed under the direction of the surgeon for the 11th Massachusetts Volunteers. And in the last decades of the century, the pages of medical journals included discussions of racial differences in musculature, disease susceptibility, vein size, pulmonary functioning, skeletal features, pain sensitivity, and other somatic "facts." Southern physicians and journals were particularly polemical in their race studies, but Northern physicians and journals concurred. Arguments against measurable differences between black and white bodies "were not to be found in the transactions and journals of the medical societies," one historian concluded after making an exhaustive survey of medical discussion of race between 1859 to 1900.[14]

The consensus was not only that the "Negro" was inferior, but that he was more fundamentally of the body—less civilized, less moral, less intellectual, and more driven by corporeal desires and appetites. The somaticization of African Americans meant they were less likely to receive anesthesia and more likely to be used for medical study after death. Between 1849–51, for example, 80 percent of all postmortems were performed on blacks according to the *Transylvania Medical Journal*. At Johns Hopkins between 1898 and 1904, two-thirds of the cadavers were black. Recent analysis of human remains found under the basement floor of the Medical College of Georgia suggest that during the years the college was open African Americans made up about 79 percent of the cadavers used by the college even though blacks accounted for only 34 percent of deaths in the region.[15]

The enormous amount of time, energy, and resources that medical professionals dedicated to documenting race as a measurable biological fact must be seen, in part, as a response to an unspoken anxiety about race as a valid category at all. The "lightening" of African Americans, the fact that some blacks could pass, and the well-known though rarely admitted history of miscegenation in the nation suggested that race might not be a stable somatic category. And yet visible race differences remained a popular expectation, distinguishing black from white was a national obsession by the end of the nineteenth century, and medicine contributed to a sense of race as a deep, organic fact permeating the entire physical body.[16]

Given this medical context—the concerted professional efforts of black physicians to increase their numbers and improve their opportunities and an anxiety in white medicine to document race as a stable, bounded category—it is not surprising that the physician earned attention from many writers, black and white, at the end of the nineteenth century as segregation became law and race violence was rampant. In fact, a flurry of novels and stories at the end of the century turn explicitly to the physician in an effort to understand what role medicine has played in the nation's race history and what role the black physician might play in the future. Appearing between 1891 and 1901, fiction by Victoria Earle Matthews, Katherine Davis Chapman Tillman, William Dean Howells, Francis Harper, and Charles Chesnutt features physicians, white and black, who live or work on the color line. Three of these— "Aunt Lindy," *The House Behind the Cedars*, and *An Imperative Duty*—place the white doctor in a racialized world. Three—*Iola Leroy*, *Beryl Weston*, and *The Marrow of Tradition*—consider what work Northern-trained black physicians might do in the South. All six texts write the physician into a national race history traversed by violence, sexual exploitation, hybridity, and desire.

In the 1889 short story "Aunt Lindy," black activist and writer Victoria Earle Matthews exposes the naivete of medicine's presumption that bodies exist outside history. Matthews was born in 1861 in Georgia and moved to New York when she was twelve. She wrote for a wide variety of black publications, and her work was often solicited by the best papers of the black and white press.[17] She became a popular speaker in the 1890s, served as chair of the executive board of what would become the National Association of Colored Women, and founded the White Rose Mission Industrial Association in New York City, the precursor to the National Urban League.[18] She was also a vocal proponent of race literature, giving a lecture on the subject in 1895 to the First Congress of Colored Women of the United States in Boston, Massachusetts. Although Matthews calls for a literature that will testify to the "intrinsic worth . . . breadth of mind . . . and boundless humanity" of blacks in this address, she was attentive in other writings to the role and power of anger in political activism. In an 1895 article for *Women's Era*, she calls upon women to "broadcast our contempt for any creature who can assail with viperous touch a subject that involves the mystery of hidden life,"[19] and in "Aunt Lindy," Matthews renders richly a black woman's contempt and rage.

Written when Matthews was twenty-eight, the story is ostensibly a tale of restraint and forgiveness. The action starts when a genial white physician fails to understand race history: "Old Dr. Bronson with his great heart and gentle, childlike manner" brings a white man injured in a fire to Aunt Lindy, an old black woman renowned for her nursing skills.[20] Oblivious to the complex relationships between blacks and whites in post-Civil War America, Dr. Bronson fails to realize that he has unwittingly brought into Aunt Lindy's house her former master, a man who whipped her and sold her children.

Aunt Lindy is a classic image of the mammy, although now she is asked to care not for the white man's children, but for the white man himself. Once she realizes that the unconscious stranger who lies in her house is Mars Jeems, she begins to tremble "like an animal at bay" and she prepares to "spring upon him, with clutching fingers extended" (15). The scene depends upon a familiar trope in which one who is wronged is given a serendipitous opportunity for revenge. Melville uses this trope in "Benito Cereno" when he elaborately describes Babo shaving Captain Delano to underscore the deadly reversal possible in every master/slave relationship, and Charles Chesnutt similarly imagines in "The Doll" a black barber shaving the man who destroyed his father. Matthews boldly imagines the nurse, a female figure we rarely suspect of murderous rage, with the same opportunity for revenge. Like Melville and Chesnutt, she probes the power of the slave, or freedman, not only to fight explicitly, as Frederick Douglass does against the overseer Covey, but subversively while serving the white man. And she underscores the somatic power of the black female who has long been intimate with white families, servicing white bodies as lover, mother, wet-nurse, and cook. Thus she undoes the gender and race codes that would portray the female black subject as a body without a will, and Aunt Lindy's readiness to pounce upon her former master bespeaks the history and rage stored within her body. The scene also testifies to a return of the nation's repressed slave past. Indeed, Matthews brings into representation that which the doctor cannot imagine—Aunt Lindy's past relations with whites, her memory of slavery, her physical rage, and her power.

Notably, the tale begins with a description of a conflagration that destroys half of Fort Valley, Georgia (the town of Matthews's birth), and it ends with a prayer meeting. Casting a "lurid glare all over the valley," the fire evokes race violence in the late nineteenth century (12), and it terrifies everyone—white and black. There are "shuddering groups of mute, frightened white faces" and "shrieking, prayerful, terror-stricken negroes" (12). The prayer meeting at the end of the tale suggests that religion may be an effective salve to the terrifying fires of race violence. As the negroes retreat to the woods, they pray to God, chanting in "doleful tones, as only the emotional Southern negro can chant or moan" (12). The prayers and songs ease the community's terror, and the "shouts of worshippers" and the "oldentime melody" rescue Aunt Lindy from her rage. When she hears the music, she runs out of her cabin, "as if impelled by unseen force," toward the camp meeting and away from the master and her rage (15).

The story's conclusion demonstrates the "boundless humanity" of Aunt Lindy and Negro spirituals, and it imagines Aunt Lindy's capacity for forgiveness and the healing power of black music. In the end, Mars Jeems recovers and secures a house for Aunt Lindy, making sure she never again "knew a sorrow," and, conveniently, her firstborn returns. But in the wildness of the fire, the music, and Aunt Lindy's "glaring eyeballs," Matthews notes a murderous rage that writers from Thomas Jefferson to W. E. B. Du Bois cautioned could be one possible consequence of a long history of racial oppression and injustice. To forget this anger is to be unconscious—like Aunt Lindy's former master—or oblivious, like Dr. Bronson. The doctor's careless act, expecting a black nurse to attend a white body, presumes that the white body is unmarked by history or race and that Aunt Lindy's racialized body is a biological fact and not an historical effect. Matthews's tale insists upon the entangled historicity of black and white bodies, and it registers the "burning contempt" that black women feel for those who "assail with viporous touch" not only their sexual purity but also their histories.

Whereas Doc Bronson is only naive and careless, the white physician in Charles Chesnutt's *The House Behind the Cedars* is arrogant, lewd, hypocritical, and an ugly representative of medical racism.[21] Much of Chesnutt's nonfiction writing, as well as his second novel, condemns explicitly the civil and political disenfranchisement of African Americans, but in *The House Behind the Cedars*, Chesnutt limns the psychology rather than the politics of race, and the central dispensary of white supremacist ideology is a doctor's office.

The novel, a cautionary tale of passing, makes the doctor instrumental in George Tryon's discovery that his betrothed, Rena Walden, has "polluted" blood.[22] As long as the lovers are in Clarence, where Rena lives with her brother, who is also passing for white, there is no danger of her secret being revealed. But when, unbeknownst to each other, the lovers both travel to Patesville, Rena's hometown, the secret will out.

Tryon goes to Patesville to collect on an old claim, and Rena to visit her sick mother. The heavily manipulated buildup to the moment of discovery features close calls, missed missives, and delayed messengers, all woven through with the presence of Dr. Green. When Tryon arrives in Patesville, he goes first to see the doctor, an old family friend. Finding the doctor out, Tryon settles into his chair and picks up a medical journal that explains the "special tendency of negro blood to revert to the African type" (71). Tryon then falls asleep and dreams of walking with his arm around Rena's waist. Later, after eating lunch with the doctor's family, Tryon accompanies Dr. Green to a pharmacy where the doctor sees Rena. Tryon, who is outside waiting in the doctor's carriage, is only slightly interested in seeing the woman the doctor has called a beautiful negro. But, as Rena exits, Tryon sees his betrothed, and realizing that she is, as Dr. Green knows her, a mulatta, his "love and yearning" turn to "anger and disgust" (95). That night he has a second dream, a nightmare influenced by the medical journal he read in Dr. Green's office, in which Rena reverts to a dark savage, slowly morphing from the beautiful white woman he loves into a terrifying, "hideous black hag" (98). "With agonized eyes he watched her beautiful tresses become mere wisps of coarse wool, wrapped around with dingy cotton strings; he saw her clear eyes grow bloodshot, her ivory teeth turn to unwholesome fangs" (98).

Medical theories of race atavism were popular and credible at this time, and in *The House Behind the Cedars*, Chesnutt reveals how such theories culpably deepen white anxiety about the taint of blackness. As long as Tryon believes Rena is white, he dreams of her beauty. He believes his fiancée is the embodiment of purity, and when asked by Dr. Green's wife about her, Tryon briefly reports that "she was a girl of no family" but feels a "decided satisfaction in being able to present for his future wife a clean bill of social health" (92). Purity is so essential to his love that he even finds contamination by proximity distasteful. While deep in his first dream, he hears a voice that mingles with Rena's image in his dream, and he is annoyed to learn from the doctor's much maligned black office assistant that it was the voice of "a young cullud 'oman" (72). Tryon feels a "touch of annoyance that a negro woman should have intruded herself into his dream" (72). This near meeting—it was, of course, Rena in the outer office leaving a message for the doctor—is repeated when Dr. Green crassly comments on the beauty of a patient and her daughter. Unaware that Dr. Green speaks of Molly Walden and her daughter Rena, Tryon finds the doctor's interest in negro beauty "tiresome." Since he is "engaged to be married to the most beautiful white woman on earth," he finds the mere mention of "a negro woman in the same room where he was thinking of Rena" to be "little short of profanation" (76). Finally, the second dream enacts the very profanation Tryon fears. Medical discourse, Chesnutt suggests, both writes race theories deep into the psyche of Southern men such as Tryon, and, ironically, makes whiteness a purity always under siege.

Dr. Green is Chesnutt's study of a white supremacist, and in the doctor's character Chesnutt traces the intertwining of arrogance, anxiety, and desire in supremacist ideology. Always eager to fortify his embattled cause, the doctor presses himself upon Tryon, presuming that this son of an old family friend is a "real Southern gentleman, whom one can invite into one's house without fear of contamination, and before whom one can express his feelings freely and be sure of perfect sympathy" (77). Fantasies of purity and superiority, Chesnutt notes, are seductive. At lunch the doctor offers a toast to the Anglo-Saxon race, and Tryon seconds the toast, feeling "in this company a thrill of that pleasure which accompanies conscious superiority" (92). Lest such toasts seem nothing more than gentlemanly racism, Chesnutt makes it clear that the thrill of superiority is heightened by titillating sexual taboos. Not only is Tryon's libidinous first dream made possible by the medical journal's confirmation of a visible distinction between white purity and black savagery, the doctor also boldly admits his lust for a body his profession defines as savage. In a meeting with Tryon and Judge Straight, Dr. Green presumes upon male camaraderie and crudely indulges the sexual license that racism authorizes. He crassly assesses Rena—"a beautiful woman, if she is a nigger"—and he admits that if it were twenty-five years ago, "I could not have answered for myself'" (75, 76). The implication is purposefully vague. Does he imagine a loving but never legalized relationship such as Rena's mother had with Rena's white father? Or, does he mean to justify rape as a response to dusky beauty? Although the novel is sensitive to the possibility of gentle love across the color line, it also, with Dr. Green's crudity, underscores the power differentials in interracial relationships.

The doctor's hypocrisy—his profession's theories of racial hierarchies and his own sexual fascination with racially contaminated bodies—bespeaks the tensions between politics and desire in the ideology of white supremacy. To reserve political power for whites after the Fifteenth Amendment, supremacist ideology branded the black race as inferior, the black intellect as servile, and even "the smallest trace of negro blood" as a contaminant (71). And yet, or perhaps because of this othering, the mulatta is a profoundly sexual figure. Exposing Dr. Green's participation in the sordid sexual underworld of white supremacy ideology, Chesnutt embarrasses the scientific and cultural prestige of the Southern white physician whose journals legitimize his political agenda and whose desires expose his fetish.

We have not done full justice to Dr. Green's role, however, if we stop here. Although the doctor viciously polices and crudely toys with a color line that Chesnutt and the legal spokesman in the novel deem arbitrary and oppressive, he rights a wrong when he unwittingly returns Rena to her mother. Although Rena's brother may pass without too much sacrifice, Rena's decision to pass means that the daughter abandons the mother. Her brother's departure may be sad but is, the novel suggests, acceptable. John Walden's decision to leave Patesville and set up as a white lawyer elsewhere is made possible by the kindest white man in the novel—Judge Archibald Straight. Rena's brother can recreate his legal identity with impunity, it seems, and law is not only the profession he takes up, it is the discourse that shapes his life. Rena, by contrast, is known by her body (not her legal mind or civil rights), and medicine is the discourse that shapes her life. As a woman, Rena is written so deeply into a domestic and somatic identity that leaving her mother becomes impossible. So, while John is freed from racism by Judge Straight, Rena is returned to her caste, "my own people," and her mother, by Dr. Green (121). In other words, the doctor is an agent of a gender ideology that Chesnutt seems to endorse—"A man may make a new place for himself—a woman is born and bound to hers" (121). That Chesnutt makes the ugliest white supremacist in the novel a physician is not surprising given medicine's role in legitimizing racism. That he makes the doctor an agent of Rena's return to her mother is more surprising, but perhaps it should not be. Chesnutt resists medicine's efforts to make race a biological category—there is nothing to define John as black or white, other than one-drop laws, which, as Judge Straight notes, vary from state to state.[23] But Chesnutt cannot imagine Rena apart from her female biology, a biology that ties her physically, emotionally, and morally to her mother. Either he simply could not see his way to thinking of Rena as he thinks of John, as an independent self-making individual, or he did not want to suggest that John's choice was an appropriate choice for a woman.

Much like *The House Behind the Cedars*, William Dean Howells's novel *An Imperative Duty* (1891) is devoted to unraveling and exposing the lineaments of racialist discourse in the mind of a white doctor. But unlike Chesnutt's novel, which explores the ugly arrogance and sordid desires produced by a medicalized race discourse, Howells's novel finds in medicine a forward-thinking scientific realism that might help the nation solve its race troubles. Like some of the *Atlantic* writers discussed in Chapter 4, Howells allied his realist literary project with science, and in *Dr. Breen's Practice* (see Chapter 5) Dr. Mulbridge's rough style is an antidote to melodrama and the feminization of medicine. With the death of his daughter, however, Howells's confidence in medicine and realism was shaken.

Winifred's complaints began in earnest in 1880, and over the next eight years her parents sought help from the homeopathic physician Dr.

Walter Wesselhoeft, the allopathic nerve specialist Dr. James Jackson Putnam, the rest cure inventor Dr. S. Weir Mitchell, and various gymnasiums and sanitariums.[24] When she died in 1889, at the age of twenty-six, Howells was devastated and bewildered. He continued to write, but he began to pay more attention to the shadowy world of the unconscious, or, in the words of a physician in Howells's 1904 novel *The Son of Royal Langbrith*, to those "cognitions which refuse anything more positive than intimation."[25]

In *The Shadow of a Dream*, serialized in *Harper's* a year after Winifred's death, a nerve specialist is valorized as a realist who authoritatively dismisses romantic and psychological explanations of illness. Dr. Wingate explains to those inclined to take an ill man's manic dreams as the origins of his physical ailment, "There's where you outsiders are apt to make your mistakes in these recondite cases. You want something dramatic—like what you've read of—and you're fond of supposing that man's trouble of mind caused his disease, when it was his disease caused his trouble of mind: the physical affected the moral, and not the moral the physical."[26] But Dr. Wingate is not merely a materialist. As the narrator explains:

I found in him, as I think one finds in most intelligent physicians, a sympathy for human suffering unclouded by sentiment, and a knowledge of human nature at once vast and accurate, which fascinated me far more than any forays of the imagination in that difficult region. Like physicians everywhere, he was less local in his feelings and interests than men of other professions.[27]

The Shadow of a Dream was, as one reviewer noted "a new departure in his art," a foray into "occult psychological forces," but Howells insisted that the "treatment [was] very realistic."[28] In fact, both Howells and the reviewer were right. Although the tale hints at a shadowy psychological world, it never undermines Dr. Wingate's somatic determinism, and although no physician was able to cure his daughter, Howells was unwilling to dethrone the physician. In his next work, *The Son of Royal Langbrith*, Howells envisions another doctor whose sensitivity to the psychological as well as his understanding of the body make him "a character of rare strength."[29]

In *An Imperative Duty*, however, the physician is not immune to melodrama, and Howells considers the physician's vulnerability to the "occult psychological forces" of race. When the novel opens, Dr. Olney has just returned from Italy, and he walks the streets of Boston, examining his countrymen, and in particular the Irish working class. He finds their voices "coarse and weak," their walk "awkward" and "undeveloped," and "their bearing apt to be aggressive."[30] Perhaps because of his own admitted dislike for the Irish, Howells lavishly details Olney's discomfort when an Irish waiter leans over him, stomach bulging against the doctor's chair, "a hairy paw" offering bread, and the waiter's hot breath "coming and going on the bald spot on his [Olney's] crown" (5).[31] Olney believes his assessment of the Irish race is professional, he looks at the Irish "scientifically," and he assesses the future potential of the race. By contrast, his response to African Americans is sentimental, but no less racist. A conversation with his soon-to-be love interest, Rhoda Aldgate, about the "soft voices" and "hopeful and happy" demeanor of African Americans is riddled with condescending generalizations about "them." Rhoda says, "I never see one of them without loving them" and declares about a black waiter: " And he's so sweet! I should like to *own* him, and keep him as long as he lived. Isn't it a shame that we can't *buy* them, Dr. Olney, as we used to do?" (19, 39). The doctor, for his part, confesses to feeling "a distinct pleasure whenever I've met any one of them" (19).[32]

Although Howells treats this delight in African Americans ironically, Olney's medical views on amalgamation are given more credence. Early in the novel, Olney patronizingly disabuses Rhoda's guardian—one of those "tiresome" women who "judge the world by the novels they have read"—of her interest in the "persistence of ancestral traits" (24, 6). He explains to Mrs. Meredith that atavism is "a notion that some writers rather like to toy with," concluding that although "it's very effective as a bit of drama," there "isn't a great deal of absolute fact there" (27, 26). Considering the case of the offspring of a white and an octoroon, he opines:

The chances of atavism, or reversion to the black great-great-great grandfather are so remote that they may be said hardly to exist at all. They are outside of the probabilities, and only on the verge of the possibilities. But it's so thrilling to consider such a possibility that people like to consider it. (27)

Of course, Olney's and Rhoda's sentimental paternalism and his scientific detachment crumble when they discover that the blackness they fetishize in others runs in Rhoda's veins. For Rhoda, the news induces an attack of feminine melodrama. For Olney, it tests his ability to live by his science. He may scoff at atavism and he may like the African American he sees on the streets, but can he love a girl descended from a slave?

Rhoda's response upon learning that her grandmother was a slave and a mistress to a white man is to head to a black neighborhood to confront the truth of her identity. Her nighttime sojourn is another version of Tryon's nightmare in Chesnutt's novel of the white beloved reverting to hideous savagery:

there was something in the way they turned their black eyes in their large disks of white upon her, like dogs, with a mute animal appeal in them. . . . She never

knew before how hideous they were, with their flat wide-nostriled noses, their
out-rolled thick lips, their mobile, bulging eyes set near together, their retreating
chins and foreheads, and their smooth, shining skin: they seemed burlesques of
humanity, worse than apes, because they were more like them. (58)

Although the race politics of the novel and the degrading images in this
passage have legitimately troubled commentators, this passage condemns
rather than condones the corporeality of blackness in the white imagination.[33] Rhoda believes that to be black is to be more "bodily," and she
takes the news of her mixed blood as a death sentence. Her white self is
no more, and she tells her aunt, "It's as if—as if—you were to come to a
perfectly well person, and tell them that they were going to die in half
an hour" (52). In an effort to come to terms with this news, she seeks a
bracing encounter with "her people." During her walk, Rhoda can see
nothing but bodies, and Howells traces how the disgust she feels for
these bodies becomes shame when she sees them as a reflection of her
own. Encountering a light-skinned negro girl, she thinks: "I am like her,
and my mother was darker, and my grandmother darker, and my great-
grander like a mulatto, and then it was a horrible old negress, a savage
stolen from Africa, where she had been a cannibal" (59).[34]

For Howells, Rhoda's walk on the wild side, a waking version of
Tryon's nightmare, is sheer melodramatic claptrap. And Dr. Olney is the
Howellsian spokesman for a literary and medical realism that will dispel
"thrilling" race fantasies of savage bodies in our midst, or in our past.
While Rhoda believes that she must "go down there and help them; try
to educate them, and elevate them; give my life to them," Olney rejects
this proposal as akin to Mrs. Meredith's melodramatic fantasies of race
atavism. In fact, what Rhoda feels as "tragedy" affects Olney "comically,"
and his "tender mockery" and deep "faithful love" rescue her from
impractical notions of duty (98). As Howells would have it, one-drop theories of race identity and titillating anxieties about race atavism are
swept away by a physician's love.[35] "Their love performed the effect of
common-sense for them, and in its purple light they saw the every-day
duties of life plain before them" (99). But as Kenneth W. Warren notes,
Olney's "commonsense response to Rhoda's proposed sacrifice quietly
slides questions of black education into the container of the romanti-
cized" (66). Through Olney, Howells recasts the important and urgent
question of black education (and the dedication that led whites and
blacks to become teachers in Reconstruction schools) as nothing more
than a silly, romantic, feminine effort at philanthropy.

Notably, Olney does not come by this "commonsense" response easily.
Upon first learning from Mrs. Meredith that Rhoda has a black ancestor,
Olney is very agitated. Although Howells calls upon medical science and

realism to counter the melodrama that taints race discourse, he is interested in the underworld of America's race fantasies and nightmares, and he is committed to uncovering the workings of race shame in white America. He acknowledges that white America's kinship with black bodies, slavery, and sexual relations outside marriage is more intimate than many might want to imagine, and he suggests that transcending racial disgust is not easy. In the most tangled, tortured paragraph in the novel, Howells traces the workings of race shame in Olney, who, upon learning of Rhoda's tainted ancestry,

> recoiled from the words in a turmoil of emotion for which there is no term but disgust. His disgust was profound and pervasive, and it did not fail, first of all, to involve the poor child herself. He found himself personally disliking the notion of her having negro blood in her veins: before he felt pity he felt repulsion; his own race instinct expressed itself in a merciless rejection of her beauty, her innocence, her helplessness because of her race. The impulse had to have its course; and then he mastered it. (31)

Although Dr. Olney may subscribe to an enlightened race ideology, Howells's Northern nerve specialist is not immune to racial disgust.

To understand Olney's immediate disgust to be the result of "race instinct" (a popular phrase at the end of the century), as Howells does, is to give it somatic legitimacy. Howells, it would seem, shared Olney's confidence in the superiority of whites. Although as a young man Howells was an ardent abolitionist (he wrote a poem about an abused octoroon and one about John Brown) and although he promoted writers such as Paul Laurence Dunbar and Charles Chesnutt and was a founding member of the National Association for the Advancement of Colored People, his fictional treatment of African Americans is sporadic and most often an occasion for examining a moment of psychological fragmentation that, for the most part, he rejected as melodramatic. As Henry B. Wonham notes, the black body in Howells's fiction is "obscurely drawn," and race is a "vehicle for dramatizing the eruption into consciousness of psychic states that ought to remain beyond the realist's representational grasp."[36]

Wonham and others have read Dr. Olney as a man who is struggling with incipient neurasthenia. His life is unsteady: his financial security has collapsed with the market, he finds his native land "bewilderingly strange," and the ethnic spectacle of the city in summer when those of his class have retired to the seashore leaves him nearly swooning. Olney's psychic instability peaks when he discovers that the woman he loves has negro blood. As Wonham suggests, in this novel blackness is a license for Howells to explore the destabilizing effects of desire across the color line. Olney loves what disgusts him, and Howells seeks both to render and then undo the power of "race instinct." The task is not easy. Although Howells gives Olney's revulsion no moral legitimacy and in the last lines of the novel he has Olney suggest to Rhoda that color prejudice is really class prejudice against those who have labored with their hands, his efforts to represent Olney mastering his initial disgust are convoluted. Indeed, Howells's awkward prose suggests that he himself struggled to master a disgust he might have sometimes understood as a natural race instinct.

Olney overcomes his race instinct by transforming his disgust for Rhoda's blackness into pity for her feminine helplessness.[37] To do this, he turns his residual disgust upon Mrs. Meredith. Presuming sexual violation is part of Rhoda's heritage, he becomes "red with shame for having heard what he had been told against his will" (31). To learn of Rhoda's negro ancestry is, given the history of race, to learn that her mother or grandmother or some other female ancestor was raped or consented to intimacy outside marriage. This sexual revelation embarrasses Olney and strips him of his professional equanimity: his "professional view . . . seemed to have lost all dignity" (31). Now his disgust focuses on sexual misconduct (rather than race), and he blames Mrs. Meredith for disclosing such a private matter (the sexual misconduct of one of Rhoda's ancestors). It "was atrocious for this old woman to have allowed her hypochondriacal anxieties to dabble with the mysteries of the young girl's future," he decides. Olney feels that "there was inherent outrage in the submission of such questions to one of the opposite sex," concluding that "there should be women to deal with" such matters (31). Thus, Howells traces, albeit awkwardly, how Olney cleanses his desire for a body that momentarily disgusts him by casting his disgust upon the woman who contaminates his love for Rhoda. Howells's half-conscious and muddled depiction of racism-become-misogyny is astute and disturbing. In the title of the novella, Howells reaches for familiar ground, the danger of melodramatic notions such as Mrs. Meredith thinking she must tell Rhoda of her heritage or Rhoda imagining she must go south to educate her people. But the novella offers a tellingly awkward record of medicine's and the nation's vulnerability to the disturbing history and discourse of race.

Ultimately, the novel makes blackness a tonic that the realist, serving as the nation's nerve specialist, can add to his armamentarium. After his daughter's death and with the advent of new literary modes, Howells began to doubt realism as an effective therapeutic against melodrama's dangerous appetite for psychological mayhem. The occult world of the mind seemed to merit further investigation and not just stonewalling. In *An Imperative Duty*, Howells dives briefly into the underworld of racialized desire but returns to the safe world of the everyday with a new tonic.

If science and realism cannot inoculate Dr. Olney from a nervousness brought on by discovering Boston is overrun with immigrants and blacks, then perhaps the best cure is for the overcivilized white man to marry a "dusky" beauty with a "tragic mask" and "gentle and gay" personality (13). Race and class ideologies were intimately woven into neurasthenic discourse: nervousness afflicted those who were sensitive and who lacked the hardiness of the nonwhite races and the working class. Olney's agitation when the novel opens is a sign of his sensitivity to the dangerously fluid world of democracy, and Howells implies that mixing the blood of the sensitive Anglo Saxon with a tincture of a hardier race might be a good remedy for Dr. Olney and the nation.[38]

Fiction featuring black physicians offers a different remedy for the nation's race maladies. On one level, the figure of a competent black physician challenges theories of negro inferiority and counters the flood of degrading images of childlike, degenerate, or lazy African Americans that filled the pages of the popular press.[39] On another level, fictional portraits of black physicians reflect the hope attached to the emergence of a class of black medical professionals. Although some black physicians at the turn of the century reported that they were not always called upon by their own people because of a lack of trust, many reported that they were accorded instant prestige within the black community.[40] Black physicians often assumed important roles in churches, social clubs, and service organizations, and many of them felt emboldened by a sense of obligation and possibility. In 1886 the first commencement valedictory address at Leonard Medical School in Raleigh, North Carolina, for example, was entitled "Medical Education as a Factor in the Elevation of the Colored Race." The valedictorian, Lawton A. Scruggs, called upon his classmates to be "pioneers of the medical profession of our race" and to teach the "practical and important truths" of health.[41] Black physicians also spoke out against racism. In an 1895 Emancipation Day speech, Luther Burbridge spoke of the racism black physicians encountered in the South, and in his work *The Philadelphia Negro: A Social Study*, W. E. B. Du Bois noted that black physicians were denied access to most white hospitals, and thus to the professional training possible only in well-equipped and well-funded facilities. Determined to get training and professional opportunities, black physicians started their own societies as well as their own hospitals and schools. By 1914 there were, in addition to the NMA, twenty-three state or regional societies and seventeen city societies.[42]

The black physician in fiction also promises something more than intellectual achievement, middle-class success, community leadership, and good health care for his own people. He represents an expertise that subverts the master's corporeal power, or in Houston Baker's term, he figures a "mastery of form." Claiming expertise in a medical world dominated by whites, the black physician is a thorn in the white man's side. He conforms to normative bourgeois codes, he seizes signs of professional success usually denied the black man, and he masters a somatic discourse that empowers him to help those bodies, like his own, that have been violated by the master. Thus he stands as a direct challenge to white supremacy. As Baker notes, "The mastery of form conceals, disguises, floats like a trickster butterfly in order to sting like a bee."[43] Two of the four fictional portraits I discuss below underscore the power of the black physician to sting the white man.

Rebecca Harding Davis, always alert to the nuances of class, gender, and race issues, took up the topic of the black physician just as blacks began to enter the profession in the 1860s. Serialized in *Scribner's* 1867, *Waiting for the Verdict* probes the psyche of a mulatto physician who establishes a thriving practice in Philadelphia because he can pass for white. For the most part, though not completely, Davis avoids race melodrama. Only on occasion does the doctor's "negro blood" threaten to become "visible." An air of mystery hovers around the doctor, but it is not caused by a physical identity incompletely concealed. Davis's portrait focuses on the psychology of passing rather than the inevitable revelation of the presumed physiological "facts" of race. She is more interested in the psychological consequences of his lie than in outing some indelible feature of his racial identity. Like most tales of passing, this one ends with the "truth" being told. Race, even when invisible, is still a fact for Davis, and yet the novel suggests that there is nothing about the doctor to make him biologically black. Davis is aware of notions of "race instinct." When Dr. Broderip's beloved learns that he is black, she shivers and recoils, and the doctor concludes that the "instinct that held the races apart was unconquerable." But the novel discredits this reaction. Doctor Broderip is renowned as a surgeon, and Davis gives no account of patients recoiling from his touch. In this the novel is subtly daring: a black surgeon cutting white bodies violates a basic creed of racism that prohibits blacks from touching white bodies. But tenderness towards all bodies, and compassion for all mortals is what Davis called for as the Civil War came to an end. The novel probes insistently the question of what will happen with the end of slavery, and it ends in the liminal space of waiting: "Broderip, in his grave yonder, has not saved his people from their balked, incomplete lives. The country which he and they have served is still silent, while they stand waiting its verdict."[44]

By the end of the century, many African Americans were still waiting for the country's verdict, but they were not only waiting. They were also taking matters into their own hands. During the Civil War this had meant joining black regiments, as Dr. Broderip does. After the collapse of Reconstruction, this meant various efforts often summed up in the phrase "racial uplift." Before emancipation, uplift referred to the group's struggle for freedom, and it was often articulated in broad, egalitarian terms. By the 1890s, after blacks had lost power in Congress and in local governments across the South, the term had come to mean the improvement of the degraded masses with the help of the civilized elite.[45] The term and the writers associated with it (including the three writers I will consider next) have not always faired well in post-1960s criticism. Uplift has, until recently, been understood as nothing more than accommodationist politics. But I want to suggest that when the vision of uplift includes leadership by black physicians, the notion is not only cultural uplift but also care of the black body, the site of the nation's ugliest racism.

In Katherine Davis Chapman Tillman's 1893 "Beryl Weston's Ambition," a serialized novella for the *A. M. E. Church Review*, the doctor bridges the gap between domestic duty and lofty ambition and between competing programs for uplift. Although in other works Tillman takes on issues such as black disenfranchisement, urban temptations, dialect, and white duplicity, here she imagines what an educated physician can do in an all-black rural community. Dr. Norman Warren's slave birth and separation from his mother at a tender age mark him as a "true" black—a Southern, Booker T. Washington Negro. But an elite, post-Civil War Northern education funded by his white mistress and a medical education in England also suggest he is one of Du Bois's talented tenth. The doctor makes no show of his European experience when he returns to the South to search for his mother, an archetypal quest in post-Reconstruction fiction, but there are hints of his worldly experience. Life abroad shapes his initial reactions to the South, and he notes that "he never saw as much rank prejudice" during his fifteen years in England as he "witnessed during one day spent in the city of New Orleans."[46] But in the end, the "princely" and "rugged" doctor casts down his bucket where he is and marries the heroine, Beryl Weston, who is herself a mixed product of a dainty, former "lady's maid" and an "uncouth" freedman who, with Washingtonian "pluck and thrift," has acquired a "snug bank account" and acres of "rich land" (212–13).

By the end of this allegory of uplift, each character earns an appropriate destiny. An Oberlin-educated, "womanish" minister who initially rejects emigration is headed to Africa with his indolent and gay bride to serve "those who sit in great darkness," work that will surely temper his and his wife's love of finery (246). A "burdened and disfigured, discontented and full of despair" servant girl becomes an artist so that she can record in her art the dark truths of poverty and racism registered in her body (224–25). At the center of the final tableaux reigns the doctor, who has a "neat little office on the principal street," and his wife Beryl, who is a "teacher of modern languages" at "one of the leading Afro-American colleges in the United States" (246).

It is not surprising that Tillman rests her optimistic and conciliatory vision upon the figure of the doctor. He embodies highbrow learning and practical knowledge. At his side, Beryl learns the sentimental heroine's lesson that she must set aside selfish ambitions for broader ideals— domestic duties and race uplift. The doctor also wins the hearts and respect of others. He is "fairly idolized" by the villagers, he has "many Anglo-Saxon patients as well as Afro-American ones," and he is "frequently called in to consult with the other leading physicians of the place" (231). Together Beryl and the doctor represent an attractive amalgamation of several models for racial uplift, including liberal education, women's economic self-sufficiency, and agricultural success. They stay in the South, uplift the community with the financial support of her father's agricultural self-reliance, teach the cultural lessons they have learned at elite institutions, and "are everywhere recognized as leaders in every movement for the advancement of their own oppressed race" (246).

There may not be much sting to the uplift that Beryl and her doctor husband offer, but in finding a promising future for every character, Tillman binds together all African Americans, suggesting that while some might be leaders, all, regardless of class or history, are part of a family that must remain devoted to each other. A sense of the elite's ties to the masses was an important democratizing element in some uplift rhetoric, and it is particularly clear in Tillman's story that when Beryl learns to accept the ugly servant girl, who offends her snobbish preference for refined people and things, she is learning an important democratic lesson. And by giving the doctor roots in slavery (class hierarchies often made free-issue blacks superior to freedmen), Tillman makes it clear that anyone might rise and the elite must always remember that their destiny is inseparable from that of the masses.[47]

Frances Harper's novel, *Iola Leroy*, ends with a similar image: the black heroine and her physician husband are headed south to bring the hallmarks of uplift—"literacy, bourgeois sensibility, and standard English diction"—to a "dialect-speaking 'Negro' folk."[48] But in *Iola Leroy*, Harper's project is not only uplift. She turns to medicine not only as a profession that will produce race leaders with taste, expertise, and good English, but also as a challenge to the entrenchment of racism in science and as a promise of love and care for black bodies. When Harper's Dr. Latimer enters late in the novel, he directly challenges racist medicine. He has a sting as sharp as Baker's trickster bee when he dupes and then exposes the folly of a white Southern physician who believes that his "practiced" eye can see even the slightest "taint of blood."[49] He also wins the beautiful Iola, who has been courted throughout the novel by a gallant white Northern physician. In short, he seizes the terms and object of medical science. Moreover, with his expertise, gained at white institutions, and his mulatta bride, he heads South where he may bring to those bodies demonized and violated a care that has been figured in the first two-thirds of the novel in the love of the mother and the attention of the nurse.

Before the black physician enters, Harper first considers and rejects the claims of the white physician in a plot that would seem to be a revision of Howells's *Imperative Duty*. Published a year after *An Imperative Duty* came out in book form, *Iola Leroy* also tells the story of a liberal white physician who proposes to a beautiful mulatto who has only recently discovered her racial heritage. But unlike Howells, Harper neither endows her heroine's physiognomy with telling race traits—her "eyes are as blue and complexion as white" as her suitor's—nor settles her happily in a white world of wealth and leisure (232). Thus Harper undermines the myth of race visibility that Howells indulges.[50] For Harper, the white physician's marriage proposal is inadequate; it is a feeble answer to the history of oppression, exile, and violence that the novel richly represents as the inheritance of all African Americans. Harper, like Matthews, is very attentive to the burden of history, and she rewrites the stereotype of the tragic mulatta by rooting her in the history of slavery, the Civil War, and Reconstruction. Given this history, the mulatta cannot marry a white physician and run off to Italy. Instead, she marries a black physician and heads South, where she and her husband take up the cause of their people. Like Tillman's physician and wife, Iola and Dr. Latimer are, at the end of the novel, reported to be active in "every reform movement for the benefit of the community" (279). In other words, while both Howells and Harper turn to the physician as one who offers a cure for the nation's race ills, Howells uses a white physician to articulate a masculinized and medicalized discourse of literary realism that will rescue the nation from race melodrama. Harper, by contrast, depends upon a black physician who knows first hand the trials of slavery to attend those bodies that have suffered physical degradation and the stigma of racialization.

It is important to note that in Howells's novel when Olney is initially unnerved by the news of Rhoda's ancestry, Howells may be suggesting that the white doctor is overwhelmed by the nation's violent race history as embodied in Rhoda. But ultimately Howells imagines Olney regaining his equanimity and mastering all that the mulatta's body represents by writing her out of race history (she is hardly black, he insists) and into a gender discourse in which she needs his protection and love. In

Harper's representation of the liberal white physician, by contrast, the white man is enfolded in a race story he cannot master or rewrite.

Dr. Gresham is as liberal in his race thinking as Howell's nerve specialist—he is eager to marry Iola despite her race heritage, and he, like Olney, believes that "the final solution" of the race question "will be the absorption of the negro into our race" (228). But for Harper, the "pity" that "stirred Dr. Gresham's heart" and his prediction of some future race erasure through amalgamation is no solution to the current needs of Southern blacks. Harper gently but firmly rejects the gender politics that would sentimentalize race oppression. As Dr. Olney is moved by Rhoda's "helplessness because of her race," so Dr. Gresham sentimentalizes Iola's "misfortunes" (110).

To him the negro was a picturesque being, over whose woes he had wept when a child, and whose wrongs he was ready to redress when a man. But when he saw a lovely girl who had been rescued by the commander of the post from the clutches of slavery, all the manhood and chivalry in his nature arose in her behalf, and he was ready to lay on the altar of her heart his first grand and over-mastering love. (110)

Gresham's chivalric love is genuine, and Harper often calls it noble, but it does not offer Iola the fullest possibilities for a life devoted to what Harper identified in her one short story as the noblest calling—"the dignity of reality."[51] In "The Two Offers" (1859), Harper demonstrates her talent for sentimental fiction, but she juxtaposes lush descriptions of love, loss, and death with a starker image of a life devoted to "the good, the true and right" (427).[52] Dr. Gresham, for all his personal commitment to good work in medicine and race relations, offers Iola only the sentimental world of a husband's undying devotion. In "The Two Offers," Harper notes the dangers for women who build their lives on such husbandly promises. In *Iola Leroy*, Harper rewrites the plot of her earlier story, a tale about women's choices with no mention of race, as a story in which women's choices are profoundly shaped by race. Iola can choose to replicate her mother's choice—marry a white man who promises love and comfort—or she can choose a life committed to race work. In fact, the novel revises the story's warning. In "The Two Offers," when the husband falls into philandering and leaves his wife, she dies from unhappiness. When Iola's father dies, Iola and her mother are remanded into slavery by his relatives. In both, a husband's protection is not reliable. But in the story the consequence is fatal unhappiness, and a sentimental sense of the power of unhappiness makes death by unhappiness possible. In the novel, the consequence of losing a husband's protection is thoroughly historicized: slavery rather than death by unhappiness is the result.

Although Dr. Gresham's love provides a sentimental interest, his promise of ease and wealth stands in stark contrast to the race realities the novel foregrounds. His first proposal inspires not an immediate answer but four chapters that fill in Iola's history—a happy childhood that teeters precariously upon her mother's race secret, a brief stint at a Northern school, and the collapse of her privileged life when she is identified as black. This new black identity, Harper makes clear, is a profoundly disenfranchised sexual identity. The lawyer hired to bring Iola back to the South grabs her while she is asleep and presses a "burning kiss" upon her (103), and the man who buys her means "to break her in" and drag her down to his own low level of sin and shame (38, 39). Although Iola tells her story to Dr. Gresham, he fails to understand that the "fiery ordeal" of racialization cannot be undone by his assertion that "Your complexion is as fair as mine" (116). His love cannot make her white again. Despite all his liberal intentions, he is not free of what Robyn Wiegman calls "epidermal hierarchy." When Iola asks how he might respond if their child should "show unmistakable signs of color" (117), he looks away and then flushes with embarrassment at the realization that his own race tolerance might not extend to his own offspring should it visibly reveal Iola's history.

At this moment, Dr. Gresham admits the difficulty of loving a dark body, even if it were his own child. Dr. Gresham also assumes that his love is more compelling than the familial love Iola gets from her dark relatives. His marriage proposal is based on a sense that his cleansing white love would, as amalgamation would for the nation, wash away the stain of the national sin made visible in the dark body. Amalgamation, Harper warns and Howells hopes, will erase the past. For Harper, amalgamation denies the mother. Thus in a passionate speech Iola ends Dr. Gresham's entreaties by declaring her devotion to her mother:

I will relieve you from all embarrassment by simply saying I cannot be your wife. When the war is over I intend to search the country for my mother. Doctor, were you to give me a palace-like home, with velvet carpets to hush my tread, and magnificence to surround my way, I should miss her voice amid all other tones, her presence amid every scene. Oh, you do not know how hungry my heart is for my mother! (118)

Oblivious to the significance of the mother, Dr. Gresham is also deaf to the political call that comes from the mother to her black sons and daughters to care for their brethren. When Dr. Gresham and Iola meet again after the war his liberal politics are still noble. In a conversation with Iola, her mother, and her brother about the nation's race troubles, he rightly identifies the "problem with the nation" not as what should be done "with the negro" but as what must be done to curb "the reckless, lawless white men who murder, lynch, and burn their fellow-citizens" (217). But Harper carefully notes that even a liberal, well-intentioned man may not be free from an unconscious presumption of race hierarchy. Dr. Gresham acknowledges that each race has had an impact on the other: white men "fettered" black men and thus "cramped" their own souls. The negro, for his part, came from "the heathenism of Africa" and brought a "stream of barbaric blood" into the "early civilization" of the "young colonies" of the South. The negro, he concludes with a note of Northern pride and a touch of white supremacist rhetoric, has played a part in making the South less civilized; the negro "has laid his hands on our Southern civilization and helped mould its character" (217).

Iola's mother gives a powerful rebuttal to his argument when she suggests that the impact of the Negro's contribution to the South is not savagery but maternal kindness. She explains that "the colored nurse could not nestle her master's child in her arms, hold up his baby footsteps on their floors, and walk with him through the impressible and formative period of his young life without leaving upon him the impress of her hand" (217). Black women, Iola's mother points out, have not taught savage ways to the masters' children. They have showered them with tender care. In fact, the novel makes black women's maternal love visible, and, in an ironic recasting of the old slave law that requires the child to assume the racial identity of its mother, it champions loyalty to the mother.

"Stand by mamma" are Iola's sister's last words, and when Iola rejects Dr. Gresham, she does so with reference to her mother and her grandmother. She refuses his first offer by explaining that she has decided not to marry until she finds her mother. Her second refusal echoes her first. She explains, "My dear grandmother is one of the excellent of the earth, and we all love her too much to ignore our relationship with her" (235). Iola's choice is not only about dedication to her mother; it is also a political choice. And in linking the two, Harper makes the mother the font of political identity and action. Dr. Gresham cannot understand this because white men, including white physicians, who have not lived race, cannot fathom the richly complex psychology of living in a marked body. As Dr. Latimer explains, "it seems almost impossible for a white man to put himself completely in our place. No man can feel the iron which enters another man's soul" (263). Nor can he know the political allegiance born of a mother's love.

Dr. Gresham's counterpart, the black Dr. Latimer, does, of course, understand race and thus is a fitting partner for Iola. Like Iola and her brother, Dr. Latimer is fair and blue-eyed. But, unlike John in *House Behind the Cedars*, he refuses "to forsake his mother's people" (238). Born to a slave woman who after the war "went out into the wide world to seek a living for herself and her child," he gains an elite medical education at the "University of P——" (239), presumably a reference to the University of Pennsylvania, where the first African American was admitted in 1879 and graduated in 1882.[53] Like Iola, he rejects an offer of comfort that entails a denial of his maternal heritage. His paternal grandmother invites him to join her family, but he is "a man of too much sterling worth" to deny his mother in exchange for "the richest advantages his grandmother could bestow" (240). Thus Harper imagines a race identity that is not somatic and yet is profoundly loyal to the maternal body.

In a scene that gathers together three doctors, Harper explicitly refutes the "economy of visibility" that makes race a corporeal rather than a political identity. Drs. Gresham, Latimer, and Latrobe (a Southern white supremacist) meet each other at a medical conference. Like the sting that Houston Baker associates with the trickster, Dr. Latimer fools Latrobe, a man who believes he can "detect the presence of negro blood when all physical traces had disappeared" (239). In an otherwise high-toned novel infused with Christian fervor for good works, Latimer's trick (he briefly passes for white and thus humiliates Latrobe) is a noteworthy exception to the novel's commitment to earnest truth telling. In this scene, Harper imagines a well-educated physician playing the role of trickster to make his point. In fact, coming at the end of the novel, Dr. Latimer's trick is a reminder of the novel's opening scene in which we hear the language tricks that slaves use to pass information among themselves about the progress of the war. As Dr. Latimer's body cannot be read by medical science as black, so the language of the slaves cannot be understood by the masters.

In addition to challenging the myth of race visibility, Harper also challenges the theory of race instinct. "Race disgust," as Howells termed it in *An Imperative Duty*, was often considered an innate, biological response. In "Hybridity in Animals, Considered in Reference to the Question of the Unity of the Human Species," an essay published in the *American Journal of Sciences and Arts*, Samuel Morton noted a natural repugnance that worked against mixing. Race mixing, many believed, would lead to degenerate individuals, and Morton postulated a natural disgust across race lines as nature's way of reducing the weakening of a species. For Howells, Dr. Olney's race disgust is, it seems, almost a biological response, though it is a response he can master and that will fade as race differences disappear with amalgamation. For Harper, by contrast, race disgust is a false sentiment best corrected within the family circle because children naturally love their mother. As Iola's brother, Henry, a young man who has grown up white, explains when he decides to join a black regiment, "love for my mother overcame all repugnance" (203).

Undoing repugnance for black bodies is an important part of Harper's novel, and the first third of the novel culminates in a nursing triangle that brings together three historically imbricated black bodies—the mulatta; the male, light-skinned, educated house slave; and the dark, illiterate field slave. Over the course of several scenes, Iola, Robert, and Tom attend to each other, nursing, kissing, and calling out to each other. In war, and in the great battle for freedom, bodies variously marked by history and racialist identity politics provide intimate corporeal care and love for one another.[54] These are bodies written out of stereotypes and into loving, physical intimacy.

In the second third of the novel, the quest for the mother is figured as a quest for the kind of love and care that Iola, Robert, and Tom give to each other. The mother is a reminder of a child's race-free years. The mother-child relationship is forged before the child learns she is black, and the scene of race discovery has been figured by writers from Frank Webb to Zora Neale Hurston as a discovery that separates the child both from her body and from the mother (or grandmother). Du Bois calls the resulting psychology "double consciousness." The "Negro" is born into a world "which yields no true self-consciousness, but only lets him see himself through the revelation of the other world. It is a peculiar sensation, this double-consciousness, this sense of always looking at one's self through the eyes of others, of measuring one's soul by the tape of the world that looks on in amused contempt and pity."[55] Frantz Fanon similarly notes the alienation of watching one's self and one's body through the gaze of the colonizer. The mother, according to Harper, can heal this wound. When Robert is reunited with his mother, he remembers that she used to "steal out at night to see me, fold me in her arms, and then steal back to her work" (181–82). In this memory and in the nursing scenes earlier in the novel, the black body is made visible not as spectacle. Rather, the black body is loved and nursed. The final third of the novel imagines the institutionalization of care and love for black bodies in the work of the newly professionalized black physician. Dr. Latimer will provide loving and scientific care for the bodies of his people.

In *The Marrow of Tradition*, Charles Chesnutt also envisions the black physician as an agent of moral and cultural uplift and as a man who will improve the health of his people. But the novel picks up where Harper's leaves off, and as a result it is a darker work. While her novel ends optimistically with the black physician heading south, Chesnutt's novel begins with the doctor arriving in the South and immediately encountering the ugly world of Southern racism. Working in the South, according to Chesnutt, is not as easy as Harper or Tillman envision in their rosy endings. For Chesnutt, cheery theories of race uplift ignore political realities, and his novel traces the political education of a naive physician, Dr. Miller. The novel vividly chronicles the vast sore of racism as manifested in the 1898 Wilmington riot, and ends, enigmatically, as a black doctor is headed upstairs to perform a "delicate operation"—a tracheotomy—on the son of riot provocateur Major Carteret.[56] The act seems unimaginable for two reasons. One, Dr. Miller's son has been killed in the riot, "struck down," he tells Carteret, "as much by your hand as though you had held the weapon with which his life was taken!" (320). In fact, Carteret admits that "pure, elemental justice" permits Dr. Miller to withhold his medical services (321). Two, the act will violate a central tenet of race relations: "From time immemorial it had been bred in the Southern white consciousness, and in the negro consciousness, for that matter, that the person of a white man was sacred from the touch of a negro" (303). The novel ends with the physician on the stairs because the medical act he goes to perform—a black man cutting a white body in order to heal it—exists on the boundary of what is imaginable, that place, according to Homi Bhabha, "from which something begins."[57]

To understand fully the role Chesnutt imagines for the black physician, we must recognize the role of the black professional historically. At the turn of the century, the number and power of black professionals troubled white supremacists. In Wilmington, before the riot, blacks played a significant role in the economic and social structures of the city as three of ten aldermen, one of three on the school committee, and half the city's policemen were black. There were black professionals, including lawyers, judges, sanitation officers, and doctors, and the health board was all black.[58] These professionals were regularly attacked in the North Carolina press and, after the riot, black community leaders fled or were banished. For example, Thomas Miller, a wealthy black real estate broker, and several others were held in jail and then escorted past a jeering crowd to a north-bound train.[59] In the white supremacist's calculus, each black official or professional represented a measurable loss of white power. Unlike Du Bois's cautious hope of living side-by-side amid peace and order, Wilmington Democrats proposed to disenfranchise blacks. Alfred Moore Waddell, the white supremacist installed as mayor after the riot, warned that "we will never surrender to a ragged raffle of negroes, even if we have to choke the Cape Fear River with carcasses."[60]

While there is only hearsay evidence that the river was in fact choked with carcasses after the Wilmington massacre (a more accurate term than riot, according to historians and Chesnutt), at least ten and perhaps as many as a hundred died. For Chesnutt, the violence was deeply disturbing. In a letter to Walter Hines Page posted the day after the massacre, he writes, "I am deeply concerned and very much depressed at the condition of affairs in North Carolina. . . . I find myself obliged to revise some of my judgments. . . . It is an outbreak of pure, malignant and altogether indefensible race prejudice, which makes me feel personally humiliated."[61] In a biography of her father, Helen Chesnutt notes that he "had been very much affected by the savage race riots."[62] Just two months after the massacre he imagined writing a novel based on the events. In a notebook entry dated January 1900, Chesnutt writes, "Doctor. Settled South serving his people. Ruined by a riot."[63] In the novel, Chesnutt details how race violence could destroy a determined, educated, idealistic professional man, but he also suggests that such violence might provide an important political education for Du Bois's talented tenth.

On one level, Dr. Miller is a symbol of the achievements of black physicians by the turn of the century. Like his real world counterparts who founded hospitals in Atlanta, Montgomery, Durham, Clarksville, Selma, and Lexington in the 1890s, Dr. Miller founds a hospital, and like many black physicians in the 1890s, he starts a training school for Negro nurses. Like Dr. Miles V. Lynk, who mortgaged part of his home to found the Medical Department of the University of West Tennessee, Dr. Miller uses part of his own inheritance to fund his hospital.[64] Dr. Miller is also like many Northern-trained black physicians who were committed to working in the South. The narrator notes, "He had been strongly tempted to leave the South. . . . But his people had needed him" (51). Indeed, without hospitals such as Dr. Miller's, black patients and physicians often had no access to hospitals at all, and the need for black physicians was acute. Although the national ratio in 1910 was one physician for 684 people, segregated health care made this ratio meaningless for African Americans. In 1910, there was only one black physician for 2883 African Americans, despite the fourfold increase in black physicians in the previous twenty years.[65] Chesnutt himself considered studying medicine, noting in an 1875 journal entry that he had "conversed with several M.D.'s on the subject of studying Medicine" and that the "best of the whole lot advised me to go to a Medical College."[66]

On another level, Dr. Miller serves to counter theories of black degeneracy. As an example of what a black man can achieve, Dr. Miller's education and professional success challenge theories of the innate inferiority of blacks and mulattos. His training in Vienna and Paris puts him among America's elite physicians, and Dr. Burns, "a distinguished specialist of national reputation," admires "his evident talent" and notes he is "a surgeon of unusual skill" (50, 70). Even Southern physicians acknowledge his competence: they receive Dr. Miller "with a cordiality generally frank, and in no case much reserved." The narrator admits the economic factor in their cordiality—the "colored population of the city was large, but in the main poor, and the white physicians were not unwilling to share this unprofitable practice"—but concludes that they consider the "colored doctor worthy of confidence" (64). In short, Dr. Miller is an antidote to the outpouring of black caricatures in magazines, newspapers, song sheets, and memorabilia and to the racist social Darwinism of the times that was so compelling and rampant, according to Henry Louis Gates, that "all of black intellectual thought between 1800 and 1930 can be read as a complex response to it."[67]

Acknowledging Dr. Miller's skill is, of course, precisely what Carteret refuses to do early in the novel but must do later when his son needs help and the riot has led all the white physicians to flee the town. Twenty years earlier Chesnutt was naively optimistic about the power of talent and achievements to elicit respect across the color line. In 1879 in a letter he submitted for publication, he declares, "I believe that the American People will recognize worth[,] ability or talent, whenever it shows itself, and that as the colored people, as a group, show themselves worthy of respect and recognition, the old prejudice will vanish, or wear away, and the *Colored Man* in America will be considered, not as a separate race, not as a stranger and a pariah, but as a friend and brother."[68] In 1900, Chesnutt was no longer so optimistic, and *The Marrow of Tradition* is, in part, a record of the violence whites were willing to use to maintain the status quo.

At the familial level, Chesnutt calls upon whites to acknowledge their blood ties with blacks when he makes Carteret's wife the half-sister of Dr. Miller's wife. He also chronicles just hard this can be for whites. As Samira Kawash notes, Olivia Carteret finds it almost impossible to recognize Janet Miller as her sister because to do so is to contaminate her own white identity and admit her culpability in the wrong done to Janet.[69] Nationally, to recognize the black man's "ability or talent" would be to give the lie to white supremacy and to make black disenfranchisement intolerable. Upon acknowledging Dr. Miller's skill, Carteret must relinquish "certain principles," including the one that "forbids the recognition of the negro as a social equal" (71). For Carteret, "Negro citizenship was a grotesque farce—Sambo and Dina raised from the kitchen to the cabinet were a spectacle to make the gods laugh." But when he must turn to Dr. Miller for his skills as a surgeon, he can no longer maintain that the negro must be confined "to that inferior condition for which nature had evidently designed him" (79).

Dr. Miller is also a response to racist scientific theories of black degeneracy because his medical work speaks directly to contemporary debates about black morbidity and mortality rates. In these years, some cities reported death rates twice as high for blacks as for whites, and according to the 1890 national census, the death rate per 1000 was 27.4 for blacks, 19.5 for whites.[70] In *Race Traits and Tendencies of the American Negro* (1896), Frederick L. Hoffman offered statistical support for popular racist interpretations of these numbers. German-born, and thus presumed to offer an outsider's impartiality, Hoffman drew upon the 1890 census report to prove that with emancipation the "tendency of the race had been downward" and that the final result would be "the extinction of the race." According to Hoffman, a high rate of sickness and death among blacks was the result of "inferior organisms and constitutional weaknesses," and "an immense amount of immorality which is a race trait" was the cause of high rates of scrofula, syphilis, and even consumption.[71] A landmark statistical analysis of African American mortality, Hoffman's *Race Traits and Tendencies of the American Negro* was published by the prestigious American Economic Association, and his statistics and conclusions were quickly endorsed by others, including the chief statistician of the U.S. Census Bureau.

Although arguments against racist science from within science were not yet common in the 1890s, Dr. Kelly Miller of Howard University countered with a review of Hoffman's work. Published by the newly founded American Negro Academy, an intellectual forum dedicated, in part, to countering scientific racism, Miller's review noted errors in Hoffman's work and refuted his thesis by using census data from various cities that recorded an increase in the African American population. Miller also used morbidity rates for working-class white Europeans to suggest that high black morbidity and mortality was a result not of biology but of social conditions. In particular, Miller cited the role of medicine: fifty percent of Negro children who died under the age of five had never seen a doctor.[72] In the context of this debate, Chesnutt's physician (who shares, perhaps not coincidentally, Kelly Miller's last name) underscores Professor Miller's argument for the role that medicine must play in the future of African American political and physical health.

In fact, like Professor Miller, Chesnutt posits that the physical well-being of the black body is a political matter, a lesson Chesnutt's physician learns during the course of the novel. Early in the novel, Dr. Miller refuses to accept a race identity mired in the past. Although he is repeatedly humiliated, for example, when he is banished to the Coloreds Only car on his journey south and subjected to tobacco smoke and spit when McBane, the son of an overseer, uses the Colored car for his spittoon, he insists, "I'll reach my destination just as surely in the other car" (55). Here, Chesnutt nostalgically records and relinquishes his own youthful optimism about the power of talent and hard work to earn its just rewards. Dr. Miller's optimism, Chesnutt makes clear, is a class privilege. His humiliation is minor compared to what Josh Green, Miller's shadowy double on the train ride south, has suffered. Miller resents being "branded and tagged and set apart . . . like an unclean thing" (57), and McBane's "expectoration" on the floor is truly offensive, but as a boy Green watched when McBane "tuck my daddy out an' shot 'im ter death, an' skeered my mammy so she ain' be'n herse'f f'm dat day ter dis" (111). While the doctor can respond philosophically, Josh Green nurtures a "dark and revengeful" dedication to killing the white man who killed his father (113). While Dr. Miller spends the hours of the riot looking for his wife and child, Green enacts the mythological folk hero's self-sacrifice by rushing into a barrage of gunfire in order to kill the most reprehensible white supremacist in the novel.

In pairing these figures, however, Chesnutt not only contrasts what one of Du Bois's talented tenth fails to do in the fires of race violence with what a poor man will do, he also notes what they share—bodies, lives, and loved ones vulnerable to racial violence. Josh Green has lost his father, Miller his son. During the riot, Dr. Miller is stopped repeatedly by white men who search him and refuse to call him by his name or acknowledge his status. The color line cannot be transcended or avoided, not even by a black professional. As he travels across town during the riot searching for his wife, the doctor passes the dead. In this metaphoric Middle Passage, each Negro body he sees is "huddled," destroyed, mutilated, oozing blood, or groaning. These images recall the real African American bodies produced by slavery and racism, and, as John Wideman notes, after this "literal and symbolic descent," Dr. Miller is left with the "bone-deep knowledge that men are either black or white and nothing can occur between them that does not first take into account that dichotomy."[73] It is a powerful lesson: "Never will the picture of that ride fade from his memory. In his dreams he repeats it night after night, and sees the sights that wounded his eyes, and feels the thoughts— the haunting spirits of the thoughts—that tore his heart as he rode through hell" (286).

Given this "bone-deep knowledge," why does Dr. Miller go to Carteret's house to save the life of a boy who will inherit the political power his father has seized illegally and violently? As Eric Sundquist notes, Dr. Miller's "agonizing restraint" as he goes to the Carteret home suggests that "the good of the community outweighs the right of personal retribution."[74] Kawash makes a similar observation: if Dr. Miller refuses to operate and allows the boy to suffocate from croup, he has committed a "form of judicial strangulation" that is akin to lynching.[75] What interests me is that Chesnutt gives the power of judgment to a physician. Racism depends upon corporeal power, the power to buy, sell, whip, rape, or kill darker-skinned bodies. As a physician, Miller claims a different kind of somatic power, a power based on knowledge rather than violence, and a medical and scientific power that was often denied black physicians by local medical societies and hospitals. As I noted earlier, in *The House Behind the Cedars*, Chesnutt offers a powerful representation of the alliance between medicine and racism when he depicts Tryon with his feet propped up on a doctor's desk reading a medical journal article about black inferiority.

In *The Marrow of Tradition*, Chesnutt gives the power of medicine to a black physician. Instead of focusing on the power of white medical discourse to define and legitimate a hierarchical relationship between black and white bodies, Chesnutt considers how a black doctor will touch a white body. When Chesnutt articulates the social law that the "person of a white man was sacred from the touch of a negro," he knows, of course, that this law seeks to deny the very thing it admits—a national anxiety about and fascination with somatic border crossings. The law sanctifies the violence done to black men who are guilty the moment they are charged with touching a white woman or harming a white man. Images of violent contact and sexual contact across the color line dominate race discourse in the United States. Chesnutt himself uses both— Josh Green plunging his knife into McBane's body and, offstage, the white/black sexual affair made public and problematic in the light skin of the mulatto. But Chesnutt also offers another kind of touch across the color line, a medical touch that is both violent and healing. Dr. Miller must slit the boy's throat to save his life. This is a "very delicate operation," a phrase that appears in the novel and in both extant preparatory sketches. The scene echoes the moment in Matthews's short story when Aunt Lindy is asked to attend the unconscious body of her former master. It also echoes a scene in Chesnutt's short story "The Doll" in which Chesnutt explicitly renders the desire for revenge and the agonizing restraint necessary if a barber is to refrain from cutting the throat of the man who killed his father. In *The Marrow of Tradition*, Chesnutt revises this powerful and subversive image of black power. The novel acknowledges the violence of surgery, but it never explicitly considers that Dr. Miller might use his scalpel for revenge; rather, it ends with the suggestion that the white body politic needs radical surgery, and that the black doctor's touch will be both violent and, perhaps, transformative. He will cut, and he will suture.

The surgeon's suture promises closure—textual, bodily, and political—but Chesnutt does not provide such closure. In one early sketch for the novel, the boy's father offers his protection in gratitude, and he encourages the black doctor to stay. The doctor, however, refuses and rides back to the North in a Jim Crow car. Chesnutt writes, "he does not want protection but wants the rights and opportunities of a man."[76] Here Chesnutt imagines an ending that condemns the South and issues a clarion call for civil rights. He was also following history: many Wilmington blacks, including elites such as Thomas Miller, left willingly and unwillingly. As Leon Prather notes, the continued presence of men such as

Miller to whom whites owed money would have made "a travesty of white supremacy."[77] In the final version, however, Dr. Miller has not left, yet, and his skills, unlike Thomas Miller's property, cannot be seized. The somatic skills of the physician make the man himself indispensable. Surgery has long been understood as the most physical of the medical arts, and Carteret needs, quite specifically, Dr. Miller's physical talents. Chesnutt rewrites the old assumptions that blacks are more physical, more animal, more driven by their bodies than whites, or, as Thomas Jefferson explained, more prone to "sensation than reflection." Dr. Miller's somatic mastery also challenges the control of black bodies that post-Reconstruction white supremacists used in desperation to prop up their illegal political power.

Significantly, at the end of the novel, Chesnutt leaves the doctor suspended in the liminal space of the staircase. Dr. Miller approaches the room of the white child but still remembers his own child. He is on the verge of being engrossed in his work as a surgeon, and yet he carries the bone-deep knowledge of the color line as it was violently drawn during the riot. Although he has just witnessed the white man's murderous, reckless, slashing of black bodies, he will touch a white body with skill, cutting and suturing carefully. "Love, duty, sorrow, *justice*" give the doctor the right to refuse Carteret's request (324, original emphasis). The ethical code of his profession, his somatic expertise, and the pleas of a "fellow creature" in distress command him to go. And he does. But the novel ends before he enters the child's room. It ends as he ascends the stairs. In this liminal space, Dr. Miller remains suspended, and so does the reader. The novel resolutely foregrounds the power of the past to shape the present, and it also strains toward some unknowable and different future.

When, in the sixth chapter of *The Souls of Black Folk*, W. E. B. Du Bois calls for a "social surgery at once the delicatest and nicest in modern history," he calls for a surgery, like the one Dr. Miller will perform on Dodie, that negotiates past and future, anger and hope, cutting and suturing. Du Bois's essay, though famous for finding hope in black leadership, is also attentive to black anger and the Josh Greens who are ready to fight. Du Bois's chapter reaches its highest pitch of rhetorical energy when he imagines the possible angry responses to the "systematic concubinage and prostitution" practiced by white masters and the immorality of lynching that "daily present themselves in the guise of terrible truth" to nine million Negroes.[78] Beside this image of nine million justifiably angry Josh Greens, Du Bois also imagines "broad-minded, upright men" and "skilled thinkers" who can establish a "loving comradeship" with the "black lowly" and can also work with "their white neighbors toward a larger, juster and fuller future."[79] Thus in a moment of optimism, Du Bois imagines what black leaders may achieve.

Chesnutt's novel is not so optimistic. Unlike Du Bois, who rhetorically figures the educated man leading his angry comrades away from violence, Chesnutt suggests that Dr. Miller is not an effective leader in the middle of a race riot. Nor is Chesnutt sanguine about the power of black institutions and professions to earn respect and full civil rights for themselves and their brethren. And yet, Dr. Miller's hospital serves as a fortress for blacks who fight against the white supremacists, and in Dr. Miller, Chesnutt celebrates the early history of black-physician leadership. Chesnutt acknowledges that doctors may not be in the vanguard of armed struggle, but in a novel that puts so much into question, the professional doctor, though not a hero, makes a small gesture "from which something [might] begin."

In 1924, Walter F. White published a bitter revision of Chesnutt's novel. Like Chesnutt's novel, *The Fire in the Flint* chronicles a Northern-trained physician's fall from innocence as his eager optimism crumbles under the violence of Southern white supremacy. White came to write this novel, his first, after spending several years investigating lynchings. Able to pass, he witnessed thirty-six lynchings and mingled among white perpetrators.[80] The Georgia-born White began working for the NAACP as an assistant secretary in 1918 at the encouragement of Dr. Louis T. Wright, an Atlanta surgeon who had just returned from a "spectacularly successful" career at Harvard Medical School.[81] Beginning in 1919, White started passing in order to eavesdrop on the plans of white supremacists and to expose the extent of lynching in the nation. In 1919 he infiltrated meetings of the racist Hyde Park-Kenwood Association in Chicago in order to learn about the details of a plan to shut down a black hospital on the South Side.[82] Two years later, after attending the Pan-African Congress London meetings with Du Bois, White joined Dr. Wright, now back in New York, in a fight to expose poor care at Harlem Hospital and to demand that the city abandon the unwritten law prohibiting black doctors and nurses from working in the New York City hospitals.[83]

The Fire in the Flint is informed by White's political work, both as an infiltrator of white supremacist meetings and as an advocate for black physicians' professional rights. The protagonist, Dr. Kenneth Harper, is at the outset as optimistic as Harper's and Tillman's physicians. Dr. Harper imagines that a well-equipped office will attract paying patients, and he rejects his brother's cynicism and bitterness about black life in the South. Predictably, the doctor discovers that he must battle for respect from poor blacks and patronage from white and black professional colleagues. But, he proves his skills and even wins the confidence of a white man who needs secret care for a sexually transmitted disease.[84] He also impresses the community with his modernity when he rescues a white patient whose case was bungled by a local, old-fashioned white physician.[85]

But Dr. Harper's professional work cannot in the end protect him from racism and race violence. After attending a black man who has been killed by a white man, Harper reports, as he should, the death to the county health commissioner, including the cause and the name of the murderer. His report is rejected, and he is warned never to make a report about a white man killing a black man again. Thus the doctor is drawn into the "insidious embrace" of the "race problem," and he relinquishes his "effort to keep to a 'middle-of-the-road' course," which had only made him "morose."[86] Dr. Harper rereads his "battered textbooks on economics" and learns from the local minister how to use inspirational rhetoric to persuade uneducated black farmers to organize a cooperative.

In the end, however, White is not optimistic about such efforts, and the novel, punctuated with images of black bodies whipped and violated by the KKK, moves to an inevitable battle between Dr. Harper and a posse of white supremacists. Like Chesnutt's Dr. Miller, Dr. Harper sees his family destroyed: his sister is raped and his brother kills himself in order to escape a lynching. Also like Dr. Miller, Dr. Harper is called in the heat of a supremacist rampage to heal a white body, the daughter of a prominent white citizen. But White does not leave his physician climbing the stairs in a white man's house to cut and, presumably, suture the throat of a young scion of white privilege. White's physician, like Chesnutt's, goes to the white body, and he rescues her from near death though he contemplates the ironic justice of letting her die. But her life is paid for by his death. As he leaves, he is ambushed and killed by supremacists who will claim that his visit was not to heal the daughter but to rape the mother. Dr. Harper fights, like his brother a few chapters earlier, with "superhuman strength born of hatred, bitterness, and despair" (297), and he becomes the multitude of angry blacks that Du Bois and others warned were ripe for action.

In the darkness his assailants could not lay hands on him, first he was here, there, everywhere—hitting, kicking, whirling, ducking blows, jumping this way and that—a veritable dervish of the deserts in his gyrations! One after another his opponents went down at his feet! (298)

The battle scene may be a staple of narratives of masculinity, and it follows the tradition established with Douglass's fight against Covey, but to imagine a doctor fighting bitterly is to suggest that racial uplift, self-improvement, education, and professional ethos have little to offer in the battle against white supremacy.

Tillman and Harper make the physician an image of cultural refinement and physical tenderness. In the 1890s they did not dare suggest a black physician might act violently because this would have only endorsed stereotypes of black men as animalistic and violent. Chesnutt is also reluctant to stain the image of the professional with rage and violence. He understands the necessity of fighting back, but he makes the working-class Josh the leader of physical resistance and keeps the image of Dr. Miller free from uncontrolled rage. Like so many of the fictional physicians I have discussed, he maintains his composure. While Chesnutt suggests that the black professional can act in accordance with the dictates of professional disinterest even after his son has been killed, White is not so sure. When Dr. Harper turns into a whirling dervish driven by a "blind, unreasoning hatred and furious rage" he has felt since the KKK had tarred and pummeled a black woman (188), White suggests that professional composure cannot withstand the political, economic, and physical assault blacks were suffering under Jim Crow.

In his autobiography, White reports that he learned the bone-deep meaning of his racial identity in the 1906 Atlanta riot. On the second day, White hid with his family in their darkened house as rioters ransacked the neighborhood and White waited, with a gun in his hand, to shoot upon his father's command. "I knew then who I was. I was a Negro, a human being with an invisible pigmentation which marked me as a person to be hunted, hanged, abused, discriminated against, kept in poverty and ignorance." Individual achievement would do nothing to protect him from such hatred and nothing for African Americans as a group: "It made no difference how intelligent or talented my millions of brothers and I were, or how virtuously we lived. . . . There were white men who said Negroes had no souls."[87] Uplift would not work, and when Dr. Harper fights ferociously he proves, as Frederick Douglass proved by fighting Covey, that he is a man. By 1924 the ideology of professionalism and the myth of the reasonable man seemed useless against white supremacist violence. It was time, White suggests, for the physician and other elites to fight back.[88]

Epilogue:
From the Clinic to the Research
Laboratory: A Case Study of Three Stories

In 1906, John Singer Sargent completed a group portrait titled *The Four Doctors*. The doctors, depicted in academic regalia, are William Welch, William Stewart Halstead, Howard Kelly, and William Osler, all professors at the Johns Hopkins Medical School. The painting was commissioned by Mary Elizabeth Garrett, a major contributor who urged the school to require college preparation in biology, physics, and chemistry for admission. This requirement, adopted with slight modifications, was the most rigorous in the nation. It set a standard for medical education that emphasized knowledge in the basic sciences and laboratory research, and the immense canvas (it now hangs in the West Reading Room of the William H. Welch Medical Library) was a fitting emblem of the preeminent role the school would assume in U.S. medicine and medical science. The faculty at Hopkins was a roll call of the most famous physicians in the nation, but three of the four sitters for the Sargent portrait were particularly famous for their work in laboratory research and surgical advances. Welch was a pathologist with extensive experience in German laboratories, Halstead, a professor of surgery, had also studied in Germany, and Kelly was a professor of gynecology, a field dominated by new surgical techniques. Only Osler, a professor of medicine and an erudite, cultured man of letters, represented the older tradition of clinical medicine.

In his study of nineteenth-century European fiction and medicine, Lawrence Rothfield suggests that realism depends upon "conceptions of character, truth, and narrative authority" central to clinical medicine.[1] Clinical medicine provided a "set of cognitive rules or presuppositions about the structure of the living body" that realists adapted to thinking about the structure of the self, and the realist narrator, like the clinical physician, is distant, compassionate, observant, and committed to some larger, beneficent humanist project.[2] In addition, the narrative mode of realism, like the diagnostic epistemology of clinical medicine, takes the embodied subject as its primary focus, telling stories by observing "individual development [that] was bound to the finitude of organic

embodiment."[3] In short, clinical medicine and nineteenth-century realism share notions about professional identity, ethical ideals, and narrative and somatic coherence. But, as Rothfield acknowledges, in the last
decades of the nineteenth century, the image of the beneficent, master
physician began to fade as realism gave way to naturalism and modernism and as clinical medicine was replaced with a new emphasis on
labs and science.

The opening of the Johns Hopkins Medical School was, of course,
only one example of significant shifts in medicine at the end of the nineteenth century as hospital care replaced home visits and as advances in
surgery and pathology radically changed the fundamentals—diagnosis
and treatment—of medical practice. For most of the nineteenth century,
medical care happened in homes, but after 1880, almshouses began to
transform themselves into hospitals that served not poor but middle-
upper-class Americans.[4] Shaped not by notions of charity but by theories
of institutional management,[5] the goal of the hospital, as one observer
noted, was to focus on the patient as strictly a medical subject.[6] During
these same years, surgery came into its heyday. Previously, invasion of
the abdominal cavity was only a last resort because infection was common and often deadly. By 1880, however, the implications of Joseph
Lister's work on antisepsis had been established, and between 1890 and
1910 there was a "dramatic increase in the amount, scope and daring of
surgery."[7] Surgery became a field of distinction, and "body cavities were
no longer forbidding obstacles . . . but enticing opportunities."[8] As one
physician proclaimed in 1888, "Abdominal surgery is now the field where
the most brilliant successes are to be attained."[9] The prestige of the
Mayo Clinic and its founders William and Charles Mayo derived in part
from their surgical skills and inventions. In fact, as their practice grew,
they hired other physicians to work as diagnosticians to select the cases
so that they could devote more time to becoming surgical specialists.[10]
With the rise of surgery, pathology also became a field for professional
distinction. Pathologists were now useful not only for postmortems but
also in diagnostics. At the Mayo clinic, for example, the eminent pathologist Louis B. Wilson discovered a quick way to stain tissues and thus
provide quick and definitive answers to the diagnostic questions faced
by clinicians.[11]

Theodore Dreiser's portrait of the physician who cared for him and
his family when he was a boy laments the passing of the old medical
ways.[12] Published in 1919, but probably written in 1902, "The Country
Doctor" offers Dr. Gridley as the epitome of the nineteenth-century "good
doctor." He never charges the poor, he gets out of bed late at night to
attend to Dreiser's sister, and he uses old-fashioned, country cures. He is
a clinician whose diagnoses depend not on lab tests and microscopes but

upon knowledge of individuals, their history, and their character, and he is identified not with institutions but with home visits and advice offered at the "principal street corner" where the "school children were wont to congregate."[13] Dr. Gridley is cultured, kind, well loved, and wise; he reads literature, receives gifts from patients, sits with the dying, and accepts his own death peacefully.

"The Country Doctor" is clearly intended to be hagiography, but it fails. One of a dozen portraits in Dreiser's gallery of worthy men that was published as *Twelve Men*, "The Country Doctor" is the weakest in the collection. The prose is lame, Dr. Gridley is not interesting, and the result is a saccharine-sweet, nostalgic portrait of a "man of soft tones . . . of gentle touch and gentle step," a man "full of the human qualities of wonder, sympathy, tenderness, and trust" (125, 131).

Not all the portraits in *Twelve Men* are so feeble. In fact, one of the most energetic is a portrait of another body worker, a physical trainer at a sanitarium where Dreiser stayed in 1903 to recover from depression.[14] The son of a peasant farmer, Culhane has trained wrestlers and boxers, worked in the circus and the meat packing industry, waited tables and bounced drunks.[15] Now he cures fat, decadent bodies by subjecting the lawyers, preachers, merchants, doctors, and writers who come to the sanitarium to strenuous regimes of cold baths, plain meals, early morning calisthenics, and lots of ridicule. In this sketch, the prose, like Culhane, is energetic, and Dreiser delights in depicting powerful men as naked, shivering, pudgy bodies, while the farmer's son towers above them as a Greek god. In short, Culhane is the embodiment of what Walter Benn Michaels suggests often excites naturalists—the "organized individual's ambitious energies."[16]

Of all the systems organized at the end of the nineteenth century, hospitals were among the most successful, and although Culhane is not a physician, the financial and public success of his spa testifies to the profit and prestige to be gained by institutional management of bodies. As William Welch and William Osler could accumulate intellectual capital and excellent incomes at Johns Hopkins, so Culhane makes a name and money by directing a well-managed, vigorous institution.

Taken together, these two portraits mark the shift from nineteenth- to early twentieth-century definitions of individualism. Dr. Gridley and his patients are nineteenth-century individuals, defined by the local, idiosyncratic details of their lives and personalities. Culhane, by contrast, represents organization, regimentation, management, ambition, and a physical strength and brutality that makes him an iconic manager of the "blazing material world" (160). Dr. Gridley and his practice are no longer viable in a world of Culhanes and their institutions for energetic, scientific management of the somatic decadence that afflicts the nation.[17] On the one hand, Culhane represents an energy that Dreiser finds impressive, and in writing about Culhane, his prose achieves a manliness that he desired.[18] On the other hand, as a character in the narrative, Dreiser is one of the weaklings—pathetic, skinny, and naked. Dreiser cannot find a role for the artist in the world of managed systems and managed bodies, a problem that emerges again and again in *Twelve Men*. The first portrait in the collection presents an iconoclastic, talented writer who is "free—spiritually, morally, in a thousand ways," but is tempted by the frivolous and dies young (1). "Du Maupassant, Junior," another portrait of a writer, also describes the early demise of a radical thinker. Robert Ames in *Sister Carrie*, is, of course, another example of Dreiser's inability to imagine the artist or intellectual as a vital, physical presence in the material and economic worlds he chronicles. Torn between his nostalgia for nineteenth-century individualism as embodied in the clinician Dr. Gridley and his awe for the ruthless energy of such body workers as Culhane operating within strictly regimented systems, Dreiser finds no home for himself or the artist.

Like Dreiser, Jack London is impressed with the arrogance, masculinity, and iconoclasm of "strong men," and in his short story "Semper Idem," London finds energy and authority in the figure of a brutal hospital surgeon. Like Dreiser, Jack London is impressed with the arrogance, masculinity, and iconoclasm of "strong men." But unlike Dreiser, London is ready, even eager, to appropriate such authority and methods for himself as a writer. London rejects the professional ethos of compassion and objectivity of clinical medicine and nineteenth-century realism, and the surgeon rather than the clinician is his model.

"Semper Idem" is a short, violent story. Dr. Bicknell deploys methods that shock his colleagues—"People who knew him were prone to brand him a butcher"—and the central medical act of the story is an aesthetically perfect but horrible-to-witness act of stitching together the throat of a man who slit his own throat.[19] Although the hospital staff presumes the case is hopeless, Dr. Bicknell sutures together the windpipe and jugular with surgical methods that cause the staff "to shudder" (66). After completing his work, Dr. Bicknell explains to the patient the correct method for successfully slicing one's throat, and the next day the man is brought to the hospital, dead on arrival. Dr. Bicknell approves of violence done right with a gentlemanly pronouncement: "Properly done, upon my life, sir, properly done" (68). The reader, like the hospital staff, shudders. The plot of "Semper Idem" is ruthless, and London offers gruesome descriptions of the near decapitation and also of an unrelated accident involving "a child's body which had been ground and crunched beneath the wheels of an electric car" (67, 66).

For London, truth is marked by the violence it does to conventional pieties, and in this story he suggests that writers must, like surgeons, embrace brutality. As Dr. Bicknell gazes at Semper Idem's hideous scar, the symbol of the doctor's brutal but virtuoso surgical skill, he is "like the artist gazing upon a finished creation" (67). In fact, the prestige of surgeons at the turn of the century depended in large measure upon a public sense of their courage and technical virtuosity, as well as upon a lingering respect for what had been in the recent past bloody, hard physical work on fully awake, resisting patients. London's story taps both images—butcher and virtuoso—and he claims both for the writer as well as the surgeon.

London borrows from surgery, in addition to its authority, its method. Surgery, in contrast to clinical medicine, is radically antinarrative. Surgery is performed upon body parts, and upon silenced bodies, with little regard for the voice or the story of the patient. As I noted in Chapter 1, when anesthesia was first introduced in the middle of the nineteenth century, doctors worried that silencing the patient was "virtually choking off Nature's voice" and that the patient's words and groans were the "true physician's best guide to the seat and character of the cause of the pain."[20] By the end of the century, the role of the patient's voice was negligible, and surgeons understood their work as a matter not of interpretation, but of technique. London's story is equally antinarrative. No character is given a history because history is not relevant. Dr. Bicknell is defined solely by his work, and the patient refuses to talk.

Clinical medicine values physical examinations and direct knowledge, as I have noted previously, but it is dependent upon narrative.[21] The doctor listens to the patient's story, retells the story in his own words as a case history, intervenes in the narrative by prescribing a cure, and takes the story into the future by offering a prognosis. Neither Dr. Bicknell nor Semper Idem values storytelling. The story may seem to be a medical case history, but Dr. Bicknell's cure does not require hearing or interpreting the patient's story. London acknowledges the reader's desire for a narrative but mocks those who seek Semper Idem's story. Those who are unwilling to know the man simply as a "cut throat," police detectives, sleuths, and reporters who have an "unseemly yet highly natural curiosity" about the case, are those with a lust for plot and an inability to appreciate the pure aesthetics of technique and violence (66).

London offers a few tantalizing hints of a narrative: Semper Idem has the hands of a gentleman but wears the clothes of a laborer and in his room is found a photograph of a woman inscribed in a feminine hand with the words, "Semper idem; semper fidelis." These facts provoke "uncontrollable public curiosity and interminable copy to the space-writers," but they do not tell a story (67). Nor do these few facts provide an identity beyond the enigmatic name the patient is given by the hospital workers, Semper Idem, an amusingly apt name for a body with no history, voice, or identity. Indeed, London so successfully eschews narrative that he almost manages to tell no story at all. There is no development of characters, no action, and the plot is structured to assert one simple, brutal, ironic, and iconic image of a technically brilliant surgeon who considers lives "the unpleasant but inevitable incidents of the profession" (65).

Critics have noted the anemic plots in London's fiction. Some have connected this to a general tendency in naturalist fiction to define writing as a material practice of putting marks on a page, and some have linked London's interest in the materiality of writing with his interests in publication and circulation and with the influence of commodity fetishism.[22] I would add that in "Semper Idem" the aesthetics of surgery also have an influence on London. In realist literature and clinical medicine, texts and bodies are organic forms with interiorities rich with latent symbols. In "Semper Idem," bodies and texts are inorganic objects known by their surfaces and not their interiorities. Semper Idem's body is a surface upon which the surgeon leaves his mark, and "Semper Idem," the text, is equally flat, explicitly thwarting efforts to find depth and meaning.[23]

William Carlos Williams's portrait of an old doctor in the short story "Old Doc Rivers" is, like Dreiser's portrait, nostalgic. Like Dreiser's Dr. Gridley, Rivers is a good diagnostician, a quiet, inscrutable man who remains aloof from the greed of commercialism, a man revered by all. He performs surgery on kitchen tables, never specializes, and if he is sometimes cruel and crude, he is also gentle and patient. As T. Hugh Crawford notes, the story offers a "sustained impression of the charismatic power of [the medical] profession.[24]

But unlike Dr. Gridley, there is nothing quaint, saccharine, or out-of-date about Doc Rivers. He is a dope addict, and a compelling figure of modernist angst. He abuses morphine, ether, heroin, cocaine, and alcohol, spends time in sanitariums drying out, depends upon drugs to get him through the day, and kills at least one patient. While a host of nineteenth-century writers, including, as I noted in Chapters 4 and 5, Sarah Orne Jewett, Henry James, Francis Harper, and Charles Chesnutt, offer the doctor as a figure of wisdom and truth telling, in the first decades of the twentieth century, the patient rather than the doctor speaks truths. Indeed, doctors are often obtuse: in *Mrs. Dalloway*, Sir William Bradshaw fails to understand the significance of Septimus's madness, and in *Main Street*, Dr. Kennicott is oblivious. Doctors who do feel the weight of the modernist despair are sick doctors. The doctors in Franz Kafka's "A Country Doctor" and Sherwood Anderson's *Winesburg, Ohio* can no longer distinguish between the pathological and the healthy, and they represent not professional competence but rather the collapse of professional mastery in the modern world.

The pathology of Doc Rivers's mind is dramatized in the fragmented narrative of the story as it moves abruptly from case to case, and from details about Rivers's odd friendships to scenes in the doctor's office. Dialogue is never marked by quotation marks, speakers remain unidentified, pronouns have unclear referents, and shifts in time and place are made without transitions. Although the story seeks to understand a man and a life, it does so as a fragmentary postmortem.[25] All the evidence comes from the memories of patients, colleagues, and acquaintances, and hospital records, and each narrative fragment is inconclusive. The stories that others tell about the doctor offer no complete image of the man, and the anecdotes fail to embody or even suggest the whole. Unlike Dreiser's Dr. Gridley, whose moral virtues are evident in every home visit or casual witticism, Doc Rivers cannot be known by metonymy. The parts do not represent the whole, but remain only parts. Nor can Doc Rivers be known through his technique, for it is improvisatory, inconsistent, and idiosyncratic. Lives can only be known and stories can only be told, Williams suggests, in bits and pieces.

As disease was increasingly understood as specific, somatic, and mechanistic, so diagnosis became increasingly dependent upon fragments of the body studied under the microscope.[26] More concerned with biopsies, laboratories, and microscopes, pathology is a science of bits and pieces, and with little interest in the body as a unified, coherent, organic extension of a lived subject. In Williams's story, the body simply is not present. A pelvic exam seems to have nothing to do with the patient or her body: "He made a quick examination, slipping on a rubber glove without removing his coat, washing his hands after at the basin in the corner of the room. The whole thing hadn't taken six minutes."[27] The brutality lies not in a description of what is done to a body, but rather in the very denial of the somatic presence of a patient.

A similar somatic absence marks the account given by a young doctor who as a boy occasionally assisted Doc River: "I do remember one woman, though. God, it was a crime. You can imagine what I mean. Here I was, a kid never knowing anything at all. I was having the time of my life. Yes, everything, you're right. I held her while he did the job. I often think of it (95)." The woman's body is absent, and we cannot even be sure what procedure Rivers performed. Was it an abortion, hysterectomy, tubal ligation, cyst removal, or rape, as one critic has suggested?[28] We know nothing about the patient, and her distress—emotional and physical—is represented only as it is refracted through the painful memories and inchoate language of the witness. Even Rivers himself is never fully realized as a somatic presence. Although he drinks and uses drugs, there is little sense of his physical decline. His psyche is the subject of the story, and the story avoids representing the psyche through the somatic. If, as Rothfield has suggested, realism asserts a unified subject by fixing consciousness in a physical body that "serves as an empirical grounding-point," then modernism achieves a sense of fragmentation through a rejection of the somatic as a reliable ground.[29] In Williams's story, patients and doctors float as disembodied subjects.

But this does not mean that the doctor has lost his authority, although his power is not as one who can manage others or provide the nation with answers and leadership. Doc Rivers has been an impressive physician, but it is his breakdown that testifies to the strenuous demands—physical and psychological—of his work and to his real engagement with the troubles, truths, and ugliness of the modern world. His breakdown is also a challenge to the coherence and efficiency valued in the emerging culture of management, and thus Williams suggests that case studies—medical and literary—must relinquish narrative coherence in order to be true to the pathological. It is important to note, however, that although Williams draws upon the methods of pathology, offering only bits and pieces, he rejects the distance and totalizing perspective claimed by the pathologist, who wears a white lab coat and names diseases. Instead, coherence comes only as a narrator/young doctor tries to make sense of Doc Rivers's life. Like both Virginia Woolf's Clarrisa Dalloway and Sherwood Anderson's George Willard, Williams's narrator stands close to but not quite in the madness, offering a compromised Archimedean point of reference for understanding and reporting on the pathology of the modern condition.

Traditionally, naturalist fiction has been read against the background of such scientific writers and social philosophers as Charles Darwin, Thomas Huxley, and Herbert Spencer, and modernist fiction has been situated within the context of post-World War I despair. More recently, naturalist and modernist texts have been read in the context of contemporaneous political and social issues, including immigration, nativism, and the gold standard. I conclude my study of literature and medicine in nineteenth-century America with an epilogue dedicated to reading three early twentieth-century stories in part to suggest what comes next in the history of the relationship between these two discourses as medicine's prestige and authority were largely accepted and as elite literature responded to the nation's call for strenuous masculinity and increased intervention in international affairs.

I also end with brief readings of three fictional portraits of physicians because I want to suggest one last time what is gained by reading literature and medicine together. Medicine is neither simply the pursuit of biological facts nor only a hegemonic discourse that seeks to legitimate an elite professional class. Medicine is a cultural practice, and a practice, like literature, eager to do good and right, to assert its truths, and to claim authority. It is also, like literature, a practice that has to negotiate its position within and against competing discourses. Beginning in the middle of the nineteenth century, medicine rapidly became a dominant force in U.S. society, shaping our deepest convictions about embodiment and who should have the authority to enter the sick room, attend to the ailing body, and witness at the deathbed. In these same years, literature professionalized, developed an elite wing of writers authoring "serious" literature, and negotiated a deepening divide between empirical and imaginative ways of knowing. Literature sometimes challenged the class, race, and gender politics of professional medicine and often suggested that the experience of embodiment was not fully understood by medicine. At the same time, the fictional doctor was a useful figure for envisioning what it might mean to encounter fully the pleasures and pains, hopes and anxieties, associated with living in mortal flesh.

This book was born out of my interest in the body and out of a deep conviction of the power of culture to shape the body. In part, my conviction attests to the influence of the constructivist position in literary studies over the last thirty years. Perhaps because I came of age as a literary scholar in the late 1980s, I began this project with a presumption that both medicine and literature offered somatic constructs that might further their authority, their discourse, their power, their ideology. My sense that bodies are deeply cultural also comes from my work as a dancer and choreographer. Within dance, there is a discourse of somatic authenticity. But the idea that there are natural and unnatural, healthy and unhealthy, anatomically correct and anatomically incorrect ways to move goes against what dance as an art tells us. As it creates meaning through and on the body, dance offers constant reminders of just how deeply embedded the body is in culture. Dance offers humbling reminders of the body's materiality, mortality, and real-world constraints, and it also reminds us that the body is never unmediated by culture. Every body on the stage is experienced by dancers and viewers in relation to a dense web of possible meanings layered upon every movement and every anatomical feature.

Terry Eagleton and others have issued important warnings about the excesses of constructivist thinking. All bodies, even culturally constructed bodies, bleed when pricked, and the fact that the body comes into meaning through culture does not give us license to ignore real bodies and real injustices visited upon the body. Race may be a cultural construct, but race violence is real. And yet, ending violence against the body depends, at least in part, upon challenging the very notion of normal or natural. Efforts to end race violence, for example, have been aided by the deconstruction of somatic categories that were deemed biological, innate, and stable less than a hundred years ago. Reconsidering what is inherent in the body and what is, in fact, of our own making has been one of the most important contributions of body studies. My project seeks to join this effort to know richly how the body comes into meaning. Thus I began this project because I wanted to think about the body—how it has been represented and the consequences of those representations. I turned to literature and medicine because it is in fiction and medicine that the body and its meanings were most intensely debated in the nineteenth century, and I focused on the period between the 1830s and the first years of the 1900s because in these years religion faded as a discourse for understanding embodiment and visual culture had not yet emerged as the powerful force it has become in thinking about the body. Finally, this project came to focus on the physician because my interest in the body narrowed into an interest in the rise of the authority of medicine—one of the most dramatic developments in the nineteenth century—and I decided to focus on literature's response to medicine because of my own sense of literature as a source for compelling and varied meditations upon the meaning of embodiment.

Notes

Introduction: What's a Doctor, After All?

1. Susan Sontag suggests that illness is "the night-side of life," and she believes that it is nearly impossible to "take up one's residence in the kingdom of the ill unprejudiced by the lurid metaphors with which it has been landscaped." Susan Sontag, *Illness as Metaphor* (New York: Farrar, Straus and Giroux, 1978), 3, 4. Making a similar argument, Sander Gilman suggests that in the image of the patient there is a "demarcation between ourselves and the chaos represented in culture by disease." Sander Gilman, *Disease and Representation: Images of Illness from Madness to AIDS* (Ithaca, N.Y.: Cornell University Press, 1988), 4.

2. Homeopathy falls outside these two categories. On the one hand, homeopathy had all the signs of professional legitimacy: a national society, well-staffed schools, and a commitment to scientific methods. Before 1860 many homeopathic physicians were regulars who believed that homeopathic treatments were often effective. In both the 1848 and 1853 yellow fever epidemics, for example, homeopathy seemed to yield better results than the heroic treatments commonly associated with regulars. Nevertheless, many regulars branded homeopathy as quackery. Oliver Wendell Holmes wrote passionately in 1842 against homeopathy, and the consultation clause in the AMA code of ethics barred regulars from consulting with practitioners who had allegiance to a single method (homeopathy came under this rubric). In 1855 the AMA required state and local societies to adopt the national code of ethics and thus to exclude homeopaths from membership, and in the 1870s the AMA required member societies to purge homeopaths from their rosters. Elite women physicians also shunned homeopathy. Although some women practitioners and some feminist health reformers embraced homeopathy, those who sought to ally themselves with regulars distanced themselves from homeopathic leaders. Elizabeth Blackwell, for example, had little respect for the founder of the homeopathic New York Medical College for Women, an institution that competed for students with Blackwell's Woman's Medical College of the New York Infirmary. See Martin Kaufman, *Homeopathy in America: The Rise and Fall of a Medical Heresy* (Baltimore: Johns Hopkins University Press, 1971); William G. Rothstein, *American Physicians in the Nineteenth Century: From Sects to Science* (Baltimore: Johns Hopkins University Press, 1972); Joseph F. Kett, *The Formation of the American Medical Profession: The Role of Institutions, 1780–1860* (New Haven, Conn.: Yale University Press, 1968); John Duffy, *The Healers: A History of American Medicine* (Urbana: University of Illinois Press, 1979),

112–19; Paul Starr, *The Social Transformation of American Medicine* (New York: Basic Books, 1982), 96–98; Regina Markell Morantz-Sanchez, *Sympathy and Science: Women Physicians in American Medicine* (New York: Oxford University Press, 1985), 72–74.

3. The histories of medicine cited above acknowledge that although sectarian battles would suggest deep divisions between various schools of healing, the boundaries were, in fact, often blurred. Lamar Riley Murphy's history of domestic medicine makes this particularly clear. She notes the emergence of different conceptions of medical legitimacy and authority (one stressing folk traditions, the other formal training), but she also suggests that stressing "the antipathies blurs significant areas of tacit or explicit consensus." She notes that hydropaths as well as homeopaths often had regular training; and she outlines shared thinking on "the management of illnesses; the importance of preventive living; the proper care of the sick; and the necessity of educating Americans about medical matters." Lamar Riley Murphy, *Enter the Physician: The Transformation of Domestic Medicine, 1760–1860* (Tuscaloosa: University of Alabama Press, 1991), 186–87. A detailed local picture emerges in Charles Rosenberg's study of health care in New York City in 1866. He documents the wide variety of medical care options available: those who would have called themselves doctors included about eight hundred regulars, about seventy homeopaths, and about six hundred irregulars. (This meant that the doctor/patient ratio was one to five hundred.) In addition, midwives and "old ladies" (the regulars' term for laypersons) offered their advice freely, as did apothecaries. As Rosenberg concludes, in this crowded health care market, patients availed themselves, regardless of class, of a variety of practitioners. See "The Practice of Medicine in New York a Century Ago," in *Explaining Epidemics and Other Studies in the History of Medicine* (New York: Cambridge University Press, 1992), 127–28.

4. John Harley Warner, *Against the Spirit of System: The French Impulse in Nineteenth-Century American Medicine* (Princeton, N.J.: Princeton University Press, 1998), 14.

5. *New York Evening Star*, December 27, 1833, as cited in *Thomsonian Recorder* 3 (January 17, 1835): 127; as cited in Starr, 56.

6. Critical reaction to *The Gross Clinic* suggests that, although the public was ready to accept professional medicine as a dignified authority, it did not want a vivid reminder of medicine's fleshy and bloody work. Now *The Gross Clinic* is widely revered as a great American painting, and in a review of the John Eakins show at the Philadelphia Art Museum, one critic celebrates Eakins as "a prophet of American inventiveness and self-invention." Of Eakins's representations of surgeons in *The Gross Clinic* and *The Agnew Clinic*, the critic notes that "Eakins renders them as demigods incandescent with pride and the world's applause." He observes, as has Michael Fried, that these surgeons are "plainly surrogates of the artists" with "brush still in hand." See Peter Schjeldahl, "The Surgeon: Philadelphia Celebrates Its Most Prodigious Son," *New Yorker*, October 22, 2001, 78. Hinckley began his painting in 1892 and made a point of including as many leading physicians as he could, which meant he stretched history and included some who were not present at the first demonstration of ether but were at the second or third. For more about Hinckley's painting and its reception, see Richard J. Wolfe, *Robert C. Hinckley and the Recreation of the First Operation Under Ether* (Boston: Boston Medical Library, 1993).

7. James Harvey Young, *American Health Quackery: Collected Essays* (Princeton, N.J.: Princeton University Press, 1992), 92.

8. Ralph Waldo Emerson and T. W. Higginson both noted the decline in the clergyman's manly authority. Emerson, who quit the ministry in 1832, believed the Unitarian belief was "effete" and that a clergyman "cannot be a man, quite and whole." See James Eliot Cabot, *A Memoir of Ralph Waldo Emerson* (Boston: Houghton Mifflin, 1887), 1: 167, 329. In 1858, in his first article for the *Atlantic Monthly*, Higginson felt compelled to defend clergymen from presumptions about "the supposed deficiency" of a "vigorous manly life." T. W. Higginson, "Saints and Their Bodies," *Atlantic Monthly* (March 1858): 584. As Ann Douglas notes, the number of Americans who belonged to a religious society actually increased between 1800 and 1850, and yet ministers were increasingly "severed from their traditional sources of power" and essentially disestablished. Ann Douglass, *The Feminization of American Culture* (New York: Anchor, 1988), 23. In his summary of the shifting fortunes of the professions in America, Samuel Haber concludes that physicians "rose to a new preeminence among the professions in the late nineteenth century." Samuel Haber, *The Quest for Authority and Honor in the American Professions, 1750 - 1900* (Chicago: University of Chicago Press, 1991), xiii.

9. Stuart F. Spicker, "Terra Firma and Infirma Species: From Medical Philosophical Anthropology to Philosophy of Medicine," *Journal of Medicine and Philosophy* 1 (1976): 119; as cited in Barbara Duden, *The Woman Beneath the Skin: A Doctor's Patients in Eighteenth-Century Germany*, trans. Thomas Dunlap (Cambridge, Mass.: Harvard University Press, 1991), 192, n.2.

10. I want to thank both anonymous readers for helping me to see the larger shape of this project. Some phrases and insights in this introduction and in subsequent chapters are taken from their reports.

11. Francis Barker, *The Tremulous Private Body: Essays on Subjection* (London: Methuen, 1984).

12. Karl Figlio, "The Historiography of Scientific Medicine: An Invitation to the Human Sciences," *Comparative Studies in Society and History* 19 (1977): 277.

13. See Michel Foucault, *The Birth of the Clinic: An Archeology of Medical Perception*, trans. A. M. Sheridan Smith (New York: Vintage, 1975), for the role of early nineteenth-century Paris clinical medicine in the making of the modern body. See Warner, *Against the Spirit*, for a fine, thorough account of "What Paris medicine meant in nineteenth-century America" (4).

14. David Armstrong, *Political Anatomy of the Body: Medical Knowledge in Britain in the Twentieth Century* (Cambridge: Cambridge University Press, 1983), xi.

15. Catherine Gallagher, "The Body Versus the Social Body in the Works of Thomas Malthus and Henry Mayhew." *Representations* 14 (1986): 86.

16. As quoted in John S. Haller, *Outcasts from Evolution: Scientific Attitudes about Racial Inferiority, 1859–1900* (Urbana: University of Illinois Press, 1971), 23.

17. Sarah E. Chinn, *Technology and the Logic of American Racism* (London: Continuum, 2000), 51; see 24–52 for a reading of Mark Twain's *Puddn'head Wilson* in the context of the history of palmistry and fingerprinting in the U.S.

18. There is a long tradition of linking physical disease and social disorder. For an analysis of how the eminent practitioner and political leader in colonial America Benjamin Rush equates disease with sedition and social fragmentation, see Dana Nelson, *National Manhood: Capitalist Citizenship and the Imagined Fraternity of White Men* (Durham, N.C.: Duke University Press, 1998), 11–22. In the nineteenth century, the rhetoric of public health often presumed that physical health would bring national order. For example, during a cholera epidemic some believed that the disease distinguished between the virtuous rich and the "most filthy, intemperate, and imprudent portion of the population." Charles

Rosenberg, *The Cholera Years: The United States in 1832, 1849, and 1866* (Chicago: University of Chicago Press, 1987), 55.

19. The modern body is the material complement to Enlightenment notions of democratic citizenship. Citizenship is, in theory, universally available. But, in practice, not everyone had equal access to citizenship in the nineteenth century, and in the representational habits of the day some are more "of the body" than others.

20. Michael Warner, "The Mass Public and the Mass Subject," in *Habermas and the Public Sphere*, ed. Craig Calhoun (Cambridge, Mass.: MIT Press, 1992), 382; as cited in Robyn Wiegman, *American Anatomies: Theorizing Race and Gender* (Durham, N.C.: Duke University Press, 1995), 49.

21. Wiegman, 4.

22. Nelson, *National Manhood*, 10.

23. Nelson, 103.

24. Haber, *Quest*, 204. Haber argues that the professions in America "transmit, with some modifications, a distinctive sense of authority and honor that has its origins in the class position and occupational prescriptions of eighteenth-century English gentlemen" (ix).

25. Burton Bledstein, *The Culture of Professionalism: The Middle Class and the Development of Higher Education in America* (New York: Norton, 1976), 88, 90.

26. Max Weber, *Economy and Society*, 2 vols., (Berkeley: University of California, Press, 1978), 2: 1121–23.

27. Edward Spencer, "A Good Word for Quacks," *Atlantic Monthly* (March 1873): 328.

28. For a particularly good history of the "segmentation of American literary cultures," see Richard Brodhead, *Cultures of Letters: Scenes of Reading and Writing in Nineteenth-Century America* (Chicago: University of Chicago Press, 1993), 80–106.

29. As Karen Sanchez-Eppler notes, "Reading sentimental fiction is thus a bodily act, and the success of a story is gauged, in part, by its ability to translate words into pulse beats and sobs." Karen Sanchez-Eppler, "Bodily Bonds: The Intersecting Rhetorics of Feminism and Abolition," in *The Culture of Sentiment: Race, Gender, and Sentimentality in Nineteenth-Century America*, ed. Shirley Samuels (New York: Oxford University Press, 1992), 100.

30. Nancy Glazener, *Reading for Realism: The History of a U.S. Literary Institution, 1850–1910* (Durham, N.C.: Duke University Press, 1997), 93–146.

31. Glazener, p. 6.

32. As Glazener notes, "professional authors sought to secure some of the status privileges created by capital, but they found their public mission in the more or less loyal critique of capitalism's excesses, a position that posited culture as a vantage point outside society's economic life" (109).

33. Lawrence Rothfield, *Vital Signs: Medical Realism in Nineteenth-Century Fiction* (Princeton: Princeton University Press, 1992), xvi.

34. Starr, *Social Transformation*, 6.

35. Cynthia Davis, *Bodily and Narrative Forms: The Influence of Medicine on American Literature, 1845–1915* (Stanford, Calif.: Stanford University Press, 2000), 1.

36. Charles Rosenberg, "The Therapeutic Revolution," in *Explaining Epidemics and Other Studies in the History of Medicine* (New York: Cambridge University Press, 1992), 11.

37. Warner, *Against the Spirit*, 4.

38. Henry James, *Notes of a Son and Brother*, ed. Frederick W. Dupee (New York: Criterion Books, 1956), 416.

Chapter 1. Professional Medicine, Democracy, and the Modern Body:
The Discovery of Etherization

1. Paul Starr, *The Social Transformation of American Medicine* (New York: Basic Books, 1982), 54.

2. Allen De Ville, *Medical Malpractice in Nineteenth-Century America: Origins and Legacy* (New York: New York University Press, 1990); Joseph Kett, *The Formation of the American Medical Profession: The Role of Institutions, 1780–1860* (New Haven, Conn.: Yale University Press, 1968); and Starr, *Social Transformation.* John Harley Warner, "Power, Conflict, and Identity in Mid-Nineteenth-Century American Medicine: Therapeutic Change at the Commercial Hospital in Cincinnati," *Journal of American History* 73 (1987): 934–56, offers both a summary of how other historians have interpreted the consequences of the sectarian challenge to regulars and a slightly alternative interpretation, suggesting that the popularity of Thomsonianism and other practices posed a challenge less to the economic well-being of regulars than to the identity, status, and authority of the profession.

3. The efforts of regulars to represent themselves as both democrats and professionals are also evident in how orthodox physicians thought about their approach to therapeutics. They often suggested that their emphasis on individualized treatments was more scientific than the populist, one-size-fits-all therapeutics of many folk healers, but they also believed that their sensitivity to the specifics of each case reflected a democratic commitment to the individual. John Harley Warner, *The Therapeutic Perspective: Medical Practice, Knowledge, and Identity in America, 1820–1885* (Cambridge, Mass.: Harvard University Press, 1986), 58–80; Martin S. Pernick, *A Calculus of Suffering: Pain Professionalism, and Anaesthesia in Nineteenth-Century America* (New York: Columbia University Press, 1985), 132–41.

4. David B. Morris, *The Culture of Pain* (Berkeley: University of California Press, 1991), 54.

5. See June Howard, *Form and History in American Literary Naturalism* (Chapel Hill: University of North Carolina Press, 1985), 19– 29.

6. For the following summary of the discovery of ether and the ether controversy, I have drawn upon the many versions that I discuss later in the chapter, including Richard Dana, "A History of the Ether Discovery," *Littell's Living Age* 16 (1848): 529–71, and Nathan P. Rice, *Trials of a Public Benefactor, as Illustrated in the Discovery of Etherization* (New York: Pudney and Russell, 1859), although both of these, as I discuss later, are heavily biased accounts. For scholarly twentieth-century histories, see Barbara Duncum, *The Development of Inhalation Anaesthesia, with Special Reference to the Years 1846–1900* (London: Oxford University Press and Wellcome Institute, 1947); Thomas E. Keys, *The History of Surgical Anesthesia* (1945; reprint New York: Dover, 1963); and Stanley Sykes, *Essays on the First Hundred Years of Anaesthesia,* vol. 3 (London: Longman, 1982). The most recent work on the history of anesthesia was an exhibition at the Wellcome Institute for the History of Medicine. The catalog offers a useful introductory essay. Christopher Lawrence and Ghislaine Lawrence, *No Laughing Matter: Historical Aspects of Anaesthesia,* Catalog of a Wellcome Institute for the History of Medicine Exhibition (London: Wellcome Institute, 1987). For the most recent telling of the ether story, see Julie M. Fenster, *Ether Day: The Strange Tale of America's Greatest Medical Discovery and the Haunted Men Who Made It* (New York: HarperCollins, 2001).

7. Quoted in Duncum, *Development,* 128.

8. Quoted in Rice, *Trials,* 373.

9. The debate over who discovered anesthesia may seem foolish at times, but

questions of priority are significant. Recent charges that the Nobel Prize Committee has overlooked deserving candidates remind us that politics—gender, race, national, and international—play a role in awarding of public recognition and financial rewards.

10. Quoted in John Harley Warner, "Remembering Paris: Memory and the American Disciples of French Medicine in the Nineteenth Century," *Bulletin of the History of Medicine* 65 (1991): 315.

11. Republished in Oliver Wendell Holmes, *Medical Essays* (New York: Riverside, 1891), 94, 97.

12. A. Biggs, *The Botanico Medical Reference Book* (Memphis, Tenn.: Wells and Care Print, 1846), 1.

13. Holmes, *Medical Essays*, 98.

14. Quoted in Dana, *History*, 544.

15. Quoted in Dana, 544. Dana reprints several other condemnations as well. William C. Roberts, editor of the *New York Annalist*, wrote that the discovery would ultimately "descend to the bottom of that great abyss, which has already engulfed so many of its predecessor novelties, but which continues, alas! to gape, until a humbug yet more prime shall be thrown into it." The editors of the *New Orleans Medical and Surgical Journal* suggested that mesmerism "has done a thousand times greater wonders, and without any of the dangers here threatened" (quoted in Dana, 544). Pernick, *Calculus*, 66–76, also offers examples of the condemnation of anesthesia as quackery by professional medicine, including a denunciation by the Massachusetts Medical Society.

16. Henry Bigelow, "Insensibility During Surgical Operations," *Boston Medical and Surgical Journal* 35 (1846): 309–17. Also see Henry R. Viets, "The Earliest Printed References in Newspapers and Journals to the First Public Demonstration of Ether Anesthesia in 1846," *Journal of the History of Medicine* 4 (Spring 1949): 149–69, for a list of newspaper articles and advertisements concerning Morton's discovery.

17. Henry Bigelow, "Anaesthetic Agents, Their Mode of Exhibition and Physiological Effects," *Transactions of the American Medical Association* 1 (1848); and Henry Bigelow, *Ether and Chloroform: A Compendium of Their History, Surgical Uses, Dangers, and Discovery* (Boston: David Clapp, 1848).

18. All quotes in this and the next two paragraphs are from Bigelow, *Ether.*

19. In 1876, at the request of Edward H. Clarke, professor of Materia Medica at Harvard, and for a centennial celebration of American medicine, Bigelow wrote another account of the history of the discovery of ether. Now an established professor of surgery at Harvard and a member of a profession no longer under attack as it was in the 1840s, Bigelow does not bother to define a role for the medical profession in the discovery. Instead, he praises Morton lavishly, comparing him to Jenner and suggesting that Morton was more than a common inventor. He insists that what allowed Morton to make the discovery was his reckless disregard for danger and convention. He describes Morton as "[f]ertile in expedients and singularly prompt in execution . . . earnest and persevering beyond conception." Henry J. Bigelow, "A History of the Discovery of Modern Anaesthesia," *American Journal of the Medical Sciences* 71 (1876): 175.

20. The work of the committee continued and is recorded in *Proceedings on Behalf of the Morton Testimonial*, Lilly Library, Special Collections, Bloomington, Indiana, which includes "Testimonial of members of the medical profession of Philadelphia on behalf of William T. G. Morton," Philadelphia, 1861; "Testimonial to William T. G. Morton," Boston, April 1861; and "Testimonial of the New York Committee," New York, 1861.

21. Viets, "Earliest Printed References," 157; Duncum, *Development,* 120; Sarah H. Hale, "The Discovery of Ether," *Godey's Lady's Book* 46 (1853): 205–12.

22. Quoted in Richard J. Wolfe, *Robert C. Hinckley and the Recreation of the First Operation Under Ether* (Boston: Boston Medical Library, 1993), 70.

23. Elizabeth Whitman Morton, "Trials of a Public Benefactor," *McClure's Magazine* (September 1896): 311–18. Richard Manning Hodges, *A Narrative of Events Connected with the Introduction of Sulphuric Ether into Surgical Use* (Boston: Little Brown, 1891).

24. Hodges, *Narrative,* 9, 138–39.

25. Hodges, 76, 136.

26. See Stephanie P. Browner, "Ideologies of the Anesthetic: Professionalism, Egalitarianism, and the Ether Controversy," *American Quarterly,* 51, 1 (March 1999): 120–23, for a discussion of other twentieth-century versions of the ether story.

27. Sherwin Nuland, *Doctors: The Biography of Medicine* (New York: Vintage, 1988), 265, 287–89.

28. Quoted in Viets, "Earliest Printed References," 160.

29. Viets, 160.

30. Viets, 226.

31. Dr. Edwards, "Patent Medicines: Report No. 52," House of Representatives, 30th Congress, 2nd Sess., February 6, 1849, 1.

32. Edwards, 1–2.

33. Bigelow, "Insensibility," 316.

34. J. F. Flagg, "The Inhalation of an Ethereal Vapor to Prevent Sensibility to Pain During Surgical Operations," *Boston Medical and Surgical Journal* 35 (December 1846): 356–59.

35. Henry Bigelow, "A Response to J. F. Flagg," *Boston Medical and Surgical Journal* 35 (1846): 382.

36. Bigelow, "Response," 379.

37. This is clear in the handbill Morton sent to physicians and surgeons and published in the *Medical Journal Advertising Sheet* of the *Boston Medical and Surgical Journal.* See Viets, "Earliest Printed References," 161. The language in this debate can be confusing since popular tonics were commonly called patent medicines. But those who wanted to keep their concoctions secret did not patent their products at all; they sold them in bottles patented for their design or under copyrighted labels. Other healers who did patent their remedies—Samuel Thomson, for example—identified all ingredients for the patent register, a regularly published document with information on all patents granted. James Harvey Young makes this distinction clear in his history of patent medicine, though he, like nineteenth-century regulars, labels all vendors of such tonics quacks. See James Harvey Young, *The Toadstool Millionaires: A Social History of Patent Medicines in America Before Federal Regulation* (Princeton, N.J.: Princeton University Press, 1961).

38. Bigelow, *Ether,* p. 13.

39. In a history of the discovery written thirty years later, Bigelow again confuses the issue. He defines the discovery as being more of a "business character" and suggests that it was a "very small advance in strictly scientific knowledge," concluding that the discovery "was not in science but in art." And yet, he avoids any mention of Morton's patent. Instead, Bigelow issues a very general call for some kind of compensation, from what source he never indicates, for Morton's family (Morton had died a few years earlier) as evidence of the world's gratitude. Bigelow, "A History," 165, 181, 165.

40. Bigelow, *Ether,* p. 3.

41. Bigelow, *Ether*, 23, 22.

42. James Bono has argued that science "is not in complete control of its metaphors and analogies," and it would seem that Bigelow's texts are a good example. James J. Bono, "Science, Discourse, and Literature: The Role/Rule of Metaphor in Science," in *Literature and Science: Theory and Practice,* ed. Stuart Peterfreund (Boston: Northeastern University Press, 1990), 59–89.

43. Foucault is, of course, the scholar most often credited with the now widely accepted notion of the emergence of a modern body as a political construction of social and scientific discourses at the end of the eighteenth century, and my description of the modern body owes much to his work on the history of French medicine. But the work of Georges Canghuilhem, *The Normal and the Pathological* (1943), trans. Carolyn R. Fawcett (New York: Zone Books, 1991) on the development of the normal and pathological as medical categories in the nineteenth century, an important influence on Foucault, is also central to our understanding of the modern body as a political and economic construction. My description of the distinction between the modern body and the premodern body owes much to the work on body perception by Barbara Duden, *The Woman Beneath the Skin: A Doctor's Patients in Eighteenth-Century Germany,* trans. Thomas Dunlap (Cambridge, Mass.: Harvard University Press, 1991), 1–31, and to work on the history of medical therapeutics in nineteenth-century America by Charles Rosenberg, "The Therapeutic Revolution: Medicine, Meaning, and Social Change in Nineteenth-Century America," in *Explaining Epidemics and Other Studies in the History of Medicine* (New York: Cambridge University Press, 1992), 9–31.

44. Quoted in Pernick, *Calculus*, 137.

45. Pernick, 138, 141, 189. 189.

46. Pernick is too thorough not to consider arguments for the widespread use of anesthesia, and he offers persuasive interpretations of the professional ideology that motivated such arguments. But this side of the anaesthesia debate is not his primary focus, and to his brief sketch of advocates of anaesthesia constructing a philanthropic image of the profession as saviors of mankind from the evils of pain, I want to add a more specifically political analysis that suggests that the defense of anaesthesia by the medical elite was also shaped by the dominant political values in America in the 1840s—Jacksonian egalitarianism—and by the clinical ideology of the new medical science. In fact, my interest in the populist and democratic impulse in the construction of the modern body stands as a complement to Pernick's reading of the theory of the individualized body as indicative of a conservative ideology in medical therapeutics. Pernick, *Calculus,* 77–92.

47. Bigelow, *Ether*, 4.

48. Bigelow, "Insensibility," 315.

49. Bigelow, "Anaesthetic," 4.

50. Bigelow, "Anaesthetic," 4.

51. Bigelow, "Insensibility," 311–12.

52. In his biography of Morton, Rice made the improvements in surgery a major advantage offered by anesthesia. In elaborate and gory detail, he describes the surgical theater before the advent of anaesthesia, making it clear that ether was a boon to both doctor and patient. See Pernick, *Calculus,* 82–83, for other examples of celebrations of the improvements in surgery decorum with the advent of ether.

53. Quoted in Pernick, 53.

54. Bigelow, *Ether*, 4.

55. James C. Whorton, *Crusaders for Fitness: The History of American Health*

Reformers (Princeton, N.J.: Princeton University Press, 1982), 3–61 and Pernick, *Calculus*, 19–20.

56. Quoted in Pernick, 53.

57. See Warner, *Therapeutic Perspective*, 85–91, for a discussion and statistical analysis of the shift from "natural" to "normal" as the preferred term.

58. Morris, *Culture*, 4–5, 279.

59. Warner, *Therapeutic Perspective*, 58.

60. Pernick, *Calculus*, 190.

61. Quoted in Warner, *Therapeutic Perspective*, 275.

62. Bigelow, *Ether*, 4.

63. Bigelow, 4.

Chapter 2. Reading the Body: Hawthorne's Tales of Medical Ambition

Epigraph: Virginia Woolf, *Mrs. Dalloway* (New York: Harcourt, 1925), 184–85.

1. Nathaniel Hawthorne, *The Letters, 1813–1843*, The Centenary Edition of the Works of Nathaniel Hawthorne, vol. 15, ed. Thomas Woodson, L. Neal Smith, and Norman Holmes Pearson (Columbus: Ohio State University Press, 1984), 138–139.

2. The text has been given various titles, including "The Ancestral Footstep," "Etherege," and "Grimshawe." Julian Hawthorne published a version of the manuscript as *Doctor Grimshawe* in 1882.

3. Nathaniel Hawthorne, *The American Claimant Manuscripts*, Centenary Edition 12, ed. Edward H. Davidson, Claude M. Simpson, and L. Neal Smith (1977).

4. Nathaniel Hawthorne, *The Elixir of Life Manuscripts*, Centenary Edition 13, ed. Edward H. Davidson, Claude M. Simpson, and L. Neal Smith (1977), 458, 495.

5. See Russell C. Maulitz, "The Pathological Tradition," *Companion Encyclopedia of the History of Medicine*, ed. W. F. Bynum and Roy Porter (New York: Routledge, 1993), 169–79.

6. The phrase "significatory excess" comes from Mary Ann O'Farrell's lively study of the blush in the nineteenth century. Mary Ann O'Farrell, *Telling Complexions: The Nineteenth-Century English Novel and the Blush* (Durham, N.C.: Duke University Press, 1997).

7. Nathaniel Hawthorne, *American Notebooks*, Centenary Edition 8, ed. Claude M. Simpson (1972), 20.

8. Henry James, *Hawthorne* (1879; New York: Macmillan, 1966), 38.

9. Hawthorne, *American Notebooks*, 388.

10. Nathaniel Hawthorne, "The Birth-mark," *Mosses from an Old Manse*, Centenary Edition 10, ed. Fredson Bowers, L. Neal Smith, John Manning, and J. Donald Crowley (1974), 49. Future parenthetical references in the text are to this edition of the tale.

11. Hawthorne, *American Notebooks*, 184. Hawthorne did not write the tale imagined in the journal entry, and the narrator's empathy with Aylmer's failures does not lessen our horror at his reckless arrogance. In fact, by turning a critique of Faustian ambition against himself in this passage, Hawthorne enacts a self-awareness that Aylmer never achieves. Although Georgiana tells Aylmer with her last breath, "You have aimed loftily!—you have done nobly!" (55), these words are more generous than true. The story does not suggest that Aylmer has "done nobly" or even "aimed loftily." Aylmer does not, as far as we know, even recognize the magnitude of his failure, and the proposed treatment has no

redeeming holiness. As John Limon suggests, the tale enacts a disciplinary purification that demonizes "scientific professionalization" just when Hawthorne and other writers were "variously failing to establish themselves as professional men of letters." See John Limon, *The Place of Fiction in the Time of Science: A Disciplinary History of American Writing* (Cambridge: Cambridge University Press, 1990), 19. Limon's assessment of Hawthorne's professional achievement is severe, but the competition with science he notes in Hawthorne and other writers is right.

12. Sophia's devotion to Nathaniel's career and her eagerness to accommodate him is evident in her letters. In an April 6, 1845, letter to her sister, Sophia wrote, "If I could help my husband in his labors, I feel that that would be the chief employ of my life." In a January 9, 1844, letter to her mother, she wrote, "I can comprehend the delicacy & tricksiness of his mood when he is evolving a work of art by a small degree of the same in my own case—And his must be far greater, because he is so much greater, & his thoughts go far out of sight." Quoted in Luanne Jenkins Hurst, "The Chief Employ of Her Life," in *Hawthorne and Women: Engendering and Expanding the Hawthorne Tradition* (Amherst: University of Massachusetts Press, 1999), 45, 48. It should also be noted that Sophia, her family, and Nathaniel took her work seriously. Her letters from Cuba were collected and circulated by her family, and Hawthorne copied sixteen excerpts into his own journal. See Hyatt Waggoner, "A Hawthorne Discovery: The Lost Notebook, 1835–1841," *New England Quarterly* 49 (1976): 624.

13. See T. Walter Herbert, *Dearest Beloved: The Hawthornes and the Making of the Middle-Class Family* (Berkeley: University of California Press, 1993), 138–48.

14. Aylmer's confidence in scientific knowledge and in an aggressive treatment plays directly into nineteenth-century debates about medical science and therapeutics. In the early 1800s, heroic therapies came under attack, and not only by alternative healers. Some regulars, including many prestigious physicians trained in Paris, called for a scaling back of medicine's claims and therapies. In 1834 Jacob Bigelow published "Self-Limiting Diseases," in the 1840s Elisha Bartlett continued the call for therapeutic skepticism, and in the 1850s and 1860s Oliver Wendell Holmes took up the cause. Therapeutic skepticism, or "nature-trusting," rejected heroic dosing and called upon the physician to let nature take its course whenever possible. Other physicians rejected their colleagues' skepticism. One physician insisted, "we ought to study every disease, and interfere." The editor of the *Western Lancet* charged in 1842 that the skeptics were more concerned with proving a diagnosis "in a post mortem examination than in the administration of medicine to cure the disease," charging that the, "triumph of these physicians is in the dead room." Quoted in John Harley Warner, *Against the Spirit of System: The French Impulse in Nineteenth-Century American Medicine* (Princeton, N.J.: Princeton University Press, 1998), 285. The debate over therapeutic skepticism (some called it nihilism) was bitter, and Hawthorne satirizes both sides of the debate. In his efforts to interfere in a matter that needs no medical attention, Aylmer serves as a critique of aggressive therapies. In his obsessive commitment to science, he resembles caricatures of the new Paris-trained physicians who were decried as uninterested in the patient and the art of healing.

15. Hawthorne, *Letters, 1813–1843*, 513, 326. Also see Hawthorne, *American Notebooks*, 317–18; Herbert, *Dearest Beloved*, 145–46; and Edwin Haviland Miller, *Salem Is My Dwelling Place: A Life of Nathaniel Hawthorne* (Iowa City: University of Iowa Press, 1991), 175–86.

16. Quoted in Herbert, *Dearest Beloved*, 146–47.

17. Quoted in Herbert, 47.

18. As Herbert notes, Hawthorne's fiction exposes how the flip side of husbandly reverence for feminine purity is the male despot's misogynist loathing for female sexuality that can seem a dark stain on what should be untrammeled purity.

19. The trope of the sexualized medical laboratory was common in sensational fiction. As David Reynolds notes, in the early 1840s the "sensational, erotic and pseudoscientific" were often linked, most explicitly in fictional laboratories where somatic work is disturbingly erotic and grotesque. David S. Reynolds, *Beneath the American Renaissance: The Subversive Imagination in the Age of Emerson and Melville* (New York: Knopf, 1988), 170.

20. Letter to Mrs. Peabody, September 29, 1850, quoted in Hurst, *Chief Employ*, 49.

21. For an essay that is warmly attentive to Hawthorne's humor, see Carol Marie Bensick, "World Lit Hawthorne: Or, Re-Allegorizing 'Rappaccini's Daughter,'" in *New Essays on Hawthorne's Major Tales*, ed. Millicent Bell (Cambridge: Cambridge University Press, 1993), 67–82

22. It is worth noting that Hawthorne imagines sexual excitement for husband and wife. See Cindy Weinstein, "The Invisible Hand Made Visible: 'The Birthmark,'" *Nineteenth-Century Literature* 48 (June 1993): 49, for a discussion the significance of a "thematics of circulation" that links their bodies.

23. Hawthorne, *American Notebooks*, 235–36.

24. Quoted in Theodore M. Brown, "Mental Disease," in *Companion Encyclopedia of the History of Medicine*, ed. W. F. Bynum and Roy Porter (London: Routledge, 1997), 442. Pinel, despite the concern I note here, was very much a part of the Paris medical world. He wrote on the importance of clinical observation and of teaching practical medicine in the hospital wards in *La Médicine clinique* (1802), and on mental illness in "Treatise on Insanity" (translated into English in 1806).

25. See Andrew Combe, *The Physiology of Digestion* (Boston: Marsch, Capen & Lyon, 1837; reprint GastroLab Homepage, Historical Texts, *http://www.kolumbus.fi/hans/welcome.htm.*, December 7, 2003). For more on the influence of phrenology and the suggestion from Orson and Lorenzo Fowler of the importance of regular exercise of both the organ of amativeness (heterosexual love) and adhesiveness (same-sex comradeship), see Reynolds, *Beneath the American Renaissance*, 214, 326. See George Combe, "The Life and Correspondence of Andrew Combe" (1850; reprint "The History of Phrenology on the Web," ed. John van Wyhe, May 9, 2003, *http://pages.britishlibrary.net/phrenology/texts.htm*, December 7, 2003).

26. Critics have noted Hawthorne's attention to male violence against women and his impulse to make the female body intensely and ambivalently significant. This has led some to charge Hawthorne with misogyny and others to read his tales as indictments of male despotism. Some critics discount the "overwriting of the narrator" and any "cautionary" morals the tales offer, finding instead "a distrust of corporeality," an obsession with female monstrosity, and a similarity between Aylmer's science and Hawthorne's art. See Nina Baym "Thwarted Nature: Nathaniel Hawthorne as Feminist," in *American Novelists Reconsidered: Essays in Feminist Criticism*, ed. Fritz Fleischmann (Boston: G.K. Hall, 1982), 62; Gillian Brown, *Domestic Individualism: Imagining Self in Nineteenth-Century America* (Berkeley: University of California Press, 1990), 68; Judith Fetterley, *The Resisting Reader: A Feminist Approach to American Fiction* (Bloomington: Indiana University Press, 1978), 26–27. Others find an "implicit feminism in 'The Birthmark' that is

considerable" or note an "identification between Hawthorne and Georgiana." See Fetterley, 31; Weinstein, "Invisible Hand," 43. Perhaps most useful is Nina Baym's summary that Hawthorne represents "male inability to deal with women's body" sometimes as "his own oddity, sometimes as his culture's curse, and sometimes as the nature of men." See Baym, "Thwarted Nature," 68. In "The Birth-mark," Hawthorne indicts medicine and limns the violence that results.

27. Nathaniel Hawthorne, "Main-Street," *The Snow-Image and Uncollected Tales*, Centenary Edition 11, ed. Fredson Bowers, L. Neal Smith, John Manning, and J. Donald Crowley (1974), 70.

28. Quoted in Warner, *Against the Spirit*, 275. Initially female purity was only the pet theory of such reformers as Samuel Gregory, Sylvester Graham, and William Alcott, but this view quickly gained currency in established medicine. For a history of the rise of notions of female asexuality and purity, see Carroll Smith-Rosenberg, *Disorderly Conduct: Visions of Gender in Victorian America* (Oxford: Oxford University Press, 1985), 302, n.23. Notably, at the same time there was an explosion in erotic and pornographic literature in which women are typically wild, eager, and sexually active. See Reynolds, *Beneath the American Renaissance*, 211–24.

29. "Report of the Trial: The People versus Dr. Horatio N. Loomis, for Libel. Tried at the Erie County Oyer and Terminer, June 24, 1850" (Buffalo, N.Y., 1850); reprint in *The Male Mid-Wife and the Female Doctor: The Gynecology Controversy in Nineteenth-Century America*, ed. Charles Rosenberg and Carroll Smith-Rosenberg (New York: Arno Press, 1974), 11.

30. "Report of the Trial," 13.

31. In his account of his discovery, Laennec reported, "The patient's age and sex did not permit me to resort to [direct application of ear to chest]. . . . Taking a sheet of paper I rolled it into a very tight roll, one end of which I placed on the precordial region, whilst I put my ear to the other. I was both surprised and gratified at being able to hear the beating of the heart with much greater clearness and distinctness than I had ever before by direct application of my ear." Quoted in Roy Porter, *The Greatest Benefit to Mankind: A Medical History of Humanity* (New York: Norton, 1997), 308–9.

32. William P. Dewees, *A Compendious System of Midwifery, Chiefly Designed to Facilitate the Inquiries of Those Who May Be Pursuing This Branch of Study* (Philadelphia: Carey, Lea, and Blanchard, 1843), quoted in Judith Walzer Leavitt, "'Science' Enters the Birthing Room: Obstetrics in America since the 18th Century," in *Sickness and Health in America: Readings in the History of Medicine and Public Health* (Madison: University of Wisconsin Press, 1985), 83.

33. Leavitt, "Science," 83.

34. Quoted in Leavitt, 83.

35. Samuel Gregory, "Man-Midwifery Exposed and Corrected: or, The Employment of Men to Attend Women in Childbirth, Shown to be a Modern Innovation" (Boston and New York, 1848); rpt. in *The Male Mid-Wife and the Female Doctor: The Gynecology Controversy in Nineteenth-Century America*, ed. Charles Rosenberg and Carroll Smith-Rosenberg (New York: Arno Press, 1974), 40.

36. Gregory, "Man-Midwifery," 41.

37. As Warner notes, Sue "captured the imagination of American physicians who traveled to Paris." See Warner, *Against the Spirit*, 260–62.

38. Quoted in Herbert, *Dearest Beloved*, 253. Herbert suggests that Sophia was thrilled by the doctor's commanding manner, and that she was "stirred by him sexually and transferred to him the ardent hero worship her husband had earlier inspired."

39. For a discussion of Hawthorne's interest in signs, interpretation, and ambiguity in *The Scarlet Letter* and this interest in relation to medicine, see Stephanie P. Browner, "Authorizing the Body: Scientific Medicine and *The Scarlet Letter*," *Literature and Medicine* 12, 2 (Fall 1993): 146–51.

40. For the fullest articulation of this idea, see C. B. Macpherson, *The Political Theory of Possessive Individualism: Hobbes to Locke* (New York: Oxford University Press, 1962).

41. Quoted in Barbara Duden, *The Woman Beneath the Skin: A Doctor's Patients in Eighteenth-Century Germany*, trans. Thomas Dunlap (Cambridge: Cambridge University Press, 1991), 192, n.2.

42. See John, B. Blake, "Anatomy," in *The Education of American Physicians*, ed. Ronald L. Numbers (Berkeley: University of California Press, 1980), 29–47; Warner, *Against the Spirit*, 71–72; and Duden, *The Woman Beneath the Skin*, 1–31.

43. Certainly U.S. physicians who studied in Paris understood the new clinical method they were learning as possibly dangerous because it valued knowledge over healing and turned the patient into a subject. See Warner, *Against the Spirit*, 253–80.

44. See Weinstein, "Invisible Hand," 71.

45. Peter Brooks, *Body Work: Objects of Desire in Modern Narrative* (Cambridge, Mass.: Harvard University Press, 1993), xi, 7.

46. Brooks, 8.

47. Michel Foucault, *The Birth of the Clinic: An Archaeology of Medical Perception*, trans. A. M. Sheridan Smith (New York: Vintage, 1975), 114.

48. Porter, *Greatest Benefit*, 312.

49. W. F. Bynum, "Nosology," in *Companion Encyclopedia of the History of Medicine*, ed. W. F. Bynum and Roy Porter (New York: Routledge, 1997), 348.

50. In the eighteenth-century novel, as Mary Ann O'Farrell suggests, the blush testifies to the body's will and yet also can be pressed to serve mannerly ethics. Thus the blush may reveal what a smile might deny, but it also expresses desire that is, conveniently, directed toward the proper marriage partner. In race science, the blush bespeaks whiteness—Darwin insisted that dark-skinned people could not blush.

51. Medical science explored the possible pathology of vascular congestion, suggesting that repeated and extensive vascular dilation (the cause of blushing and also sexual arousal) could cause permanent and pathological lesions. See S. E. D. Short, *Victorian Lunacy: Richard M. Bucke and the Practice of Late Nineteenth-Century Psychiatry* (Cambridge: Cambridge University Press, 1986).

52. As Brodhead notes, Hawthorne refused to naturalize his symbols and refused to allow material explanations to supplant the sign. See Richard Brodhead, *The School of Hawthorne* (New York: Oxford University Press, 1989), 187–88.

53. O'Farrell, *Telling Complexions*, 3.

54. Foucault, *Birth of the Clinic*, 114.

55. Foucault, 81.

56. Hawthorne, "Rappaccini's Daughter," *Mosses from an Old Manse*, 110, 110, 110, 124. Future parenthetical references in the text are to this edition of the tale.

57. Quoted in Miller, *Salem*, 246.

58. Hawthorne, *Letters, 1843–1853*, 105.

59. Hawthorne, "The Old Manse," *Mosses from an Old Manse*, 32–33.

60. Nathaniel Hawthorne, *Passages from the American Note-Books of Nathaniel Hawthorne* (Boston: Houghton Mifflin, 1883), 334–35. No date is given for this entry, but it follows an entry for April 8, 1843.

61. Richard Brodhead, *Cultures of Letters: Scenes of Reading and Writing in Nineteenth-Century America* (Chicago: University of Chicago Press, 1993), 67.

62. See Katharine Eisman, *Inwardness and Theater in the English Renaissance* (Chicago: University of Chicago Press, 1995), 1–34. She notes the importance in the English Renaissance of both a belief in the self as "obscure, hidden, ineffable" and a belief in the self as "fully manifest" (28).

63. See Brodhead, *Cultures*, 48–68, for a discussion of Hawthorne's response to publicity, and for a reading of *The Blithedale Romance* that mediates the publicized, spectatorial world of stage entertainment and the privatized domestic world through the figure of Coverdale.

64. As many critics have noted, the gaze that pokes and pries fascinated Hawthorne. It was, on occasion, his model for authorship, as in "Sights from a Steeple" and *The Blithedale Romance*. See Browner, "Authorizing," for a discussion of the distinction Hawthorne makes between the prying gaze of the author and that of the physician.

65. Hawthorne, *The Scarlet Letter*, 129.

66. The image was a response to medicine's need for cadavers in order to teach anatomy and pathology. Beginning in the 1830s with efforts such as the one led by Dr. Abel Lawrence Peirson of Salem, the medical profession lobbied for legal access to cadavers. At the same time, and in response to alleged and actual grave-robbing, there were complaints, invocations of the famous anti-doctor riots of 1788, and several disturbances, including a riot in 1824 at the Yale Medical School and another in 1830 at Castleton Medical College in Vermont. Between 1830 and 1850, five states passed anatomy acts, of which three were repealed within a decade because the public was anxious not only about dishonoring bodies laid to rest, but also about medicine's eagerness to open the body and probe its interior. See Blake, "Anatomy," 37; Gary Laderman, *The Sacred Remains: American Attitudes Toward Death, 1799–1883* (New Haven, Conn.: Yale University Press, 1996), 83; and Frederic C. Waite, "The Development of Anatomical Laws in the States of New England," *New England Journal of Medicine* 233 (December 1945): 720–21.

67. For a connection between Alessandro Benedetti and Hawthorne's Baglioni (the historical anatomist and the fictional medical professor both commission a vial from Benvenuto Cellini), see Carol Marie Bensick, *La Nouvelle Beatrice: Renaissance and Romance in "Rappaccini's Daughter"* (New Brunswick, N.J.: Rutgers University Press, 1985), 105–8. I would add that his fame as an anatomist and his link to Cellini (who is directly cited in Hawthorne's tale) brings anatomy explicitly into Hawthorne's tale of the Paduan medical department in the early sixteenth century. Moreover, his emphasis on the role of the senses (he coined the term *anatomia sensibilis* to indicate that teaching and anatomical knowledge must be based solely on what is perceptible through the senses) echoes Rappaccini's dedication to sensory knowledge. See R. K. French, "Berengario da Carpi and the Use of Commentary in Anatomical Teaching," in *The Medical Renaissance of the Sixteenth Century*, ed. A. Wear, R. K. French, and Iain M. Lonie (Cambridge: Cambridge University Press, 1985), 42–74.

Benedetti launched the University of Padua into the limelight with his "The Account of the Human Body: Or Anatomy" (1502). See Porter, *Greatest Benefit*, 178. Soon after, several other anatomical texts appeared, and in 1531 a dissection manual by Galen was rediscovered and published that revealed that Galen had extrapolated from animal dissections for his knowledge of human anatomy. This prompted a revolution in anatomy: now anatomists could follow Galen's injunction to dissect and thus to see for themselves—the very definition of "autopsy." But, they could also make their own reputations by correcting Galen and contributing to a more accurate map of the human body. With these opportunities suddenly available, anatomy became, like geography, a field in which new worlds beckoned and parts had to be named. Like a lucky discoverer who memorializes himself by putting his name on a strait, lake, or continent, the anatomist might discover and put his name on an organ, vessel, or tube. Falloppia and others achieved such fame. The decision to appoint Vesalius, a young physician expert in dissection, was a bold move calculated to confirm the university's dominant role in the new field of anatomy.

68. "Rappaccini's Daughter" is set in the years Vesalius was doing his work. In an exhaustive and seminal study of the historical contexts for Hawthorne's tale, Bensick carefully identifies the setting. Based on very precise references in the tale to the development of botanic gardens in Padua, to the Borgia family, and to a vial made by Cellini, Bensick narrows the setting to the early sixteenth century.

69. See William S. Heckscher, *Rembrandt's Anatomy of Dr. Nicolaas Tulp: An Iconological Study* (New York: New York University Press, 1958), 139, n. 73. Heckscher's date comes from Charles Pickering, *Chronological History of Plants* (Boston: Little, Brown, 1879). Bensick, depending on Peter Laven, *Renaissance Italy: 1464–1534* (London: B. T. Batsford, 1966), gives 1545 as the date of the first botanical garden at the University of Padua and 1533 for the endowment of the first chair in botany. Bensick also notes that private gardens appeared before the University garden. See Bensick, *La Nouvelle Beatrice*, 31. While Bensick's dates are important for her argument that the story is set between 1527 and 1533, I would suggest that the more important significance of the references to botanical gardens at Padua is the link between botany and anatomy—the shared desire in both to anatomize, to map, and to name.

70. See Charles Russell Bardeen, "Anatomy in America," *Bulletin of the University of Wisconsin* 3, 4 (1905): 87.

71. Charles D. O'Malley, *Andreas Vesalius of Brussels* (Berkeley: University of California Press, 1965), 99.

72. See J. B. Saunders and Charles D. O'Malley, "Introduction," in *The Illustrations from the Works of Andreas Vesalius of Brussels* (New York: World Publishing, 1950), 17–18; and see O'Malley, *Vesalius*, 94–97.

73. See Porter, *Greatest Benefit*, 182.

74. Jonathan Sawday, *The Body Emblazoned: Dissection and the Human Body in Renaissance Culture* (London: Routledge, 1995).

75. For a fictional meditation upon dissection and intimacy, see John David Morley, *The Anatomy Lesson* (New York: St. Martin's, 1995); and for a nonfiction account written by someone who had never before seen an autopsy, see Michael Dibdin, "The Pathology Lesson," *Granta: The Body* 39 (Spring 1992): 91–102.

76. See Heckscher, *Rembrandt's Anatomy*, 43.

77. See Katherine Park, "The Criminal Body and the Saintly Body: Autopsy and Dissection in Renaissance Italy," *Renaissance Quarterly* 41, 1 (1994): 1–33.

78. See Heckscher, *Rembrandt's Anatomy*, 32.

79. See O'Malley, *Vesalius*, 113.

80. See Porter, *Greatest Benefit*, 181, for a brief comment on the *Fabrica* title page as a statement of medicine's new authority and methods.

81. Quoted in O'Malley, *Vesalius*, 113–14.

82. Francis Barker, *The Tremulous Private Body: Essays on Subjection* (London: Methuen, 1984), 100.

83. Barker focuses on Rembrandt's painting, *Anatomy of Dr. Nicholaas Tulp*, but her suggestion that anatomy both claimed an authority directly from the body

and yet continued to invoke the text as part of its domain is applicable to Vesalius's *Fabrica* as well.

84. For a reading of "Rappaccini's Daughter" as a tale that thematizes Hawthorne's interest in and appropriation of female creativity, see Joel Pfister, *The Production of Personal Life: Class, Gender, and the Psychological in Hawthorne's Fiction* (Stanford, Calif.: Stanford University Press, 1991), 59–79.

85. Hawthorne has little interest, it would seem, in later models of somatic interiority—the mechanical models developed by Descartes, Harvey, and Boyle, for example.

86. Morgagni occupied the anatomy chair at the University of Padua (the same position Vesalius had held years earlier), and his work was translated into all the major Western languages by the end of the eighteenth century.

87. Russell C. Maulitz, *Morbid Appearances: The Anatomy of Pathology in the Early Nineteenth Century* (Cambridge: Cambridge University Press, 1987), 18.

88. Quoted in Esmond R. Long, *Selected Readings in Pathology from Hippocrates to Virchow* (Springfield, Ill.: Charles C. Thomas, 1939), 139.

89. Foucault, *Birth of the Clinic*, 135.

90. Foucault, 122.

91. Warner, *Against the Spirit*, 270.

92. Porter, *Greatest Benefit*, 312.

93. In a December 6, 1844, letter to Sophia, Hawthorne writes of a marital "bliss" that is "as clear as crystal in my heart," but goes on to acknowledge, "though now and then, in great stress of earthly perplexities, a mist bedims its surface." See Hawthorne, *Letters, 1843–1853*, 70.

94. Other disease theories were emerging in the late 1830s and early 1840s. By 1836 the idea of "trans-microscopic" organic "corpuscles" produced by fermentation had gained some credibility, and in general there was interest in the idea of organic parasites that entered and then sickened the body. See Charles Rosenberg, *The Cholera Years: The United States in 1832, 1849, and 1866* (Chicago: University of Chicago, Press, 1987), 164–72, and Porter, *Greatest Benefit*, 409–15.

95. Quoted in Peter Stallybrass and Allon White, *The Politics and Poetics of Transgression* (Ithaca, N.Y.: Cornell University Press, 1986), 139.

96. See Franny Nudelman, "'Emblem and Product of Sin': The Poisoned Child in *The Scarlet Letter* and Domestic Advice Literature," *Yale Journal of Criticism* 10, 1 (Spring 1997): 193–213, for an excellent discussion of poison and women in Hawthorne's writing and in nineteenth-century culture. In the first half of the century, the image of the female poisoner negotiated complicated questions about female bodies. In an 1840 Massachusetts trial of a female poisoner, the prosecutor warned that poison as "an instrument of death is not manifest like a sword, pistol or dagger; but generally invisible, prepared in secret, disguised and administered in an unsuspected form, in food or medicine, presented by hands beloved." The female poisoner, he cautioned, is equally duplicitous, and a jury should not be misled by her physical appearance, by the "living, breathing, palpitating flesh and blood, full of tremor and anxiety, which stands in danger before our eyes." The female poisoner also appeared in nineteenth-century crime literature, where she similarly represented the threat of concealed female deviance and thus served as a nightmarish inversion of maternity. Mothers, it was commonly asserted in advice manuals, pass to their children their deepest emotions. These transmissions were understood to be somatic, inevitable, and always with visible results. Underlying both images is a notion of the female body as naturally expressive. Female bodies will reveal female character,

and when they do not it is a perversion of femininity that ends in such monstrosities as the female poisoner.

97. "Historical Commentary" in Hawthorne, *American Notebooks,* 697.

98. Edwin Percy Whipple, "Tragic Power," *Graham's Magazine* 36 (May 1850): 345–46, reprinted in Hawthorne, *The Scarlet Letter: An Authoritative Text, Essays in Criticism, and Scholarship* (New York: Norton, 1988), 183; Evert A. Duyckinck, "Great Feeling and Discrimination," *Literary World* 6 (March 30): 323–25, reprinted, 181.

99. In Rose Hawthorne Lathrop, *Memories of Hawthorne* (Boston: Houghton Mifflin, 1897), 121.

100. The earliest citation in the *OED* for "morbid" is 1656.

101. Quoted in Nancy Glazener, *Reading for Realism: The History of a U.S. Literary Institution, 1850–1910* (Durham, N.C.: Duke University Press, 1997), 100, 101.

102. Laderman, *Sacred Remains,* 81. There were some attempts to legislate medical access to bodies, but none was successful before the Civil War.

103. Hidden rooms and basements in novels such as Lippard's *The Quaker City* (and many other city novels) figure urban corruption and psychological interiority. See Karen Halttunen, "Gothic Mystery and the Birth of the Asylum: The Cultural Construction of Deviance in Early-Nineteenth-Century America," in *Moral Problems in American Life: New Perspectives on Cultural History,* ed. Karen Halttunen and Lewis Perry (Ithaca, N.Y.: Cornell University Press, 1998), 41–58.

104. For an analysis of the class implications of interiority in fiction, see Deidre Shauna Lynch's study of British fiction from Defoe to Austen, in which she connects an "inward turn" at the end of the eighteenth century and the emergence of characters with psychological depths to social processes. Lynch suggests that in these years, there was "an increasing demonization of the literacies of the crowd" and "a new insistence that reading was an activity pursued by individuals." With the emergence of a hierarchy in literature, "characters acquired inner lives." Deidre Shauna Lynch, *The Economy of Character: Novels Market Culture, and the Business of Inner Meaning* (Chicago: University of Chicago Press, 1998), 6.

105. Bensick, *La Nouvelle Beatrice.*

106. Thus, when the narrator suggests Beatrice is "pure whiteness" within, we are offended. The conclusion is too easy; it cloys. It may do justice to Beatrice's character, but it does not do justice to her body.

Chapter 3. Carnival Bodies and Medical Professionalism in Melville's Fiction

Epigraph: John Stuart Mill, "Civilization," *Westminster Review* 30 (April 1836): 1–28; reprinted in George Levine, *The Emergence of Victorian Consciousness* (New York: Free Press, 1967), 99.

1. Herman Melville, *Billy Budd, Sailor,* in *Herman Melville* (New York: Library of America, 1984), 1427.

2. Peter Stallybrass and Allon White, *The Politics and Poetics of Transgression* (Ithaca, N.Y.: Cornell University Press, 1986), 123–24.

3. The only physician not satirized in Melville's oeuvre is the unnamed, impoverished physician in "Two Temples" who sneaks into an elite New York church after being denied entrance by a beadle. In the second of these paired sketches, the physician goes to London as a medical escort and gains admittance

to an elite London theater when a working man gives him a ticket. For a discussion of these tales, see Stephanie P. Browner, "Documenting Cultural Politics: A *Putnam's* Short Story," *PMLA* (March 2001): 397–405.

4. Herman Melville, *Typee: A Peep at Polynesian Life*, vol. 1 of The Writings of Herman Melville, Northwestern-Newberry Edition, ed. Harrison Hayford, Hershel Parker, and G. Thomas Tanselle (Evanston: Northwestern University Press, 1968), 6. Future parenthetical references are to this edition.

5. Richard Brodhead, *Cultures of Letters: Scenes of Reading and Writing in Nineteenth-Century America* (Chicago: University of Chicago Press, 1993), 67.

6. Stallybrass and White, *Politics and Poetics*, 202.

7. See Leon Howard, "Historical Note," 282–91, and Harrison Hayford, Hershel Parker, and G. Thomas Tanselle, "Note on the Text," 306–11, both in Melville, *Typee*; and John Bryant, "Textual Expurgations," in Melville, *Typee: A Peep at Polynesian Life* (New York: Penguin, 1996), 275–87.

8. Stallybrass and White, *Politics and Poetics*, 201.

9. Nathaniel Hawthorne, *The Marble Faun*, vol. 4 of The Centenary Edition of the Works of Nathaniel Hawthorne, ed. Roy Harvey Pearce, Claude M. Simpson, Fredson Bowers, and L. Neal Smith (Columbus: Ohio State University Press, 1968), 123.

10. Ibid.

11. Thomas Thorne, "America's Earliest Nude?" *William and Mary Quarterly* 6, 5 (October 1949): 565; Lillian B. Miller, "Paintings, Sculpture, and the National Character, 1815–1860," *Journal of American History* 53, 4 (March 1967): 702.

12. See Samuel Otter, *Melville's Anatomies* (Berkeley: University of California Press, 1999), 20–24.

13. Stallybrass and White, *Politics and Poetics*, 22.

14. Robert K. Martin suggests that in both tales of nakedness the "Westerners see a sexual gesture where none is intended" and that they prefer "concealment to display, taking display as a sign of sexual freedom." I would simply add that Melville is fully aware that his readers will find the scenes sexually suggestive. See Robert K. Martin, *Hero, Captain, and Stranger: Male Friendship, Social Critique, and Literary Form in the Sea Novels of Herman Melville* (Chapel Hill: University of North Carolina Press, 1986), 24.

15. In his study of Melville and colonialism, Gregory Sanborn suggests that Melville understands savagery as the "ceaseless ornamentation of one's self with signs" and that he achieves a degree of postcolonial wisdom because he suggests that "the discursive authority of the colonialist is more anxious than we might think, and the subjectivity of the native more opaque." Gregory Sanborn, *The Sign of the Cannibal: Melville and the Making of a Postcolonial Reader* (Durham, N.C.: Duke University Press, 1998), 116.

16. Judith Butler, *Bodies That Matter: On the Discursive Limits of "Sex"* (New York: Routledge, 1993), 31.

17. Melville's exploration of the role of the body in Taipi culture lands him right in the middle of our own current debates about the body. Recently, critics of poststructuralism have warned that there is danger in reading everything, and especially bodies, as texts. They remind us that all bodies, even culturally constructed bodies, bleed when pricked. As Terry Eagleton notes, current discussions of the somatic rarely talk of real violence and real bodily injury. In response, Judith Butler offers a warning: in our eagerness to retrieve a real body we may turn the body into "a sign of irreducibility," a sign of a historical and innocent materiality. As Butler astutely notes, however, we might be able to have our cake and eat it too; we need not give up a category just because we deconstruct

it. "Surely, it must be possible," she asserts, "both to use [a] term, to use it tactically . . . and also to subject the term to a critique which interrogates" it (29). This is Melville's project: he invokes the trope of the "natural body" and interrogates this construct at the same time. The beauty of the naked houris and the simple somatic pleasures of island life do indeed stand for an innocent materiality that the West violates cruelly by bringing civilization—disease, violence, and destruction (as well as French clothes)—to the islands. Thus, Melville makes powerful, tactical use of the natural body so central to primitivist romance. At the same time, however, Melville understands the native body as not merely innocent or natural. For a discussion of Melville's refusal to sentimentalize innocence, see Nancy Ruttenburg, "Melville's Handsome Sailor: The Anxiety of Influence," *American Literature* (March 1994): 83–103.

18. The somatic pleasures endorsed in the opening tales of nakedness give way in the second half of the novel to somatic anxieties. Pleasures continue to beckon, but Tommo also worries for his physical safety and for his unmarked (white) Western body. Karky's interest in tattooing Tommo is unnerving, and a confirmation of cannibalism among the Taipi leaves Tommo terrified for his own safety, so he flees. The violence of Tommo's exit is troubling, and critics have sought to explain why Melville has his alter ego leave Nukuheva in such a brutal scene—having climbed into a rescue boat, Tommo stabs at a native in the water who is pursuing him. Contemporary reviewers suggested that Tommo's violent departure reveals the truth about living with the savages. Primitive life may seem idyllic but in the end Tommo "felt himself a prisoner" in a world of cannibals. See Brian Higgins and Hershel Parker, eds., *Herman Melville: The Contemporary Reviews* (Cambridge: Cambridge University Press, 1995), 29. Nearly a hundred years later, D. H. Lawrence made essentially the same point, suggesting that the flight was a necessary and inevitable rejection of the "vast vacuum" of an aimless life of pleasure. More recently, critics have read Tommo's flight not so much as a critique of the emptiness of savage life, but as evidence of Tommo's (and Melville's) inability to maintain the primitivist ideology both he and Melville initially embrace. According to Samuel Otter, Tommo abandons paradise because the local tattoo artist's eagerness to ornament him threatens the white man's fantasy that his body is pure and thus distinct from the tattooed, darker skin of non-Europeans. Otter, *Melville's Anatomies*.

19. Higgins and Parker, *Melville*, 7.

20. Biographers note Melville's love of the body. One biographer suggests that Melville "loved high and irresponsible talk for the mere and sufficient majesty it gave the diaphragm to expand." See Raymond M. Weaver, *Herman Melville: Mariner and Mystic* (New York: George H. Doran, 1921), vi. Another writes of "the vigorous, tactile Herman." See Hershel Parker, *Herman Melville: A Biography*, vol. 1, *1819–1851* (Baltimore: Johns Hopkins University Press, 1996), 450.

21. Howard, "Historical Note," 294.

22. Quoted in Ann Douglas, *The Feminization of American Culture* (New York: Anchor, 1988), 289.

23. More recent critics have focused almost exclusively on the novel's political commentary, and some have lost an awareness of the intimate link between Melville's political commentary and his love of the body and its pleasures.

24. Leon Howard, *Herman Melville: A Biography* (Berkeley: University of California Press, 1951), 72. But while most critics have accepted Melville's political agenda in *Typee* at face value (more or less), they have been inclined to find political posturing in *White-Jacket*. Critics have suggested that Melville's polemic against flogging was not particularly daring (some call it opportunistic), and several

have argued that Melville's identification with the common sailor is not genuine, noting that his own class snobbery lies not far below the work's democratic rhetoric. I want to suggest, however, that Melville's political critique in *White-Jacket* is pointed and passionate.

25. Herman Melville, *White-Jacket, or The World in a Man-of-War*, Northwestern-Newberry Edition 5 (1970), 248. Future parenthetical citations are to this edition.

26. Herman Melville, *Journals*, Northwestern-Newberry Edition 15 (1989), 40, 174, 357.

27. The travel guide/memoir appeared in a second, revised edition in 1850 under the title, *The French Metropolis. Paris; As Seen during the Spare Hours of a Medical Student*, 2nd ed., rev. (New York: Francis, 1850).

28. As quoted in Melville, *Journals*, 341–42.

29. See Parker, *Melville*, vol. 1, 652, 680. At the pathology museum in Paris, Melville saw in glass jars of pickling solution a heart with a gold coin embedded in it, a baby with a tail, and a baby with two heads. Hershel Parker imagines that the visit to the museum allowed Melville to soothe "a lifelong curiosity about abnormal human anatomy." In his journal, Melville noted, "Went to the Museum Dupuytren. Pathological. Rows of cracked skulls. Skeletons & things without a name." See Melville, *Journals*, 33.

30. Wai Chee Dimock, *Empire for Liberty: Melville and the Poetics of Individualism* (Princeton, N.J.: Princeton University Press, 1989), 317.

31. Robyn Wiegman, *American Anatomies: Theorizing Race and Gender* (Durham, N.C.: Duke University Press, 1995), 6.

32. The physicality of friendships among sailors fosters what Robert K. Martin calls a "democratic eros," his term for the "seminal power" of male friendships that are "not directed to control or production." See Martin, *Hero, Captain, and Stranger*.

33. David Arnold, *Colonizing the Body: State Medicine and Epidemic Disease in Nineteenth-Century India* (Berkeley: University of California Press, 1993), 6.

34. Quoted in Dana Nelson, *National Manhood: Capitalist Citizenship and the Imagined Fraternity of White Men* (Durham, N.C.: Duke University Press, 1998), 123.

35. As Colette Guillaumin explains, in some societies visibility is claimed by those in power, and difference is the declared property of the dominant group. This was precisely what Melville noted about the use of tattoos among the Taipi: power is made visible through an intensification of embodiment (men in positions of power have elaborate tattoos while younger men have fewer distinguishing marks). See Colette Guillaumin, *Racism, Sexism, Power and Ideology* (New York: Routledge, 1995).

36. Quoted in Cynthia J. Davis, *Bodily and Narrative Forms: The Influence of Medicine on American Literature, 1845–1915* (Stanford, Calif.: Stanford University Press, 2000), 27.

37. Quoted in Davis, 21. U.S. physicians were sensitive to the possibility that too much equanimity might suggest to a wary public that doctors were becoming cold-hearted scientists. Perhaps with an eye to these concerns, regulars saw a role for sentimentality as well as self-control in their bedside manners. Holmes and others who studied in Paris believed that while the scientific methods they were learning were invaluable, the cold bedside manners (as well as the scientific obsessions) of their mentors were not to be emulated. As Davis notes, early AMA documents and Holmes's novel *Elsie Venner* imagine kindness at the bedside or an occasional tear at the end of a case as acceptable and even appropriate signs of a physician's humanity. See Davis, 13–48, for a discussion of sentimentality in medicine and in Holmes's novel *Elsie Venner*.

38. Melville, *Billy Budd, Sailor*, 1427–28.

39. According to the text's editors, Melville also touched on the limitations of the man of science in a deleted passage on "Lawyers, Experts, and Clergy." See Hershel Parker, *Reading* Billy Budd (Evanston: Northwestern University Press, 1990), 154–56, 170–72, and see the notes with Harrison Hayford's 1962 edition of *Billy Budd, Sailor*.

40. Herman Melville, "Hawthorne and His Mosses," *Literary World* (August 1850).

41. Quoted in Jay Leyda, *The Melville Log: A Documentary Life of Herman Melville, 1819–1891*, 2 vols. (New York: Gordian Press, 1969), 469. For more on the financial pressure Melville felt shortly before and during the writing of *The Confidence-Man* and the health problems he was suffering at the same time, see Elizabeth S. Foster, Introduction to *The Confidence-Man* (New York: Hendricks House, 1954), xx–xxiii. Although there is little on the relationship between Melville and Holmes, they clearly enjoyed each other's company. Maunsell Field records in his *Memories of Many Men* (1874) a discussion between Holmes and Melville which, he reports, "was conducted with the most amazing skill and brilliance on both sides. It lasted for hours, and Darley and I had nothing to do but listen. I never chanced to hear better talking in my life. It was so absorbing that we took no note of time, and the Doctor lost his dinner, as we lost ours" (quoted in Leyda, 506). Based on Elizabeth Melville's journal, Jay Leyda also reconstructs the details of Holmes's professional visit to Melville, and he adds this note from a biographical sketch published in the *Evening Journal* after Melville's death: "when at one time Mr. Melville was seriously ill Dr. Holmes visited him with fraternal tenderness, incidentally of course giving him his best medical advice, without—that also, of course—intruding upon the province of the local practitioner" (quoted in Leyda, 502). Significantly, the note takes care to point out that Holmes only acted as a neighbor, and thus he did not transgress the rules of the AMA and infringe upon the practice of another physician.

42. Michael T. Gilmore, *American Romanticism and the Marketplace* (Chicago: University of Chicago Press, 1985), 150.

43. Dimock, *Empire*, 212; Elizabeth Renker, *Strike Through the Mask: Herman Melville and the Scene of Writing* (Baltimore: Johns Hopkins University Press, 1996), 69. More generally, critical commentary on *The Confidence-Man* describes the novel as a cry of despair from an author who has lost all confidence in man, truth, kindness, and generosity. When Melville was rediscovered in the 1920s, and the novel was declared worthy of greater attention (it had been dismissed as unreadable for decades), even those who celebrated its aesthetic achievements read it as evidence of the author's Timonism. Lewis Mumford in 1929 called it "an indictment of humanity" and insisted that it was "far more deeply corrosive than anything in Bierce or Twain." In 1938, Ivor Winters wrote that it depicted a world of moral confusion; in 1948, Thorpe wrote in *Literary History of the United States* that Melville had clearly "abandoned his humanist faith in the decency and dignity of man"; in 1949, Richard Chase suggested that the novel "represents all that is wrong with the liberalism of Melville's day." In her 1954 introduction to *The Confidence-Man*, Elizabeth S. Foster offered a magisterial study that significantly expanded critical interest in the novel, suggesting that it was not only a treatise on man's foibles and an expose of nineteenth-century philosophical optimism and millennial religiosity, but also a study of evil. After Foster, H. Bruce Franklin suggested that in the novel all gods are con-men, and James Miller concluded that "Christ's heavenly doctrine of charity (love) is unworkable" in Melville's world. More recently, with the advent of deconstruction, poststructuralism, and new historicism, some critics have found virtues in the con-man.

In his introduction to the Oxford paperback edition, for example, Tony Tanner suggests that Melville was seeking a "new kind of fidelity, a fidelity to the radical discontinuity and plurality of the self." Others suggest that Melville's novel exposes the evils of capitalism—alienation, reification, commodification. And yet even these critics conclude that the novel is nihilistic. Tanner, for example, admits that "the end leaves us nothing to stand on and nothing to see by." Gilmore suggests that the "rage and alienation . . . everywhere . . . amount to an acknowledgement that the conditions of production and exchange emergent under capitalism permit no exception." Dimock suggests that the novel reduces everything, including persons, to a product of economic practice. See Lewis Mumford, *Herman Melville* (New York: Harcourt Brace, 1929), 248; Willard Thorpe, "Melville," in *Literary History of the Unites States,* ed. Robert E. Spiller et al. (New York: Macmillan, 1948), 463; Richard Volney Chase, *Herman Melville: A Critical Study* (New York: Macmillan, 1949), 463; H. Bruce Franklin, *The Wake of the Gods, Melville's Mythology* (Stanford, Calif.: Stanford University Press, 1963); James Miller, *A Reader's Guide to Herman Melville* (New York: Farrar, 1962), 180; Tony Tanner, Introduction to *The Confidence-Man* (New York: Oxford University Press, 1989), xxxiv–xxxvi; Gilmore, 151.

44. Carolyn Karcher notes that we can never know if Black Guinea is a white man in blackface, or if the avatars that come after him are black men masquerading as white. See *Shadow Over the Promised Land: Slavery, Race, and Violence in Melville's America* (Baton Rouge: Louisiana State University Press, 1980).

45. Herman Melville, *The Confidence-Man, A Masquerade,* Northwestern-Newberry Edition 10 (1984), 226. Future parenthetical references will be to this edition.

46. Michael Rogin, *Subversive Genealogy: The Politics and Art of Herman Melville* (New York: Knopf, 1983), 244.

47. Eric Lott, *Love and Theft: Blackface Minstrelsy and the American Working Class* (New York: Oxford University Press, 1993), 15.

48. Susan Ryan, "Misgivings: Melville, Race, and the Ambiguities of Benevolence," *American Literary History* 12, 4 (Winter 2000): 685–712.

49. Most critics presume that Black Guinea is an able-bodied white man. For a contrary view, see Karcher, *Shadow,* 186–257.

50. Robert P. Nevin, "Stephen C. Foster and Negro Minstrelsy," *Atlantic Monthly* 20 (November 1867): 609. The image of financial desperation and somatic willingness that is captured in the catching-pennies trick was cast into iron a few years later when mechanical banks became popular. The banks, however, and in particular those models in which black pickaninnies and other degrading black stereotypes catch coins in their mouths, enact a slightly different economic equation. While Cuff and Black Guinea offer a "singular temptation at once to diversion and charity," toy banks offer an invitation at once to diversion and thrift, with the black body providing enticement to help oneself rather than another. The first bank was patented in 1869, and they were popular from 1870 to 1930. Their rise coincided with self-help and thrift as themes in popular fiction, such as Horatio Alger's Ragged Dick series, which began in 1867.

51. See James Harvey Young, *The Toadstool Millionaires: A Social History of Patent Medicine in America Before Federal Regulation* (Princeton, N.J.: Princeton University Press, 1961), 44–57.

52. Appeals to the sage traditions of Native Americans were common in patent medicines at mid-century as well as a signature of Thomson's method. See James Harvey Young, *American Health Quackery* (Princeton, N.J.: Princeton University Press, 1992), 54.

53. For more on the evangelical rhetoric of alternative medicine, see James C. Whorton, *Crusaders for Fitness: The History of American Health Reformers* (Princeton, N.J.: Princeton University Press, 1982), 1–92 and Robert C. Fuller, *Alternative Medicine and American Religious Life* (New York: Oxford University Press, 1989), 12–37.

54. A. Biggs, *The Botanico Medical Reference Book* (Memphis, Tenn.: Wells and Care, 1846), 25–26.

55. Reprinted in Ann Novotny and Carter Smith, *Images of Healing: A Portfolio of American Medical & Pharmaceutical Practice in the 18th, 19th, and Early 20th Centuries* (New York: Macmillan, 1980), 51.

56. See Paul Starr, *The Social Transformation of American Medicine* (New York: Basic Books, 1982), 53.

57. Quoted in Richard Shyrock, *Medical Licensing in America* (Baltimore: Johns Hopkins University Press, 1967), 417.

58. Quoted in Martin Kaufman, *Homeopathy in America: The Rise and Fall of a Medical Heresy* (Baltimore: Johns Hopkins University Press, 1971), 56.

59. Oliver Wendell Holmes, *Medical Essays* (New York: Riverside, 1891), 2.

60. Karen Haltunnen, *Confidence Men and Painted Women: A Study of Middle-Class Culture in America, 1830–1870* (New Haven, Conn.: Yale University Press, 1982), 1–32, has examined the pervasive and powerful tropes of deception, counterfeiting, and con games in mid-nineteenth-century culture, a result, she argues, of the widespread uncertainty engendered by the rise of cities and a more fluid class structure. In medicine these changes were further aggravated by the popularity and success of alternative practitioners and the consequent challenge to economic security and professional identity of regulars. It is not surprising, then, that much of mid-nineteenth-century medical discourse, like American culture in general, focused on truth and deception.

61. The poem also suggests that Major Melvill's achievements and era are things of the past. The Melville family was not immediately pleased with the poem, but as it grew in fame, it grew in their esteem. See Parker, *Melville*, 54–55.

62. Reports indicate that on the outing Holmes, as usual, was the debonair gentleman. At the summit, he pulled a champagne bottle out of his medical bag, and he had a spirited debate with Melville and others when he asserted the superiority of Englishmen to Americans. See Leyda, *Melville Log*, 383–86.

63. Leyda makes suggestive connections between a lost report from Dr. Holmes to Melville and the surveyor's note to the chimney owner in "I and My Chimney." See Leyda, 502–3.

64. "It is folly for the physician to boast," writes Hooker, "that he worships in a temple, upon whose altars no strange fires ever burn, while he looks out with contempt upon what he regards as the almost heathenish observances and worship of the unscientific and unlearned people" (quoted in Young, *American Health Quackery*, 39).

65. Thomas Richards, *The Commodity Culture of Victorian England: Advertising and Spectacle, 1851–1914* (Stanford, Calif.: Stanford University Press, 1990), 187.

66. Barnum's part in patent medicine included selling, exposing, and using various nostrums. He tried to sell bear's grease as a hair restorer, scoffed in his book *Humbugs of the World* at one seller's claim that his Hasheesh Candy could cure seventy-one diseases, and regularly swallowed for his own complaints Benjamin Brandreth's Universal Vegetable Pills. See Young, *American Health Quackery*, 90.

67. As a term from anatomy, hypochondrium (singular of hypochondria) refers to the region under the lower ribs, the viscera of the epigastric region,

including the liver, gall-bladder, and spleen. In classical medicine, this area was understood to be the seat of melancholy, and in the 1855 *Webster's Dictionary* hypochondria was defined as a "combination of melancholy and dyspepsia, consisting in gloomy ideas of life, dejected spirits, and indisposition to activity." By the mid-nineteenth century, of course, Galen's humoral theory of disease etiology was no longer in use, but words such as hypochondria, dyspepsia, and melancholia continued to identify temperament as a factor in disease. Thus, in calling the Titan a hypochondriac, Melville allows that his pains are real and also suggests that he is temperamentally given to suffering.

68. Melville was not the only writer attentive to the fundamental inefficacy of language in the face of pain. Emily Dickinson writes of the empty, timeless nature of pain:

Pain—has an element of Blank—
It cannot recollect
When it begun—or if there were
A time when it was not—

It has no Future—but itself—
Its Infinite contain
Its Past—enlightened to perceive
New Periods—of Pain.

The Complete Poems of Emily Dickinson, ed. Thomas H. Johnson (Boston: Little, Brown, 1960), # 650, 323–24. In her essay "On Being Ill," Virginia Woolf comments, "English which can express the thoughts of Hamlet and the tragedy of Lear has not words for the shiver or the headache . . . let a sufferer try to describe a pain in his head . . . and language at once runs dry." *Collected Essays,* vol. 4 (New York: Harcourt, 1967), 194.

69. Elaine Scarry, *The Body in Pain: The Making and Unmaking of the World* (New York: Oxford University Press, 1985).

70. Susan Ryan has noted that doubt was an integral feature in the discourse of charity in the nineteenth century. As she explains, those who flaunted their misery were deemed untrustworthy and public signs of need—in particular, crutches—became suspect as signs readily commandeered by conniving, and undeserving mendicants.

71. See Charles Rosenberg, *The Care of Strangers: The Rise of America's Hospital System* (New York: Basic Books, 1987), 15–69, for a history of class bias in nineteenth-century hospital care.

72. In the short story "The Poor Man's Crumbs," Melville satirizes easy, condescending judgments made by "the well-housed, well-warmed, and well-fed." In this 1854 *Putnam's* tale, he lampoons the facile optimism of "Poet Blandmour," a man much like the herb-doctor. The Poet calls a spring snow "Poor Man's Manure" since the snow moistens the ground, and he dubs cold rainwater "Poor Man's Egg," since water can substitute for eggs. Determined to judge for himself, the narrator goes to dine with a poor farmer and his wife, and he discovers nothing romantic about their poverty.

73. See Keith Thomas, "Wrapping It Up," review of Natalie Zemon Davis, *The Gift in Sixteenth-Century France, New York Review of Books,* 21 December 2000, 69–72.

74. Daniel Hack, "Literacy Paupers and Professional Authors: The Guild of Literature and Art," *Studies in English Literature* 39, 4 (Autumn 1999): 691–714.

75. David Caputo, "Roundtable," in *Deconstruction in a Nutshell: A Conversation with Jacques Derrida* (New York: Fordham University Press, 1997), 19.

76. Caputo, 144.

77. Caputo, 19.

78. Foster, "Introduction," lxxxviii.

Chapter 4. Class and Character: Doctors in Nineteenth-Century Periodicals

Epigraph: Edward Spencer, "A Good Word for Quacks," *Atlantic Monthly* 31 (March 1873): 328.

1. The scholarship on the history of the professions is extensive. Samuel Haber, *The Quest for Authority and Honor in the American Professions, 1750–1900* (Chicago: University of Chicago Press, 1991), is a particularly thorough history and it focuses on the professions' rise and fall during these years.

2. For a full history of heroic medicine, see William G. Rothstein, *American Physicians in the Nineteenth Century: From Sects to Science* (Baltimore: Johns Hopkins University Press, 1972), 41–62.

3. Haber, *Quest*, 103–7.

4. Eliot Freidson, *Profession of Medicine: A Study of the Sociology of Applied Knowledge* (New York: Dodd, Mead, 1970), 72.

5. Antonio Gramsci, *Selections from the Prison Notebooks*, ed. and trans. Quintin Hoare and Geoffrey Nowell Smith (New York: International Publishers, 1971), 6.

6. Magali Sarfatti Larson, *The Rise of Professionalism: A Sociological Analysis* (Berkeley: University of California Press, 1977), xv. Many other historians and sociologists make the same point. Peter Dobkin Hall, *The Organization of American Culture, 1700–1900: Private Institutions, Elites, and the Origins of American Nationality* (New York: New York University Press, 1982), notes that the success of medical professionalizing arose not from advances in science, diagnosis, or therapeutics (these were not significant, rarely visible, and not yet capable of transforming medical practice), but from medicine's association with "the institutions and social groups in which political, financial, and cultural power resided" and from the "patronage of powerful groups" (145, 150). Regarding alliances between professionals and the ruling elite, also see Chantel Mouffe, "Hegemony and Ideology in Gramsci," in *Gramsci and Marxist Theory*, ed. Chantal Mouffe (Boston: Routledge, 1979), 168–204. As Mouffe says, hegemony is "the ability of one class to annex the interests of other social groups to its own" (183). This is not illegitimate, as Nancy Glazener, *Reading for Realism: The History of a U.S. Literary Institution, 1850–1910* (Durham, N.C.: Duke University Press, 1997), points out, though hegemony usually means that the process by which groups get power is occluded or misrepresented (pp. 31–32).

7. "Short Essays on the Medical Profession," *Southern Literary Messenger* 9 (May 1843): 297.

8. Worthington Hooker, "The Present Mental Attitude and Tendencies of the Medical Profession," *New Englander* 10 (1852); reprinted as *Inaugural Address* (New Haven, Conn.: T. J. Stafford Printer, 1852).

9. "Doctors," *Putnam's* 2 (1853): 66–71; "The Medical Profession," *Putnam's* 2 (1853): 315–18.

10. Glazener, *Reading*, 6.

11. Shirley Samuels, "Miscegenated America: The Civil War," *American Literary History* 9 (1997): 483. For the effects of the European revolutions, see Larry

Reynolds, *European Revolutions and the American Literary Renaissance* (New Haven, Conn.: Yale University Press, 1988); and for suggestions about the role of daguerreotypes in a commodity culture in which copies and originals, image and substance, facade and truth, seem interchangeable, see Alan Trachtenberg, "Seeing and Believing: Hawthorne's Reflections on the Daguerreotype in *The House of the Seven Gables*," *American Literary History* 9 (1997): 460–81.

12. Larson, *Rise*, 106–10.

13. Whitfield J. Bell, Jr., *John Morgan, Continental Doctor* (Philadelphia: University of Pennsylvania Press, 1965), 17–25, 54–90, 178–205. Also see R. French Stone, M.D., ed., *Biography of Eminent American Physicians and Surgeons* (Indianapolis: Carlon and Hollenbeck, 1894), 336–38.

14. Quoted in Carl Binger, M.D., *Revolutionary Doctor: Benjamin Rush, 1746–1813* (New York: Norton, 1966), 99; see also 108–9, 112–13, 159–60; and Stone, *Biography*, 435–30.

15. Quoted in Nathan G. Goodman, *Benjamin Rush: Physician and Citizen, 1746–1813* (Philadelphia: University of Pennsylvania Press, 1934), 74–75.

16. John Cary, *Joseph Warren: Physician, Politician, Patriot* (Urbana: University of Illinois Press, 1961), 127.

17. Cary, 1–10, 26–29, 223–25. Cary argues that Warren was true to anti-aristocratic politics his entire life. He suggests that Warren toned down his radical view because he wanted to gain as many supporters as possible for the Liberty Party, but that he remained loyal to artisans and laborers.

18. In addition to Cary's biography of Joseph Warren, for more on John Warren and his son, see John Collins Warren, *To Work in the Vineyard of Surgery: The Reminiscences of J. Collins Warren, 1842–1927*, ed. Edward D. Churchill, M.D. (Cambridge, Mass.: Harvard University Press, 1958).

19. John Morgan, *A Discourse upon the Institution of Medical Schools in America* (1765; New York: Arno Press, 1975), i-xxvi.

20. Morgan, xvi.

21. See Haber, *Quest*, 52–54, for a discussion of the prestige associated with medical theory.

22. As Haber notes, between 1830 and 1845 "the number of medical colleges doubled," while apprenticeships "fell into disuse" (104).

23. Gramsci, *Selections*, 7.

24. James Jackson, *Letters to a Young Physician* (Boston: Phillips, Sampson, 1855), 9.

25. Alexander Hamilton, "Federalist # 35" (5 January 1788); reprint, *The Avalon Project at Yale Law School: Documents in Law, History, and Diplomacy. http://www. yale.edu/ lawweb/avalon/federal/fed35.htm*, 9 December 2003.

26. James Madison, "Federalist #38" (15 January 1788); reprint, *The Avalon Project at Yale Law School: Documents in Law, History, and Diplomacy.* http://www. yale.edu/lawweb/avalon/federal/fed38.htm, 9 December 2003.

27. Morgan, *Discourse*, 2, xviii.

28. Quoted in Hall, *Organization*, 141.

29. Hall, *Organization*, 148.

30. Jackson, *Letters*, 22.

31. The letter is quoted in full in N. I. Bowditch, *A History of the Massachusetts General Hospital* (1851; reprint in Medicine and Society in America Series, New York: Arno Press, 1972), 3–9.

32. Bowditch, 5, 8, 9, 3, 9.

33. Bowditch, 3, 9.

34. Robert F. Dalzell, Jr., *Enterprising Elite: The Boston Associates and the World They Made* (Cambridge, Mass.: Harvard University Press, 1987), 113–15.

35. Ronald Story, *The Forging of an Aristocracy: Harvard and the Boston Upper Class, 1800–1870* (Middletown, Conn.: Wesleyan University Press, 1980), 10–12.

36. Dalzell, *Enterprising Elite*, 114.

37. See Hall, *Organization*, 122, and Glazener, *Reading*, 29.

38. Dalzell, *Enterprising Elite*, 103–5

39. Story, *Forging*, 12.

40. Story, 10–12.

41. John C. Gunn, *Domestic Medicine . . .* (New York: Saxton, Barker, 1860).

42. *Harper's Weekly*, 20 August 1859, 544.

43. Quoted in Larson, *Rise*, 118.

44. According to Haber's calculations, in 1800 almost all states had medical licensing laws but by 1860 almost none did (*Quest*, 105). Also see Richard Shyrock, *Medical Licensing in America* (Baltimore: Johns Hopkins University Press, 1967), 30.

45. See Rothstein, *American Physicians*, 76; Larson, *Risk*, 112.

46. The AMA was founded, in part, with the hopes of bolstering the profession's reputation, and although many, including the first president, were able to enter the profession because entrance barriers had been lowered, he and others sought to articulate the grounds on which the profession might elevate itself and earn once again the confidence of the nation. See Haber, *Quest*, 107.

47. Max Weber, *The Theory of Social and Economic Organization*, trans. A. M. Henderson and Talcott Parsons (New York: Oxford University Press, 1947), 328. For a discussion of Weber's analysis of the professions within the context of nineteenth-century European medicine, see Lawrence Rothfield, *Vital Signs: Medical Realism in Nineteenth-Century Fiction* (Princeton, N.J.: Princeton University Press, 1992), 73–75.

48. "Minutes of the First Annual Meeting of the American Medical Association," *Transactions of the American Medical Association* 1 (1848): 7.

49. See Haber, *Quest*, 100, for further discussion of regulars' response to elitism.

50. Glazener points out that the habit of reading for character—for how individual characters develop, fail in a moment of crisis, triumph, and make decisions—mitigated against reading for "systematic ideological effects" and instead endorsed the notion of self-making (115).

51. As Dana D. Nelson, *National Manhood: Capitalist Citizenship and the Imagined Fraternity of White Men* (Durham, N.C.: Duke University Press, 1998), notes in her discussion of Benjamin Rush's essay on education, rigorous self-mastery was "the precondition for the white man's authorization as a civic manager" (11).

52. Karen Haltunnen, *Confidence Men and Painted Women: A Study of Middle-Class Culture in America, 1830–1870* (New Haven, Conn.: Yale University Press, 1982).

53. Chauncy D. Leake, *Percival's Medical Ethics* (Baltimore: Williams and Wilkins, 1927); Donald E. Konold, *History of American Medical Ethics, 1847–1912* (Madison: University of Wisconsin Press, 1962), 9–10. Percival was concerned to uphold the higher prestige of the physician as compared to the surgeon or apothecary in England. This was the kind of distinction that Morgan had found appealing in the mid-eighteenth century, and although by the mid-nineteenth century the physician's superiority to the surgeon was no longer asserted, Percival's general concern with the status of the medical profession was shared by the AMA.

54. Haber, *Quest*, 54–55.

55. See Daniel Walker Howe, *Making the American Self: Jonathan Edwards to Abraham Lincoln* (Cambridge, Mass.: Harvard University Press, 1997), 1- 10.

56. Pierre Bourdieu, *Distinction: A Social Critique of the Judgment of Taste,* trans. Richard Nice (Cambridge, Mass.: Harvard University Press, 1984), 6–7.

57. John Harley Warner, *Against the Spirit of System: The French Impulse in Nineteenth-Century American Medicine* (Princeton, N.J.: Princeton University Press, 1998), 3.

58. Warner, 40.

59. Bell, *John Morgan,* 54–99.

60. James Thacher, *American Medical Biography: or Memoirs of Eminent Physicians who have flourished in America . . .* (Boston: Richardson and Lord, 1828), 406.

61. Goodman, *Benjamin Rush,* 14–24.

62. Quoted in Warner, *Against the Spirit,* 40. For more on the elitism of Paris-trained physicians, the resentment from "homebred" physicians, and the fraternity and career-building among those who had studied in Paris, see 144–52.

63. Stone, *Biography,* 337.

64. "Minutes," 7.

65. Abraham Flexner, Introduction to facsimile of John Morgan, *A Discourse upon the Institution of Medical Schools in America,* Publications of the Institute of the History of Medicine 4th ser. (Baltimore: Johns Hopkins University Press, 1937).

66. See Stanley B. Blair, "A Dose of Exquisite Aesthetics: Literature in American Medicine, 1902–1906," *Journal of Popular Culture* 28, 4 (1995): 103–12.

67. Richard Brodhead, *Cultures of Letters: Scenes of Reading and Writing in Nineteenth-Century America* (Chicago: University of Chicago Press, 1993), 80–106.

68. John T. Morse, Jr., *Oliver Wendell Holmes: Life and Letters,* 2 vols. (Boston: Houghton, Mifflin, 1896), 1: 107–9.

69. See Haber, 3–15, for a history of the role of eighteenth-century notions of the English gentleman in definitions of professionalism in nineteenth-century United States.

70. Oliver Wendell Holmes, "Experiments in Medicine," *Boston Medical and Surgical Journal* 30 (1844): 202; cited in Warner, *Against the Spirit,* 262.

71. See Barry Menikoff, "Oliver Wendell Holmes," *Dictionary of Literary Biography,* vol. 1 (Detroit: Gale Research, 1978), 110.

72. See Barry Menikoff, "Oliver Wendell Holmes," in *Fifteen American Authors Before 1900: Bibliographic Essays on Research and Criticism,* ed. Robert A. Rees and Earl N. Harbert (Madison: University of Wisconsin Press, 1971), 215, 220–22. Others who focus on Holmes as a physician and scientist include Eleanor M. Tilton, *Amiable Autocrat: A Biography of Dr. Oliver Wendell Holmes* (New York: Henry Schuman, 1947), and Miriam R. Small, *Oliver Wendell Holmes* (New York: Twayne, 1962).

73. No critic can avoid the class issues raised by Holmes—the man, his image, his life, his literary style. See Glazener, *Reading,* 23–27, for an astute history of the Boston Brahmins and the complex relationship between class and professionalism at mid-century.

74. In 1850, Harvard considered a proposal to admit women and admitted three African Americans—Martin Delany, Daniel Laing, and Isaac H. Snowden. The objection to women in the school was strong, and the proposal to admit women was turned down. The proposal to admit blacks was debated, and although there was a petition against the proposal, there was also strong support. Laing and Snowden had received support from the American Colonization Society and entered with the promise to serve in Liberia. Delany applied and gained admission without ties to the Society and did not plan to go to Liberia. Holmes initially supported the admissions, but when the three African American students were dismissed the next spring after vocal student and faculty protests

he wrote the dismissal at the direction of the medical faculty. He wrote: "This experiment had satisfied the medical faculty that the intermixing of the white and black races in their lecture rooms is distasteful to a large portion of the class and injurious to the interests of the school." Laing went on to get an M.D. from Dartmouth. Harvard conferred its first degree on a black physician, Edward Clarence Joseph Turpin Howard, in 1869. See Wilbur H. Watson, *Against the Odds: Blacks in the Profession of Medicine in the United States* (New Brunswick, N.J.: Transaction Publishers, 1999), 49–50. Also see Robert S. Levine, *Martin Delany, Frederick Douglass, and the Politics of Representative Identity* (Chapel Hill: University of North Carolina Press, 1997), 61–66.

75. Ellery Sedgwick, *The Atlantic Monthly 1857–1909: Yankee Humanism at High Tide and Ebb* (University of Massachusetts Press, 1994), 6, 7.

76. Glazener, *Reading*, 31.

77. See Glazener, *Reading*, 21, 50, 111.

78. Calvin Wheeler Phillio, "Akin by Marriage," *Atlantic Monthly* 1 (November 1857): 94–110; (December 1857): 229–39; (January 1858): 279–88.

79. L. P. Hale, "The Queen of the Red Chessmen," *Atlantic Monthly* 1 (February 1858): 431–45.

80. Rose Terry, "Eben Jackson," *Atlantic Monthly* 1 (March 1858): 525–36.

81. W. C. Prime, "The Infant Heir," *Harper's New Monthly Magazine* 8 (May 1854): 824–32; "Mary Rankin: A Physician's Story," *Harper's New Monthly Magazine* 10 (May 1855): 789–94.

82. Linda E. Speth, "The Married Women's Property Acts, 1839–1865: Reform, Reaction, or Revolution?" *Women in the Law*, vol. 1, ed. D. Kelly Weisberg (Cambridge, Mass.: Schenkman, 1982), 69–91.

83. Hugh A. Garland, "The Death of John Randolph," *Harper's New Monthly Magazine* 2 (December 1850): 80–84.

84. See Henry Adams, *John Randolph* (Boston: Houghton Mifflin, 1882, 1898); Russell Kirk, *Randolph of Roanoke: A Study in Conservative Thought* (Chicago: University of Chicago Press, 1951).

85. See Martin Pernick, "Medical Profession: I, Medical Professionalism," *Bioethics Encyclopedia*, 4 vols., ed. Warren T. Reich (New York: Free Press, 1978), 1028.

86. Quoted in Warner, *Against the Spirit*, 264.

87. Jackson, *Letters*, 23.

88. Oliver Wendell Holmes, "The Professor's Story," *Atlantic Monthly* 5, 6, 7 (January 1860–April 1861). Republished as *Elsie Venner*, 1861. Subsequent parenthetical citations are to *Elsie Venner* (New York: New American Library, 1961).

89. For an excellent analysis of the novel's critique of marketplace economics, see Anne Dalke, "Economics, of the Bosom Serpent: Oliver Wendell Holmes's *Elsie Venner: A Romance of Destiny*," *American Transcendental Quarterly* 2 (1988): 57–68.

90. Oliver Wendell Holmes, *The Autocrat of the Breakfast Table* (Boston: Houghton Mifflin, 1888), 244–45.

91. See Hall, *Quest*, 198–206 for a reading of *Elsie Venner* as Holmes's interest in an aristocracy of men motivated by intellect and higher purposes. For a discussion of the tension between realism and sentiment in Holmes's fiction see Cynthia Davis, *Bodily and Narrative Forms: The Influence of Medicine on American Literature, 1845–1915* (Stanford, Calif.: Stanford University Press, 2000), 13–48.

92. Henry James, "A Most Extraordinary Case," *Atlantic Monthly* 21 (April 1868): 461–85.

93. Rebecca Harding Davis, "Life in the Iron Mills," *Atlantic Monthly* 7 (April

1861): 430–51; reprinted as *Life in the Iron Mills*, ed. Cecelia Tichi, Bedford Cultural Editions (Boston: Bedford, 1998). Future parenthetical citations are to this edition.

94. C. F. Briggs, "Elegant Tom Dillar," *Putnam's* 1 (1853): 525–30. For a reprint and fuller version of the commentary I offer here, see Stephanie P. Browner, "Documenting Cultural Politics: A *Putnam's* Short Story," *PMLA* 116, 2 (March 2001): 397–405.

95. Bette S. Weidman, "Charles Frederick Briggs," in *Antebellum Writers in New York and the South*, ed. Joel Meyerson, *Dictionary of Literary Biography*, vol. 3 (Detroit: Gale Research, 1979), 22.

96. Francis's other medical contributions include editing *The American Medical and Philosophical Register*, founding Rutgers Medical College, and serving as president of the medical board of Bellevue Hospital for fourteen years. He also wrote a chronicle of New York, culminating in *Old New York, or Reminiscences of the Past Sixty Years*.

97. For Francis's role in the New York literary scene, see Perry Miller, *The Raven and the Whale: The War of Words and Wits in the Era of Poe and Melville* (New York: Harcourt, 1956), 16–19, 102–3.

98. The description of Dr. Francis's soirees comes from an 1850 letter written by a New York journalist (maybe Henry T. Tuckerman, who was a regular at Francis's home) and sent to a New Orleans newspaper. See Hershel Parker, *Herman Melville: A Biography*, vol. 1, *1819–1851* (Baltimore: Johns Hopkins University Press, 1996), 652.

99. Notably, while *Putnam's* offered ample coverage of opera in a regular "Music" column, it did not comment on minstrelsy or other popular theater, except for J. J Trux, "Negro Minstrelsy—Ancient and Modern," *Putnam's Monthly* 5 (January 1855): 72–79.

100. In noting the democratic energy of minstrelsy, I do not mean to overstate the case, and it is important to remember, as Eric Lott notes, that minstrelsy "divested black people of control over elements of their culture" (18). Indeed, "Elegant Tom Dillar" may suggest that only when a European aristocrat "does" black culture does it become art refined enough for a professional man to find interesting. But Briggs's story also, in detailing the doctor's eagerness to see Higgins every night, testifies to a "profound white investment in black culture." Eric Lott, *Love and Theft: Blackface Minstrelsy and the American Middle Class* (New York: Oxford University Press, 1993), 18.

101. See Lott, 149, for a discussion of vulgarity and the libidinal body politics of minstrelsy. Lott also notes the homosocial bonds across race lines that minstrelsy explores and the gesture to gender bending in some performances. Dr. Laurens's willingness to allow himself but not his daughter the somatic pleasures of minstrelsy speaks to the homoerotic undertones in minstrelsy.

102. Glazener, *Reading*, 109.

103. Rebecca Harding Davis, *Bits of Gossip* (Boston: Houghton Mifflin, 1904), pp. 32–33. See Sharon M. Harris, *Rebecca Harding Davis and American Realism* (University of Pennsylvania Press, 1991), 56–57, for more on Davis's decision to submit "Life in the Iron Mills" to the *Atlantic*. Also see Jane Atteridge Rose, *Rebecca Harding Davis* (New York: Twayne, 1993), pp. 33–35, for more on Davis's reactions to Boston's literati, including Hawthorne and Holmes.

104. See Harris, *Davis*, 61–68; Brodhead, *Cultures*, 79, 87.

105. Quoted in Glazener, *Reading*, 127. As Glazener notes, James's criticism should be read in the context of high-brow disregard for sentimentalism more

generally, and the power of this critique to dismiss polemical literature that took up social justice issues and called for social change. See Glazener, 126–27.

106. F. J. O'Brien, "The Diamond Lens," *Atlantic Monthly* 1 (January 1858): 354–67; Moncure Daniel Conway, "My Lost Art," *Atlantic Monthly* 10 (August 1862): 228–35.

107. Oliver Wendell Holmes, "The Stereoscope and the Stereograph," *Atlantic Monthly* 3 (June 1859): 748.

108. Oliver Wendell Holmes, "Sun-Painting and Sun-Sculpture," *Atlantic Monthly* 8 (July 1861): 13–29; "Doings of the Sunbeam," *Atlantic Monthly* 12 (July 1863): 1–15.

109. Jonathan Crary, *Techniques of the Observer: On Vision and Modernity in the Nineteenth Century* (Cambridge, Mass.: MIT Press, 1990), 70.

110. David Reynolds, *Beneath the American Renaissance* (New York: Knopf, 1988), 170, 171–224.

111. See Susan Belasco Smith and Kenneth M. Price, "Introduction: Periodical Literature in Social and Historical Context," in *Periodical Literature in Nineteenth-Century America*, ed. Kenneth M. Price and Susan Belasco Smith (Charlottesville: University Press of Virginia, 1995), 5; Glazener, *Reading*, 93–146.

Chapter 5. Gender, Medicine, and Fiction in Postbellum Fiction

1. Mary E. Wager, "Women as Physicians," *Galaxy* 6, 6 (December 1868): 788.

2. Two of these illustrations appeared in *Frank Leslie's Illustrated Newspaper*, April 16, 1870. The third is attributed to *Frank Leslie's Illustrated Newspaper* with date unknown. My source for all three is Regina Morantz-Sanchez, *Conduct Unbecoming a Woman: Medicine on Trial in Turn-of-the-Century Brooklyn* (Oxford: Oxford University Press, 1999), 81–82. For an overview of women, science, and letters in the nineteenth century, see Nina Baym, *American Women of Letters and the Nineteenth-Century Sciences: Styles of Affiliation* (New Brunswick, N.J.: Rutgers University Press, 2001). For a provocative study of the writings of women physicians, see Susan Wells, *Out of the Dead House: Nineteenth-Century Women Physicians and the Writing of Medicine* (Madison: University of Wisconsin Press, 2001).

3. Martha Banta, "Men, Women, and the American Way," in *Cambridge Companion to Henry James*, ed. Jonathan Freeman (Cambridge: Cambridge University Press, 1998), 26.

4. Richard Brodhead, *Cultures of Letters: Scenes of Reading and Writing in Nineteenth-Century America* (Chicago: University of Chicago Press, 1993), 170.

5. Regina Morantz-Sanchez, *Sympathy and Science: Women Physicians in American Medicine* (Oxford: Oxford University Press, 1985), 16.

6. Quoted in Morantz-Sanchez, *Sympathy and Science*, 45.

7. Morantz-Sanchesz, *Sympathy and Science*, 35.

8. Morantz-Sanchez, *Sympathy and Science*, 45.

9. Although many in the first generation of women doctors earned degrees from sectarian institutions, this did not ghettoize them. Distinctions between medical paradigms were not rigid, and sectarian graduates, male or female, were bona fide professional doctors in the eyes of most.

10. See Morantz-Sanchez, *Sympathy and Science*, 314, 49, and Mary Roth Walsh, *"Doctors Wanted, No Women Need Apply": Sexual Barriers in the Medical Profession, 1835–1975* (New Haven, Conn.: Yale University Press, 1977), 186.

11. Quoted in Morantz-Sanchez, *Sympathy and Science*, 196.

12. Quoted in Morantz-Sanchez, *Sympathy and Science*, 59.

13. Morantz-Sanchez, *Sympathy and Science*, 6.

14. Londa Schiebinger, *The Mind Has No Sex? Women in the Origins of Modern Science* (Cambridge, Mass.: Harvard University Press, 1989), 134.

15. Schiebinger, 121, 158–59.

16. Thomas Laqueur, *Making Sex: Body and Gender From the Greeks to Freud* (Cambridge, Mass.: Harvard University Press, 1990).

17. Schiebinger, *Mind*, 189–213.

18. Ludmilla Jordanova, *Sexual Visions: Images of Gender in Science and Medicine Between the Eighteenth and Twentieth Centuries* (Madison: University of Wisconsin Press, 1989), 94.

19. E. Anthony Rotundo, *American Manhood: Transformations in Masculinity from the Revolution to the Modern Era* (New York: Basic Books, 1993).

20. Quoted in Wells, *Out of the Dead House*, 211. For a detailed and well-researched account of the jeering incident and Dr. Agnew's resistance to women in medicine, see 193–211.

21. Marc Simpson, "The 1880s," in *Thomas Eakins*, ed. Darrel Sewell (Philadelphia: Philadelphia Museum of Art, 2001), 114–15.

22. Simpson, 118.

23. Michael Fried, *Realism, Writing, Disfiguration: On Thomas Eakins and Stephen Crane* (Chicago: University of Chicago Press, 1987), 61.

24. Fried, 59–61, 64, 66, 69.

25. Dana D. Nelson, *National Manhood: Capitalist Citizenship and the Imagined Fraternity of White Men* (Durham, N.C.: Duke University Press, 1998), 173.

26. Robyn Wiegman, *American Anatomies: Theorizing Race and Gender* (Durham, N.C.: Duke University Press, 1995), 88.

27. William Dean Howells, "The Man of Letters is a Man of Business," *Scribner's Magazine* (October 1893): 438.

28. See Brodhead, *Cultures of Letters*, 19.

29. Nancy Glazener, *Reading for Realism: The History of a U.S. Literary Institution, 1850–1910* (Durham, N.C.: Duke University Press, 1997), 145.

30. "Literary Virility," *Scribner's* (March 1876): 737.

31. Glazener, *Reading*, 120–21.

32. Quoted in Carol Troyen, "Eakins in the Twentieth Century," in *Thomas Eakins*, ed. Sewell, 369. Another critic noted that Eakins possessed "the qualities of manhood that are not too conspicuous in American painting," and a preparatory study for *The Agnew Clinic* that features just the doctor was called in 1914 the "greatest portrait ever painted by an American." Quoted in Troyen, 368, 369.

33. Theodore Roosevelt, *American Ideals and Other Essays Social and Political* (New York: G.P. Putnam's Sons, 1897), 24–25.

34. David Noble, *Death of a Nation: American Culture and the End of Exceptionalism* (Minneapolis: University of Minnesota Press, 2002).

35. T. Gaillard Thomas, M.D., *A Practical Treatise on the Diseases of Women*, 3rd ed. (Philadelphia: Henry C. Lea, 1872), 56, 599.

36. Thomas, 599–600.

37. Edward H. Clarke, M.D., *Sex in Education; or, A Fair Chance for Girls* (Boston: Houghton, Mifflin, 1873), 35.

38. Clarke, 37–38.

39. Clarke, 62, 168.

40. Clarke, 12.

41. Mary Putnam Jacobi, *The Question of Rest for Women During Menstruation* (New York: G.P. Putnam's Sons, 1886), 165. Quoted in Laqueur, *Making Sex*, 224.

42. Louisa May Alcott, *Rose in Bloom: A Sequel to "Eight Cousins"* (1876; reprint New York: A.L. Burt, 1918). Alcott briefly acknowledges women's public roles. Rose considers studying medicine and sternly lectures her skeptical cousins that "women have succeeded in this profession" (12). Phebe, Rose's maid, friend, and alter ego, leaves the familial sphere, earns a living, makes a name for herself as a soloist in a church choir, and lives for a year as an independent woman. Jo March's brief stint as a writer and Christie Devon's as an actress reveal Alcott's commitment in other novels, albeit ambivalent, to representing women's work beyond the domestic world. For more on Alcott's negotiation of her political commitment to representing women in the public sphere and her devotion to domestic ideology, see Glenn Hendler, "The Limits of Sympathy: Louisa May Alcott and the Sentimental Novel," *American Literary History* 4 (1991): 685–706.

43. Louisa May Alcott, *Eight Cousins; or The Aunt Hill* (1874; reprint Boston: Little, Brown, 1927). As in her other juvenile fiction, in *Eight Cousins* Alcott offers a schematic representation of gender in the family. The youngest generation is all male (except Rose), and the older generation is all female (except Dr. Alec and his quiet brother). This configuration not only highlights the central relationship—Rose and Dr. Alec—but also allows Alcott to explore masculine identity within the domestic sphere and to suggest that even manhood does not remove a male from the domestic world. As the oldest boys become men, they do not leave the circle: rather they stand always in a line of boys that reaches back to the youngest who still clings to his mother.

44. Alcott, *Rose in Bloom*, 100.

45. Marmee in *Little Women* and Jo in *Little Men* offer an "enclosed family space warmed by maternal affection," and their presence, "operating without the aid of overt or physical coercion, has the power almost magically to mold character in the direction of parental ideals, to transpose parental preference into an imperative from within." See Brodhead, *Cultures*, 72, 71. Feminists might take exception to Brodhead's label of Marmee as a disciplinary presence. Jean Wyatt, for example, suggests the mother bond in *Little Women* is a subversive rather than coercive force. And yet, she too notes the powerful presence of the mother in Alcott's fiction. To replace the mother completely, and to do so with a doctor, is, I want to suggest, significant. Jean Wyatt, *Reconstructing Desire: The Role of the Unconscious in Women's Reading and Writing* (Chapel Hill: North Carolina University Press, 1990).

46. Louisa May Alcott, *Little Women* (1871; reprint New York: Bantam, 1983), 86.

47. Alcott, *Little Women*, 266.

48. Alcott, *Eight Cousins*, 204. For more on the gendering of appetites, addiction, realism, and professionalism, see Glazener, *Reading*, 93–146.

49. Alcott, *Eight Cousins*, 213.

50. See Casey Finch, "'Hooked and Buttoned Together': Victorian Underwear and Representations of the Female Body," *Victorian Studies* 34 (1991): 339.

51. Lora Romero, *Home Fronts: Domesticity and Its Critics in the Antebellum United States* (Durham, N.C.: Duke University Press, 1997), 23.

52. Quoted in Romero, 23.

53. Elizabeth Wilson, *Adorned in Dreams: Fashion and Modernity* (Berkeley: University of California Press, 1985), 2. Also see Mark Selzer, "The Still Life," *American Literary History* 3, 3 (Fall 1991): 455–59, for an incisive analysis of the critique of consumer culture.

54. Mac is modeled in part on Henry David Thoreau. As a young girl Alcott admired Thoreau, and in making Mac a poet she calls up the association of literature with spiritual wisdom that the Transcendentalists cultivated.

55. Henry James, *Selected Letters*, ed. Leon Edel (New York: Farrar, Straus, Giroux), 258, n.2.

56. Morantz-Sanchez, *Sympathy and Science*, 72.

57. Rebecca Harding Davis, "A Day with Doctor Sarah," *Harper's New Monthly Magazine* (September 1878): 615.

58. Davis, 617.

59. Dana D. Nelson, "Representative/Democracy: The Political Work of Countersymbolic Representation," in *Materializing Democracy: Toward a Revitalized Cultural Politics*, ed. Russ Castronovo and Dana D. Nelson (Durham, N.C.: Duke University Press, 2002), 235.

60. William Dean Howells, *Dr. Breen's Practice* (Boston: J.R. Osgood, 1881), 12. Future parenthetical references are to this edition.

61. See Cynthia J. Davis, *Bodily and Narrative Forms: The Influence of Medicine on American Literature, 1845–1915* (Stanford, Calif.: Stanford University Press, 2000), for a reading of the ending as equivocal on Breen's medical talents.

62. Morantz-Sanchez offers a useful history of the varied compromises women in medicine were able to negotiate. For more on the choices women made and what they wrote about the issue, see Morantz-Sanchez, *Sympathy and Science*, 126–43.

63. William Dean Howells, *Heroines of Fiction* (New York: Harper and Brothers, 1901), 190.

64. Howells was also not optimistic about the fate of single independent women. In *A Hazard of New Fortunes*, Alma Leighton is lonely and unhappy.

65. William Dean Howells, *Life in Letters of William Dean Howells*, ed. Mildred Howells (New York: Doubleday, 1928), 300.

66. See Glazener, *Reading*, 138. Also see Cynthia Davis, *Bodily and Narrative Forms*, 107–13 for a more sympathetic reading of Howells's novel. Davis takes into account that Howells and his family were under a homeopath's care while he was writing the novel, and she suggests that the ending is less about women's fitness for medicine and more about achieving closure and formal balance.

67. Quoted in Cynthia Davis, 92. Also see 91–95, 113–21 for commentary on Phelps's answer to Clarke and for a reading of *Dr. Zay*.

68. For a reading of Howells's *Dr. Breen's Practice*, Phelps's *Dr. Zay*, and Jewett's *A Country Doctor*, see Jean Carwile Masteller, "The Women Doctors of Howells, Phelps, and Jewett," in *Critical Essays on Sarah Orne Jewett*, ed. Gwen L. Nagel (Boston: G.K. Hall, 1984), 135–47. Phelps was alert to the differences between her vision of a doctoress and Howells, commenting, "I don't feel that Dr. Breen is a fair example of professional women: indeed, I know she is not for I know the class thoroughly from long personal observation under unusual opportunities" (quoted in Masteller, 138).

69. See Susan Albertine, "Breaking the Silent Partnership: Businesswomen in Popular Fiction," *American Literature* 62 (1990): 238–61 for a recent reading of Phelps as a feminist; see John W. Crowley, "W. D. Howells: The Everwomanly," in *American Novelists Revisited: Essays in Feminist Criticism*, ed. Fritz Fleishmann (Boston: G.K. Hall, 1982), for a consideration of Howells's relationship to women and feminism.

70. Elizabeth Stuart Phelps, *Doctor Zay: A Novel* (1882; reprint New York: Feminist Press, 1987), 44, 50. Future parenthetical references are to this edition.

71. For more about the tension many presumed must exist between a woman's

feminine nature and the requirements of medical training and practice, see Morantz-Sanchez, *Sympathy and Science*, 90–126.

72. See Lilian Furst, "Halfway up the Hill: Doctoresses in Late Nineteenth-Century American Fiction," in *Women Healers and Physicians: Climbing a Long Hill*, ed. Lilian R. Furst (Lexington: University of Kentucky, Press, 1997), 223.

73. See Cynthia Davis, *Bodily and Narrative Forms*, for a sympathetic reading of the end of Phelps's novel. According to Davis, Dr. Zay's acquiescence to Yorke may be a defeat of sorts, but marriage is not endorsed vociferously. "The whisper with which Zay surrenders to Yorke's embrace may signal the onset of a nonnarratable (and stultifying) quiescence, but even if so, it simultaneously interrogates—"is that all?"—whether the equilibrium a novel's last words typically initiate will necessarily ensure" (121).

74. Horace Scudder, Review of *The Portrait of a Lady* and *Dr. Breen's Practice*, *Atlantic* 49 (January 1882): 129.

75. See Oscar Cargill, *The Novels of Henry James* (New York: Macmillan, 1961), 123–26.

76. Henry James, *The Bostonians* (1886; reprint New York: Penguin, 1966), 36. Future parenthetical references are to this edition.

77. Henry James, *Daisy Miller* (1878; reprint New York: Penguin Books, 1986), 110.

78. Michael Anesko, *Letters, Fictions, Lives: Henry James and William Dean Howells* (Oxford: Oxford University Press, 1997), 29.

79. *Patch Adams* (1998) is a recent example. Other recent films with variations on this plot include *City of Joy* (1992) and *The Doctor* (1991). A related medical narrative celebrates the doctor who fights against forces that would prevent him from giving humane care. The television series *Marcus Welby, M.D.* is a familiar example. Perhaps the earliest film featuring a woman doctor is *Mary Stevens, M.D.* (1933). For more on medicine and film, see Peter Dans, *Doctors in the Movies: Boil the Water and Just Say Ahh* (Bloomington, Ill.: Medi-Ed Press, 2000).

80. Annie Nathan Meyer, *Helen Brent, M.D.* (New York: Cassell, 1894), 15. Future parenthetical references are to this edition.

81. Morantz-Sanchez, *Conduct*, 118.

82. For a full account of Dixon's career, the trials, and gynecology at the end of the century, see Morantz-Sanchez, *Conduct*.

83. "Comment on New Books," *Atlantic Monthly* 70 (November 1892): 707.

84. See Morantz-Sanchez, *Conduct*, 113–37. Morantz-Sanchez is careful to note that medical theories and practices rarely line up neatly with a doctor's sex or with twentieth-century gender politics, and yet she suggests that Jones's writings resist defining "any female bodily function as inherently abnormal" (132).

85. Brodhead *Cultures*, 170.

86. Sarah Orne Jewett, *A Country Doctor* (1884; reprint New York: Meridian, 1986), 177. Future parenthetical references are to this edition.

87. Ann Romines, *The Home Plot: Women, Writing, and Domestic Ritual* (Amherst: University of Massachusetts Press, 1992), 90.

88. Margaret Roman, *Sarah Orne Jewett: Reconstructing Gender* (Tuscaloosa: University of Alabama Press, 1992), ix-xi.

89. Brodhead, *Cultures*, 160–61.

90. Brodhead, 169.

91. See Michael Holstein, "Writing as a Healing Art," *Studies in American Fiction* 16 (1988): 39–49, for an analysis of Jewett's representation of the healing arts of Almira Todd in *The Country of the Pointed Firs* as a model of the relationship

between disciple and vocation. Holstein presents a persuasive reading of Todd's healing as a lesson that Jewett offers her narrator/writer in the proper distance a healer or a writer must establish between herself and her patients or subjects. Holstein's suggestion that writing is itself a healing art for Jewett is useful, but, like many others who read Jewett sentimentally, Holstein fails to acknowledge the professional and disciplinary demands that Jewett also associates with literature and medicine. Also see Malina Snow, "'That One Talent': The Vocation as Theme in Sarah Orne Jewett's *A Country Doctor*," *Colby Library Quarterly* 16 (1980): 138–47, for a useful reading of the vocation theme in *A Country Doctor*, although Snow also resists reading Jewett's interest in vocation as part of a larger move toward the professionalization of literature.

92. Henry James, "The Middle Years," *Tales of Henry James* (New York: Norton, 1984), 266. Future parenthetical references will be to this edition.

93. For a fine study of "The Middle Years," see Julie Rivkin, "Doctoring the Text: Henry James and Revision," in *Henry James's New York Edition: The Construction of Authorship*, ed. David McWhirter (Stanford, Calif.: Stanford University Press, 1995), 142–63.

94. Andrew Taylor, *Henry James and the Father Question* (Cambridge: Cambridge University Press, 2002), 61.

95. Quoted in Taylor, 62.

96. Taylor, 160.

97. Henry James, Preface to *The Wings of the Dove*, vol. 1 (New York: Scribner's 1909), v.

98. See Jean Strouse, *Alice James: A Biography* (Boston: Houghton Mifflin, 1980), 273–95, for an examination of the role of illness in the James family; and see Howard M. Feinstein, *Becoming William James* (Ithaca, N.Y.: Cornell University Press, 1984), 45–67, for an analysis of the politics of illness in the James family. For more on the James family, illness, performance, and sympathy, see Kristin Boudreau, *Sympathy in American Literature: American Sentiments from Jefferson to the Jameses* (Gainesville: University Press of Florida, 2001).

99. Henry James, Preface, vi.

100. For more on postbellum medicine, see John S. Haller, *American Medicine in Transition, 1840–1910* (Urbana: University of Illinois Press, 1981).

101. Charles E. Rosenberg, *Explaining Epidemics and Other Studies in the History of Medicine* (Cambridge: Cambridge University Press, 1992), 266.

102. Henry James, Preface, vi.

103. Alice James, *The Diary of Alice James*, ed. Leon Edel (New York: Viking Penguin, 1982), 206.

104. Alice James, *Diary*, 206.

105. Henry James, *Notes of a Son and Brother*, ed. Frederick W. Dupee (New York: Criterion Books, 1956), 416. Leon Edel notes that James "had to reckon on the one hand with his pain and on the other 'with the strange fact of there being nothing to speak of the matter with me.'" James's "obscure hurt" has prompted as much diagnostic speculation as Milly's illness. But in writing of it years later in *Notes of a Son and a Brother*, James makes it clear that medical diagnosis cannot do justice to the psychological and physical experience of pain and disability. Writing of his struggle to choose a career, James focuses on the injury he suffered in the spring of 1861, the same year his father had refused his son's request to attend Harvard, and the same year that war broke out and many young men, including two of James's brothers, were signing up to fight. James never explicitly describes the injury and he never identifies the afflicted body part. Indeed, as Edel notes, the "details are meager" and "they bristle with ambiguities,"

and critics have variously made connections between the "obscure hurt" and James's celibacy or his failure to fight in the Civil War. Ultimately, James came up with his own interpretation: "I came to think of my relation to my injury as a "*modus vivendi.*" Interestingly, the house of the surgeon who dismissed his injury with a "comparative pooh-pooh" became a symbol of the role both the injury and the doctor's response played in his realization of his literary interests: "the house . . . put forth to me as I passed it in many a subsequent season an ironic smug symbolism of its action on my fate." Crucial to James's account of this moment in his life is the embarrassment he suffered when the Boston surgeon failed to find anything wrong. The denial of the pain—physical or psychological—that he was suffering was, James suggests, tantamount to denying his experience any meaning at all. James positions his first thoughts about becoming a writer not only in relation to a somatic experience, but also in response to medicine's failure to understand his experience. Leon Edel, *Henry James: A Life* (New York: Harper, 1985), 58. 416.

106. Henry James, *The Wings of the Dove*, 1902 (Baltimore: Penguin Books, 1976), 79, 143. Future parenthetical citations will be to this edition.

107. Henry James, Preface, xxii.

108. Rosenberg, *Explaining*, 269.

109. Henry James, "The Art of Fiction" (1888), reprinted in *The Future of the Novel*, ed. Leon Edel (New York: Vintage, 1956), 9, 25.

110. Henry James, Preface, vi–vii.

111. Charles Rosenberg, *The Care of Strangers: The Rise of America's Hospital System* (Baltimore: Johns Hopkins University Press, 1995), 7.

Chapter 6. Social Surgery: Physicians on the Color Line

1. W. E. B. Du Bois, *The Souls of Black Folk* (Chicago: McClure, 1903), 104.

2. Du Bois, *Souls*, 107, 105–6.

3. W. E. B. Du Bois, *The Philadelphia Negro: A Social Study* (Philadelphia: University of Pennsylvania Press, 1899; reprint with introduction by Elijah Anderson, 1996), 113.

4. W. Michael Byrd and Linda A. Clayton, "An American Health Dilemma: A History of Blacks in the Health System," *Journal of the National Medical Association* 84 (1992): 195; Herbert M. Morais, *The History of the Afro-American in Medicine*, in International Library of Negro Life and History (New York: Association for the Study of Afro-American Life and History, 1976), 85–86.

5. Morais, 64–66.

6. See Du Bois's response to such predictions in "What Is the Negro Problem" (1889), reprinted in *The Oxford W. E. B. Du Bois Reader*, ed. Eric Sundquist (New York: Oxford University Press, 1996), 348; and Byrd and Clayton, "An American Health Dilemma," 195.

7. Although Todd Savitt argues that black physicians subordinated the broad ideal of racial betterment to the more immediate concerns of individual careers, his own article, as well as histories by Morais and Watson and novels discussed in this chapter, testifies to the role physicians played in the reality and dreams of racial uplift. See Todd L. Savitt, "Entering a White Profession: Black Physicians in the New South, 1880–1920," *Bulletin of the History of Medicine* 61, 4 (Winter 1987): 507–40; and Wilbur H. Watson, *Against the Odds: Blacks in the Profession of Medicine in the United States* (New Brunswick, N.J.: Transaction Publishers, 1999).

8. For more on the history of nineteenth-century scientific discussions of

race, see William Stanton, *The Leopard's Spots: Scientific Attitudes Toward Race in America, 1815–1859* (Chicago: University of Chicago Press, 1960); Stephen Jay Gould, *The Mismeasure of Man* (New York: Norton, 1981); Dana Nelson, *National Manhood: Capitalist Citizenship and the Imagined Fraternity of White Men* (Durham, N.C.: Duke University Press, 1998).

9. Quoted in Stanton, 7, 20.

10. See Gould, *The Mismeasure of Man* and Nelson, *National Manhood* for excellent commentary on Morton and the significance of his belief in science as unmediated by politics.

11. Quoted in Georgina D. Feldberg, *Disease and Class: Tuberculosis and the Shaping of Modern North American Society* (New Brunswick, N.J.: Rutgers University Press, 1995), 15.

12. Quoted in John S. Haller, *Outcasts from Evolution: Scientific Attitudes of Racial Inferiority, 1859–1900* (Urbana: University of Illinois Press, 1971), 23.

13. Haller, 29.

14. Haller, 68.

15. See Robert L. Blakely and Judith M. Harrington, "Grave Consequences: The Opportunistic Procurement of Cadavers at the Medical College of Georgia," in *Bones in the Basement: Postmortem Racism in Nineteenth-Century Medical Training,* ed. Blakely and Harrington (Washington, D.C.: Smithsonian Institution Press, 1997).

16. As Robyn Wiegman puts it: "The move from the visible epidermal terrain to the articulation of the interior structure of human bodies thus extrapolated in both broader and more distinct terms the parameters of white supremacy, giving it a logic lodged fully in the body." Throughout the nineteenth century, racial characteristics were understood as permanent and "connected to the organic coherence of the organism as a whole." Robyn Wiegman, *American Anatomies: Theorizing Race and Gender* (Durham, N.C.: Duke University Press, 1995), 31.

17. Shirley Wilson Logan, *"We Are Coming": The Persuasive Discourse of Nineteenth-Century Black Women* (Carbondale: Southern Illinois University Press, 1999), 131.

18. Logan, 130–32.

19. Logan, 127.

20. Victoria Earle Matthews, "Aunt Lindy: A Story Founded on Real Life," *A.M.E. Church Review* 5 (January 1889): 246–50 (reprint, New York: J. J. Little, 1893). Future parenthetical references are to this edition.

21. Chesnutt imagined a more enlightened white physician in "Her Virginia Mammy." In this short story, when a doctor discovers that his betrothed has Negro ancestry of which she is unaware, he never tells her; and they marry happily. Charles Chesnutt, "Her Virginia Mammy," in *The Wife of His Youth, and Other Stories of the Color Line* (1899; reprint Ridgewood, N.J.: Gregg Press, 1967).

22. Charles Chesnutt, *The House Behind the Cedars* (1900; reprint, New York: Penguin, 1993), 96. Future parenthetical references are to this edition.

23. Chesnutt was very light and yet chose not to pass. He considered it when he was young, and he often felt a chasm between himself and poor blacks, noting that he was neither fish nor fowl. Interestingly, Du Bois often noted Chesnutt's light skin. In his obituary, for example, he wrote, "Chesnutt was of that group of white folk who because of a more or less remote Negro ancestor identified himself voluntarily with the darker group," W. E. B. Du Bois, "Obituary," *Crisis* (January 1933).

24. See John W. Crowley, *The Black Heart's Truth: The Early Career of W. D. Howells* (Chapel Hill: University of North Carolina Press, 1985), 114–19, for more about these years and illness in general in Howells's life.

25. William Dean Howells, *The Son of Royal Langbrith* (1904; reprint Bloomington: Indiana University Press, 1969), 227.

26. William Dean Howells, *The Shadow of a Dream* (1890; reprint Bloomington: Indiana University Press, 1970), 46–47.

27. Howells, *Shadow*, 9.

28. Quoted in Martha Banta, "Introduction," to Howells, *The Shadow of a Dream* (Bloomington: Indiana University Press, 1970), xix, xx.

29. Howells, *Son of Royal Langbrith*, 228. As one critic notes, Dr. Anther's virtues—"imaginative compassion and unselfish love combined with his common sense and trained habit of scientific or rational diagnosis"—make him central to the story and a rich example of Howells's interest in understanding what exactly medicine might offer beyond somatic therapies. George N. Bennett, *The Realism of William Dean Howells, 1889–1920* (Nashville, Tenn.: Vanderbilt University Press, 1973), 206.

30. William Dean Howells, *An Imperative Duty* (1892; reprint Bloomington: Indiana University Press, 1970), 4. Future parenthetical references are to this edition.

31. See Banta, "Introduction," for examples of how Howells's revisions of the book version lighten the anti-Irish sentiment.

32. For more on Howells and race, see Joseph R. McElrath, Jr., "W. D. Howells and Race: Charles W. Chesnutt's Disappointment of the Dean," *Nineteenth-Century Literature* 51, 4 (1997): 474–99; Henry B. Wonham, "Howells, Du Bois, and the Effect of 'Common Sense': Race, Realism, and Nervousness in *An Imperative Duty* and *The Souls of Black Folk*," in *Criticism and the Color Line: Desegregating American Literary Studies*, ed. Henry B. Wonham (New Brunswick, N.J.: Rutgers University Press, 1996), 126–39.

33. The novel never offers more human images of African Americans, and Anna Julia Cooper and other commentators took offense at the stereotyped images in the novel, suggesting that Howells had strayed far from what he knew. In the late nineteenth century, popular magazines such as *Puck* and *Judge* specialized in ethnic caricature similar to what Rhoda sees here. See Henry B. Wonham, "Writing Realism, Policing Consciousness: Howells and the Black Body," *American Literature* 67:4 (December 1995): 701- 724.

34. As Wonham notes in "Writing Realism," blackness was one way Howells could explore the unmoored self, territory he typically avoided. Wonham suggests that for Howells blackness serves as an antidote to American nervousness.

35. See Michele Birnbaum, "Racial Hysteria: Female Pathology and Race Politics in Frances Harper's *Iola Leroy* and W. D. Howells's *An Imperative Duty*," *African American Review* 33, 1 (Spring 1999): 7–17. Birnbaum, like Wonham, suggests that Howells offers miscegenation as a cure for Olney's nervousness.

36. Wonham, "Writing Realism," 710. For more on Howells's relationship with Chesnutt, see McElrath, "W. D. Howells and Race" and William L. Andrews, "William Dean Howells and Charles W. Chesnutt: Criticism and Race Fiction in the Age of Booker T. Washington," *American Literature* 48 (1976): 327–39.

37. For more on the feminization of blackness, see Wiegman, *American Anatomies*, 43–78.

38. See Tom Lutz, *American Nervousness, 1903: An Anecdotal History* (Ithaca, N.Y.: Cornell University Press, 1991), 261–75, for a discussion of African American writers and neurasthenia.

39. Plantation fiction offered condescending images of folk medicine practiced down in the slave quarters by conjurers and old mammies.

40. See Savitt, "Entering," 507–40.

41. Quoted in Savitt, 512.

42. Savitt, 534.

43. Houston Baker, *Modernism and the Harlem Renaissance* (Chicago: University of Chicago Press, 1987), 50.

44. Rebecca Harding Davis, *Waiting for the Verdict* (1867; reprint Upper Saddle, N.J.: Gregg Press, 1967), 304, 361.

45. See Kevin Gaines, *Uplifting the Race: Black Leadership, Politics, and Culture in the Twentieth Century* (Chapel Hill: University of North Carolina Press, 1996), 19–46. Gaines rightly suggests that to understand late nineteenth-century notions of uplift it is essential to understand fully the losses that came with the end of Reconstruction—a devastating period that included "disenfranchisement and the rout of blacks from electoral and third-party politics and the federal government's appeasement of the forces of reaction in the South" (20).

46. Katherine Davis Chapman Tillman, "Beryl Weston's Ambition," *The Works of Katherine Davis Chapman* (New York: Oxford University Press, 1991), 233. Future parenthetical references are to this edition.

47. Gaines sees this particular version of uplift in Francis E. W. Harper's speeches and in her novel *Iola Leroy* (see below). See Gaines, *Uplifting the Race*, 21, 36–37.

48. Daylanne English, "W. E. B. DuBois's Family *Crisis*," *American Literature* 72, 2 (June 2000): 292.

49. Frances E. W. Harper, *Iola Leroy, or Shadows Uplifted* (1892; reprint New York: Oxford University Press, 1988), 229. Future parenthetical references are to this edition.

50. As Wiegman notes, "bodies are neither black nor white, and the range of possibilities accruing to either designation contradicts the assurance of these categories to represent, mimetically, the observable body" (*American Anatomies*, 9).

51. Frances E. W. Harper, "The Two Offers" (1858), in *The Norton Anthology of American Literature*, vol. 1, ed. Nina Baym (New York: Norton, 1999), 430. Future parenthetical citations are to this edition.

52. "The Two Offers" appeared in the *Anglo-African Magazine*, and it may be the first short story published by an African American woman. See Frances Smith Foster, "Introduction" to *Iola Leroy*, xxix.

53. Nathan Francis Mossell, the first African American admitted to the University of Pennsylvania, was asked to sit behind a screen at his classes, but he refused, and although white students initially shunned him, when he graduated the applause was so prolonged the provost had to ask the audience to stop. See Morais, *History*, 80.

54. Although records are scarce, at least 181 black women and men served as contract nurses in eleven hospitals in three states. In addition, many more volunteered and accompanied regiments, serving as laundresses, cooks, and nurses. Harriet Tubman served as a nurse in the South Carolina Sea Islands during the war, and Susie King Taylor taught, cooked, and nursed at Fort Pulaski and at the battlefront. See Mary Elizabeth Carnegie, *The Path We Tread: Blacks in Nursing, 1854–1984* (Philadelphia: Lippincott, 1986), 5–11.

55. Du Bois, *Souls*, 3.

56. Charles W. Chesnutt, *The Marrow of Tradition* (1901; reprint Ann Arbor: University of Michigan Press, 1969), 317. Future parenthetical references are to this edition.

57. Homi Bhabha, *The Location of Culture* (London: Routledge, 1994), 5.

58. Leon H. Prather, *We Have Taken a City: Wilmington Racial Massacre and Coup of 1898* (Rutherford, N.J.: Fairleigh Dickinson University Press, 1984), 22.

59. Prather, 140–42.

60. Prather, 89–90.

61. Charles W. Chesnutt, *"To Be an Author": Letters of Charles Chesnutt, 1889–1905*, ed. Joseph R. McElrath, Jr., and Robert C. Leitz, III (Princeton, N.J.: Princeton University Press, 1997), 116.

62. Helen Chesnutt, *Charles Waddell Chesnutt: Pioneer of the Color Line* (Chapel Hill: University of North Carolina Press, 1952), 158.

63. Charles W. Chesnutt, Notebook, Chesnutt Collection, Fisk University Library.

64. Morais, *History*, 65–68.

65. Morais, 86.

66. Charles W. Chesnutt, *The Journals of Charles Chesnutt*, ed. Richard Brodhead (Durham, N.C.: Duke University Press, 1993), 81.

67. Henry Louis Gates, *Figures in Black: Words, Signs, and the "Racial" Self* (New York: Oxford University Press, 1987), 109.

68. Chesnutt, *Journals*, 108.

69. Samira Kawash, *Dislocating the Color Line: Identity, Hybridity, and Singularity in African-American Literature* (Stanford, Calif.: Stanford University Press, 1997), 116.

70. Morais, *History*, 50, 86.

71. Quoted in George M. Frederickson, *The Black Image in the White Mind: The Debate on Afro-American Character and Destiny, 1817–1914* (New York: Harper, 1971), 250–51.

72. Nancy Leys Stepan and Sander L. Gilman, "Appropriating the Idioms of Science: The Rejection of Scientific Racism," in *The Racial Economy of Science: Toward a Democratic Future*, ed. Sandra Harding (Bloomington: Indiana University Press, 1993), 183–84.

73. John Wideman, "Charles W. Chesnutt: *The Marrow of Tradition*," *Amercan Scholar* 42 (Winter 1972–73): 133.

74. Eric Sundquist, *To Wake the Nations: Race in the Making of American Literature* (Cambridge: Harvard University Press, 1993), 452.

75. Kawash, *Dislocating*, 121.

76. Chesnutt, Notebook.

77. Prather, *We Have Taken a City*, 140.

78. Du Bois, *Souls*, 106.

79. Du Bois, *Souls*, 108.

80. Mary White Ovington, "The National Association for the Advancement of Colored People." *Journal of Negro History* 9, 2 (April 1924): 113.

81. Walter White, *A Man Called White: The Autobiography of Walter White* (New York: Viking, 1948), 37.

82. William M. Tuttle, "Contested Neighborhoods and Racial Violence: Prelude to the Chicago Riot of 1919," *Journal of Negro History* 55, 4 (October 1970): 281.

83. White, *A Man Called White*, 63–64. White remained an active leader throughout the 1950s, visiting black troops during World War II and making recommendations on civil rights to Eisenhower and Truman. He earned accolades for his investigations but was also criticized for his willingness to "sacrifice" leftists such as Du Bois and Paul Robeson during the Cold War. For a sample of his journalism, see Ralph Lynch Hollis, compiler, *The Black Urban Condition: A Documentary History, 1866–1971* (New York: Crowell, 1975).

84. Savitt notes that this was a service black physicians sometimes provided— discreet care of white men for sexually transmitted diseases.

85. The acceptance of black professionals within their own community was a much discussed issue in the first decades of the twentieth century. Booker T. Washington confidently told medical students at Howard University in 1909 that "There is a great demand for negro doctors." And, in fact, seniors were courted by representatives from large cities and small towns across the South (Savitt, "Entering," 513). Yet some doctors reported that they were not always accepted, even by their own. One wrote that there seems to be an "indefinable something" that "disinclines the Negro to give countenance and patronage to members of his own race" (Savitt, 518), and both Du Bois and Carter G. Woodson noted that black professionals were not always used extensively within their own community. Notably, while Du Bois and Woodson note that this is only the case in some places, and both seek to understand the racial self-hatred behind such behavior, the issue could also be turned against blacks, as it was in a 1949 film, *Lost Boundaries*, about a black physician who passes when he fails to get work as an African American.

86. Walter White, *The Fire in the Flint* (New York: Knopf, 1924), 98, 147. Future parenthetical references are to this edition.

87. White, *A Man Called White*, 11.

88. Two more recent images of the black physician and two very different responses to the intersection of race, medicine, and professionalism can be found in the popular television series *The Bill Cosby Show* and in Carolivia Herron's novel *Thereafter Johnnie* (1991). On prime-time television, the black physician is an obstetrician and a good father. In Herron's novel, he is a surgeon who teaches at Howard and a domineering father of three daughters (he touches one daughter sexually when she is young and has a consensual relationship with her when she is older).

Epilogue: From the Clinic to the Research Laboratory: A Case Study of Three Stories

1. Lawrence Rothfield, *Vital Signs: Medical Realism in Nineteenth-Century Fiction* (Princeton, N.J.: Princeton University Press, 1992), 153.

2. Rothfield, xiii.

3. Rothfield, 149.

4. Charles Rosenberg, *The Care of Strangers: The Rise of America's Hospital System* (New York: Basic Books, 1987), 244–52.

5. See Alan M. Chesney, *The Johns Hopkins Hospital and the Johns Hopkins University School of Medicine*, vol. 1, *Early Years, 1867–1893* (Baltimore: Johns Hopkins University Press, 1943); and see Paul Starr, *The Social Transformation of American Medicine* (New York: Basic Books, 1982), 115–16.

6. See Starr, *Social Transformation*, 159, 467 n.29.

7. Starr, 156; see also, Rothfield, *Vital Signs*, 144–50.

8. Rosenberg, *Care of Strangers*, 148.

9. M. H. Richardson to Dr. Eliot, March 29, 1888, quoted in Rosenberg, *Care of Strangers*, 148.

10. See Helen Clapesattle, *The Doctors Mayo* (Minneapolis: University of Minnesota Press, 1941), 297–338, 388, 392; and Starr, *Social Transformation*, 156–57, 210.

11. Starr, 210.

12. Ellen Moers, *Two Dreisers* (New York: Viking Press, 1969), 186, 341 n. 9.

13. Theodore Dreiser, *Twelve Men* (New York: Boni and Liveright, 1919), 119. All subsequent parenthetical citations are to this edition.

14. Richard Lingeman, *Theodore Dreiser: An American Journey, 190 -1945* (New York: Putnam's, 1990), 174. Also see Tom Lutz, *American Nervousness, 1903: An Anecdotal History* (Ithaca, N.Y.: Cornell University Press, 1991), 38–46, for an interpretation of Dreiser's health problems in 1903 as part of a cultural habit of interpreting neurasthenia and mental health problems as evidence of the patient's sensitivity and upper-class sensibilities.

15. For excellent, nuanced commentary on the role of physicality and animal vitality, see June Howard, *Form and History in American Literary Naturalism* (Chapel Hill: University of North Carolina Press, 1985), 70–103. Culhane is defined by his animal energy, and by the "profanity and brutality" he uses to turn spiritually sick men into fit animals (186). Dreiser's portrait of Culhane also clearly participates in the nativist ideology that Howard suggests underlies naturalist images of the brute. He is an Irish immigrant, and he has links to the criminal world.

16. Walter Benn Michaels, "An American Tragedy, or the Promise of American Life," *Representations* 25 (Winter 1989): 73.

17. See Martha Banta, *Taylored Lives: Narrative Productions in the Age of Taylor, Veblen, and Ford* (Chicago: University of Chicago Press, 1993).

18. See Lutz, *American Nervousness*, 38–62.

19. Jack London, *Short Stories of Jack London*, ed. Earle Labor, Robert C. Leitz III, and I. Milo Shepard (New York: Macmillan, 1991). All subsequent parenthetical citations are to this edition.

20. Quoted in Martin Pernick, *A Calculus of Suffering: Pain, Professionalism, and Anesthesia in Nineteenth-Century America* (New York: Columbia University Press, 1985), 53.

21. See Kathryn Montgomery Hunter, *Doctors' Stories: The Narrative Structure of Medical Knowledge* (Princeton, N.J.: Princeton University Press, 1991), 4–30, 47–48.

22. Jonathan Auerbach, "Congested Mails: Buck and Jack's Call," *American Literature* 67 (March 1995): 51–76. Walter Benn Michaels, *The Gold Standard and the Logic of Naturalism: American Literature at the Turn of the Century* (Berkeley: University of California Press, 1987).

23. Michael Fried, in a reading of "The Monster" (another turn-of-the-century story featuring a doctor) argues that in Stephen Crane's short story the act of writing is "thematized as *violent* disfigurement" and associated with producing the effects of "horror and repugnance." The same is true in "Semper Idem." Disfigurement is a central theme figured in the inscribed photograph, in the scar left by the doctor's sutures, and in the violence of London's story itself. Michael Fried, *Realism, Writing, Disfiguration: On thomas Eakins and Stephen Crane* (Chicago: University of Chicago Press, 1987), 101.

24. T. Hugh Crawford, *Modernism, Medicine, and William Carlos Williams* (Norman: University of Oklahoma Press, 1993), 25.

25. Robert F. Gish, *William Carlos Williams: A Study of the Short Fiction* (Boston: Twayne, 1989), 57, calls the story "a kind of diagnosis after the fact—biography as postmortem."

26. Rosenberg, *Care of Strangers*, 290.

27. William Carlos Williams, *The Collected Stories of William Carlos Williams* (New York: New Directions, 1996). Future parenthetical references are to this edition.

28. My inclincation is to read this passage as a description of an abortion. Gish interprets it as a description of Rivers raping the patient (*William Carlos Williams*, 58–59).

29. Rothfield, *Vital Signs*, 166; see also 148–74 for an excellent discussion of the relationship between pathology and modernism.

Bibliography

Adams, Henry. *John Randolph*. Boston: Houghton Mifflin, 1882, 1898.

Albertine, Susan. "Breaking the Silent Partnership: Businesswomen in Popular Fiction." *American Literature* 62 (1990): 238–61.

Alcott, Louisa May. *Eight Cousins; or The Aunt Hill*. 1874. Reprint Boston: Little, Brown, 1927.

———. *Little Women*. 1871. Reprint New York: Bantam, 1983.

———. *Rose in Bloom: A Sequel to "Eight Cousins"*. 1876. Reprint New York: A.L. Burt, 1918.

Andrews, William L. "William Dean Howells and Charles W. Chesnutt: Criticism and Race Fiction in the Age of Booker T. Washington." *American Literature* 48 (1976): 327–39.

Anesko, Michael. *Letters, Fictions, Lives: Henry James and William Dean Howells*. Oxford: Oxford University Press, 1997.

Armstrong, David. *Political Anatomy of the Body: Medical Knowledge in Britain in the Twentieth Century*. Cambridge: Cambridge University Press, 1983.

Arnold, David. *Colonizing the Body: State Medicine and Epidemic Disease in Nineteenth-Century India*. Berkeley: University of California Press, 1993.

Auerbach, Jonathan. "Congested Mails: Buck and Jack's Call." *American Literature* 67 (March 1995): 51–76.

Baker, Houston. *Modernism and the Harlem Renaissance*. Chicago: University of Chicago Press, 1987.

Banta, Martha. "Introduction" to William Dean Howells, *The Shadow of a Dream*. Bloomington: Indiana University Press, 1970.

———. "Men, Women, and the American Way." In *Cambridge Companion to Henry James*, ed. Jonathan Freeman. Cambridge: Cambridge University Press, 1998.

———. *Taylored Lives: Narrative Productions in the Age of Taylor, Veblen, and Ford*. Chicago: University of Chicago Press, 1993.

Bardeen, Charles Russell. "Anatomy in America." *Bulletin of the University of Wisconsin* 3, 4 (1905): 85–208.

Barker, Francis. *The Tremulous Private Body: Essays on Subjection*. London: Methuen, 1984.

Baym, Nina. *American Women of Letters and the Nineteenth-century Sciences: Styles of Affiliation*. New Brunswick, N.J.: Rutgers University Press, 2001.

———. "Thwarted Nature: Nathaniel Hawthorne as Feminist." In *American Novelists Reconsidered: Essays in Feminist Criticism*, ed. Fritz Fleischmann. Boston: G.K. Hall, 1982.

Bell, Whitfield J., Jr. *John Morgan, Continental Doctor*. Philadelphia: University of Pennsylvania Press, 1965.

Bennett, George N. *The Realism of William Dean Howells, 1889–1920*. Nashville, Tenn.: Vanderbilt University Press, 1973.

Bensick, Carol Marie. *La Nouvelle Beatrice: Renaissance and Romance in "Rappaccini's Daughter"*. New Brunswick, N.J.: Rutgers University Press, 1985.

———. "World Lit Hawthorne: Or, Re-Allegorizing 'Rappaccini's Daughter.'" In *New Essays on Hawthorne's Major Tales*, ed. Millicent Bell. Cambridge: Cambridge University Press, 1993.

Bhabha, Homi. *The Location of Culture*. London: Routledge, 1994.

Bigelow, Henry. "Anaesthetic Agents, Their Mode of Exhibition and Physiological Effects." *Transactions of the American Medical Association* 1 (1848).

———. *Ether and Chloroform: A Compendium of Their History, Surgical Uses, Dangers, and Discovery*. Boston: David Clapp, 1848.

———. "A History of the Discovery of Modern Anaesthesia." *American Journal of the Medical Sciences* 71 (1876): 164–84.

———. "Insensibility During Surgical Operations." *Boston Medical and Surgical Journal* 35 (1846): 309–17.

———. "A Response to J. F. Flagg." *Boston Medical and Surgical Journal* 35 (1846): 382.

Biggs, A. *The Botanico Medical Reference Book*. Memphis, Tenn.: Wells and Care, 1846.

Binger, Carl, M.D. *Revolutionary Doctor: Benjamin Rush, 1746–1813*. New York: Norton, 1966.

Birnbaum, Michele. "Racial Hysteria: Female Pathology and Race Politics in Frances Harper's *Iola Leroy* and W. D. Howells's *An Imperative Duty*." *African American Review* 33, 1 (Spring 1999): 7–17.

Blair, Stanley B. "A Dose of Exquisite Aesthetics: Literature in American Medicine, 1902–1906." *Journal of Popular Culture* 28, 4 (1995): 103–12.

Blake, John B. "Anatomy." In *The Education of American Physicians*, ed. Ronald L. Numbers. Berkeley: University of California Press, 1980.

Blakely, Robert L. and Judith M. Harrington. "Grave Consequences: The Opportunistic Procurement of Cadavers at the Medical College of Georgia." In *Bones in the Basement: Postmortem Racism in Nineteenth-Century Medical Training*, ed. Robert L. Blakely and Judith M. Harrington. Washington, D.C.: Smithsonian Institution Press, 1997.

Bledstein, Burton. *The Culture of Professionalism: The Middle Class and the Development of Higher Education in America*. New York: Norton, 1976.

Bono, James J. "Science, Discourse, and Literature: The Role/Rule of Metaphor in Science." In *Literature and Science: Theory and Practice*, ed. Stuart Peterfreund. Boston: Northeastern University Press, 1990.

Boudreau, Kristin. *Sympathy in American Literature: American Sentiments from Jefferson to the Jameses*. Gainesville: University Press of Florida, 2001.

Bourdieu, Pierre. *Distinction: A Social Critique of the Judgment of Taste*. Translated by Richard Nice. Cambridge, Mass.: Harvard University Press, 1984.

Bowditch, N. I. *A History of the Massachusetts General Hospital*. 1851. Reprint Medicine and Society in America Series. New York: Arno Press, 1972.

Briggs, C. F. "Elegant Tom Dillar." *Putnam's* 1 (1853): 525–30.

Brodhead, Richard. *Cultures of Letters: Scenes of Reading and Writing in Nineteenth-Century America*. Chicago: University of Chicago Press, 1993.

———. *The School of Hawthorne*. New York: Oxford University Press, 1989.

Brooks, Peter. *Body Work: Objects of Desire in Modern Narrative*. Cambridge, Mass.: Harvard University Press, 1993.

Brown, Gillian. *Domestic Individualism: Imagining Self in Nineteenth-Century America*. Berkeley: University of California Press, 1990.

Brown, Theodore M. "Mental Disease." In *Companion Encyclopedia of the History of Medicine*, ed. W. F. Bynum and Roy Porter. London: Routledge, 1997.

Browner, Stephanie P. "Authorizing the Body: Scientific Medicine and *The Scarlet Letter*." *Literature and Medicine* 12, 2 (Fall 1993): 146–51.

———. "Documenting Cultural Politics: A *Putnam's* Short Story." *PMLA* 116, 2 (March 2001): 397–405.

———. "Ideologies of the Anesthetic: Professionalism, Egalitarianism and the Ether Controversy." *American Quarterly* 51, 1 (March 1999): 108–43.

Bryant, John. "Textual Expurgations." In Herman Melville, *Typee: A Peep at Polynesian Life*. New York: Penguin, 1996.

Butler, Judith. *Bodies That Matter: On the Discursive Limits of "Sex"*. New York: Routledge, 1993.

Byrd, W. Michael and Linda A. Clayton. "An American Health Dilemma: A History of Blacks in the Health System." *Journal of the National Medical Association* 84 (1992): 189–200.

Bynum, W. F. "Nosology." In *Companion Encyclopedia of the History of Medicine*, ed. W. F. Bynum and Roy Porter. New York: Routledge, 1997.

Cabot, James Eliot. *A Memoir of Ralph Waldo Emerson*. Vol. 1. Boston: Houghton Mifflin, 1887.

Canghuilhem, Georges. *The Normal and the Pathological*. 1943. Trans. Carolyn R. Fawcett. New York: Zone Books, 1991.

Caputo, David. "Roundtable." In Jacques Derrida, *Deconstruction in a Nutshell: A Conversation with Jacques Derrida*. New York: Fordham University Press, 1997.

Cargill, Oscar. *The Novels of Henry James*. New York: Macmillan, 1961.

Carnegie, Mary Elizabeth. *The Path We Tread: Blacks in Nursing, 1854–1984*. Philadelphia: Lippincott, 1986.

Cary, John. *Joseph Warren: Physician, Politician, Patriot*. Urbana: University of Illinois Press, 1961.

Chase, Richard Volney. *Herman Melville: A Critical Study*. New York: Macmillan, 1949.

Chesney, Alan M. *The Johns Hopkins Hospital and the Johns Hopkins University School of Medicine*. Vol. 1, *Early Years, 1867–1893*. Baltimore: Johns Hopkins University Press, 1943.

Chesnutt, Charles. "Her Virginia Mammy." In *The Wife of His Youth, and Other Stories of the Color Line*. 1899. Reprint Ridgewood, N.J.: Gregg Press, 1967.

———. *The House Behind the Cedars*. 1900. Reprint New York: Penguin, 1993.

———. *The Journals of Charles Chesnutt*. Ed. Richard Brodhead. Durham, N.C.: Duke University Press, 1993.

———. *The Marrow of Tradition*. 1901. Reprint Ann Arbor: University of Michigan Press, 1969.

———. Notebook. Chesnutt Collection, Fisk University Library, Nashville, Tenn.

———. *"To Be an Author": Letters of Charles Chesnutt, 1889–1905*. Ed. Joseph R. McElrath, Jr., and Robert C. Leitz, III. Princeton, N.J.: Princeton University Press, 1997.

Chesnutt, Helen. *Charles Waddell Chesnutt: Pioneer of the Color Line*. Chapel Hill: University of North Carolina Press, 1952.

Chinn, Sarah E. *Technology and the Logic of American Racism*. London: Continuum, 2000.

Churchill, Edward D., M.D., ed. *To Work in the Vineyard of Surgery: The Reminiscences of J. Collins Warren, 1842–1927.* Cambridge, Mass.: Harvard University Press, 1958.

Clapesattle, Helen. *The Doctors Mayo.* Minneapolis: University of Minnesota Press, 1941.

Clarke, Edward H., M.D. *Sex in Education; or, A Fair Chance for Girls.* Boston: Houghton Mifflin, 1873.

Combe, Andrew. "The Physiology of Digestion." Boston: Marsch, Capen and Lyon, 1837. Reprinted on the *GastroLab Homepage, Historical Texts. http://www.kolumbus.fi/hans/welcome.htm.* 7 December 2003.

Combe, George. "The Constitution of Man in Relation to External Objects." 8th ed. 1847. Reprinted in "The History of Phrenology on the Web," ed. John van Wyhe. 9 May 2003. *http://pages.britishlibrary.net/phrenology/texts.htm.* 7 December 2003.

———. "The Life and Correspondence of Andrew Combe." 1850. Reprinted in "The History of Phrenology on the Web," ed. John van Wyhe. *http://pages.britishlibrary.net/phrenology/texts.htm.* 7 December 2003.

"Comment on New Books." *Atlantic Monthly* 70 (November 1892): 704–14.

Conway, Moncure Daniel. "My Lost Art." *Atlantic Monthly* 10 (August 1862): 228–35.

Crary, Jonathan. *Techniques of the Observer: On Vision and Modernity in the Nineteenth Century.* Cambridge, Mass.: MIT Press, 1990.

Crawford, T. Hugh. *Modernism, Medicine, and William Carlos Williams.* Norman: University of Oklahoma Press, 1993.

Crowley, John W. *The Black Heart's Truth: The Early Career of W. D. Howells.* Chapel Hill: University of North Carolina Press, 1985.

———. "W. D. Howells: The Everwomanly." In *American Novelists Revisited: Essays in Feminist Criticism,* ed. Fritz Fleishmann. Boston: G.K. Hall, 1982.

Dalke, Anne. "Economics, of the Bosom Serpent: Oliver Wendell Holmes's *Elsie Venner: A Romance of Destiny.*" *American Transcendental Quarterly* 2 (1988): 57–68.

Dalzell, Robert F., Jr. *Enterprising Elite: The Boston Associates and the World They Made.* Cambridge, Mass.: Harvard University Press, 1987.

Dana, Richard. "A History of the Ether Discovery." *Littell's Living Age* 16 (1848): 529–71.

Dans, Peter E. *Doctors in the Movies: Boil the Water and Just Say Aah.* Bloomington, Ill. : Medi-Ed Press, 2000.

Davis, Cynthia J. *Bodily and Narrative Forms: The Influence of Medicine on American Literature, 1845–1915.* Stanford, Calif.: Stanford University Press, 2000.

Davis, Rebecca Harding. *Bits of Gossip.* Boston: Houghton Mifflin, 1904.

———. "A Day with Doctor Sarah." *Harper's New Monthly Magazine* 57 (September 1878): 611–17.

———. "Life in the Iron Mills," *Atlantic Monthly* 7 (April 1861): 430–51. Reprint, ed. Cecelia Tichi. Bedford Cultural Edition. Boston: Bedford, 1998.

———. *Waiting for the Verdict.* 1867. Reprint Upper Saddle, N.J.: Gregg Press, 1967.

De Ville, Allen. *Medical Malpractice in Nineteenth-Century America: Origins and Legacy.* New York: New York University Press, 1990.

Dibdin, Michael. "The Pathology Lesson." *Granta: The Body* 39 (Spring 1992): 91–102.

Dickinson, Emily. *The Complete Poems of Emily Dickinson.* Ed. Thomas H. Johnson. Boston: Little, Brown, 1960.

Dimock, Wai Chee. *Empire for Liberty: Melville and the Poetics of Individualism.* Princeton, N.J.: Princeton University Press, 1989.

"Doctors." *Putnam's* 2 (1853): 66–71.

Douglas, Ann. *The Feminization of American Culture*. New York: Anchor, 1988.

Dreiser, Theodore. *Twelve Men*. New York: Boni and Liveright, 1919.

Du Bois, W. E. B. "Obituary." *Crisis*, January 1933.

———. *The Philadelphia Negro: A Social Study*. Philadelphia: University of Pennsylvania Press, 1899. Reprint with introduction by Elijah Anderson, 1996.

———. *The Souls of Black Folk*. Chicago: McClure, 1903.

———. "What Is the Negro Problem." 1889. In *The Oxford W. E. B. Du Bois Reader*, ed. Eric Sundquist. New York: Oxford University Press, 1996.

Duden, Barbara. *The Woman Beneath the Skin: A Doctor's Patients in Eighteenth-Century Germany*. Trans. Thomas Dunlap. Cambridge, Mass.: Harvard University Press, 1991.

Duffy, John. *The Healers: A History of American Medicine*. Urbana: University of Illinois Press, 1979.

Duncum, Barbara. *The Development of Inhalation Anaesthesia, with special reference to the Years 1846–1900*. London: Oxford University Press and Wellcome Historical Medical Museum, 1947.

Duyckinck, Evert A. "Great Feeling and Discrimination." *Literary World* 6 (March 30): 323–25. Reprinted in Nathaniel Hawthorne, *The Scarlet Letter: An Authoritative Text, Essays in Criticism, and Scholarship*, ed. Seymour Gross, Sculley Bradley, Richmond Croom Beatty, E. Hudson Long, and E. Sculley Bradley. Norton Critical Edition. New York: Norton, 1988.

Edel, Leon. *Henry James: A Life*. New York: Harper, 1985.

Edwards, Dr. "Patent Medicines: Report No. 52." U.S. House of Representatives, 30th Congress, 2nd Sess., 6 February 1849.

Eisman, Katharine. *Inwardness and Theater in the English Renaissance*. Chicago: University of Chicago Press, 1995.

English, Daylanne. "W. E. B. DuBois's Family *Crisis*." *American Literature* 72, 2 (June 2000): 291–320.

Feinstein, Howard M. *Becoming William James*. Ithaca, N.Y.: Cornell University Press, 1984.

Feldberg, Georgina D. *Disease and Class: Tuberculosis and the Shaping of Modern North American Society*. New Brunswick, N.J.: Rutgers University Press, 1995.

Fenster, Julie M. *Ether Day: The Strange Tale of America's Greatest Medical Discovery and the Haunted Men Who Made It*. New York: HarperCollins, 2001.

Fetterley, Judith. *The Resisting Reader: A Feminist Approach to American Fiction*. Bloomington: Indiana University Press, 1978.

Figlio, Karl. "The Historiography of Scientific Medicine: An Invitation to the Human Sciences." *Comparative Studies in Society and History* 19 (1977): 262–86.

Finch, Casey. "'Hooked and Buttoned Together': Victorian Underwear and Representations of the Female Body." *Victorian Studies* 34 (1991): 337–63.

Flagg, J. F. "The Inhalation of an Ethereal Vapor to Prevent Sensibility to Pain During Surgical Operations." *Boston Medical and Surgical Journal* 35 (2 December 1846): 356–59.

Flexner, Abraham. Introduction to facsimile edition of John Morgan, *A Discourse upon the Institution of Medical Schools in America*. Publications of the Institute of the History of Medicine 4th ser. Baltimore: Johns Hopkins University Press, 1937.

Foster, Elizabeth S. Introduction to Herman Melville, *The Confidence-Man*. New York: Hendricks House, 1954.

Foster, Frances Smith. Introduction to Francis E. W. Harper, *Iola Leroy*. New York: Oxford University Press, 1988.

Foucault, Michel. *The Birth of the Clinic: An Archeology of Medical Perception*. Trans. A. M. Sheridan Smith. New York: Vintage, 1975.

Franklin, H. Bruce. *The Wake of the Gods: Melville's Mythology.* Stanford, Calif.: Stanford University Press, 1963.

Frederickson, George M. *The Black Image in the White Mind: The Debate on Afro-American Character and Destiny, 1817–1914.* New York: Harper, 1971.

Freidson, Eliot. *Profession of Medicine: A Study of the Sociology of Applied Knowledge.* New York: Dodd, Mead, 1970.

French, R. K. "Berengario da Carpi and the Use of Commentary in Anatomical Teaching." In *The Medical Renaissance of the Sixteenth Century,* ed. A. Wear, R. K. French, and Iain M. Lonie. Cambridge: Cambridge University Press, 1985.

Fried, Michael. *Realism, Writing, Disfiguration; On Thomas Eakins and Stephen Crane.* Chicago: University of Chicago Press, 1987.

Fuller, Robert C. *Alternative Medicine and American Religious Life.* New York: Oxford University Press, 1989.

Furst, Lillian R. "Halfway up the Hill: Doctoresses in Late Nineteenth-Century American Fiction." In *Women Healers and Physicians: Climbing a Long Hill,* ed. Lillian R. Furst. Lexington: University Press of Kentucky, 1997.

Gaines, Kevin. *Uplifting the Race: Black Leadership, Politics, and Culture in the Twentieth Century.* Chapel Hill: University of North Carolina Press, 1996.

Gallagher, Catherine. "The Body Versus the Social Body in the Works of Thomas Malthus and Henry Mayhew." *Representations* 14 (1986): 83–106.

Garland, Hugh A. "The Death of John Randolph." *Harper's New Monthly Magazine* 2 (December 1850): 80–84.

Gates, Henry Louis. *Figures in Black: Words, Signs, and the "Racial" Self.* New York: Oxford University Press, 1987.

Gilman, Sander. *Disease and Representation: Images of Illness from Madness to AIDS.* Ithaca, N.Y.: Cornell University Press, 1988.

Gilmore, Michael T. *American Romanticism and the Marketplace.* Chicago: University of Chicago Press, 1985.

Gish, Robert F. *William Carlos Williams: A Study of the Short Fiction.* Boston: Twayne, 1989.

Glazener, Nancy. *Reading for Realism: The History of a U.S. Literary Institution, 1850–1910.* Durham, N.C.: Duke University Press, 1997.

Goodman, Nathan G. *Benjamin Rush: Physician and Citizen, 1746–1813.* Philadelphia: University of Pennsylvania Press, 1934.

Gould, Stephen Jay. *The Mismeasure of Man.* New York: Norton, 1981.

Gramsci, Antonio. *Selections from the Prison Notebooks.* Ed. and trans. Quintin Hoare and Geoffrey Nowell Smith. New York: International Publishers, 1971.

Gregory, Samuel. "Man-Midwifery Exposed and Corrected: or, The Employment of Men to Attend Women in Childbirth, Shown to be a Modern Innovation." Boston and New York, 1848. Reprinted in *The Male Mid-Wife and the Female Doctor: The Gynecology Controversy in Nineteenth-Century America,* ed. Charles Rosenberg and Carroll Smith-Rosenberg. New York: Arno Press, 1974.

Guillaumin, Colette. *Racism, Sexism, Power and Ideology.* New York: Routledge, 1995.

Gunn, John C. *Domestic Medicine . . .* New York: Saxton, Barker, 1860.

Haber, Samuel. *The Quest for Authority and Honor in the American Professions, 1750–1900.* Chicago: University of Chicago Press, 1991.

Hack, Daniel. "Literacy Paupers and Professional Authors: The Guild of Literature and Art." *Studies in English Literature* 39, 4 (Autumn 1999): 691–714.

Hale, L. P. "The Queen of the Red Chessmen." *Atlantic Monthly* 1 (February 1858): 431–45.

Hale, Sarah H. "The Discovery of Ether." *Godey's Lady's Book* 46 (1853): 205–12.

Hall, Peter Dobkin. *The Organization of American Culture, 1700–1900: Private Institutions, Elites, and the Origins of American Nationality.* New York: New York University Press, 1982.

Haller, John S. *American Medicine in Transition, 1840–1910.* Urbana: University of Illinois Press, 1981.

———. *Outcasts from Evolution: Scientific Attitudes of Racial Inferiority, 1859–1900.* Urbana: University of Illinois Press, 1971.

Halttunen, Karen. *Confidence Men and Painted Women: A Study of Middle-Class Culture in America, 1830–1870.* New Haven, Conn.: Yale University Press, 1982.

———. "Gothic Mystery and the Birth of the Asylum: The Cultural Construction of Deviance in Early-Nineteenth-Century America." In *Moral Problems in American Life: New Perspectives on Cultural History,* ed. Karen Halttunen and Lewis Perry. Ithaca, N.Y.: Cornell University Press, 1998.

Hamilton, Alexander. "Federalist # 35." 5 January 1788. Reprint in *The Avalon Project at Yale Law School: Documents in Law, History, and Diplomacy.* http://www.yale.edu/lawweb/avalon/fed35.htm. 9 December 2003.

Harper, Frances E. W. *Iola Leroy, or Shadows Uplifted.* 1892. Reprint New York: Oxford University Press, 1988.

———. "The Two Offers," 1858. Reprinted in *The Norton Anthology of American Literature,* vol. 1, ed. Nina Baym. New York: Norton, 1999.

Harris, Sharon M. *Rebecca Harding Davis and American Realism.* Philadelphia: University of Pennsylvania Press, 1991.

Hawthorne, Nathaniel. *The American Claimant Manuscripts.* Volume 12 of The Centenary Edition of the Works of Nathaniel Hawthorne, ed. Edward H. Davidson, Claude M. Simpson, and L. Neal Smith. Columbus: Ohio State University Press, 1977.

———. *American Notebooks.* Centenary Edition 8, ed. Claude M. Simpson. Columbus: Ohio State University Press, 1972.

———. "The Birth-mark." In *Mosses from an Old Manse,* Centenary Edition 10, ed. Fredson Bowers, L. Neal Smith, John Manning, and J. Donald Crowley. Columbus: Ohio State University Press, 1974.

———. *The Elixir of Life Manuscripts.* Centenary Edition 13, ed. Edward H. Davidson, Claude M. Simpson, and L. Neal Smith. Columbus: Ohio State University Press, 1977.

———. *The Letters, 1813–1843.* Centenary Edition 15, ed. Thomas Woodson, L. Neal Smith, and Norman Holmes Pearson. Columbus: Ohio State University Press, 1984.

———. *The Letters, 1843–1853.* Centenary Edition 16, ed. Thomas Woodson, L. Neal Smith, and Norman Holmes Pearson. Columbus: Ohio State University Press, 1985.

———. "Main-Street." In *The Snow-Image and Uncollected Tales,* Centenary Edition 11, ed. Fredson Bowers, L. Neal Smith, John Manning, and J. Donald Crowley. Columbus: Ohio State University Press, 1974.

———. *The Marble Faun.* Centenary Edition 4, ed. Roy Harvey Pearce, Claude M. Simpson, Fredson Bowers, and L. Neal Smith. Columbus: Ohio State University Press, 1968.

———. "The Old Manse." In *Mosses from an Old Manse,* Centenary Edition 10, ed. Fredson Bowers, L. Neal Smith, John Manning, and J. Donald Crowley. Columbus: Ohio State University Press, 1974.

———. *Passages from the American Note-Books of Nathaniel Hawthorne.* Boston: Houghton Mifflin, 1883.

———. "Rappaccini's Daughter." In *Mosses from an Old Manse*, Centenary Edition 10, ed. Fredson Bowers, L. Neal Smith, John Manning, and J. Donald Crowley. Columbus: Ohio State University Press, 1974.

———. *The Scarlet Letter*. Centenary Edition 1, ed. William Charvat, Roy Harvey Pearce, Claude M. Simpson, Fredson Bowers, and Matthew J. Bruccoli. Columbus: Ohio State University Press, 1962.

———. *The Scarlet Letter: An Authoritative Text, Essays in Criticism, and Scholarship*. Ed. Seymour Gross, Sculley Bradley, Richmond Croom Beatty, E. Hudson Long, and E. Sculley Bradley. Norton Critical Edition. New York: Norton, 1988.

Hawthorne, Rose Lathrop. *Memories of Hawthorne*. Boston: Houghton Mifflin, 1897.

Heckscher, William S. *Rembrandt's* Anatomy of Dr. Nicolaas Tulp: *An Iconological Study*. New York: New York University Press, 1958.

Hendler, Glenn. "The Limits of Sympathy: Louisa May Alcott and the Sentimental Novel." *American Literary History* 4 (1991): 685–706.

Herbert, T. Walter. *Dearest Beloved: The Hawthornes and the Making of the Middle-Class Family*. Berkeley: University of California Press, 1993.

Higgins, Brian and Hershel Parker, eds. *Herman Melville: The Contemporary Reviews*. Cambridge: Cambridge University Press, 1995.

Higginson, Thomas Wentworth. "Saints and Their Bodies." *Atlantic Monthly* 1 (March 1858): 582–95.

Hodges, Richard Manning. *A Narrative of Events Connected with the Introduction of Sulphuric Ether into Surgical Use*. Boston: Little Brown, 1891.

Hollis, Ralph Lynch, compiler. *The Black Urban Condition: A Documentary History, 1866–1971*. New York: Crowell, 1975.

Holmes, Oliver Wendell. *The Autocrat of the Breakfast Table*. Boston: Houghton Mifflin, 1888.

———. "Doings of the Sunbeam." *Atlantic Monthly* 12 (July 1863): 1–15.

———. *Elsie Venner*. 1861. Reprint New York: New American Library, 1961.

———. "Experiments in Medicine." *Boston Medical and Surgical Journal* 30 (1844): 202.

———. *Medical Essays*. New York: Riverside, 1891.

———. "The Stereoscope and the Stereograph." *Atlantic Monthly* 3 (June 1859): 738–49.

———. "Sun-Painting and Sun-Sculpture." *Atlantic Monthly* 8 (July 1861): 13–29.

Holstein, Michael. "Writing as a Healing Art." *Studies in American Fiction* 16 (1988): 39–49.

Hooker, Worthington. "The Present Mental Attitude and Tendencies of the Medical Profession." *New Englander* 10 (1852). Reprinted as *Inaugural Address*. New Haven, Conn.: T. J. Stafford Printer, 1852.

Howard, June. *Form and History in American Literary Naturalism*. Chapel Hill: University of North Carolina Press, 1985.

Howard, Leon. *Herman Melville: A Biography*. Berkeley: University of California Press, 1951.

———. "Historical Note." In Herman Melville, *Typee: A Peep at Polynesian Life*, Northwestern-Newberry Edition.

Howe, Daniel Walker. *Making the American Self: Jonathan Edwards to Abraham Lincoln*. Cambridge, Mass.: Harvard University Press, 1997.

Howells, William Dean. *Dr. Breen's Practice*. Boston: J.R. Osgood, 1881.

———. *Heroines of Fiction*. New York: Harper and Brothers, 1901.

———. *An Imperative Duty*. 1892. Reprint Bloomington: Indiana University Press, 1970.

———. *Life in Letters of William Dean Howells*. Ed. Mildred Howells. New York: Doubleday, 1928.

———. "The Man of Letters Is a Man of Business." *Scribner's Magazine* (October 1893): 429–46.

———. *The Shadow of a Dream.* 1890. Reprint Bloomington: Indiana University Press, 1970.

———. *The Son of Royal Langbrith.* 1904. Reprint Bloomington: Indiana University Press, 1969.

Hunter, Kathryn Montgomery. *Doctors' Stories: The Narrative Structure of Medical Knowledge.* Princeton, N.J.: Princeton University Press, 1991.

Hurst, Luanne Jenkins. "The Chief Employ of Her Life." In *Hawthorne and Women: Engendering and Expanding the Hawthorne Tradition,* ed. John L. Idol, Jr., and Melinda M. Ponder. Amherst: University of Massachusetts Press, 1999.

Jackson, James. *Letters to a Young Physician.* Boston: Phillips, Sampson, 1855.

James, Alice. *The Diary of Alice James.* Ed. Leon Edel. New York: Viking Penguin, 1982.

James, Henry. "The Art of Fiction." 1888. Reprinted in *The Future of the Novel,* ed. Leon Edel. New York: Vintage, 1956.

———. *The Bostonians.* 1886. Reprint New York: Penguin, 1966.

———. *Daisy Miller.* 1878. Reprint New York: Penguin, 1986.

———. *Hawthorne.* 1879. Reprint New York: Macmillan, 1966.

———. "The Middle Years." 1893. In *Tales of Henry James,* ed. Christof Wegelin. New York: Norton, 1984.

———. "A Most Extraordinary Case," *Atlantic Monthly* 21 (April 1868): 461–85.

———. *Notes of a Son and Brother.* Ed. Frederick W. Dupee. New York: Criterion Books, 1956.

———. Preface to *The Wings of the Dove.* Vol. 1. New York: Scribner's, 1909.

———. *Selected Letters.* Ed. Leon Edel. New York: Farrar, Straus, Giroux.

———. *The Wings of the Dove.* 1902. Baltimore: Penguin, 1976.

Jewett, Sarah Orne. *A Country Doctor.* 1884. Reprint New York: Meridian, 1986.

Jordanova, Ludmilla. *Sexual Visions: Images of Gender in Science and Medicine Between the Eighteenth and Twentieth Centuries.* Madison: University of Wisconsin Press, 1989.

Karcher, Carolyn. *Shadow over the Promised Land: Slavery, Race, and Violence in Melville's America.* Baton Rouge: Louisiana State University Press, 1980.

Kaufman, Martin. *Homeopathy in America: The Rise and Fall of a Medical Heresy.* Baltimore: Johns Hopkins University Press, 1971.

Kawash, Samira. *Dislocating the Color Line: Identity, Hybridity, and Singularity in African-American Literature.* Stanford, Calif.: Stanford University Press, 1997.

Kett, Joseph F. *The Formation of the American Medical Profession: The Role of Institutions, 1780–1860.* New Haven, Conn.: Yale University Press, 1968.

Keys, Thomas E. *The History of Surgical Anesthesia.* 1945. Reprint New York: Dover, 1963.

Kirk, Russell. *Randolph of Roanoke: A Study in Conservative Thought.* Chicago: University of Chicago Press, 1951.

Konold, Donald E. *History of American Medical Ethics, 1847–1912.* Madison: University of Wisconsin Press, 1962.

Laderman, Gary. *The Sacred Remains: American Attitudes Toward Death, 1799–1883.* New Haven, Conn.: Yale University Press, 1996.

Laqueur, Thomas. *Making Sex: Body and Gender from the Greeks to Freud.* Cambridge, Mass.: Harvard University Press, 1990.

Larson, Magali Sarfatti. *The Rise of Professionalism: A Sociological Analysis.* Berkeley: University of California Press, 1977.

Lawrence, Christopher and Ghislaine Lawrence. *No Laughing Matter: Historical Aspects of Anaesthesia.* Catalog of Wellcome Institute for the History of Medicine exhibition. London: Wellcome Institute, 1987.

Leake, Chauncey D. *Percival's Medical Ethics.* Baltimore: Williams and Wilkins, 1927.

Leavitt, Judith Walzer. "'Science' Enters the Birthing Room: Obstetrics in America Since the 18th Century." In *Sickness and Health in America: Readings in the History of Medicine and Public Health,* ed. Judith Walzer Leavitt and Ronald L. Numbers. Madison: University of Wisconsin Press, 1985.

Levine, Robert S. *Martin Delany, Frederick Douglass, and the Politics of Representative Identity.* Chapel Hill: University of North Carolina Press, 1997.

Leyda, Jay. *The Melville Log: A Documentary Life of Herman Melville, 1819–1891.* 2 vols. New York: Gordian Press, 1969.

Limon, John. *The Place of Fiction in the Time of Science: A Disciplinary History of American Writing.* Cambridge: Cambridge University Press, 1990.

Lingeman, Richard. *Theodore Dreiser: An American Journey, 1908–1945.* New York: Putnam's, 1990.

"Literary Virility." *Scribner's* (March 1867): 727–37.

Logan, Shirley Wilson. *"We Are Coming": The Persuasive Discourse of Nineteenth-Century Black Women.* Carbondale: Southern Illinois University Press, 1999.

London, Jack. *Short Stories of Jack London.* Ed. Earle Labor, Robert C. Leitz III, and I. Milo Shepard. New York: Macmillan, 1991.

Long, Esmond R. *Selected Readings in Pathology from Hippocrates to Virchow.* Springfield, Ill.: Charles C. Thomas, 1939.

Lott, Eric. *Love and Theft: Blackface Minstrelsy and the American Working Class.* New York: Oxford University Press, 1993.

Lutz, Tom. *American Nervousness, 1903: An Anecdotal History.* Ithaca, N.Y.: Cornel University Press, 1991.

Lynch, Deidre Shauna. *The Economy of Character: Novels, Market Culture, and the Business of Inner Meaning.* Chicago: University of Chicago Press, 1998.

Macpherson, C. B. *The Political Theory of Possessive Individualism: Hobbes to Locke.* New York: Oxford University Press, 1962.

Madison, James. "Federalist #38." 15 January 1788. Reprint in *The Avalon Project at Yale Law School: Documents in Law, History, and Diplomacy.* http://www.yale.edu/lawweb/avalon/federal/fed38.htm. 9 December 2003.

Martin, Robert K. *Hero, Captain, and Stranger: Male Friendship, Social Critique, and Literary Form in the Sea Novels of Herman Melville.* Chapel Hill: University of North Carolina Press, 1986.

"Mary Rankin: A Physician's Story." *Harper's New Monthly Magazine* 10 (May 1855): 789–794.

Masteller, Jean Carwile. "The Women Doctors of Howells, Phelps, and Jewett." In *Critical Essays on Sarah Orne Jewett,* ed. Gwen L. Nagel. Boston: G.K. Hall, 1984.

Matthews, Victoria Earle. "Aunt Lindy: A Story Founded on Real Life." *A.M.E. Church Review* 5 (January 1889): 246–50. Reprint New York: J.J. Little, 1893.

Maulitz, Russell C. *Morbid Appearances: The Anatomy of Pathology in the Early Nineteenth Century.* Cambridge: Cambridge University Press, 1987.

———. "The Pathological Tradition." In *Companion Encyclopedia of the History of Medicine,* ed. W. F. Bynum and Roy Porter. New York: Routledge, 1993.

McElrath, Joseph R., Jr. "W. D. Howells and Race: Charles W. Chesnutt's Disappointment of the Dean." *Nineteenth-Century Literature* 51, 4 (1997): 474–99.

"The Medical Profession." *Putnam's* 2 (1853): 315–18.

Melville, Herman. *Billy Budd, Sailor.* Ed. Harrison Hayford and Merton Sealts, Jr. Chicago: University of Chicago Press, 1962.

————. *Billy Budd, Sailor.* New York: Library of America, 1984.

————. *The Confidence-Man, A Masquerade.* The Writings of Herman Melville, the Northwestern-Newberry Edition, vol. 10, ed. Harrison Hayford, Hershel Parker, and G. Thomas Tanselle. Evanston: Northwestern University Press, 1984.

————. "Hawthorne and His Mosses." *Literary World* (August 1850).

————. *Journals.* Northwestern-Newberry Edition 15, ed. Howard C. Horsford and Lynn Horth. Evanston: Northwestern University Press, 1989.

————. *Typee: A Peep at Polynesian Life.* Northwestern-Newberry Edition 1, ed. Harrison Hayford, Hershel Parker, and G. Thomas Tanselle. Evanston: Northwestern University Press, 1968.

————. *White-Jacket, or The World in a Man-of-War.* Northwestern-Newberry Edition 5, ed. Harrison Hayford, Hershel Parker, and G. Thomas Tanselle. Evanston: Northwestern University Press, 1970.

Menikoff, Barry. "Oliver Wendell Holmes." In *Dictionary of Literary Biography*, vol. 1. Detroit: Gale Research, 1978.

————. "Oliver Wendell Holmes" In *Fifteen American Authors Before 1900: Bibliographic Essays on Research and Criticism,* ed. Robert A. Rees and Earl N. Harbert. Madison: University of Wisconsin Press, 1971.

Meyer, Annie Nathan. *Helen Brent, M.D.* New York: Cassell, 1894.

Michaels, Walter Benn. "An American Tragedy, or the Promise of American Life." *Representations* 25 (Winter 1989): 71–98.

————. *The Gold Standard and the Logic of Naturalism: American Literature at the Turn of the Century.* Berkeley: University of California Press, 1987.

Mill, John Stuart "Civilization." *Westminster Review* 30 (April 1836): 1–28. Reprinted in *The Emergence of Victorian Consciousness,* ed. George Levine. New York: Free Press, 1967.

Miller, Edwin Haviland. *Salem Is My Dwelling Place: A Life of Nathaniel Hawthorne.* Iowa City: University of Iowa Press, 1991.

Miller, James. *A Reader's Guide to Herman Melville.* New York: Farrar, 1962.

Miller, Lillian B. "Paintings, Sculpture, and the National Character, 1815–1860." *Journal of American History* 53, 4 (March 1967): 696–707.

Miller, Perry. *The Raven and the Whale: The War of Words and Wits in the Era of Poe and Melville.* New York: Harcourt, 1956.

"Minutes of the First Annual Meeting of the American Medical Association." *Transactions of the American Medical Association* 1 (1848): 1–15.

Moers, Ellen. *Two Dreisers.* New York: Viking, 1969.

Morais, Herbert M. *The History of the Afro-American in Medicine.* International Library of Negro Life and History. New York: Association for the Study of Afro-American Life and History, 1976.

Morantz-Sanchez, Regina. *Conduct Unbecoming a Woman: Medicine on Trial in Turn-of-the-Century Brooklyn.* Oxford: Oxford University Press, 1999.

————. *Sympathy and Science: Women Physicians in American Medicine.* New York: Oxford University Press, 1985.

Morgan, John. *A Discourse upon the Institution of Medical Schools in America.* 1765. New York: Arno Press, 1975.

Morley, John David. *The Anatomy Lesson.* New York: St. Martin's, 1995.

Morris, David. *The Culture of Pain.* Berkeley: University of California Press, 1991.

Morse, John T., Jr. *Oliver Wendell Holmes: Life and Letters.* 2 vols. Boston: Houghton Mifflin, 1896.

Morton, Elizabeth Whitman. "Trials of a Public Benefactor." *McClure's Magazine* 7 (September 1896): 311–18.

Mouffe, Chantel. "Hegemony and Ideology in Gramsci." In *Gramsci and Marxist Theory*, ed. Chantal Mouffe. Boston: Routledge, 1979.

Mumford, Lewis. *Herman Melville*. New York: Harcourt Brace, 1929.

Murphy, Lamar Riley. *Enter the Physician: The Transformation of Domestic Medicine, 1760–1860*. Tuscaloosa: University of Alabama Press, 1991.

Nelson, Dana D. *National Manhood: Capitalist Citizenship and the Imagined Fraternity of White Men*. Durham, N.C.: Duke University Press, 1998.

———. "Representative/Democracy: The Political Work of Countersymbolic Representation." In *Materializing Democracy: Toward a Revitalized Cultural Politics*, ed. Russ Castronovo and Dana D. Nelson. Durham, N.C.: Duke University Press, 2002.

Nevin, Robert P. "Stephen C. Foster and Negro Minstrelsy." *Atlantic Monthly* 20 (November 1867): 608–16.

Noble, David. *Death of a Nation: American Culture and the End of Exceptionalism*. Minneapolis: University of Minnesota Press, 2002.

Novotny, Ann and Carter Smith. *Images of Healing: A Portfolio of American Medical and Pharmaceutical Practice in the 18th, 19th, and Early 20th Centuries*. New York: Macmillan, 1980.

Nudelman, Franny. "'Emblem and Product of Sin': The Poisoned Child in *The Scarlet Letter* and Domestic Advice Literature." *Yale Journal of Criticism* 10, 1 (Spring 1997): 193–213.

Nuland, Sherwin. *Doctors: The Biography of Medicine*. New York: Vintage, 1988.

O'Brien, F. J. "The Diamond Lens." *Atlantic Monthly* 1 (January 1858): 354–67.

O'Farrell, Mary Ann. *Telling Complexions: The Nineteenth-Century English Novel and the Blush*. Durham, N.C.: Duke University Press, 1997.

O'Malley, Charles D. *Andreas Vesalius of Brussels*. Berkeley: University of California Press, 1965.

Otter, Samuel. *Melville's Anatomies*. Berkeley: University of California Press, 1999.

Ovington, Mary White. "The National Association for the Advancement of Colored People." *Journal of Negro History* 9, 2 (April 1924): 107–16.

Park, Katherine. "The Criminal Body and the Saintly Body: Autopsy and Dissection in Renaissance Italy." *Renaissance Quarterly* 41, 1 (1994): 1–33.

Parker, Hershel. *Herman Melville: A Biography*. Vol. 1, *1819–1851*. Baltimore: Johns Hopkins University Press, 1996.

———. *Reading* Billy Budd. Evanston, Ill.: Northwestern University Press, 1990.

Pernick, Martin S. *A Calculus of Suffering: Pain, Professionalism, and Anaesthesia in Nineteenth-Century America*. New York: Columbia University Press, 1985.

———. "Medical Profession: I, Medical Professionalism" In *Bioethics Encyclopedia*, 4 vols., ed. Warren T. Reich. New York: Free Press, 1978.

Pfister, Joel. *The Production of Personal Life: Class Gender, and the Psychological in Hawthorne's Fiction*. Stanford, Calif.: Stanford University Press, 1991.

Phelps, Elizabeth Stuart. *Doctor Zay: A Novel*. 1882. Reprint New York: Feminist Press, 1987.

Phillio, Calvin Wheeler. "Akin by Marriage," *Atlantic Monthly* 1 (November 1857): 94–110; (December 1857): 229–39; (January 1858): 279–88.

Porter, Roy. *The Greatest Benefit to Mankind: A Medical History of Humanity*. New York: Norton, 1997.

Prather, Leon H. *We Have Taken a City: Wilmington Racial Massacre and Coup of 1898*. Rutherford, N.J.: Fairleigh Dickinson University Press, 1984.

Prime, W. C. "The Infant Heir." *Harper's New Monthly Magazine* 8 (May 1854): 824–32.

Proceedings on Behalf of the Morton Testimonial. Lilly Library, Special Collections. Indiana University, Bloomington.

Renker, Elizabeth. *Strike Through the Mask: Herman Melville and the Scene of Writing.* Baltimore: Johns Hopkins University Press, 1996.

"Report of the Trial: The People versus Dr. Horatio N. Loomis, for Libel. Tried at the Erie County Oyer and Terminer, June 24, 1850." Buffalo, 1850. Reprinted in *The Male Mid-Wife and the Female Doctor: The Gynecology Controversy in Nineteenth-Century America,* ed. Charles Rosenberg and Carroll Smith-Rosenberg. New York: Arno Press, 1974.

Reynolds, David S. *Beneath the American Renaissance: The Subversive Imagination in the Age of Emerson and Melville.* New York: Knopf, 1988.

Reynolds, Larry. *European Revolutions and the American Literary Renaissance.* New Haven, Conn.: Yale University Press, 1988.

Rice, Nathan P. *Trials of a Public Benefactor, as illustrated in the Discovery of Etherization.* New York: Pudney and Russell, 1859.

Richards, Thomas. *The Commodity Culture of Victorian England: Advertising and Spectacle, 1851–1914.* Stanford, Calif.: Stanford University Press, 1990.

Rivkin, Julie. "Doctoring the Text: Henry James and Revision." In *Henry James's New York Edition: The Construction of Authorship,* ed. David McWhirter. Stanford, Calif.: Stanford University Press, 1995.

Rogin, Michael. *Subversive Genealogy: The Politics and Art of Herman Melville.* New York: Knopf, 1983.

Roman, Margaret. *Sarah Orne Jewett: Reconstructing Gender.* Tuscaloosa: University of Alabama Press, 1992.

Romero, Lora. *Home Fronts: Domesticity and Its Critics in the Antebellum United States.* Durham, N.C.: Duke University Press, 1997.

Romines, Ann. *The Home Plot: Women, Writing and Domestic Ritual.* Amherst: University of Massachusetts Press, 1992.

Roosevelt, Theodore. *American Ideals and Other Essays Social and Political* New York: G.P. Putnam's Sons, 1897.

Rose, Jane Atteridge. *Rebecca Harding Davis.* New York: Twayne, 1993.

Rosenberg, Charles. *The Care of Strangers: The Rise of America's Hospital System.* New York: Basic Books, 1987.

———. *The Cholera Years: The United States in 1832, 1849, and 1866.* Chicago: University of Chicago Press, 1987.

———. *Explaining Epidemics and Other Studies in the History of Medicine.* New York: Cambridge University Press, 1992.

———. "The Practice of Medicine in New York a Century Ago." In *Explaining Epidemics and Other Studies in the History of Medicine.* New York: Cambridge University Press, 1992.

———. The Therapeutic Revolution: Medicine, Meaning, and Social Change in Nineteenth-Century America." In *Explaining Epidemics and Other Studies in the History of Medicine.* New York: Cambridge University Press, 1992.

Rothfield, Lawrence. *Vital Signs: Medical Realism in Nineteenth-Century Fiction.* Princeton, N.J.: Princeton University Press, 1992.

Rothstein, Willliam G. *American Physicians in the Nineteenth Century: From Sects to Science.* Baltimore: Johns Hopkins University Press, 1972.

Rotundo, E. Anthony. *American Manhood: Transformations in Masculinity from the Revolution to the Modern Era.* New York: Basic Books, 1993.

Ruttenburg, Nancy. "Melville's Handsome Sailor: The Anxiety of Influence." *American Literature* (March 1994): 83–103.

Ryan, Susan. "Misgivings: Melville, Race, and the Ambiguities of Benevolence." *American Literary History* 12, 4 (Winter 2000): 685–712.

Samuels, Shirley. "Miscegenated America: The Civil War." *American Literary History* 9 (1997): 482–501.

Sanborn, Gregory. *The Sign of the Cannibal: Melville and the Making of a Postcolonial Reader.* Durham, N.C.: Duke University Press, 1998.

Sanchez-Eppler, Karen. "Bodily Bonds: The Intersecting Rhetorics of Feminism and Abolition." In *The Culture of Sentiment: Race, Gender, and Sentimentality in Nineteenth-Century America*, ed. Shirley Samuels. New York: Oxford University Press, 1992.

Saunders, J. B. and Charles D. O'Malley. "Introduction." In *The Illustrations from the Works of Andreas Vesalius of Brussels.* New York: World Publishing, 1950.

Savitt, Todd L. "Entering a White Profession: Black Physicians in the New South, 1880–1920." *Bulletin of the History of Medicine* 61, 4 (Winter 1987): 507–40.

Sawday, Jonathan. *The Body Emblazoned: Dissection and the Human Body in Renaissance Culture.* London: Routledge, 1995.

Scarry, Elaine *The Body in Pain: The Making and Unmaking of the World.* New York: Oxford University Press, 1985.

Schiebinger, Londa. *The Mind Has No Sex? Women in the Origins of Modern Science.* Cambridge, Mass.: Harvard University Press, 1989.

Schjeldahl, Peter. "The Surgeon: Philadelphia Celebrates Its Most Prodigious Son." *New Yorker* 77 (October 22, 2001): 78–81.

Scudder, Horace. Review of *The Portrait of a Lady* and *Dr. Breen's Practice. Atlantic* 49 (January 1882): 126–30.

Sedgwick, Ellery. *The Atlantic Monthly 1857–1909: Yankee Humanism at High Tide and Ebb.* Amherst: University of Massachusetts Press, 1994.

Selzer, Mark. "The Still Life." *American Literary History* 3, 3 (Fall 1991): 455–86.

Short, S. E. D. *Victorian Lunacy: Richard M. Bucke and the Practice of Late Nineteenth Century Psychiatry.* Cambridge: Cambridge University Press, 1986.

"Short Essays on the Medical Profession." *Southern Literary Messenger* 9 (May 1843): 297–301.

Shyrock, Richard. *Medical Licensing in America.* Baltimore: Johns Hopkins University Press, 1967.

Simpson, Marc. "The 1880s." In *Thomas Eakins*, ed. Darrel Sewell. Philadelphia: Philadelphia Museum of Art, 2001.

Small, Miriam R. *Oliver Wendell Holmes.* New York: Twayne, 1962.

Smith, Susan Belasco and Kenneth M. Price. "Introduction: Periodical Literature in Social and Historical Context." In *Periodical Literature in Nineteenth-Century America*, ed. Kenneth M. Price and Susan Belasco Smith. Charlottesville: University Press of Virginia, 1995.

Smith-Rosenberg, Carroll. *Disorderly Conduct: Visions of Gender in Victorian America.* Oxford: Oxford University Press, 1985.

Snow, Malina. "'That One Talent': The Vocation as Theme in Sarah Orne Jewett's *A Country Doctor.*" *Colby Library Quarterly* 16 (1980): 138–47.

Sontag, Susan. *Illness as Metaphor.* New York: Farrar, Straus and Giroux, 1978.

Spencer, E. "A Good Word for Quacks." *Atlantic Monthly* 31 (March 1873): 322–29.

Speth, Linda E. "The Married Women's Property Acts, 1839–1865: Reform, Reaction, or Revolution?" In *Women in the Law*, vol. 1, ed. D. Kelly Weisberg. Cambridge, Mass.: Schenkman, 1982

Stallybrass, Peter and Allon White. *The Politics and Poetics of Transgression.* Ithaca, N.Y.: Cornell University Press, 1986.

Stanton, William. *The Leopard's Spots: Scientific Attitudes Toward Race in America, 1815–1859.* Chicago: University of Chicago Press, 1960.

Starr, Paul. *The Social Transformation of American Medicine.* New York: Basic Books, 1982.

Stepan, Nancy Leys and Sander L. Gilman. "Appropriating the Idioms of Science: The Rejection of Scientific Racism." In *The Racial Economy of Science: Toward a Democratic Future,* ed. Sandra Harding. Bloomington: Indiana University Press, 1993.

Stone, R. French, M.D., ed. *Biography of Eminent American Physicians and Surgeons.* Indianapolis: Carlon and Hollenbeck, 1894.

Story, Ronald. *The Forging of an Aristocracy: Harvard and the Boston Upper Class, 1800–1870.* Middletown, Conn.: Wesleyan University Press, 1980.

Strouse, Jean. *Alice James: A Biography.* Boston: Houghton Mifflin, 1980.

Sundquist, Eric. *To Wake the Nations: Race in the Making of American Literature* Cambridge, Mass.: Harvard University Press, 1993.

Sykes, Stanley. *Essays on the First Hundred Years of Anaethesia,* vol. 3. London: Longman, 1982.

Tanner, Tony. Introduction to Herman Mellville, *The Confidence-Man.* New York: Oxford University Press, 1989.

Taylor, Andrew. *Henry James and the Father Question.* Cambridge: Cambridge University Press, 2002.

Terry, Rose. "Eben Jackson." *Atlantic Monthly* 1 (March 1858): 525–36.

Thacher, James. *American Medical Biography: or Memoirs of Eminent Physicians who have flourished in America . . .* Boston: Richardson and Lord, 1828.

Thomas, Keith "Wrapping It Up." Review of Natalie Zemon Davis, *The Gift in Sixteenth-Century France. New York Review of Books,* December 21, 2000, 69–72.

Thomas, T. Gaillard. *A Practical Treatise on the Diseases of Women.* 3rd ed. Philadelphia: Henry C. Lea, 1872.

Thorne, Thomas. "America's Earliest Nude?" *William and Mary Quarterly* 6, 5 (October 1949): 565–68.

Thorpe, Willard. "Melville." In *Literary History of the United States,* ed. Robert E. Spiller et al. New York: Macmillan, 1948.

Tillman, Katherine Davis Chapman. "Beryl Weston's Ambition." In Katherine Davis Chapman, *The Works of Katherine Davis Chapman.* New York: Oxford University Press, 1991.

Tilton, Eleanor M. *Amiable Autocrat: A Biography of Dr. Oliver Wendell Holmes* New York: Henry Schuman, 1947.

Trachtenberg, Alan. "Seeing and Believing: Hawthorne's Reflections on the Daguerreotype in *The House of the Seven Gables." American Literary History* 9 (1997): 460–81.

Troyen, Carol. "Eakins in the Twentieth Century." In *Thomas Eakins,* ed. Darrel Sewell. Philadelphia: Philadelphia Museum of Art, 2001.

Trux, J. J. "Negro Minstrelsy—Ancient and Modern." *Putnam's Monthly* 5 (January 1855): 72–79.

Tuttle, William M. "Contested Neighborhoods and Racial Violence: Prelude to the Chicago Riot of 1919." *Journal of Negro History* 55, 4 (October 1970): 266–88.

Viets, Henry R. "The Earliest Printed References in Newspapers and Journals to the First Public Demonstration of Ether Anesthesia in 1846." *Journal of the History of Medicine* 4 (Spring 1949): 149–69.

Wager, Mary E. "Women as Physicians." *Galaxy* 6, 6 (December 1868): 774–90.

Waggoner, Hyatt. "A Hawthorne Discovery: The Lost Notebook, 1835–1841." *New England Quarterly* 49 (1976): 618–26.

Waite, Frederick C. "The Development of Anatomical Laws in the States of New England." *New England Journal of Medicine* 233 (December 1945): 720–21.

Walsh, Mary Roth. *"Doctors Wanted, No Women Need Apply": Sexual Barriers in the Medical Profession, 1835–1975*. New Haven, Conn.: Yale University Press, 1977.

Warner, John Harley. *Against the Spirit of System: The French Impulse in Nineteenth-Century American Medicine*. Princeton, N.J.: Princeton University Press, 1998.

———. "Power, Conflict, and Identity in Mid-Nineteenth-Century American Medicine: Therapeutic Change at the Commercial Hospital in Cincinnati." *Journal of American History* 73 (1987): 934–56.

———. "Remembering Paris: Memory and the American Disciples of French Medicine in the Nineteenth Century." *Bulletin of the History of Medicine* 65 (1991): 301–25.

———. *The Therapeutic Perspective: Medical Practice, Knowledge, and Identity in America, 1820–1885*. Cambridge, Mass.: Harvard University Press, 1986.

Watson, Wilbur H. *Against the Odds: Blacks in the Profession of Medicine in the United States*. New Brunswick, N.J.: Transaction Publishers, 1999.

Weaver, Raymond M. *Herman Melville: Mariner and Mystic*. New York: George H. Doran, 1921.

Weber, Max. *Economy and Society*. 2 vols. Berkeley: University of California, Press, 1978.

———. *The Theory of Social and Economic Organization*. Trans. A. M. Henderson and Talcott Parsons. New York: Oxford University Press, 1947.

Weidman, Bette S. "Charles Frederick Briggs." In *Antebellum Writers in New York and the South*, ed. Joel Meyerson. *Dictionary of Literary Biography*, vol. 3. Detroit: Gale Research, 1979.

Weinstein, Cindy. "The Invisible Hand Made Visible: 'The Birth-mark.'" *Nineteenth-Century Literature* 48 (June 1993): 44–73.

Wells, Susan *Out of the Dead House: Nineteenth-Century Women Physicians and the Writing of Medicine*. Madison: University of Wisconsin Press, 2001.

White, Walter. *The Fire in the Flint*. New York: Knopf, 1924.

———. *A Man Called White: The Autobiography of Walter White*. New York: Viking, 1948.

Whipple, Edwin Percy. "Tragic Power." *Graham's Magazine* 36 (May 1850): 345–46. Reprinted in Nathaniel Hawthorne, *The Scarlet Letter: An Authoritative Text, Essays in Criticism, and Scholarship*, ed. Seymour Gross, Sculley Bradley, Richmond Croom Beatty, E. Hudson Long, and E. Sculley Bradley. Norton Critical Edition. New York: Norton, 1988.

Whorton, James C. *Crusaders for Fitness: The History of American Health Reformers*. Princeton, N.J.: Princeton University Press, 1982.

Wideman, John. "Charles W. Chesnutt: *The Marrow of Tradition*." *American Scholar* 42 (Winter 1972–73): 128–34.

Wiegman, Robyn. *American Anatomies: Theorizing Race and Gender*. Durham, N.C.: Duke University Press, 1995.

Williams, William Carlos. *The Collected Stories of William Carlos Williams*. New York: New Directions, 1996.

Wilson, Elizabeth. *Adorned in Dreams: Fashion and Modernity*. Berkeley: University of California Press, 1985.

Wolfe, Richard J. *Robert C. Hinckley and the Recreation of the First Operation Under Ether*. Boston: Boston Medical Library, 1993.

Wonham, Henry B. "Howells, Du Bois, and the Effect of 'Common Sense': Race, Realism, and Nervousness in *An Imperative Duty* and *The Souls of Black Folk*." In

Criticism and the Color Line: Desegregating American Literary Studies, ed. Henry B. Wonham. New Brunswick, N.J.: Rutgers University Press, 1996.

———. "Writing Realism, Policing Consciousness: Howells and the Black Body." *American Literature* 67, 4 (December 1995): 701–24.

Woolf, Virginia. *Mrs. Dalloway.* New York: Harcourt, 1925.

———. "On Being Ill." In *Collected Essays.* New York: Harcourt, 1967.

Wyatt, Jean. *Reconstructing Desire: The Role of the Unconscious in Women's Reading and Writing.* Chapel Hill: University of North Carolina Press, 1990.

Young, James Harvey. *American Health Quackery: Collected Essays.* Princeton, N.J.: Princeton University Press, 1992.

———. *The Toadstool Millionaires: A Social History of Patent Medicine in America Before Federal Regulation.* Princeton, N.J.: Princeton University Press, 1961.

Index

Acknowledgments

This book has been more than ten years in the making, and thus so many have provided support that I cannot thank here all who have helped.

I have benefited from the support of several institutions. Indiana University provided a fellowship in 1991 that freed me from teaching. Berea College and the Appalachian College Association provided summer faculty/student research grants that supported research assistants for two summers, and both the College and the Association have provided funds for conferences where I was able to present some of these ideas and get feedback from colleagues across the nation and in Europe. Most importantly, both the College and the Appalachian College Association supported a year-long sabbatical that allowed me to complete the project.

Earlier versions of portions of this work have been previously published as follows and are reprinted by permission: "Doctors, Bodies, and Fiction," in *Blackwell Companion to American Fiction, 1780–1865*, ed. Shirley Samuel (London: Blackwell, 2003); "Documenting Cultural Politics: A Putnam's Short Story," *PMLA* 116 (March 2001): 397–415; "Ideologies of the Anesthetic: Professionalism, Egalitarianism, and the Ether Controversy," *American Quarterly* 51 (March 1999): 108–43; "'Profound Science' and 'Elegant Literature': Doctors in Nineteenth-Century U.S. Periodical Fiction," *Texas Studies in Language and Literature* 42 (Winter 2000): 363–83; and "'Social Surgery': Uplift, Liberation, and Professionalism in Chesnutt," in *Black Liberation in the Americas*, ed. Fritz Gysin and Christopher Mulvey (Munich: LitVerlag, 2002).

The librarians at Hutchins Library, Berea College, and especially Steve Gowler, Janey Wilson, Susan Henthorn, Patty Tartar, Shannon Wilson, and Barbara Powers, have generously helped me track down answers, make interlibrary loan requests, and work in Special Collections and the nineteenth-century journals collection. In addition, John

Bolin as Dean of the Faculty, Steve Boyce as Provost, and President Larry Shinn have provided support and encouragement often over the last ten years. I also want to thank my colleagues in the Department of English, Theatre, and Speech Communication, and my colleagues in Draper and across the College, and especially Phyllis Gabbard for her help with preparing the manuscript.

I am grateful to Jonathan Elmer, David Nordloh, and Pat Brantlinger who helped me shape the project in its earliest stages and to Anne Matthews, William Little, Elizabeth Rosdeitcher, and Paul Wack for their willingness to read and talk about literature, medicine, doctors with me over many years. Allison Berg and Lori Robison have been invaluable partners as we have shared work in preparation for conference panels, and conversations about literature with Mary Favret and Andrew Miller are among those I treasure most. Ellen Weinauer has set aside her own work time and again to read drafts and to share her wide-ranging insights and knowledge on nineteenth-century American literature; her suggestions are embedded in every chapter.

My mother helped me find a title and her provocative questions during our weekly long-distance phone conversations have helped me understand the broader contours of the project. My father proofread the final draft, catching small errors and offering elegant alternatives to clumsy phrases. My sisters' unconditional love and support make it possible to work hard year after year. I also thank my two sons, Miles and Brendan, for great dinner conversations and their interest in my work.

My most profound debt of gratitude is to my husband, Stephen Pulsford. His belief in the project and in me has never flagged; his intellectual companionship, humor, generosity, and love sustain me.